MW00677965

KIERKEGAARD'S LITERARY FIGURES AND MOTIFS

TOME II: GULLIVER TO ZERLINA

Kierkegaard Research: Sources, Reception and Resources
Volume 16, Tome II

Kierkegaard Research: Sources, Reception and Resources
is a publication of the Søren Kierkegaard Research Centre

General Editor
JON STEWART
Søren Kierkegaard Research Centre,
University of Copenhagen, Denmark

Editorial Board
FINN GREDAL JENSEN
KATALIN NUN
PETER ŠAJDA

Advisory Board
LEE C. BARRETT
MARÍA J. BINETTI
ISTVÁN CZAKÓ
HEIKO SCHULZ
CURTIS L. THOMPSON

Kierkegaard's Literary Figures and Motifs

Tome II: Gulliver to Zerlina

Edited by
KATALIN NUN AND JON STEWART

ASHGATE

© Katalin Nun, Jon Stewart and the contributors 2015

All rights reserved. No part of this publication may be reproduced, stored in a retrieval system or transmitted in any form or by any means, electronic, mechanical, photocopying, recording or otherwise without the prior permission of the publisher.

Katalin Nun and Jon Stewart have asserted their right under the Copyright, Designs and Patents Act, 1988, to be identified as the editors of this work.

Published by
Ashgate Publishing Limited
Wey Court East
Union Road
Farnham
Surrey, GU9 7PT
England

Ashgate Publishing Company
110 Cherry Street
Suite 3-1
Burlington, VT 05401-3818
USA

www.ashgate.com

British Library Cataloguing in Publication Data
A catalogue record for this book is available from the British Library

The Library of Congress has cataloged the printed edition as follows:
Kierkegaard's literary figures and motifs / edited by Jon Stewart and Katalin Nun.
    volumes cm.—(Kierkegaard research : sources, reception and resources ; volume 16)
    Includes index.
    Contents: Tome I. Agamemnon to Guadalquivir—Tome II. Gulliver to Zerlina
    ISBN 978-1-4724-4136-2 (v. 1 : hardcover)—ISBN 978-1-4724-4884-2 (v. 2 : hardcover)
1. Kierkegaard, Søren, 1813–1855—Knowledge—Literature. 2. Literature—Philosophy. I. Stewart, Jon (Jon Bartley)
    B4377.K514 2014
    198'.9—dc23

2014013575

ISBN 9781472448842 (hbk)

Cover design by Katalin Nun

MIX
Paper from
responsible sources
FSC
www.fsc.org   FSC® C013985

Printed in the United Kingdom by Henry Ling Limited, at the Dorset Press, Dorchester, DT1 1HD

Contents

List of Contributors

Julie K. Allen, University of Wisconsin-Madison, Department of Scandinavian Studies, 1302 Van Hise Hall, 1220 Linden Drive, Madison, WI 53706, USA.

Joseph Ballan, Institut for Engelsk, Germansk og Romansk, Københavns Universitet, Njalsgade 130, 2300 Copenhagen S, Denmark.

Matthew Brake, George Mason University, 4400 University Dr., Fairfax, VA 22030, USA.

F. Nassim Bravo Jordan, Universidad Iberoamericana, Prolongción Paseo de la Reforma 880, Lomas de Santa Fe, 01210, Mexico City, Mexico.

Nicholas John Chambers, Lincoln Christian University, 100 Campus View Dr., Lincoln, IL 62656, USA.

Sara Ellen Eckerson, Instituto de Filosofia da Linguagem, Faculdade de Ciências Sociais e Humanas—Universidade Nova de Lisboa, Av. de Berna, 26—4º piso, 1069–061 Lisbon, Portugal.

Fernando Manuel Ferreira da Silva, Centro de Filosofia da Universidade de Lisboa, Faculdade de Letras, Alameda da Universidade, 1600–214 Lisbon, Portugal.

Antonella Fimiani, Univertà degli Studi di Salerno, Dipartimento di Scienze del Patrimonio Culturale (DISPAC), Via Giovanni Paolo II, 132, 84084 Fiscianao (Salerno), Italy.

Gabriel Guedes Rossatti, Universidade Federal de Santa Catarina—UFSC, Programa de Pós-Graduação em Filosofia, Campus Universitário—Trindade—CEP 88.040-970—Florianópolis, Santa Catarina, Brazil.

Malgorzata Grzegorzewska, Institute of English Studies, University of Warsaw, Nowy Swiat 4, 00-497 Warsaw, Poland.

Karen Hiles, Stevenson School, 3152 Forest Lake Road, Pebble Beach, CA 93953, USA.

Ana Pinto Leite, University of Lisbon, Departamento de Filosofia da Faculdade de Letras, Alameda da Universidade, 1600–214 Lisbon, Portugal.

Leonardo F. Lisi, The Humanities Center, The Johns Hopkins University, Gilman Hall 213, 3400 N. Charles St., Baltimore, MD 21218, USA.

Laura Liva, Università G. D'Annunzio—School of Advanced Studies, via dei Vestini 31, 66013 Chieti Scalo, Italy.

Marcia Morgan, Muhlenberg College, Department of Philosophy, 2400 Chew Street, Allentown, PA 18104, USA.

Anne Louise Nielsen, Aarhus University, Institut for Kultur og Samfund, Systematisk Teologi, Jens Chr. Skous Vej 3, bygning 1453, lokale 321, 8000 Aarhus C, Denmark.

Frederico Pedreira, Instituto de Filosofia da Linguagem (IFL), Programa em Teoria da Literatura, Faculdade de Letras, Alameda da Universidade, 1600-214 Lisbon, Portugal.

Markus Pohlmeyer, Universität Flensburg, Auf dem Campus 1, 24943 Flensburg, Germany.

David D. Possen, Institut for Medier, Erkendelse og Formidling, Det Humanistiske Fakultet, Københavns Universitet, Karen Blixens Vej 4, 2300 Copenhagen S, Denmark.

Robert B. Puchniak, St Paul's High School, 2200 Grant Ave, Winnipeg, Manitoba, R3P 0P8, Canada.

Anders Rendtorff Klitgaard, Københavns Voksenuddannelsescenter, Vognmager-gade 8, 1120 Copenhagen K, Denmark.

Telmo Rodrigues, Instituto de Filosofia da Linguagem, Faculdade de Ciências Sociais e Humanas—Universidade Nova de Lisboa, Av. de Berna, 26—4° piso, 1069–061 Lisbon, Portugal.

Elisabete M. de Sousa, Centro de Filosofia da Universidade de Lisboa, Faculdade de Letras, Alameda da Universidade, 1600–214 Lisbon, Portugal.

Sean Anthony Turchin, University of Maryland University College, Academic Center at Largo, 1616 McCormick Drive, Largo, MD, 20774, USA.

Nataliya Vorobyova Jørgensen, Institute of English Studies, University of Warsaw, Nowy Swiat 4, 00–497 Warsaw, Poland.

Will Williams, Baylor University, Morrison 101.8, One Bear Place #97350, Waco, TX 76798–7350, USA.

List of Abbreviations

BA   *The Book on Adler*, trans. by Howard V. Hong and Edna H. Hong, Princeton: Princeton University Press 1998.

C   *The Crisis and a Crisis in the Life of an Actress*, trans. by Howard V. Hong and Edna H. Hong, Princeton: Princeton University Press 1997.

CA   *The Concept of Anxiety*, trans. by Reidar Thomte in collaboration with Albert B. Anderson, Princeton: Princeton University Press 1980.

CD   *Christian Discourses*, trans. by Howard V. Hong and Edna H. Hong, Princeton: Princeton University Press 1997.

CI   *The Concept of Irony*, trans. by Howard V. Hong and Edna H. Hong, Princeton: Princeton University Press 1989.

CIC   *The Concept of Irony*, trans. with an Introduction and Notes by Lee M. Capel, London: Collins 1966.

COR   *The Corsair Affair; Articles Related to the Writings*, trans. by Howard V. Hong and Edna H. Hong, Princeton: Princeton University Press 1982.

CUP1   *Concluding Unscientific Postscript*, vol. 1, trans. by Howard V. Hong and Edna H. Hong, Princeton: Princeton University Press 1992.

CUP2   *Concluding Unscientific Postscript*, vol. 2, trans. by Howard V. Hong and Edna H. Hong, Princeton: Princeton University Press 1992.

CUPH   *Concluding Unscientific Postscript*, trans. by Alastair Hannay, Cambridge and New York: Cambridge University Press 2009.

EO1   *Either/Or*, Part I, trans. by Howard V. Hong and Edna H. Hong, Princeton: Princeton University Press 1987.

EO2   *Either/Or*, Part II, trans. by Howard V. Hong and Edna H. Hong, Princeton: Princeton University Press 1987.

EOP   *Either/Or*, trans. by Alastair Hannay, Harmondsworth: Penguin Books 1992.

EPW   *Early Polemical Writings*, among others: *From the Papers of One Still Living*; *Articles from Student Days*; *The Battle Between the Old and the New Soap-Cellars*, trans. by Julia Watkin, Princeton: Princeton University Press 1990.

EUD   *Eighteen Upbuilding Discourses*, trans. by Howard V. Hong and Edna H. Hong, Princeton: Princeton University Press 1990.

.

FSE   *For Self-Examination*, trans. by Howard V. Hong and Edna H. Hong, Princeton: Princeton University Press 1990.

FT   *Fear and Trembling*, trans. by Howard V. Hong and Edna H. Hong, Princeton: Princeton University Press 1983.

FTP   *Fear and Trembling*, trans. by Alastair Hannay, Harmondsworth: Penguin Books 1985.

JC   *Johannes Climacus, or De omnibus dubitandum est*, trans. by Howard V. Hong and Edna H. Hong, Princeton: Princeton University Press 1985.

JFY   *Judge for Yourself!*, trans. by Howard V. Hong and Edna H. Hong, Princeton: Princeton University Press 1990.

JP   *Søren Kierkegaard's Journals and Papers*, vols. 1–6, ed. and trans. by Howard V. Hong and Edna H. Hong, assisted by Gregor Malantschuk (vol. 7, Index and Composite Collation), Bloomington and London: Indiana University Press 1967–78.

KAC   *Kierkegaard's Attack upon "Christendom," 1854–1855*, trans. by Walter Lowrie, Princeton: Princeton University Press 1944.

KJN   *Kierkegaard's Journals and Notebooks*, vols. 1–11, ed. by Niels Jørgen Cappelørn, Alastair Hannay, David Kangas, Bruce H. Kirmmse, George Pattison, Vanessa Rumble, and K. Brian Söderquist, Princeton and Oxford: Princeton University Press 2007ff.

LD   *Letters and Documents*, trans. by Henrik Rosenmeier, Princeton: Princeton University Press 1978.

LR   *A Literary Review*, trans. by Alastair Hannay, Harmondsworth: Penguin Books 2001.

M   *The Moment and Late Writings*, trans. by Howard V. Hong and Edna H. Hong, Princeton: Princeton University Press 1998.

P   *Prefaces / Writing Sampler*, trans. by Todd W. Nichol, Princeton: Princeton University Press 1997.

PC   *Practice in Christianity*, trans. by Howard V. Hong and Edna H. Hong, Princeton: Princeton University Press 1991.

PF   *Philosophical Fragments*, trans. by Howard V. Hong and Edna H. Hong, Princeton: Princeton University Press 1985.

PJ   *Papers and Journals: A Selection*, trans. by Alastair Hannay, Harmonds-
        worth: Penguin Books 1996.

PLR   *Prefaces: Light Reading for Certain Classes as the Occasion May Require*,
        trans. by William McDonald, Tallahassee: Florida State University Press
        1989.

PLS   *Concluding Unscientific Postscript*, trans. by David F. Swenson and Walter
        Lowrie, Princeton: Princeton University Press 1941.

PV   *The Point of View* including *On My Work as an Author*, *The Point of View
        for My Work as an Author*, and *Armed Neutrality*, trans. by Howard V.
        Hong and Edna H. Hong, Princeton: Princeton University Press 1998.

PVL   *The Point of View for My Work as an Author* including *On My Work as an
        Author*, trans. by Walter Lowrie, New York and London: Oxford University
        Press 1939.

R   *Repetition*, trans. by Howard V. Hong and Edna H. Hong, Princeton:
        Princeton University Press 1983.

SBL   *Notes of Schelling's Berlin Lectures*, trans. by Howard V. Hong and Edna
        H. Hong, Princeton: Princeton University Press 1989.

SLW   *Stages on Life's Way*, trans. by Howard V. Hong and Edna H. Hong,
        Princeton: Princeton University Press 1988.

SUD   *The Sickness unto Death*, trans. by Howard V. Hong and Edna H. Hong,
        Princeton: Princeton University Press 1980.

SUDP   *The Sickness unto Death*, trans. by Alastair Hannay, London and New York:
        Penguin Books 1989.

TA   *Two Ages: The Age of Revolution and the Present Age. A Literary Review*,
        trans. by Howard V. Hong and Edna H. Hong, Princeton: Princeton
        University Press 1978.

TD   *Three Discourses on Imagined Occasions*, trans. by Howard V. Hong and
        Edna H. Hong, Princeton: Princeton University Press 1993.

UD   *Upbuilding Discourses in Various Spirits*, trans. by Howard V. Hong and
        Edna H. Hong, Princeton: Princeton University Press 1993.

WA   *Without Authority* including *The Lily in the Field and the Bird of the Air,
        Two Ethical-Religious Essays, Three Discourses at the Communion on
        Fridays, An Upbuilding Discourse, Two Discourses at the Communion*

on Fridays, trans. by Howard V. Hong and Edna H. Hong, Princeton: Princeton University Press 1997.

WL   *Works of Love*, trans. by Howard V. Hong and Edna H. Hong, Princeton: Princeton University Press 1995.

WS   *Writing Sampler*, trans. by Todd W. Nichol, Princeton: Princeton University Press 1997.

Gulliver:

Kierkegaard's Reading of Swift and *Gulliver's Travels*

Frederico Pedreira

The aim of this article is to investigate the occurrences of Lemuel Gulliver as a literary figure in Søren Kierkegaard's *oeuvre*. These occurrences seem to relate not only to Gulliver as the motif presented in *Gulliver's Travels* but also to Jonathan Swift (1667–1745) as a background force of personal motivations for the construction of his most famous character. Kierkegaard had access to a complete collection of works by Swift and also to some of the biographical aspects regarding the Irish author, more concretely the accounts that describe his mental degeneration in the last years of his life. These aspects seem to be crucial when one wishes to analyze the inseparability between Swift and Gulliver in the philosopher's perspective.

Gulliver's Travels was written between 1721 and 1725 and published anonymously. The literary figure of Gulliver "is as much an object as an instrument of satire: we need to remember that he is not Swift. He is not always admirable."[1] Nevertheless, this motif concentrated in itself the necessary balance between ardent satire and the smoothness of a sympathetic literary figure that could make the novel subsist for centuries simultaneously as a famous political and social manifesto and a comic and imaginary travels' guide suitable for both children and adults. This kind of flexibility in communication occurs, of course, mostly due to Swift's mastery of irony, in its efficient forms and subtle variations. As Irvin Ehrenpreis puts it, "By employing fictitious persons and places in a pseudo-memoir, [Swift] would escape the frustrations that had smothered his less covert speech. Thus the self-transforming energy of the unprintable essays found a new vehicle, bold enough to satisfy Swift's anger, expressive enough to convey his doctrine, but so disguised that it could be sold in London."[2]

In *Gulliver's Travels*, Lemuel Gulliver incorporates, in the different contexts in which he appears, an anatomic and psychological discordance that mimics the numerous struggles Swift experienced while fighting for the political affairs of Ireland and writing several pamphlets that put him in a vulnerable social position,

---

[1]   A. Norman Jeffares, *Anglo-Irish Literature*, Dublin: Macmillan 1982, p. 28.
[2]   Irvin Ehrenpreis, *Swift: The Man, his Works, and the Age*, vols. 1–3, London: Methuen 1983, vol. 3, *Dean Swift*, p. 446.

including *A Proposal for the Universal Use of Irish Manufacture.*[3] Swift acted in his lifetime according to a fundamental contradiction: "Though born [in Ireland], he felt himself an Englishman, and thought of his life there [sc. in Ireland] as exile. On the other hand, he felt offended at the underprivileged position that England imposed on Ireland, and at Ireland's internal failure to act in her own interest."[4]

The same seminal element of contradiction can be found in Gulliver's actions and speech, especially on the occasions when this apparently coherent and humanistic character suddenly finds himself identifying with strange acts of despondency or unethical conduct. At one point, Gulliver praises his "great Love of his Native Country"[5] and fellow humans, or calmly considers a puritan or strictly rational approach to humankind, and even claims that he has been cleansed of all the human vices, follies or ignoble feelings after his prolonged contact with the perfected race of the Houyhnhnms. Nevertheless, when he returns from his last journey to the country of the Houyhnhnms, he recounts how his wife and family received him with great joy, "but I must freely confess the sight of them filled me only with Hatred, Disgust and Contempt, and the more by reflecting on the near Alliance I had to them."[6] The irony that is invested in this book, accompanied by the imaginative work that devises an alternative world where rules of perception and morality are constantly being reshaped, create a necessary distance between the author's position and Gulliver's ethical movements. Irony provides the fundamental creative space for Swift to satirize through metaphors and sharp associations with the contemporary debates of his time, while at the same time debasing reality and providing room for the subjectivity of the reader's mind. As Ehrenpreis argues, "The harmony of Swift's book lies in comic themes—confrontations of mind and body—connected by an ironic tone which is focused in turn on the ambiguous relation of the author to his project."[7] These confrontations of mind and body presented in the book, where human limbs and embryos of ideals and utopias constantly bump into all kinds of obstacles, are what really make Gulliver's willingness to continue his travels work as a mirror of Swift's desire to interfere positively in Irish social and political spheres at all costs. Even if the author reached a point of pure skepticism about rescuing humanity from its vices and deep levels of corruption, he "could not refrain from probing, anatomising and diagnosing its malady."[8]

References to Jonathan Swift in Kierkegaard's work can be found in *Either/ Or I* and *Stages on Life's Way*. More specifically on *Gulliver's Travels*, one can find references in *Stages on Life's Way* and *The Book on Adler*. Kierkegaard's personal book collection contained a compilation of Swift's works titled *Satyrische*

---

[3]   Jonathan Swift, *A Proposal for the Universal Use of Irish Manufacture*, Dublin: E. Waters 1720.

[4]   Claude Rawson (ed.), *The Character of Swift's Satire: A Revised Focus*, Newark: University of Delaware Press 1983, p. 19.

[5]   Jonathan Swift, *Gulliver's Travels*, ed. by Robert DeMaria, Jr., London: Penguin Books 2003, p. 237.

[6]   Ibid., p. 265.

[7]   Ehrenpreis, *Swift: The Man, his Works, and the Age*, vol. 3, *Dean* Swift, p. 450.

[8]   Herbert Davis (ed.), *Jonathan Swift: Essays on his Satire and other Studies*, New York: Galaxy 1964, p. 157.

und ernsthafte Schriften von Dr. Jonathan Swift.[9] Heinrich Waser (1714–77) was responsible for this first translation of Swift's works directly from English into German. With his extensive prefaces to Swift's books, in which he tried to appraise and justify the value of the Irish author's irony and satire, Waser was "the man who presumably did more than anybody else to spread this knowledge of the Dean in Central Europe."[10] For the translation and notes of Swift's complete work, Waser used a pseudonym, Johann von Breitenfels, "a *nom de plume* [he] presumably chose to sidestep the pitfalls of Zurich censorship."[11]

In one of the Diapsalmata written by pseudonym A and included in *Either/Or I*, we can find one of the references to Swift and the recurrent theme of his lunacy, which seems to have entertained Kierkegaard in other similar passages: "Old age fulfils the dreams of youth. One sees this in Swift: in his youth he built an insane asylum; in his old age he himself entered it."[12] Plus, in the next Diapsalmata, author A writes the following:

> It is cause for alarm to note with what hypochondriac profundity Englishmen of an earlier generation have spotted the ambiguity basic to laughter. Thus Dr. Hartley has observed: *dass wenn sich das Lachen zuerst bei Kindern zeiget, so ist es ein entstehendes Weinen, welches durch Schmerz erregt wird, oder ein plötzlich gehemtes und in sehr kurzen Zwischenräumen wiederholtes Gefühl des Schmerzens* [that when laughter first makes its appearance in the child, it is a nascent cry that is excited by pain or a suddenly arrested feeling of pain repeated at very short intervals]....What if everything in the world were a misunderstanding; what if laughter really were weeping![13]

This particular passage has its origins in a particular entry from Kierkegaard's journals, dated February 21, 1839, where it reads:

> When one sees with what hypochondriacal profoundity a previous generation of Englishmen discovered the ambiguity that lies at the root of laughter, as in the comments by Dr. Hartley, I am strangely moved to anxiety. What if laughter was a sheer misunderstanding, what if the world was so bad and existence so unhappy that laughter was really weeping? What if it was a misunderstanding—a misunderstanding that was due to a compassionate genius or a mocking demon?[14]

In both cases Kierkegaard was quoting philosopher and physician David Hartley, whose words were cited by Carl Friedrich Flögel in his *Geschichte der komischen Literatur*,[15] one of Kierkegaard's sources for a critical approach to Swift's authorship.

---

9   Jonathan Swift, *Satyrische und ernsthafte Schriften*, vols. 1–8, 3rd printing, Zürich: Orell, Geßner and Compagnie 1766 (*ASKB* 1899–1906).

10   Hermann Josef Real (ed.), *The Reception of Jonathan Swift in Europe*, London: Thoemmes 2005, p. 112.

11   Ibid., p. 114.

12   *SKS* 2, 11 / *EO1*, 21.

13   Ibid.

14   *SKS* 18, 14–15, EE:28 / *KJN* 2, 10.

15   See Carl Friedrich Flögel, *Geschichte der komischen Literatur*, vols. 1–4, Liegnitz and Leipzig: David Siegert 1784–87 (*ASKB* 1396–1399), vol. 1, p. 50.

In his book on the history of comic literature, Flögel included an article on Swift with some translations of *Remarks on the Life and Writings of Dr. Jonathan Swift*, by John Boyle, Earl of Orrery, who asserted the following about *Gulliver's Travels*:

> ...[t]he venomous strokes of [Swift's] satyr, although in some places just, are carried into so universal a severity, that not only all human actions, but human nature itself is placed in the worst light....[In the] last part of his imaginary travels, Swift has indulged a misanthropy that is intolerable....The voyage to the Houyhnhnms is a real insult upon mankind.[16]

Flögel's critical approach to Swift is regarded in the same line of thought of eighteenth-century critics such as Albrecht von Haller and Christoph Martin Wieland, who, when it comes to Swift's authorship, "no longer seem in control of their own emotions when confronted with what they (mis)take to be a misanthrope's hostility towards humankind. In their eyes, it seems, *no* satirist, indeed *no* author, was entitled to the hatred of the whole human race, and to its wholesale, unconditional condemnation."[17]

Kierkegaard had access, not only to the article that Flögel dedicated to Swift and his *Gulliver's Travels*, with the aforementioned comments, but also to the extensive prefaces and accurate translations by Heinrich Waser in his eight-volume compilation of Swift's work.[18] Waser had greatly acclaimed Swift in his preface to the first volume of *Satyrische und ernsthafte Schriften von Dr. Jonathan Swift*, censuring "the common public 'disgust at satire'...extolling satire at the same time as 'useful' and 'virtuous'....'As long as virtue is respected the satirist who shames vice is, like other teachers of virtue, a valuable and honourable man.'"[19] Kierkegaard read volume 5 of Waser's translation of *Gulliver's Travels*, where the following laudatory comment can be found in the preface:

> Poor Gulliver! He is said to have degraded human nature by having exposed it in its corruption. Perhaps he has, on account of the many variegated experiences he was made to bear, indignantly charged the human race with having deviated from its first definition as an honest, innocent, rational, and virtuous being; with having yielded to passions that expelled everything good and that made life bitter. In doing so, he has criticized what everyday experience teaches, what Holy Scripture laments, what is condemned from all pulpits, what, in brief, is an irrefutable truth.[20]

This statement favors Swift's ironical strategies and charges them with a responsible and ethical side, and Kierkegaard might have found somewhat appealing this aspect of the esthetic experiment merging with the ethical concentricity. This particular movement can be related to Johannes Climacus' ironist described in the *Concluding*

[16]   John Boyle Orrery, Earl of Cork and Orrery, *Remarks on the Life and Writings of Dr. Jonathan Swift*, ed. by João Fróes, Newark: University of Delaware Press; London: Associated University Presses 2000, p. 175, p. 215, p. 217.
[17]   Real (ed.), *The Reception of Jonathan Swift in Europe*, p. 106.
[18]   Ibid., p. 117.
[19]   Ibid., p. 115.
[20]   Quoted from ibid., p. 117.

Unscientific Postscript, where irony is not treated as absolute negativity but is instead committed to make the individual momentarily detach himself from life and others in order to internalize his inclination for self-determination. As Andrew Cross puts it: "For the person in the ethical sphere…meaningfulness is to be found in the realization of one's capacity for autonomous choice and willing."[21]

Indeed, in *The Concept of Irony*, one can find a definition of a controlled irony that resembles Waser's approach to *Gulliver's Travels* and its way of telling the "irrefutable truth" about human nature in a sequence of purposeful jests: "As soon as irony is controlled, it makes a movement opposite to that in which uncontrolled irony declares its life. Irony limits, finitizes, and circumscribes and thereby yields truth, actuality, content; it disciplines and punishes and thereby yields balance and consistency."[22] Hence, the irony that we find in *Gulliver's Travels* seems to be one of the same kind (*stable irony*) that Wayne C. Booth addressed to the author of *A Modest Proposal*, one that does not relate to a straightforward conception of irony, uniquely derived from a principle of contradiction and playful reversal of meanings, one in which "the essential structure of [the] irony is not designed 'to deceive some readers and allow others to see the secret message' but to deceive *all* readers for a time and then require *all* readers to recognize and cope with their deception."[23]

Two entries about Jonathan Swift can be found in Kierkegaard's journals. The first was written between 1840 and 1841: "In the case of Swift, it was an irony of fate that in his old age he entered the insane asylum he himself had erected in his early years."[24] The second and very similar reference to the satirist is dated from 1844: "In his youth the Englishman Swift founded a lunatic asylum which he himself entered in his old age. The story goes that while there he would often look at himself in a mirror and say: Poor old man."[25] Again, we find a progression of this image in *Stages on Life's Way*: "When Swift became an old man, he was committed to the insane asylum he himself had established when he was young. Here, it is related, he often stood in front of a mirror with the perseverance of a vain and lascivious woman, if not exactly with her thoughts. He looked at himself and said: Poor old man!"[26] According to Peter P. Rohde, Kierkegaard elaborated his own fantasy over the image of Swift's mental degeneration. In his explanatory notes to his edition of Kierkegaard's journals, Rohde asserts, "Kierkegaard's rather misconstrued account was derived from the German writer J.G. Hamann," and this reference to Swift "which in the papers appear rather unmotivated, is repeated, thereby rounding off the whole entry more artistically."[27] The entry is in fact taken from philosopher Johann

---

21   Andrew Cross, "The Perils of Reflexive Irony," in *The Cambridge Companion to Kierkegaard*, ed. by Alastair Hannay and Gordon D. Marino, Cambridge: Cambridge University Press 1999, p. 148.

22   *SKS* 1, 395 / *CI*, 326.

23   Wayne C. Booth, *A Rhetoric of Irony*, Chicago: University of Chicago Press 1974, p. 106.

24   *Pap.* III B 9 / *JP* 2, 1727.

25   *SKS* 18, 212, JJ:226 / *KJN* 2, 195.

26   *SKS* 6, 187 / *SLW*, 199.

27   Peter P. Rohde, *The Diary of Søren Kierkegaard*, New York: Philosophical Library 1960, pp. 208f.

Georg Hamann,[28] and one is prone to understand this magnification of Swift's mental condition as indicative of Kierkegaard's sublimation of the concept of irony and those intertwining forces of contradiction that shape one's life, where the extremes that constitute paradox finally touch and give rise to the ironic laughter. In *Stages on Life's Way* one can find a continuation of the episode of Swift's lunacy and aging process, this time placed before the story "Quiet Despair": "Then he did not look at himself in the mirror, as did the aged Swift, for the mirror was no more, but in loneliness he comforted himself by listening to his father's voice: Poor child, you are in a quiet despair."[29]

During his lifetime, Jonathan Swift undertook several acts of charity, especially related to social outcasts, including reintegration programs for beggars and a charity school for poor children. By 1731, he had decided "to give 'the little wealth he had, / To build a house for fools and mad.' "[30] Swift tried to improve this project for several years: "Though [he] had always shown a particular interest in schools and hospitals, this plan for his own fortune did not mature until he was nearly seventy."[31] Swift's senility affected him before the project was completed, and he had to leave further negotiations to his executors. The hospital was eventually built but, as contrary to what Kierkegaard imagined, Swift died in his own house, suffering from brain lesions, deafness and severe aphasia, surrounded by various servants who took care of him devotedly until the end of his life. Swift spent his last five years unseen by the public, and many stories and anecdotes began to spread about the legend of Swift going mad. The exaggerations were ones like those Irvin Ehrenpreis quotes from two of Swift's contemporaries: "His madness appears chiefly in most incessant strains of obscenity and swearing; habits…of which his writings have some tincture,"[32] or "Dr Swift has lately awaked from a mere animal life into a thorough misanthropy and brutality of lust."[33]

Kierkegaard referred to Swift as a lunatic who observed himself in the mirror and said "Poor old man!" Although this is a literary recreation of madness, Swift indeed had a similar episode pertaining likewise to a certain degree of reflective sorrow, probably the last episode of this kind that was acknowledged during his lifetime. In one of Swift's last days, suffering the effects of aphasia, "he tried to speak to his servant, whom he sometimes called by name. Not finding words to tell what he meant, he showed some uneasiness and said, 'I am a fool'—his last recorded words."[34] The entry is taken from Swift's correspondence, and Kierkegaard might

---

[28]   See the Hongs' note, *SLW*, Explanatory Notes, p. 743. See Johann Georg Hamann, *Hamann's Schriften*, vols. 1–8, ed. by Friedrich Roth and G.A. Wiener, Berlin, Leipzig: G. Reimer 1821–43 (*ASKB* 536–544), vol. 2, pp. 61–2; letters from Hamann to Jacobi, April 25, 1786, March 30, 1788. *Friedrich Heinrich Jacobi's Werke*, vols. 1–6, Leipzig: G. Fleischer 1812–25 (*ASKB* 1722–1728), vol. 4.3, pp. 211–402.

[29]   *SKS* 6, 187–8 / *SLW*, 200.

[30]   Ehrenpreis, *Swift: The Man, his Works, and the Age*, vol. 3, *Dean Swift*, p. 818.

[31]   Ibid., p. 817.

[32]   Irvin Ehrenpreis, *The Personality of Jonathan Swift*, New York: Barnes & Noble 1969, p. 116.

[33]   Ehrenpreis, *Swift: The Man, his Works, and the Age*, vol. 3, *Dean Swift*, p. 919.

[34]   Ibid., p. 918.

have read it in volume 7 of his edition of *Satyrische und ernsthafte Schriften von Dr. Jonathan Swift*, which is dedicated to Swift's letters.[35] The explicit self-debasement and silent recognition of intellectual feebleness, even in the midst of madness, accentuates the depths of sorrow that can only be fully reflected by the sufferer who finds himself in total isolation. One can see this trait of depression in Kierkegaard's portrait of Swift and both in the son and father's figures in the story "Quiet Despair."

For Kierkegaard, the portrait of a decaying Swift functions to illustrate the internalization of sorrow and the inescapability from it, while at the same time confronting the subject with a fundamental contradiction: external struggle, which for Swift is conveyed through irony and satire, and an internal despair and depression, which is the main engine for the emergence of the comic. Laughing and crying become indistinguishable at this point since they seem to share the same essence of sorrow. After all, and following Kierkegaard's idea previously quoted, Swift seems to be one of those "Englishmen of an earlier generation…who…have spotted the ambiguity basic to laughter."[36] This also evokes Swift's necessity to create a character such as Gulliver, who in his ontological perplexities and with his ironic subtleties is infatuated as a comic *persona* that hides a fundamental despair for not being able to recover a sense of self in a psychological landscape where everything, in the visitor's (and the reader's) perspective, is subject to relativization, doubt, and subjectivity. As Ehrenpreis writes: "Behind each ironic proposition, Swift recognizes a point of view from which it will seem an expression of despair. Behind each serious proposition is a point of view from which it will seem absurd."[37] This, of course, repeats Kierkegaard's formulation, "That the outer is not always the inner,"[38] and underlines the necessity for inwardness and a well-conceived sorrow in Swift in order to create such comic apparatus as presented in *Gulliver's Travels*.

Kierkegaard excluded the following excerpt from the final version of *Stages on Life's Way*: "Misunderstanding has its comic side. I had a maid who wanted to do everything to please me and to care for me, but she could not understand anything but that it was lovely in winter to have enough firewood and to make a fire, and I could not bear warm temperatures—and she stoked the fire and yet was indescribably fond of me."[39] In the margin of the manuscript it reads: *Gulliver's Travels*. This entry relates to the comic that has its roots in a scenario of sorrow and despair for the one who recounts the irony of a personal occurrence. The confluence of opposite qualities and psychological states might have drawn Kierkegaard's attention to Swift's biographical information and the literary figure of Lemuel Gulliver.

In *Stages on Life's Way*, one can read again the dark side of the comic, when the irony works temporarily to keep the author isolated in a realm of negativity and misunderstanding that he has created around himself:

> It is tragic when an enthusiast speaks to a generation of dunderpates and is not understood,
> but it is tragic only because there is no point of contact between them because the

---

[35]   Real (ed.), *The Reception of Jonathan Swift in Europe*, p. 115.
[36]   *SKS* 2, 11 / *EO1*, 21.
[37]   Ehrenpreis, *Swift: The Man, his Works, and the Age*, vol. 3, *Dean Swift*, pp. 448–9.
[38]   *Pap.* VII B 235, p. 186 / *BA*, 100.
[39]   *Pap.* V B 148, p. 122 / *SLW*, 626.

dunderpates do not care at all for the enthusiast. *Gulliver's Travels* is comic because of fantasy verging on madness, but the effect is only comic, and comic because the substance of qualitative passion is not present in the misunderstanding, although passion is present in the poet, for without passion there is no poet, not a comic poet, either.[40]

What Kierkegaard seems to underline in this passage is the figure of Swift as a poet who has a "passion" that cannot be fully conveyed, a feature that can also be his doom, since it traps the author in his ironies and in his own failure to communicate a higher truth or meaning, since the misunderstanding does not carry this "qualitative passion" and there is no ground for mutual understanding. The tragedy of the situation is left for Swift alone to assimilate. Thus the force of his irony is also a personal despair converted into laughter of ambiguous origins. Kierkegaard appropriates Swift as an example of esthetic maladjustment with comic consequences for the public, since his irony is often translated into misunderstandings that can make the author a recluse of his apparently derisive speech. Swift's ironical tone in *Gulliver's Travels* is unique and transmits some of the author's political ideas but in a manner that scorns humanity by exacerbating its flaws and unrealistic ideals, leaving a sense of emptiness in its place. For Kierkegaard, of course, Swift's own maladjustment in his life, charged with political and social struggles, might have sounded reminiscent of Gulliver trying to adapt his own physicality to the material and social landscape of the countries he consequently visits, more specifically Lilliput and Brobdingnag, where more dynamic descriptions are available for the subject's continual and sometimes morally painful change of perspective. Two excerpts in *The Book on Adler* can illustrate the point of Kierkegaard evoking *Gulliver's Travels*, not only as an example of physical disproportion, but also as a deeper psychological experience that relates intellectual isolation to the aesthetic effect of irony when carried to its extreme consequences. Kierkegaard ascribes a comical quality to Magister Adler, the Hegelian pastor and philosopher who simply has chosen the wrong intellectual landscape to preach his thoughts, where there is a great discrepancy between his education and abstract philosophy, and the simpleminded but earnest Christian believers who have immediate spiritual necessities:

> The situation is now established: a man who is entirely occupied with Hegelian philosophy becomes a rural pastor, lives in rural remoteness and in the intellectual sense in perfect isolation. If one considers the situation purely esthetically, it is so humorous that it could be used splendidly in a sequel to *Gulliver's Travels*, because in the intellectual sense the misrelation of the situation is exactly as painfully wrong as the more physical one that Swift describes....But Magister Adler as a Hegelian is a wild, alien bird in the country, utterly without recourse, and yet is just as disproportioned in the intellectual sense in relation to his surrounding world as Gulliver was among the very tiny, little people or among the giants. Whereas Gulliver still had the advantage and the alleviation that he was only a visitor, Magister Adler, on the other hand, despite his disproportion, is essentially in the relationship by being appointed pastor, and he is also too intelligent not to perceive that in relation to simple peasants it is foolish to be proud of his philosophy.[41]

---

[40]   *SKS* 6, 388 / *SLW*, 419–20.

[41]   *Pap.* VII B 235, pp. 183–4 / *BA*, 96–7.

Kierkegaard might have found in Gulliver a vehicle for satire and irony that temporarily dismantled readers' presuppositions about their reality and social contexts. The force of irony in Swift is developed to such a degree that it creates the same kind of subjectivity that Kierkegaard saw in the constant stream of doubt and questioning conveyed by Socrates. Gulliver behaves like a pure gentleman with a kind and noble heart, being a well-educated and scientifically curious Englishman, even when he is a victim of the hatred, contempt, and prejudice of Lilliputians or Brobdingnagians. This benevolence should be considered as a result of Swift's irony in the way that it makes Gulliver immune to all kinds of personal attacks, since his self-esteem cannot be harmed. In a sense, his receptiveness to all kinds of approaches from different countries and their people can be associated with Socrates' passive attitude towards his followers. Nevertheless, and in contrast to the Socratic total or negative irony, for Gulliver the permanent re-evaluation of identity through losing the sense of self (and the ironic reaction to this permanent loss) is a way of opening up the necessary space for subjectivity and reinstating pure thought as the only valid beginning for one's approach to the nature of truth. Irvin Ehrenpreis believes that by reading *Gulliver's Travels* "we feel drawn into a radical, comical criticism of human nature which leaves us unsure of our axioms, offers no clear set of rules to replace them, and challenges us to reconsider our instinctive patterns of life."[42] Still in this perspective, "the book becomes a machine designed not to advance a set of doctrines but to start readers on the way to reflection, self-doubt, and fresh thought."[43]

Jonathan Swift's satire and irony, materialized in Gulliver as a character, contain an important ethical dimension, though engendered by a purely esthetic investment that might have seemed valuable to Kierkegaard. As John Lippitt puts it, Swift's controlled or stable irony "can, because of its important *riddling* dimension, play the role of 'setting free' the recipient of such communication. Yet, crucially, it can do this *without* falling into the trap of 'total' irony, attacked by Kierkegaard in *The Concept of Irony* for its ultimate moral nihilism."[44] Lippitt concludes that the "main point is that for irony such as this to work, it is crucial that the ironist has a *position*,"[45] which therefore proves that an author who uses irony like Swift has it firmly anchored in a defined set of values and ethical motivations, making that same use not a destructive but a valuable device for the reconfiguration of perception and thought and, more importantly, for the essential enquiry into the self.

Irony, for Johannes Climacus,[46] stands for the transitional phase between immediacy and the ethical sphere, since the ironist has managed, through doubt, subjectivity, and laughter, to dissociate himself from society, and also from his own immediate nature and finite common sense. The ironist, then, aims to get closer to the "nature that ethical self-choice involves"[47] while at the same time protecting his

---

[42]   Ehrenpreis, *Swift: The Man, his Works, and the Age*, vol. 3, *Dean Swift*, p. 454.
[43]   Ibid., p. 455.
[44]   John Lippitt, *Humour and Irony in Kierkegaard's Thought*, Basingstoke: Macmillan 2000, p. 7.
[45]   Ibid., p. 153.
[46]   *SKS* 7, 483 / *CUP1*, 531.
[47]   Cross, "The Perils of Reflexive Irony," p. 148.

inwardness,[48] and this Kierkegaard certainly found to be an important consequence of what he called the "fantasy verging on madness"[49] that permeates *Gulliver's Travels*. Although being no moralist, Swift used Gulliver as simultaneously a mirror and a window by which the reader could scrutinize himself and the others in all their feeblemindedness and natural appetence for corruption.

---

[48]   See Alastair Hannay, *Kierkegaard: A Biography*, Cambridge: Cambridge University Press 2001, p. 305: "Among ironists, however, the irony will be an indication of the inwardness that is being protected."

[49]   *SKS* 6, 388 / *SLW*, 419–20.

Bibliography

Evans, C. Stephen, *Kierkegaard on Faith and the Self: Collected Essays*, Waco: Baylor University Press 2006, p. 70.

Grimsley, Ronald, "Gulliver," in *Kierkegaard, Literary Miscellany*, ed. by Niels Thulstrup and Marie Mikulová Thulstrup, Copenhagen C.A. Reitzel 1981 (*Bibliotheca Kierkegaardiana*, vol. 9), pp. 173–4.

Lippitt, John, *Humour and Irony in Kierkegaard's Thought*, Basingstoke: Macmillan 2000, p. 7; pp. 149–57.

Hamlet:

The Impossibility of Tragedy/
The Tragedy of Impossibility

Leonardo F. Lisi

Shakespeare is one of the most often cited literary authors in Kierkegaard's *oeuvre*. In the German intellectual context, which constitutes his most important frame of reference for this topic, Kierkegaard is naturally far from unique in this respect since Shakespeare had already emerged as the paradigm *par excellence* of a new literary movement at the end of the eighteenth century. Within this general enthusiasm, moreover, *Hamlet* held particular pre-eminence as the most enigmatic and revolutionary of Shakespeare's creations. Here, too, Kierkegaard follows the general trend, insofar as the Danish Prince is the character from Shakespeare's works who is most frequently alluded to in his writings. At this point, however, the similarities with most of his precursors largely end, as Kierkegaard's discussions of *Hamlet* frequently not only draw on his own philosophy but also provide highly complex and original interpretations of Shakespeare's play.

In what follows, I unpack Kierkegaard's reception of *Hamlet* in three steps. In the first, I provide a brief outline of the view of *Hamlet* that dominated the German cultural context. In the second, I focus in greater detail on Frater Taciturnus' "A Side-Glance at Shakespeare's Hamlet" in *Stages on Life's Way*, Kierkegaard's most important, sustained, and original discussion of the play, his longest discussion of any of Shakespeare's works, in fact.[1] Part III proceeds to examine the remaining, more cursory references to *Hamlet* in Kierkegaard's *oeuvre*, most of which center on two phrases: "To be or not to be," from Hamlet's famous soliloquy in Act Three, Scene One of the play, and Goethe's description of Hamlet in *Wilhelm Meister's Lehrjahre* as an acorn tree planted in a flowerpot. It is also among such shorter allusions to Shakespeare's work that Kierkegaard at times appears to identify his own experience with Hamlet's, which is the question that has dominated the secondary literature on this topic more than any other, and with which I conclude.

---

[1]   Joel D.S. Rasmussen, "William Shakespeare: Kierkegaard's Post-Romantic Reception of 'the Poet's Poet,' " in *Kierkegaard and the Renaissance and Modern Traditions*, Tome III: *Literature, Drama, Music*, ed. by Jon Stewart, Aldershot: Ashgate 2009 (*Kierkegaard Research: Sources, Reception and Resources*, vol. 5), p. 198.

I. The German Reception of Shakespeare's Hamlet

The German reception of William Shakespeare's (1564–1616) work properly begins only towards the end of the eighteenth century, most significantly in connection with Christoph Martin Wieland's (1733–1813) prose translation of twenty-two of Shakespeare's plays, published between 1762 and 1766,[2] and the canonical verse translation of the complete works produced by August Wilhelm Schlegel (1767–1845) and Ludwig Tieck (1773–1853) between 1797 and 1833.[3] Shakespeare's importance for German literature during this period, and for the remainder of the nineteenth century, lies not least with the clear contrast he provided to the French drama that had previously dominated the German stage. Already in Gotthold Ephraim Lessing's (1729–81) seminal *Hamburgische Dramaturgie*, published between 1767 and 1769, Shakespeare appears as a counterweight to the plays of Voltaire (1694–1778),[4] and in other critics such as Johann Elias Schlegel (1719–49) Shakespeare provided the primary weapon against the neoclassicism championed by the influential critic Johann Christoph Gottsched (1700–66).[5] Where the French models emphasized the Aristotelian unities of time, space, and action, as well as the decorum of behavior and speech, Shakespeare's plays blatantly broke with all of these. His dramatic worlds shift between various locations, frequently span days, weeks and even years, and, most importantly, present characters that exhibit violent and inconsistent language and emotions wholly alien to neoclassical tastes. In the generations that followed the earliest reception of Shakespeare in Germany, these aspects of his plays became the model for literary movements such as the *Sturm und Drang* and Romanticism.

Within this appreciation of Shakespeare as the herald of a new literary form, *Hamlet* held a particularly important place in German culture. The attributes of inconsistency of character and action that appealed to German writers are of course particularly visible in this text and may well have contributed to this fascination.

---

[2]   William Shakespeare, *Shakespeares theatralische Werke*, vols. 1–8, trans. by Christoph Martin Wieland, Zürich: Orell Gessner und Comp. 1762–6.

[3]   William Shakespeare, *Shakespeare's dramatische Werke*, vols. 1–9, trans. by August Wilhelm Schlegel, supplemented and edited by Ludwig Tieck, Berlin: Reimer 1825–33. As has frequently been pointed out, Ludwig Tieck in fact only played a minor role in the translation of Shakespeare's plays, instead delegating the bulk of the labor to Wolf von Baudissin (1789–1878) and his daughter Dorothea Tieck (1799–1841). Kierkegaard owned the second edition of the Schlegel-Tieck translation (*ASKB* 1883–1888), and, as Joel Rasmussen points out, it is mostly this text that he makes use of (Rasmussen, "William Shakespeare: Kierkegaard's Post-Romantic Reception of 'the Poet's Poet,' " pp. 186–7). For detailed accounts of the German reception history of Shakespeare, see Simon Williams, *Shakespeare on the German Stage, Volume I: 1586–1914*, Cambridge: Cambridge University Press 1990, and Roger Paulin, *The Critical Reception of Shakespeare in Germany 1682–1914: Native Literature and Foreign Genius*, Hildesheim, Zürich, New York: Georg Olms Verlag 2003.

[4]   Gotthold Ephraim Lessing, *Hamburgische Dramaturgie*, in *Werke*, vols. 1–12, ed. by Wilfried Barner et al., Frankfurt a.M.: Deutscher Klassiker Verlag 1985, vol. 6, pp. 238–40.

[5]   Johann Elias Schlegel, "Vergleichung Shakespeares und Gryphus," in *Werke*, vols. 1–5, ed. by Johann Heinrich Schlegel, Copenhagen and Leipzig: Verlag der Mummischen Buchhandlung 1764–73, vol. 3, pp. 27–64.

But beyond this, the Prince's excessive reflexivity, his melancholy and inability to act became points of special identification for German intellectuals and writers, who invoked these features as characteristics of their own country's political and cultural condition. Indeed, in a poem from 1844, Ferdinand Freiligrath (1810–76) made this comparison famous with the opening assertion that "Germany is Hamlet!" (*Deutschland ist Hamlet!*).[6]

Inevitably, such identification with Hamlet generated a wealth of critical, philosophical, and artistic responses to Shakespeare's work, far above what can be discussed here.[7] One work in particular, however, must be mentioned, since it influenced these appropriations of *Hamlet* more than any other, namely, Johann Wolfgang von Goethe's (1749–1832) novel *Wilhelm Meisters Lehrjahre*, published between 1795 and 1796. The titular hero of that work, who seeks to establish himself as a theater actor, puts forward an interpretation of *Hamlet* that is the touchstone for almost all subsequent treatments of the play in nineteenth-century Germany, and which consists essentially of two parts. In the first, Wilhelm insists that the play's apparent contradictions can be resolved if the Prince's psychology is properly understood.[8] To Wilhelm, the key to Hamlet's character is his gentle and upright nature before the action of the play begins. The young Prince, as Wilhelm explains, is "pleasant of appearance, civilized by nature, obliging from his heart," and unable "to unite with someone who transgresses the boundaries of the just, good and decent."[9] It is only with the death of his father and his mother's marriage to Claudius that Hamlet falls into melancholy, since these events deprive him of his claim to the throne and thereby leave him with a sense of his own nothingness.[10] Given Hamlet's gentle and peaceful nature, the demand that he revenge his father's murder is something he cannot fulfill, placing him in a tragic contradiction.[11] As Wilhelm puts it in the passage Kierkegaard draws on repeatedly: in *Hamlet* Shakespeare represents, "a great deed placed upon a soul not up to the task....Here an oak-tree is planted in a

---

[6]   Ferdinand Freiligrath, "Deutschland ist Hamlet," *Werke*, vols. 1–6, ed. by Julius Schwering, Berlin: Bong 1909, vol. 2, pp. 71–3. For an account of the repeated use of Hamlet in German poetry, see Brigitte Sessler, *Hamlet–ein lyrisches Politikum? Hamlet in deutschsprachigen Gedichten vom 18. Jahrhundert bis heute*, Heidelberg: Universitätsverlag 2008.

[7]   For more detailed discussions of the German reception of *Hamlet*, see Paulin, *The Critical Reception of Shakespeare in Germany*, pp. 436–66, and Williams, *Shakespeare on the German Stage*, pp. 67–87.

[8]   Johann Wolfgang von Goethe, *Wilhelm Meisters Lehrjahre*, in *Werke*, Hamburger Ausgabe, vols. 1–14, ed. by Erich Trunz, Munich: Deutscher Taschenbuch Verlag 2000, vol. 7, p. 217. Kierkegaard owned the 1828–33 edition of Goethe's complete works (*ASKB* 1641–1668).

[9]   Goethe, *Wilhelm Meisters Lehrjahre*, pp. 217–18: "*Angenehm von Gestalt, gesittet von Natur, gefällig von Herzen aus...[N]iemals konnte er sich mit dem vereinigen, der die Grenzen des Rechten, des Guten, des Anständigen überschritt.*" With the exception of quotations from Kierkegaard's work, all translations in this article are my own.

[10]   Ibid., pp. 244–5.

[11]   Ibid., p. 245.

delicate vessel, which should only have contained lovely flowers in its womb; the roots expand, the vessel is destroyed."[12]

This view of Hamlet's character persists with only minor variations in most subsequent interpretations. As early as the year of *Wilhelm Meister*'s appearance, August Wilhelm Schlegel championed the novel's interpretation of the Danish Prince,[13] and it reappears in the work of Shakespeare scholars such as Franz Horn (1781–1837),[14] Georg Gottfried Gervinus (1805–71),[15] and Friedrich Kreyßig (1818–79),[16] as well as in Georg Wilhelm Friedrich Hegel's (1770–1831) influential lectures on fine arts, delivered mainly during the 1820s. The latter describe Hamlet as having a soul unsuited for the task his father gives him, and, like Juliet in *Romeo and Juliet*, ultimately too noble to survive in our world.[17] Subsequent authors influenced as much by Hegel as by Goethe, such as Eduard Gans (1797–1839),[18] Heinrich Theodor Rötscher (1803–71),[19] and Friedrich Theodor Vischer (1807–87),[20] modified their interpretation of Hamlet's delay by attributing it not merely to his emotional or psychological shortcomings but to an obstacle or risk inherent in thought at large.

In all these instances, the focus of the play is on Hamlet's character, be it in the form of his specific psychology or his particular relation to a more general aspect of human thought. In contrast to this, the second part of Goethe's discussion in *Wilhelm Meisters Lehrjahre* centers on the claim that an impersonal fate is crucially operative

---

[12]   Ibid., pp. 245–6: "*eine große Tat auf eine Seele gelegt, die der Tat nicht gewachsen ist….Hier wird ein Eichbaum in ein köstliches Gefäß gepflanzt, das nur liebliche Blumen in seinen Schoß hätte aufnehmen sollen; die Wurzeln dehnen sich aus, das Gefäß wird zernichtet.*"
[13]   A.W. Schlegel, "Etwas über William Shakespeare bei Gelegenheit Wilhelm Meisters," *Kritische Schriften*, ed. by Emil Staiger, Zürich and Stuttgart: Artemis Verlag 1962, pp. 59–60. In his subsequent, highly influential lectures on literature, Schlegel subdued this enthusiasm for Goethe's reading; see August Wilhelm Schlegel, *Vorlesungen über dramatische Kunst und Literatur*, vols. 1–2, *Kritische Schriften und Briefe*, vols. 1–6, ed. by Edgar Lohner, Stuttgart, Berlin, Cologne, Mainz: W. Kohlhammer 1967, vol. 6, p. 169.
[14]   Franz Horn, *Shakespeare's Schauspiele*, vols. 1–5, Leipzig: Brockhaus 1823–31, vol. 2, p. 32.
[15]   Georg Gottfried Gervinus Gervinus, *Shakespeare*, vols. 1–3, Leipzig: Wilhelm Engelmann 1849, vol. 3, pp. 240–98.
[16]   Friedrich Kreyssig, *Vorlesungen über Shakespeare, seine Zeit und seine Werke*, vols. 1–2, Berlin: Nicolaische Büchhandlung 1858, vol. 2, pp. 215–66.
[17]   G.W.F. Hegel, *Vorlesungen über die Ästhetik*, vols. I-III, in *Werke*, vols. 1–20, ed. by Eva Moldenhauer and Karl Markus Michel, Frankfurt a.M.: Suhrkamp 1986, vol. 15, p. 559; pp. 566–7.
[18]   Eduard Gans, "Der Hamlet des Ducis und der des Shakespeare," in *Vermischte Schriften, juristischen, historischen, staatswissenschaftlichen und ästhetischen Inhalts*, vols. 1–2, Berlin: Duncker und Humboldt 1834, vol. 2, pp. 270–1; pp. 288–9.
[19]   Heinrich Theodor Rötscher, *Der Kunst der dramatischen Darstellung*, vols. 1–3, Berlin: Wilhelm Thome 1841–46, vol. 2, pp. 99–103 (*ASKB* 1802–1803).
[20]   Friedrich Theodor Vischer, "Shakespeares Hamlet," in *Kritische Gänge*, vols. 1–6, ed. by Robert Vischer, 2nd enlarged ed., Munich: Meyer & Jessen Verlag 1922, vol. 6, pp. 64–5; pp. 87–8.

in Shakespeare's work. While the Prince himself, as Wilhelm explains, is without a plan, the play as a whole does not lack one.[21] The final lesson of *Hamlet* is that human agency is unable to master its own circumstances and environment, and that we are instead subject to a force we cannot control.[22] In spite of its apparent shift in focus, this invocation of an impersonal fate in fact cements the view that the problem of the play is specific to its hero's psychology. The contradiction between duty and abilities, or between reason and experience, it turns out, is not absolute, but rather only lasts until the order of the world sweeps the hero aside and reasserts its underlying goals.

While Wilhelm's notion of fate in *Hamlet* remains theoretically underdeveloped in the novel, it is clear that a reading of Shakespeare's play along such lines governs a number of later interventions that pick up on this second component of Goethe's interpretation. Already in 1797, Friedrich Hildebrand von Einsiedel (1750–1828) insists that *Hamlet* depends as much on the presence of fate as on the hero's character,[23] while the 1803 book-long study by F.W. Ziegler reads Fortinbras' final ascent to the throne as the workings of a providential order.[24] In the writings of Hermann Ulrici (1806–84), this claim is accentuated by presenting the workings of fate in the play as a punishment of Hamlet, justly imposed for his excessive striving for autonomy,[25] while for Eduard Gans fate reveals the reason (*Vernunft*) that Hamlet's own more limited perspective does not believe exists.[26]

Combining the two prongs of Goethe's interpretation and its reception in subsequent criticism, it is possible to claim that the standard view of *Hamlet* identifies two complementary if inversely related sources for tragedy in the play. With respect to Hamlet's relative inability to fulfill his duty, the tragedy is absolute, since his specific character makes it impossible that he follow his father's command. But in relation to the absolute condition of fate, the tragedy is merely relative, since the painful destruction of the hero that it demands serves to establish order and justice, which grants us a degree of reconciliation.

II. Hamlet *in* Stages on Life's Way

The discussion of Shakespeare's famous play in *Stages on Life's Way* is found in Frater Taciturnus' lengthy "Letter to the Reader," which provides a commentary to

---

[21]   Goethe, *Wilhelm Meisters Lehrjahre*, p. 254.
[22]   Ibid., pp. 254–5.
[23]   Friedrich Hildebrand von Einsiedel, *Grundlinien zu einer Theorie der Schauspielkunst, nebst der Analyse einer komischen und tragischen Rolle, Falstaff und Hamlet von Shakespeare*, Leipzig: Georg Joachim Göschen 1797, pp. 115–16; pp. 119–20.
[24]   F.W. Ziegler, *Hamlets Charakter nach psychologischen und physiologischen Grundsätzen durch alle Gefühle und Leidenschaften zergliedert*, Vienna: Auf Kosten des Verfassers 1803, p. 131.
[25]   Hermann Ulrici, *Ueber Shakespeare's dramatische Kunst und sein Verhältniß zu Calderon und Goethe*, Halle: Eduard Anton 1839, pp. 235–6.
[26]   Gans, "Der Hamlet des Ducis und der des Shakespeare," p. 290. Similar views can also be found in Rötscher (*Der Kunst der dramatischen Darstellung*, vol. 2, p. 132) and Vischer ("Shakespeares Hamlet," p. 65; pp. 70–1).

Quidam's diary that precedes it. The engagement with *Hamlet* itself takes up a mere five paragraphs, under the heading of "A Side-Glance at Shakespeare's Hamlet,"[27] but it occurs in the context of a complicated and frequently elliptical argument that can only be fully understood by drawing on the book more widely, and at times even on other works in Kierkegaard's *oeuvre*.

The most immediate motivation we are given for the discussion of Shakespeare's play in relation to Quidam's diary is a remark by the German author Ludwig Börne (1786–1837). As Taciturnus writes: "Börne says of *Hamlet*, 'It is a Christian drama.' To my mind this is a most excellent comment. I substitute only the word a 'religious' drama, and then declare its fault to be not that it is that but that it did not become that or, rather, that it ought not to be a drama at all."[28] As Gene Fendt in particular has stressed, Börne's original statement does not in fact read "It is a Christian drama," but rather "Hamlet is a Christian tragedy" (*Hamlet ist ein christliches Trauerspiel*),[29] meaning that Taciturnus actually makes two substitutions, rather than just one: religious for Christian and drama for tragedy.[30] The likely reasons for, and implications of, these substitutions will be addressed in greater detail below. What matters at this point is Taciturnus' distinction between "religious drama" and "drama" in his assertion that *Hamlet* did not become the first and ought not to be the second. The latter statement implies that the play indeed *is* drama (as it clearly is),[31] and that it is this fact which prevents it from becoming "religious" or "religious drama." At stake in this claim would seem to be a differentiation between content and form akin to the one deployed by Kierkegaard's aesthete in the first volume of *Either/Or*. As A argues there with respect to Mozart's *Don Giovanni*, every classical work is a seamless combination of its subject matter and particular treatment.[32] What marks Mozart's *Don Giovanni* as above all other versions of that same myth is thus that he embodied it in music, which is the medium most appropriate to the idea of sensuousness.[33] In Taciturnus' conception of *Hamlet*, however, it would appear that we have the exact opposite situation to that of a classical work: the religious subject matter is embodied in the medium *least* suited to it.[34]

---

[27]   *SKS* 6, 417 / *SLW*, 452–4.

[28]   *SKS* 6, 418 / *SLW*, 453.

[29]   Ludwig Börne, "Hamlet, von Shakespeare," *Gesammelte Schriften,* vols. 1–8, Hamburg: Hoffmann und Campe 1828–34, vol. 2, p. 197. Kierkegaard owned the second edition of Börne's complete works, from 1835–40 (*AKSB* 1627–1629).

[30]   Gene Fendt, *Is Hamlet a Religious Drama? An Essay on a Question in Kierkegaard*, Milwaukee: Marquette University Press 1998, pp. 228–9. As Fendt also points out, in Kierkegaard's draft the passage is in fact reproduced correctly (*Pap.* V B 148:16 / *JP* 2, 1561), further suggesting that the twofold change in Taciturnus' "Letter" is intentional.

[31]   It is unclear to me why Ziolkowski asserts that Taciturnus in this sentence claims that *Hamlet* is *not* a drama (Eric Ziolkowski, *The Literary Kierkegaard*, Evanston, Illinois: Northwestern University Press 2011, p. 204).

[32]   *SKS* 2, 57 / *EO1*, 49.

[33]   *SKS* 2, 64 / *EO1*, 56–7.

[34]   It is most likely that Taciturnus' claim should be understood to mean that the subject matter of *Hamlet* is simply "religious" rather than "religious drama." The latter possibility does not contradict the interpretation offered here but merely implies that whatever "religious

Taciturnus' opening claim about Shakespeare's play is accordingly that Börne is correct in viewing *Hamlet* as containing a religious subject matter, but wrong in thinking that this religiousness is actualized in its dramatic form.[35] Why the religious cannot be represented dramatically is unpacked further in Taciturnus' next sentence: "When Shakespeare does not want to give Hamlet religious presuppositions that conspire against him in religious doubt (whereby the drama ceases), then Hamlet is essentially a vacillator, and the esthetic demands a comic interpretation."[36] Three claims in this sentence are of particular significance: first, that Hamlet does not have religious presuppositions (for if he had, it would not be a drama); second, that Hamlet is "a vacillator"; and third, that as vacillator the proper aesthetic treatment of him would be comic.

It is interesting to note that the first of these assertions replicates the description repeatedly given of the girl in Quidam's diary.[37] With respect to the girl, however, her lack of religious presuppositions is related to her immediacy and lack of reflexivity,[38] attributes that do not fit particularly well with the traditional view of Hamlet as the paradigmatic hero of thought and doubt. That Taciturnus is not seeking to reject this traditional interpretation of Shakespeare's character is made clear by the second claim, that Hamlet is a vacillator (*en Ubesluttet*, someone undecided), which necessarily involves reflexivity of some sort. Indeed, Taciturnus proceeds to describe Hamlet as "morbidly reflective" (*Reflexionssyg*, literally meaning sick with reflection), a view that he attributes to Heinrich Theodor Rötscher.[39]

How are these two assertions related: that Hamlet does not have religious presuppositions and that he suffers from a sickness of reflexivity? In his essay on *Hamlet*, Rötscher refers to the hero's "sickness of reflection" (*Krankheit der Reflexion*) as the condition that keeps the theoretical and practical dimensions of his personality at odds.[40] What Rötscher has in mind is the claim that Hamlet does not want the plan he has conceived in theoretical purity to be corrupted when he enacts it in the world. As a consequence, he continually awaits conditions under which idea and actuality might meet in a more propitious manner, which only

---

drama" may be, it is not to be associated with the conventional medium of theatrical representation as we know it.

[35]   I see no reason for Joel Rasmussen's claim that Taciturnus' agreement with Börne is supposed to be ironic (Rasmussen, "William Shakespeare: Kierkegaard's Post-Romantic Reception of 'the Poet's Poet,' " p. 203). Quite to the contrary, as will also become clear below, Taciturnus has strong reasons for agreeing with Börne's reading of *Hamlet*, as long as it is ascribed to the subject matter of the play rather than its form.

[36]   *SKS* 6, 418 / *SLW*, 453, translation modified.

[37]   *SKS* 6, 211 / *SLW*, 226, and passim.

[38]   *SKS* 6, 225, 390 / *SLW*, 241, 421.

[39]   *SKS* 6, 418–19 / *SLW*, 453.

[40]   Theodor Rötscher, *Der Kunst der dramatischen Darstellung*, vol. 2, pp. 113–4. A few pages later Rötscher again describes Hamlet's reflexivity in terms of an illness: "*Hamlet erkennt sich, während seines Reflektirens, nicht zugleich als durch die Reflexion selbst krank und ohnmächtig, weil er sie in keinem Momente als die eigentliche Wurzel seiner sittlichen Schwäche auffaßt*" (ibid., p. 124).

infinitely postpones the moment of decision.[41] A slightly different characterization of what Taciturnus means by the term *Reflexionssyge* can be found in a passage from Quidam's diary earlier in *Stages on Life's Way*. As Quidam writes there:

> This is not morbid reflection [*Reflexionssyge*] on my part, for during this whole affair my principal idea has been as clear as day to me: to do everything to work her loose and to keep myself at the pinnacle of my wish. I do not think up new purposes [*Fortsæt*] every day, but my reflection certainly can think up something new in connection with my purpose [*Fortsættet*]. I wonder if the man who wants to be rich in this world is morbidly reflective [*reflexionssyg*] when he sticks firmly to his resolve but when he sees that it will not work with one method then chooses another.[42]

"Morbid reflection" is here equated with the absence of a determinate and static purpose which provides thought with an organizing *telos*. The absence of religious presuppositions is thus not simply identical with an absence of reflection in general, as is the case with the girl in Quidam's diary, but also, more specifically, with the absence of a particular kind of reflexivity, one that involves a unifying *telos* as a defining characteristic. A further trait of religious reflection is that this *telos* exceeds the finite and immediate. As Taciturnus and Quidam repeatedly point out, a religious relation is a God-relation, which is also said to be a relation to an idea.[43] The notion of idea in *Stages on Life's Way* remains extremely vague, but Quidam at one point equates it with the meaning of a life.[44] This suggests that idea should be understood as the conception of a whole that can ascribe to each of our particular experiences its proper significance and value by placing it in a synthetic relation to terms other than the ones it is connected to in our immediate experience. Such an idea can never be actualized directly and is therefore available only through a reflexive abstraction from, and elaboration of, the phenomenally given. It is for this same reason that the religious relation to an idea cannot be represented aesthetically, since the aesthetic, for Quidam as well as for Taciturnus, remains confined to sensuousness and the immediately apparent.[45]

If Shakespeare's Hamlet does *not* have religious presuppositions, since he is a character in drama, but *does* have reflexivity, since he suffers from "morbid reflexivity," this must therefore mean that he possesses a kind of reflexivity that stays strictly within the realm of the aesthetic. On the basis of the uses of *Reflexionssyge* traced here, this would seem to take two forms. The first is that found in Rötscher's analysis, in which Hamlet cannot act because he first seeks assurance that the action will immediately instantiate the moral purpose. Such thought can be described as merely finite, since it perceives the given only in its immediate relations and fails to perform the religious reflection that relates the particular to an idea it does not directly represent. The second is the notion of *Reflexionssyge* in the still more specific sense

---

[41]   Cf., for example, Rötscher, *Der Kunst der dramatischen Darstellung*, vol. 2, pp. 101–2, and passim.

[42]   *SKS* 6, 237 / *SLW*, 254, translation modified.

[43]   *SKS* 6, 211, 384 / *SLW*, 225, 414.

[44]   *SKS* 6, 236 / *SLW*, 253.

[45]   Cf. *SKS* 6, 408 / *SLW*, 441.

used by Quidam, where Hamlet not only lacks the ability to see how immediate experience could actualize his abstract purpose, but even to form a coherent purpose in the first place, or to stick to it once formed.[46]

These two kinds of aesthetic reflexivity appear to be at play in Taciturnus' further explanation of why this situation is comic, the third of the claims contained in the sentence quoted earlier. As Taciturnus writes: "Hamlet says he has conceived his grandiose plan of being the avenger to whom vengeance belongs....If the plan remains fixed, then Hamlet is a kind of loiterer [*Nølepeer*] who does not know how to act; if the plan does not remain fixed, he is a kind of self-torturer who torments himself for and with wanting to be something great. Neither of these involves the tragic."[47] As the biblical allusion makes clear, Taciturnus sees Hamlet as laying claim to a substantive, ideal purpose: divine vengeance. But if he has no external obstacles to prevent him from executing that purpose nor any internal doubts about his inherent relation to a transcendent *telos* in doing so, then his failure to act must be due to the two modes of aesthetic reflexivity sketched above that cannot serve as means for such an end: either he delays because he is unsure how his actions can embody their intended purpose and therefore waits for suitable circumstances to arise (Hamlet as *Nølepeer*),[48] or because he is unable to actually form a purpose at all and deludes himself in thinking that he is intended for such a task (Hamlet as self-torturer). What is laid bare in either case is the difference between Hamlet as he actually is (merely aesthetic) and the role he claims for himself (religious or ethical), and that contradiction is only comic. In Taciturnus' subsequent words: "the comic lies in the misrelation between an imagined possibility and actuality."[49]

---

[46]   That Kierkegaard does not view Hamlet's reflexivity as a proper reflexivity, that is, as one that transcends a merely aesthetic mode of thought, is also suggested by a journal entry in which he directly alludes to Rötscher's analysis in the course of criticizing Hegelian philosophy more generally: "One says that one must doubt everything, and then when one writes on Hamlet one is shocked at this disease of reflection—and yet Hamlet had not even brought it to the point of doubting everything" (*SKS* 18, 229, JJ: 281 / *KJN* 2, 210). The final clause of this sentence makes it clear that Hamlet's doubt, in Kierkegaard's view, is not radical enough, even if it is already too much for a Hegelian like Rötscher to tolerate.

[47]   *SKS* 6, 418 / *SLW*, 453.

[48]   The English translation of *Nølepeer* as "loiterer" obscures this point. "To loiter," in English, most commonly means: "To linger indolently on the way when sent on an errand or when making a journey; to linger idly about a place; to waste time when engaged in some particular task, to dawdle" (*Oxford English Dictionary*, Oxford: Clarendon Press 1989, loiter, v., entry 1.a.). But the Danish verb *at nøle* specifically includes the meaning of a hesitation due to doubt or uncertainty, not mere indolence or idleness: "*vente med eller være langsom til at udføre en handling eller udtale sig, fx pga. tvivl, overvejelser eller modvilje*" (*Den Danske Ordbog*, http://ordnet.dk/ddo, nøle, v.).

[49]   *SKS* 6, 435 / *SLW*, 472. It is worth noting that elsewhere in his *oeuvre* Kierkegaard also draws on what he claims is a passage in *Hamlet* to elucidate this structure of comic misrelation, namely, the Prince's oath by a fire-tong. As Climacus explains in the *Concluding Unscientific Postscript*: "Hamlet swears by the fire tongs; the comic is in the contradiction between the solemnity of the oath and the reference that annuls the oath, no matter what the object is" (*SKS* 7, 466 / *CUP1*, 514). Kierkegaard also invokes this situation in *Prefaces* (*SKS* 4, 478 / *P*, 14) and in his journals (*SKS* 18, 272, JJ: 396 / *KJN* 2, 251), but as the commentary

According to Kierkegaard's pseudonym, then, the play as we have it from Shakespeare's hands is at best a comedy, since it has a religious purpose that cannot be expressed through the aesthetic means at its disposal, the hero's merely finite forms of thought. No less interesting is Taciturnus' proposal for an alternative version of *Hamlet*, one that would avoid the comic structure that it has in Shakespeare without abandoning the aesthetic sphere. As Taciturnus repeatedly points out, this is the version of *Hamlet* we would in fact expect from an aesthetic point of view and which the hero's comic hesitation disappoints. If Hamlet does not have religious doubts about his plan or external obstacles, "then one demands quick action."[50] And further still:

> If Hamlet is kept in purely esthetic categories, then what one wants to see is that he has the demonic power to carry out such a resolution. His misgivings have no interest whatsoever; his procrastination and temporizing, his postponing and his self-deluding enjoyment in the renewed intention [*Fortsæt*] at the same time as there is no outside hindrance merely diminish him, so that he does not become an esthetic hero, and then he becomes a nonentity.[51]

Hamlet as non-entity is Hamlet as a comic figure, the insubstantial character that falsely lays claim to substantial aims, which is what Shakespeare gives us. But Hamlet as hero within the aesthetic would be a Hamlet able to execute his resolution and in that sense to stand in some positive relation to the idea that governs him.

In the context of *Stages on Life's Way*, there are three ways in which such a positive relation can be imagined. The first is that the character simply instantiates its idea in a direct and unproblematic manner. In this case Hamlet would be similar to tragic heroes such as Romeo and Juliet, who provide an immediate embodiment of the idea of love.[52] Presumably this would mean that Hamlet would fully express the idea of vengeance and set out to murder Claudius without further ado. This possibility fits well with the statement in the above passage, that in this version, "His misgivings have no interest whatsoever."[53] But it is clear that a *Hamlet* along such lines would not retain much of anything from the original play, nor would it be an option our own age since, as Taciturnus insists, no one believes any longer that immediacy can express an idea directly.[54]

The two other ways in which a positive relation to an idea can be established center on the concept of the demonic deployed by Taciturnus in the above quotation. That concept receives a more substantial discussion earlier in *Stages on Life's Way*, where Quidam writes: "every individuality who solely by himself has a relation to the idea without any middle term (here is the silence toward all others) is demonic;

---

in *Søren Kierkegaards Skrifter* points out, Hamlet does not in fact make this oath in either the English, German, or Danish editions of the text, and it is therefore unclear where the example comes from (*SKS* K7, 342).

50   *SKS* 6, 418 / *SLW*, 453.
51   Ibid.
52   *SKS* 6, 378 / *SLW*, 407.
53   *SKS* 6, 419 / *SLW*, 453.
54   *SKS* 6, 378 / *SLW*, 407–8.

if the idea is God, then the individual is religious; if the idea is that of evil, then he is in the stricter sense demonic."[55] In the context of the passage as a whole, "Silence towards all others" designates the failure to reveal one's interiority fully, a quality that Quidam ties to deceit in the form of "sagacity" (*Klogskab*) and "intrigue," and which, as he points out, is shared by the Devil and Christ.[56] To suspend the "middle term" (*Mellembestemmelse*) in our relation to the idea thus means to suspend the apparent meaning that we put forward in our interaction with others for the sake of the hidden meaning that we do not share with them. In the moment of deceit, that is, my relation to the idea that I am seeking to express is not mediated by my action's intrinsic attributes, but rather by the intention that I hide and which does not manifest itself directly in the external world. What distinguishes the two versions of the demonic identified by Quidam is the nature of this hidden meaning that provides our actions with their true value. If I suspend the meanings that govern the shared, external world for the sake of an evil purpose, the demonic is evil, if the purpose is good, the demonic is good.

The criteria of evil and goodness here remain unspecified, but an earlier passage in Quidam's diary provides a useful hint. As Quidam explains there, he would not allow himself to use any "scheming" (*Klogskab*) or "cunning" (*List*) in his efforts to win the girl, since these are the tools of "a philanderer" (*Courmager*), which he strongly rejects.[57] The statement, however, contrasts sharply with the diary's first entry, only a few days prior, in which Quidam elaborates precisely on the "cunning" (*List*) and "deception" (*Bedrag*) that he makes use of in his relation to the girl.[58] The difference between the deceit that Quidam practices and the one that he rejects, then, cannot be based on the means deployed by each (*Klogskab*, *List*, and *Intrigue* in either case), but must rather hinge on the ends they seek. Whereas the philanderer suspends his actions' apparent meanings only for the gratification of his own desires, Quidam, as he repeatedly points out, deceives the girl for her own sake.[59]

Significantly, the former option resonates with the notion of the demonic elaborated by Theodor Rötscher in the third volume of the work that Taciturnus draws on for his discussion of Shakespeare's *Hamlet*. According to Rötscher, the demonic in its specific sense refers to an individual's subordination of his or her rational powers to a purpose derived from our sensuous nature,[60] such as the seducer's use of reason to satisfy sexual desire. Transferred to *Hamlet*, this structure of the demonic in the evil sense would have two implications. On the one hand, it would avoid the problem that in modernity no one any longer believes in immediacy's ability to express ideas directly by incorporating a moment of reflection. On the other, it would sacrifice the ideality of the idea expressed in this manner, since the hero's purpose

---

[55]   *SKS* 6, 215–16 / *SLW*, 231.
[56]   *SKS* 6, 214–15 / *SLW*, 230–1.
[57]   *SKS* 6, 188 / *SLW*, 201.
[58]   *SKS* 6, 184 / *SLW*, 196.
[59]   *SKS* 6, 184–5, 188 / *SLW*, 196–7, 200. This, of course, is the difference between Quidam and Johannes the Seducer in *Either/Or*, to which the diary in *Stages on Life's Way* was originally intended as a counter-piece (cf. *SKS* K7, 53).
[60]   Rötscher, *Der Kunst der dramatischen Darstellung*, vol. 3, pp. 61ff.

remains within the sphere of the aesthetic. If the meaning of actions is *not* what they appear to be (and they therefore do not constitute a straightforward instantiation of the idea), the meaning they *do* have does not transcend the realm of the senses but rather derives from the hero's immediate nature (the desire for revenge, the lust for power, and so on). Although this *Hamlet* would also not have any use for the "misgivings" Shakespeare confers onto his character, it would be able to stay closer to the original conception of the play because it need not do away with other central aspects, such as Hamlet's deceit and pretended madness as means to reach his goal of killing Claudius.

The third option for making Hamlet into a hero by providing him with some positive relation to an idea lies with the good demonic. Insofar as the suspension of immediacy's claim to ideal meaning in this scenario occurs, as Quidam claims, for the girl's sake rather than his own, it does not impose a new aesthetic purpose derived from the subject's own sensuous nature. This fact is also described by Quidam through the assertion that his deception of the girl is "for the sake of the idea, for the sake of meaning."[61] However, such a relation to the idea, as mentioned earlier, falls outside of the aesthetic and therefore cannot be what Taciturnus has in mind in this discussion, where he proposes a non-comic but still aesthetic version of Shakespeare's play.

Of the three possible heroic Hamlets, accordingly, only two are aesthetic in a strict sense, and of these only the second, the evil demonic, appears to fit Taciturnus' argument fully. In addition to the two aesthetic *Hamlets* discussed so far—the comedy that Shakespeare gives us and the evil demonic that Taciturnus proposes as an alternative—Kierkegaard's pseudonym, however, also puts forward two religious versions of the play, raising the sum total of *Hamlet* variations in his discussion to no less than four. In the last of these, moreover, the notion of the good demonic already mentioned plays a much more central role.

The first religious version of *Hamlet* is gestured to early on in Taciturnus' discussion, through the suggestion that a Hamlet with religious presuppositions would in fact suffer from religious doubts about his plan to murder Claudius. In the sentence already partly quoted earlier, Taciturnus writes: "If Shakespeare does not give Hamlet religious presuppositions that conspire against him in religious doubt (whereby the drama ceases), then Hamlet is essentially a vacillator."[62] And a sentence later, he reiterates the same scenario: "If one does not simultaneously see [Hamlet] sink religiously under this plan (whereby the scene becomes introspective and his unpoetic doubts and misgivings in the psychological sense become a strange [*mærkelig*] form of dialectical repentance, because the repentance seems to come too early), then one demands quick action."[63] A third formulation of this situation occurs towards the very end of "A Side-Glance at Shakespeare's *Hamlet*":

> If Hamlet is to be interpreted religiously, one must either allow him to have conceived the plan, and then religious doubts divest him of it, or do what to my mind better

---

61   *SKS* 6, 236 / *SLW*, 253.

62   *SKS* 6, 418 / *SLW*, 453.

63   Ibid., translation modified.

illuminates the religious (for in the first case there could possibly also be mixed some doubts as to whether he was capable of carrying out his plan in actuality)—give him the demonic power resolutely and masterfully to carry out his plan and then let him collapse into himself and into the religious until he finds peace there.[64]

The second of the two possibilities suggested in this final quotation can be left aside for the moment. What matters here is that Taciturnus in the course of his discussion gives us three glimpses of a religious Hamlet unable to even begin action due to religious doubts about his plan. As argued above, and as Taciturnus again emphasizes in these passages, such a relation falls strictly outside the dramatic and aesthetic since the religious consists in a reflexive relationship between immediacy and an idea that it cannot exhibit in a direct manner. The qualification here of this relationship as one of "doubt" furthermore signals that it remains merely negative in Hamlet's case. The problem is not merely that immediacy cannot directly express its participation in the totality it needs in order to have meaning, but that Hamlet is prevented from perceiving a relation between the two at all (although he does have access to the idea itself, unlike his aesthetic counterpart). In the comic version of the play put forward by Taciturnus, Hamlet's vacillation was essentially grounded in failures of his particular psychology: either his misconception of the respective terms in assuming that actuality must be able to express its idea directly (Hamlet as *Nølepeer*), or his inability to grasp the idea by failing to articulate a proper purpose and stay faithful to it (Hamlet as self-torturer). In religious doubt, however, the hesitation arises from an awareness of the difference intrinsic to these spheres and the inability to find a way to overcome it.

Taciturnus nevertheless offers two closely related reasons why this particular instantiation of religious doubt in *Hamlet* is not the most suited. The first is introduced in the parenthesis to the second quotation above: "the scene becomes introspective and his unpoetic doubts and misgivings in the psychological sense become a strange [*mærkelig*] form of dialectical repentance, because the repentance seems to come too early."[65] The category of repentance introduced in this formulation is another complicated concept which must be unpacked through other moments in the text. Earlier in *Stages on Life's Way*, Quidam notes in his diary:

> My explanation that I repent but cannot undo what I am guilty of doing [*ikke gjøre det Forskyldte om*] is nonsense. In other words, if I cannot give the reason why I cannot undo it [*gjøre det om*], I will never speak of repenting, but least of all give pride as the reason (i.e., that I do not want to), for that is actually to make a fool of her. Therefore I have never represented myself as repenting before now, although I do indeed repent and have repented that I entered into that relationship and find my humiliation in not being able to undo it [*gjøre det om*], precisely what my pride desires, since it is crushed because I, who have had an almost foolhardy conception of willing, must wince because there is something I will, will with all my passion, but cannot do. Why I cannot (which is due to my relation to the idea, until either it or I am changed), I cannot tell her in such a way that she can understand it, but for this reason I have never said that I repented.[66]

---

[64]   *SKS* 6, 419 / *SLW*, 454, translation modified.
[65]   *SKS* 6, 418 / *SLW*, 453, translation modified.
[66]   *SKS* 6, 321 / *SLW*, 345, translation modified.

At the most immediate level, the object of repentance is here identified with regret for having entered into a relationship with the girl. The problem, as Quidam stresses throughout his diary, is that they are simply too different to make a marriage between them possible.[67] Repentance, moreover, involves the desire to "undo" that which one feels regret for, or, as Quidam puts it in an earlier passage: "As a rule repentance is identified by one thing, that it acts."[68] "Undo," however, is not to be understood in the sense of breaking off their relationship, since that is something Quidam clearly *is* doing, nor in the sense of literally cancelling the events surrounding his engagement with the girl, which would be an empirical impossibility. Rather, the Danish *gjøre om* means to do again or over, which here invites the specific connotations of Kierkegaard's concept of repetition. Important in the present context is the claim that the obstacle to repeating or doing over his relationship with the girl is not his personal pride (as Quidam had speculated in an earlier diary entry alluded to in the opening statement of the above quotation[69]), but rather the relation between idea and his reality. If Quidam repents having entered into a relationship with the girl, this is because he can discover no positive relation between the gulf dividing their empirical subjectivities and the idea of marriage that stipulates the lovers' identity. To repeat their relationship would accordingly require either a different idea of marriage, one that allows for the difference between the lovers to persist, or a different subjectivity, in which, for example, the attributes of hiddenness and melancholy that distance Quidam from the girl have disappeared. Under such circumstances the unity of Quidam and the girl would be possible, and their relation could be done over in a manner that positively expresses its idea.

The "strangeness" of a Hamlet, who feels religious doubt before acting, can thus be identified with the fact that it would require regret for a deed not yet done, or the realization of the incompatibility of an action with its idea prior to its manifestation. The specific problem of this situation is not only that it arguably constitutes a somewhat awkward scenario, but also that it involves the risk addressed in the second qualifying remark Taciturnus provides about this religious version, in the last of the three quotations given above: "for in the first case there could possibly also be mixed some doubts as to whether he was capable of carrying out his plan in actuality."[70] If Hamlet doubts whether his immediate action can embody the idea that he attributes to it, then hesitation *prior* to that action is not the best way to exemplify such doubt, since we might suspect that what he really is uncertain of is not the intrinsic difference between act and meaning but his particular inability to carry out the plan. The real obstacle, that is, could simply be Hamlet's cowardice or ineptitude, in which case his invocation of religious doubt would merely serve to mask that fear.

The second religious version of *Hamlet* that Taciturnus proposes is articulated in the same passage from the conclusion of his "Side-Glance," already quoted above: "give him the demonic power resolutely and masterfully to carry out his plan and

---

[67]   *SKS* 6, 207 / *SLW*, 221–2, and passim.
[68]   *SKS* 6, 315 / *SLW*, 339.
[69]   Ibid.
[70]   *SKS* 6, 419 / *SLW*, 454, translation modified.

then let him collapse into himself and into the religious until he finds peace there."[71] The first aspect to emphasize in this statement is Taciturnus' return to the notion of the demonic, which in the context of a religious Hamlet would be of the good rather than the evil kind. The former, as discussed above, consists in the suspension of the meaning that events have in virtue of their external and shared characteristics for the sake of their relation to a purpose that transcends the realm of the aesthetic. Hamlet's plan, in this scenario, would not be directly instantiated by his behavior, but rather become visible only to a mode of reflection able to perceive his actions as part of a totality that exceeds their immediate consequences and implications. The second significant aspect of this religious *Hamlet* lies with the hero's proposed collapse. It is natural to assume that this should be understood as another case of repentance, although this time one that *follows* rather than precedes the events in question, which means that Hamlet's collapse would be caused by his inability to perceive the positive relation between idea and actuality in question once the facts have been established. Finally, as a third moment in this variation, the Prince gains some sort of resolution to this condition of repentance: he suffers in the failed relation between experience and its intended meaning "until he finds peace."

The scope of this final claim is difficult to determine fully and requires a more detailed elaboration. Ultimately it depends on the larger and complicated question of how the religious is to be understood in *Stages on Life's Way*. There are at least two interpretations possible. On the one hand, the relation between actuality and idea that constitutes the religious is figured in purely negative terms, so that the transcendent *telos* that events require for their proper meaning is perceived only as incompatible with the configuration of those events themselves. In this case the religious approximates the condition that *Fear and Trembling* describes as that of the Knight of Infinite Resignation, in which the subject gives up on the possibility of expressing the infinite idea in finite experience.[72] On the other hand, however, the religious in *Stages on Life's Way* is also figured in positive terms, closer to what *Fear and Trembling* associates with the Knight of Faith, in which the subject asserts the compatibility of idea and actuality in spite of their essential difference.[73]

It is useful here to return to Ludwig Börne's statement about *Hamlet*, with which Taciturnus' discussion begins. As already indicated, the latter misquotes Börne's assertion in two important ways, and it is worth reproducing the context in which this claim originally appears at greater length. There Börne discusses the view that Shakespeare is an ironic writer, and rejects it as inapplicable to most of his plays since Shakespeare "sees no contradiction between being and appearance."[74] In *Hamlet*, however, this is different: there we do indeed get irony, and with a vengeance:

---

[71] Ibid.

[72] *SKS* 4, 136–43 / *FT*, 41–9. Versions of this view can be found in *Stages on Life's Way* on *SKS* 6, 221, 224, 241, 397, 398 / *SLW*, 236, 240, 260, 428, 430.

[73] *SKS* 4, 141 / *FT*, 46–7. Something of this kind is at stake in the notion of "doing over" through repentance examined earlier (*SKS* 6, 321 / *SLW*, 345), which Quidam desires but remains unable to perform, and elsewhere Quidam and Taciturnus explore a movement of resignation and return that approximates the double movement of faith in *Fear and Trembling* (*SKS* 6, 281–2, 391, 406–7 / *SLW*, 302–3, 422–3, 439–40; cf. *SKS* 4, 141 / *FT*, 46).

[74] Börne, "Hamlet, von Shakespeare," p. 197.

The poet, who always teaches us so kindly, who resolves all our doubts, here abandons us to weighty apprehensions and frightful concerns. It is not the righteous, the virtuous who are destroyed, no, but worse, it is virtue and justice. Nature rebels against its creator and is victorious, the moment is master and after it the next moment reigns; infinity is subjected to space, eternity to time. Without avail our own heart warns us not to mind evil just because it is strong or to spurn goodness because it is weak; we are more inclined to believe our eyes. We see that the one who has suffered much has lived little, and we waver. Hamlet is a Christian tragedy.[75]

In *Hamlet*, according to Börne, the contradiction between the infinite and finite is not only operative, but of metaphysical proportions. What we get is not simply the contradiction between an idea, such as justice or virtue, and its empirical instantiation in a specific individual, but rather the contradiction between those ideas and experience as such. Existence as a whole reveals itself as inimical to higher values in *Hamlet*, so that *no* actualization of the infinite, of goodness, or of justice becomes possible in this world, no matter who the empirical subject of those acts might be. The claim that this worldview is Christian is the claim that Christianity is essentially life-denying, that it holds an ascetic view of existence as sinful because it is devoid of any relation to spiritual values.[76]

This is a remarkable interpretation of *Hamlet*, one quite distinct from the dominant approach cemented by Goethe for at least two reasons. First, in the latter, as we saw, the problem of Hamlet is first and foremost empirical and contingent: it is grounded in the conjunction of Hamlet's particular character (his specific psychological and emotional identity), and a particular set of events (his father's death, his mother's marriage, the appearance of the ghost). In Börne, on the other hand, Hamlet becomes a representative of a condition shared by all. Second, this condition is also different from the fate discussed by Goethe and his followers. That fate, as mentioned above, consists in the negation of one sequence of events (the one generated by individuals like Hamlet) for another (that of world history, justice, and so on), but not, as is the case in Börne's reading, in the denial of action and purposes as such. To this extent Börne in fact anticipates the much later, more famous interpretation of *Hamlet* put forward by Friedrich Nietzsche (1844–1900) in *The Birth of Tragedy*, where the Prince's inability to act is grounded in his insight into the world's Dionysian

---

[75]   Ibid.: "*Der Dichter, der uns immer so freundlich belehrt, uns alle unsere Zweifel löst, verläßt uns hier in schweren Bedenklichkeiten und bangen Besorgnissen. Nicht die Gerechten, nicht die Tugendhaften gehen unter, nein schlimmer, die Tugend und die Gerechtigkeit. Die Natur empört sich gegen ihren Schöpfer und siegt; der Augenblick ist Herr und nach ihm der andere Augenblick; die Unendlichkeit ist dem Raume, die Ewigkeit ist der Zeit unterthan. Vergebens warnt uns das eigene Herz, das Böße ja nicht zu achten, weil es stark, das Gute nicht zu verschmähen, weil es schwach ist; wir glauben unsern Augen mehr. Wir sehen, daß Wer viel geduldet, har wenig gelebt, und wir wanken. Hamlet ist ein christliches Trauerspiel.*"

[76]   Such a perception of Christianity was in fact common currency in the Young Germany movement that Börne formed a part of. Interestingly, however, Young Germany's most famous representative, Heinrich Heine, claims in his highly critical account of Börne that the latter actually was an adherent of such ascetic Christianity, rather than an opponent of it, as Kierkegaard asserts. See Heinrich Heine, *Ludwig Börne. Eine Denkschrift*, in *Werke*, vols. 1–10, ed. by Oskar Walzel et al., Leipzig: Insel Verlag 1913, vol. 8, pp. 360–1; pp. 478–81.

essence.[77] And even prior to Nietzsche, a closely related view had been proposed by Arthur Schopenhauer (1788–1860) in his *Parerga und Paralipomena*, likewise with reference to Hamlet.[78] Tragedy of this kind is absolute all the way down and offers no reconciliation.

The constellation of Börne's, Schopenhauer's, and Nietzsche's interpretations of *Hamlet* indicates that a hitherto largely overlooked reception history of Shakespeare's play existed in the nineteenth century alongside the one derived from Goethe. That Kierkegaard's engagement with the play must in fact be situated in this context is already hinted at by Taciturnus' insistence that the second religious variation is preferable because it avoids the possible suggestion that Hamlet did not act simply because he doubted his personal ability to carry out the task. That insistence makes clear that Kierkegaard shares the view that the play is concerned with more than a problem based on Hamlet's particular character. And it is likewise clear that for Kierkegaard—as for Börne, Schopenhauer and Nietzsche—this "more" is specifically linked to a nihilistic view of existence. As much can be derived from a more cursory reference to *Hamlet* in the draft version of another text, the essay "The Tragic in Ancient Drama Reflected in the Tragic in Modern Drama" in the first volume of *Either/Or*. Discussing anxiety (*Angst*) as an essentially modern "reflection category," A there writes:

> If something is to be truly depressing, a presentiment must first emerge, amid all possible favorable circumstances, that, despite everything, something might nonetheless be amiss. One does not oneself become conscious of anything particularly wrong; rather, it must lie in the familial situation. Then the corrosive power of original sin manifests itself—it can rise to the level of despair and seem much more frightful than the specific detail that confirms the truth of the suspicion.[79]

In this context, the source of Hamlet's melancholy is not a particular crime that Gertrude has committed, but rather the universal condition of original sin.[80] Gertrude's offense is her life with Claudius in the Danish court, but not because it was enabled by a specific transgression, as it is in Goethe, but rather because it reveals the fallen state of human life as such.

If Hamlet's anxiety is grounded in the intimation of original sin, this means that the Prince, to Kierkegaard, finds himself in a world universally devoid of ideality. The presence of crimes is not simply due to specific actions by specific people, which could always be avoided or corrected, but rather is a consequence of the world's inherent nature, which necessarily negates the existence of all moral ideas. This resonates not only with the view of *Hamlet* in the Börne tradition gestured

---

[77] Friedrich Nietzsche, *Die Geburt der Tragödie oder Griechentum und Pessimismus*, in *Werke*, vols. 1–3, ed. by Karl Schlechta, Darmstadt: Wissenschaftliche Buchgesellschaft 1997, vol. 1, p. 48.
[78] Arthur Schopenhauer, *Parerga und Paralipomena*, in *Werke*, vols. 1–5, ed. by Ludger Lütkehaus, Zürich: Haffmans Verlag 1988, vol. 5, p. 516.
[79] *SKS* 18, 82, FF: 35 / *KJN* 2, 75–6.
[80] This is also the context for the sole reference to *Hamlet* in *The Concept of Anxiety* (*SKS* 4, 429 / *CA*, 128).

to above, but also fits quite comfortably with Kierkegaard's notion of the Knight of Infinite Resignation. Indeed, it even recalls the discussion of Religiousness A in the *Concluding Unscientific Postscript*, where access to God is conceived to be possible only by rejecting everything earthly. As Johannes Climacus writes: "Here the upbuilding is quite properly distinguishable by the negative, by the self-annihilation…because God is in the ground only when everything that is in the way is cleared out, every finitude, and first and foremost the individual himself in his finitude, in his caviling against God."[81] What the religiousness of the believer shares with the nihilism of the atheists is that both view the world as infinitely distant from ideality, even as their evaluations of this fact diverge completely.[82]

From this perspective Taciturnus' substitution of "religious" for "Christian" in his opening quotation from Börne makes perfect sense. In the *Concluding Unscientific Postscript*, Kierkegaard strictly distinguishes between the two terms,[83] stressing that the negative relation between experience and ideality is proper to the former category alone, while the latter involves the further movement of return that bestows reality with value once again. If the idea of *Hamlet* is "religious" rather than "Christian," accordingly, it must be in this specific sense. And the peace that this idea affords in Taciturnus' last variation of the play would then be the peace of the Knight of Resignation, the acceptance that ideality and experience remain incompatible, not the peace of reconciliation proper to the Christianity embodied by the Knight of Faith.[84]

This analysis likewise makes it possible to address the rationale for the second of Taciturnus' substitutions in his quotation from Börne's text: drama for tragedy. As with the religious in general, a Hamlet stuck in Religiousness A would be

---

[81]   *SKS* 7, 509–10 / *CUP1*, 560–1. That Kierkegaard associates Hamlet with Religiousness A is also suggested by Climacus' description of that stage by means of its analogy to the acorn bursting its flowerpot that Goethe uses as an image for Hamlet in *Wilhelm Meister* (*SKS* 7, 439 / *CUP1*, 484). Other uses of this image in Kierkegaard's *oeuvre* will be discussed below.

[82]   This is precisely the argument of the introductory paragraph to the "Side-glance." Taciturnus there makes two important claims: first, that nonbelievers like Börne often have a better understanding of faith than systematic thinkers who claim to be Christians; and second, that the notion of faith held by a nineteenth-century nonbeliever (Börne) is the same as a seventeenth-century believer (Shakespeare) (*SKS* 6, 417–8 / *SLW*, 452–3). Although neither Shakespeare nor Börne are here envisioned to have access to Christianity proper, the implication of both claims is that Börne is correct in his notion of the religiousness of resignation, even though his evaluation differs from that of the believer (offense rather than passion). That Kierkegaard has great respect for Börne's understanding of the religious has also been emphasized by Peter Tudvad in his *Stadier på antisemitismens vej. Søren Kierkegaard og jøderne*, Copenhagen: Rosinante 2010, p. 11, pp. 455–60.

[83]   *SKS* 7, 505 / *CUP1*, 555.

[84]   An important difference to the Börne tradition of *Hamlet* interpretations would nevertheless remain, since, from Kierkegaard's perspective, the responsibility for the failure to move from the position of the Knight of Infinite Resignation to that of the Knight of Faith lies with the individual believer. In this sense it would be more correct to say that Kierkegaard's reading of *Hamlet* in fact falls somewhere between that of Börne and Goethe. Like the former he insists that the gap between ideal and real is objective and universal, but closer to the latter, he maintains that the failure to overcome that gap is grounded in subjectivity.

incompatible with the medium of drama, since, as already argued, drama remains in immediacy and cannot represent any internal relationship to a transcendent idea. Yet the idea of Religiousness A is not incompatible with tragedy more specifically. Quite to the contrary, as Taciturnus argues at the beginning of his "Letter," when tragic *drama* has become impossible because immediacy no longer can express ideality, a new form of *tragedy* can still be posited in which the idea is related to reflexively and dialectically rather than through sensuous representation.[85] A version of *Hamlet* that stays true to its idea, that is, needs to draw on a medium that is able to encompass this reflexivity and thereby retain the tragic contradiction at stake. What the medium able to perform this task might be is not difficult to identify in *Stages on Life's Way*; it is, of course, the diary of Quidam. The very fact that Taciturnus finds the manuscript in Helsignør, Hamlet's Elsinore,[86] already signals that we are here dealing with a new version of Shakespeare's play, and the numerous resonances to the Danish Prince throughout Kierkegaard's text amply confirm this view. What form precisely the diary is imagined to be, however, is more difficult to assess.

III. Cursory References to Hamlet

There is nothing in Kierkegaard's *corpus* to match the intensity of his engagement with *Hamlet* in *Stages on Life's Way*. A number of more cursory references to Shakespeare's play nevertheless testify to the extent of Kierkegaard's interest in this work, and the deep resonances he found in it with his own philosophical concerns. A forceful indication of this fact is found in Kierkegaard's allusion to Shakespeare's Prince in a journal entry from 1844:

> Danish philosophy—should there ever be talk of such a thing—will differ from German philosophy in that in no wise will it begin with nothing or without any presupposition, or explain everything by mediating, since it begins, on the contrary, with the proposition that there are many things between heaven and earth which no philosophy has explained.[87]

The reference here is to Hamlet's famous statement to Horatio in Act One, Scene Five: "There are more things in heaven and earth, Horatio, / Than are dreamt of in your philosophy."[88] In line with Taciturnus' reading of Hamlet as an instance of Religiousness A, the claim here is that Shakespeare's hero acknowledges the impossibility of the speculative project that seeks to subsume experience under rational thought.

In a similar vein, in the *Concluding Scientific Postscript* Kierkegaard returns to Rötscher's analysis of *Hamlet* to draw one of that work's most important distinctions between objective and subjective modes of thought.[89] According to Johannes

---

85   *SKS* 6, 376–7 / *SLW*, 405–6.
86   *SKS* 6, 175 / *SLW*, 187.
87   *SKS* 18, 217, JJ: 239 / *KJN* 2, 199.
88   William Shakespeare, *The Tragedy of Hamlet, Prince of Denmark*, in *The Riverside Shakespeare*, ed. by G. Blakemore Evans et al., 2nd ed., Boston and New York: Houghton Mifflin 1997, I. v. ll. 166–7, p. 1199.
89   *SKS* 7, 112 / *CUP1*, 116.

Climacus' discussion in that context, Rötscher acknowledges that Hamlet can only put an end to his *Krankheit der Reflexion* through a moment of subjective decision, since the gap between thought and being cannot be bridged by reflexivity alone. As Taciturnus already signaled in *Stages on Life's Way*, Rötscher, who is otherwise strictly Hegelian in his conception of history and logic, is in this way forced to draw on "existence-categories" when discussing the transition into action,[90] and thereby reveals the limitations of objective reason.

As an account of Rötscher's argument, this is at best only partly faithful to the text,[91] but for the present purposes it is more important that Climacus here conceives of Hamlet as a representative of the kind of subjective thought that he is trying to defend. Later in the *Concluding Unscientific Postscript* Hamlet is again invoked when Climacus similarly rejects the possibility of a world-historical system: "What a Sophist once said, that he could carry the whole world in a nutshell, now seems to be accomplished in modern surveys of world history."[92] The passage appears to allude to Hamlet's famous statement, "I could be bounded in a nutshell, and count myself a king of infinite space,"[93] which would make Hamlet the sophist Climacus has in mind. If that is so, however, it does not mean that Hamlet has become a representative of Hegelian thought. Quite to the contrary, the weight of Climacus' point likely lies with the second part of Hamlet's statement: "where it not that I have bad dreams."[94] The passage then suggests that the desire of objective thought to compress the world into a nutshell necessarily fails when we take into account the subjective and human dimension (the fact that we "have bad dreams"), which makes existence in such an artificially constrained place impossible. Hamlet's problems, that is, arise precisely from the fact that he is a subjective thinker in an objectified world, and is conscious of the contradiction this entails.

A final passage in the *Concluding Unscientific Postscript* specifies this view of Hamlet still further:

> The way of objective reflection now leads to abstract thinking, to mathematics, to historical knowledge of various kinds, and always leads away from the subjective individual, whose existence or nonexistence becomes, from an objective point of view,

---

[90]   *SKS* 6, 419 / *SLW*, 453.

[91]   It is correct that Rötscher does not claim that Hamlet's reflexivity leads him to the "absolute beginning," but his interpretation of the killing of Claudius in Act Five does not seem to fit the point that Climacus is trying to make. In the beginning of his analysis, Rötscher seems closest to Climacus' view, when he writes: "*Das Subjekt, welches sich durch die Reflexion den rechten Moment wohlbedächtig erschaffen wollte, wird getrieben, sich im Momente der Leidenschaft hinzugeben und aus ihr zu handeln*" (Rötscher, *Der Kunst der dramatischen Darstellung*, vol. 2, p. 103). Yet in his subsequent elaboration of this claim it becomes clear that passion is here not understood as a conscious form of decision but rather as a blind force that converts the individual into an agent of, precisely, world spirit. As Rötscher writes, Hamlet acts "*als ein blindes Werkzeug, nicht als ein selbstbewußter Geist*," and "*in der That vollbringt sich nur die Forderung des sittlichen Geistes*" (ibid., p. 132).

[92]   *SKS* 7, 125 / *CUP1*, 134.

[93]   Shakespeare, *The Tragedy of Hamlet, Prince of Denmark*, II. ii. ll. 254–6, p. 1203.

[94]   Ibid., II. ii. l. 256, p. 1203.

altogether properly, infinitely indifferent, altogether properly, because, as Hamlet says, existence and nonexistence have only subjective significance.[95]

The allusion here is to Hamlet's famous "To be or not to be" soliloquy in Act Three, Scene One of the play. Climacus' point is that the problem Hamlet faces there only has importance and validity from a subjective perspective, from within the kind of thought that does not abstract existence into merely rational categories.[96]

Hamlet's musings on suicide in his famous soliloquy in this way serve Kierkegaard as a critique of the subjection of individual and concrete experience to the categories of abstract, speculative thought. More specifically, Kierkegaard uses Hamlet's speech in the context of one of the most important philosophical controversies of the Danish Golden Age: the debate on the law of excluded middle that culminated in 1839.[97] As Kierkegaard writes in a journal entry from that same year:

> In truth, we didn't need Hegel to tell us that relative contradictions can be mediated, since it is found in the ancients that they can be distinguished; personality will for all eternity protest against the idea that absolute contradictions are susceptible of mediation (and this protest is incommensurable with what mediation asserts) [and] it will for all eternity repeat its *immortal* dilemma: to be or not to be, that is the question. (Hamlet.)[98]

Kierkegaard's point appears to be that Hegelian mediation is only possible in relation to relative opposites, while absolute ones remain in place, at least from the perspective of the individual's concrete experience. A *hamletsk dialektik*, as Johannes Climacus designates it in *Philosophical Fragments*,[99] would accordingly be a dialectic that does not mediate absolute distinctions rationally, but rather overcomes them in a different way appropriate to our finite existence.

Elsewhere Kierkegaard uses Hamlet's "to be or not to be" soliloquy to indicate more specifically what this alternative solution to the problem of absolute opposites might look like: instead of speculative thought, Hamlet's dilemma is a sign of radical interiority. In a journal entry from 1848, for example, Kierkegaard rejects the idea that the revelation of truth constitutes a relation in which the recipient is merely passive. Instead, revelation is grounded on love, in which the recipient actively seeks that which is revealed and is transformed by it. That relation is described as *inderligt* by Kierkegaard and characterized by Hamlet's speech: "to be or not to be."[100] Hamlet is deployed in a similar manner in the *Concluding Unscientific Postscript*, when

---

[95]   *SKS* 7, 177 / *CUP1*, 193.

[96]   A similar claim is also made by means of Hamlet in *Philosophical Fragments* (*SKS* 4, 246 / *PF*, 41), and in Kierkegaard's journals and notebooks (*SKS* 22, 435, NB14: 50 / *JP* 1, 1057; *SKS* 22, 163, NB12:37 / *KJN* 6, 162–3).

[97]   For a detailed overview of the debate, cf. Jon Stewart, *A History of Hegelianism in Golden Age Denmark*, Tome II, *The Martensen Period, 1837–1842*, Copenhagen: C.A. Reitzel 2007, pp. 289–373. For Kierkegaard's contribution to this debate, cf. Jon Stewart, *Kierkegaard's Relations to Hegel Reconsidered*, New York: Cambridge University Press 2003, pp. 182–237.

[98]   *SKS* 18, 33–4, EE: 93 / *KJN* 2, 30.

[99]   *SKS* 4, 246 / *PF*, 41.

[100]   *SKS* 21, 172, NB8:63 / *KJN* 5, 179.

Johannes Climacus equates the difficulty of authentic prayer with the difficulty of acting Shakespeare's Prince. Both require such degrees of interiority that we may only succeed in doing them correctly once in our life.[101]

Whereas Hamlet's famous soliloquy is used to exemplify a legitimate existential position in the above cases, it is interesting to note that Kierkegaard also uses it on a number of occasions to designate an opposed, illegitimate point of view.[102] Most interesting of these dismissive interpretations of Hamlet's question, perhaps, is the one found in volume two of *Either/Or*, where Judge William tells his friend: "The old saying 'to be—or not to be' holds for the person who lives esthetically."[103] In the context of the Judge's larger discussion, the claim refers to the aesthetic person's dependence on external conditions for his happiness, as opposed to the ethical who relies on his own individuality to generate the desired outcome to his life. The meaning of Hamlet's opposition here accordingly appears to be that the aesthetic person's ideal either must exist or not exist, since he cannot bring it into being himself. That William is possibly not far off in his assessment could be said to find confirmation in one of his friend's diapsalmata from the first volume,[104] where the option of suicide is figured in the imagery of sea and voyage that Hamlet uses in his famous soliloquy, and where courage likewise remains the obstacle. If the Judge is correct in his diagnosis of his friend's malaise, then the question nevertheless remains whether he has adequately understood the conditions under which the problem the aesthete faces can be overcome; Taciturnus presumably would claim that he has not.

In many of the above cases, the use of Hamlet's famous question has moved quite far from its original meaning and is instead fully incorporated into Kierkegaard's own considerations and concerns. Another such use of *Hamlet* centers on a different phrase, although one taken not from Shakespeare's play itself but rather from Goethe's discussion in *Wilhelm Meister*, namely the assertion that Shakespeare in the Danish Prince has represented: "a great deed placed upon a soul not up to the task....Here an oak-tree is planted in a delicate vessel, which should only have contained lovely flowers in its womb; the roots expand, the vessel is destroyed."[105] Kierkegaard references this characterization in Goethe's novel as early as 1836,[106] and it reappears on a number of subsequent occasions to designate a form of radical interiority and even Christian faith.

In the first volume of *Either/Or*, the aesthete draws on Goethe's image in his discussion of Margarete from *Faust*: "What Goethe said somewhere about Hamlet, that his soul in relation to his body was an acorn planted in a flower pot, with the result, therefore, that it burst the container, is true of Margarete's love."[107] It is interesting to note that A here misquotes Goethe's formulation by making the contradiction one between body and soul rather than soul and action. Doing so implicitly frames action

---

[101]   *SKS* 7, 151 / *CUP1*, 163.
[102]   Cf., for example, *SKS* 9, 56 / *WL*, 49; *SKS* 11, 68 / *WA*, 62; *SKS* 10, 49 / *CD*, 38.
[103]   *SKS* 3, 241 / *EO2*, 253.
[104]   *SKS* 2, 46 / *EO1*, 37.
[105]   Goethe, *Wilhelm Meisters Lehrjahre*, pp. 245–6.
[106]   *SKS* 19, 100–2, Not3:4 / *KJN* 3, 97–100.
[107]   *SKS* 2, 205 / *EO1*, 210.

as a category of the physical realm and therefore as inherently in opposition to the soul. As in Taciturnus' religious versions of the play, the aesthete can be seen to raise the collision in Hamlet from one specific to the Prince's personality and situation, as it is in Goethe, to a universal problem. In addition, A also inverts the relation found in Goethe. In the latter, it is the "acorn" of action that bursts the "flower pot" of the soul, whereas in A's use it is the soul that has become too large for the body. This significantly changes the diagnosis of Hamlet's condition by making his internal state too powerful for the fragile world, rather than, as in Goethe, making the demands of the world too powerful for his fragile spirit. This too could be seen to anticipate Taciturnus' view of the "idea" of *Hamlet*, at least if the body's weakness is understood as an inability to give ideality actual existence.

Such a reading of Hamlet also underlies Kierkegaard's use of the same image from Goethe in a later instance. Writing in 1854, Kierkegaard invokes Wilhelm Meister's description in relation to the condition of genius that he wishes to attribute to himself: "Genius is a disproportionate composition. Goethe's comment on Hamlet gives a striking picture of the genius: He is an acorn planted in a flower pot. So too the genius: a superabundance without the strength to bear it."[108] Here it is again the excess of interiority that defeats genius' capacities for externalization. The problem, that is, lies not with the collision of two opposed demands—an encroachment on the soul by an external obligation incompatible with it—but with the impossibility of expressing the internal due to the shortcomings of the external world as such. Where Hamlet in Wilhelm Meister's interpretation would have avoided his tragedy if his father's death had not actively imposed the duty of vengeance on him, Kierkegaard's genius is inherently at odds with his existence.

In the preceding passage Kierkegaard is eager to distinguish the condition of genius exemplified by Hamlet from the religious, but in *Philosophical Fragments* he notably uses Goethe's image to describe nothing less than the Incarnation itself. As Johannes Climacus writes in that text: "When an oak nut is planted in a clay pot, the pot breaks; when new wine is poured into old leather bottles, they burst. What happens, then, when the god plants himself in the frailty of a human being if he does not become a new person and a new vessel!"[109] The incompatibility of internal and external that Hamlet represents has here been raised to its highest level, beyond a merely human contradiction to the metaphysical one of God's infinity having to find impossible instantiation in the finitude of our world. To the extent that Christ succeeds, he resolves Hamlet's dilemma, which again suggests that Kierkegaard primarily conceives of Shakespeare's hero as the stage immediately prior to the paradoxical fulfillment afforded by Christianity.

One last aspect of Kierkegaard's relation to Hamlet should briefly be mentioned, particularly in light of the extensive attention it has received in the secondary literature, namely his personal identification with the Danish Prince. The interest in this topic goes as far back as Kierkegaard's own niece, Henriette Lund, who in her book, *Erindringer fra Hjemmet*, gives the following account:

---

[108] *SKS* 26, 94, NB31:124 / *JP* 6, 6903.
[109] *SKS* 4, 240 / *PF*, 34.

Once in the last years of his life, when I met uncle Søren on the street, I recall that he
expressed surprise at the interest in Shakespeare's Hamlet that brought me to read and
re-read it both in the original and translation, as well as to follow every performance
into the smallest details. I tried to win him over by asking whether he wasn't himself
captivated by this strange play, whether it didn't move him as well. "Yes, but with me it
is a completely different matter," and when I looked at him inquisitively, he added a kind
of explanation: "You can't understand that now—perhaps someday you will understand
it!"[110]

Lund's own interpretation of her uncle's statement is that he was thinking of his
battle against the Danish State Church, which constituted a duty and obligation akin
to Hamlet's revenge and which Kierkegaard was similarly reluctant to carry out until
the very end.[111] Subsequent critics have emphasized this as well as other similarities,
in particular Hamlet and Kierkegaard's common melancholy, the rejection of their
lovers in the service of a higher idea, their relationships to their fathers, their rapid
shifts in mood, their isolation from the rest of society, and so on.

Although most of these discussions are highly speculative, it is possible to find
support for the view that Kierkegaard himself perceived a certain similarity between
himself and Shakespeare's hero with respect to the two crucial issues in his life: his
relation to Regine Olsen, and what Kierkegaard took to be his service to a higher
plan or purpose. The similarity to Hamlet as concerns the latter point in particular
is suggested by a number of journal entries from the mid-1840s, where Kierkegaard
repeatedly returns to Hamlet's death. What preoccupies Kierkegaard in this scene
is that Hamlet here finally can reveal the plan he has been working for in secret all
along, and which has prevented him from being understood by others up until that
point. In Kierkegaard's view, however, Hamlet's attempt to explain himself in these
terms prior to dying is in fact a moment of weakness which constitutes a betrayal
of the idea he serves. It would have been better, Kierkegaard explains, if Hamlet
had kept his secret even in the moment of death, even if that meant that he would
necessarily be misunderstood.[112] It is not difficult to find analogues in this scenario to
Kierkegaard's conception of his own activity as a religious writer, although the fact
that he finally "revealed" his project in posthumous works like *The Point of View for
My Work as an Author* suggests he too fell victim to the temptation he here ascribes
to Hamlet.

In a late entry from 1854, Kierkegaard turns to the implications of Hamlet's
secret plan for his relation to Ophelia:

---

[110]   Henriette Lund, *Erindringer fra Hjemmet*, Copenhagen, Bianco Luno 1880, p. 187:
"*En Gang i de sidst Aar af hans Liv, da jeg mødte Onkel Søren paa Gaden, erindrer jeg, han
ytrede Forundring over den Interesse af Shakespeares 'Hamleth', der bragte mig til at læse
og atter læse den baade i Grundsprog og Oversættelse, samt med Spænding følge Opførelsen
i de mindste Detailler. Jeg søgte at gjøre ham Part i Sagen ved at spørge, om han da ikke selv
fængsledes af dette mærkelige Drama, om det ikke ligeledes bevægede ham. 'Jo, men med
mig er det en hel anden Sag', og da jeg spørgende betragtede ham, tilføjede han som en Art
Forklaring: 'Det kan Du ikke forstaa nu—engang maaske vil Du forstaa det!'*"
[111]   Ibid., pp. 187–8.
[112]   *SKS* 20, 30, NB:21 / *KJN* 4, 28.

Hamlet cannot be regarded as really being in love with Ophelia. It must not be interpreted in this way, even though psychologically it is quite true that a person who is going about hatching a great plan is the very one who needs momentary relaxation and therefore can well use a love affair. Yet I do not believe that Hamlet is to be interpreted this way. No, what is indefensible in Hamlet is that, intriguing in grand style as he is, he uses a relationship to Ophelia to take the attention away from what he actually is keeping hidden. He misuses Ophelia. This is how it should be interpreted, and one can also add that precisely because he is so overstrained he almost goes so far that momentarily he actually is in love.[113]

The conflict between Hamlet's adherence to his secret plan and his public relation to Ophelia has strong resonances with Kierkegaard's own understanding of the contradiction between his religious calling and his engagement to Regine Olsen. To what extent his break with Regine is here to be seen as akin to or different from Hamlet's behavior towards Ophelia is difficult to assess, but it seems unlikely that Kierkegaard would not have had the similarity in mind.

---

[113] *SKS* 26, 121, NB32:3 / *JP* 2, 1562.

Bibliography

Bellessort, André, "Le crépuscule d'Elseneur," *Revue des deux Mondes*, vol. 84, 1914, pp. 49–83.

Boehlich, Walter, "Sören, Prinz von Dänemark," *Der Monat*, vol. 6, no. 66, 1954, pp. 628–34.

Børge, Vagn, "Kierkegaard und Hamlet," *Wissenschaft und Weltbild: Zeitschrift für Grundfragen der Forschung und Weltanschauung*, vol. 23, 1970, pp. 50–8.

Christensen, Villads, *Søren Kierkegaard i Lys af Shakespeares Hamlet*, Copenhagen: Rosenkilde og Bagger 1960.

Erichsen, Valborg, "Hamlet og Søren Kierkegaard," *Edda*, vol. 15, 1921, pp. 75–80.

Madariaga, Salvadore de, "Noch Einmal: Kierkegaard und Hamlet," *Der Monat*, vol. 6, no. 66, 1954, pp. 625–8.

Oppel, Horst, "Shakespeare und Kierkegaard. Ein Beitrag zur Geschichte der Hamlet-Deutung," *Shakespeare-Jahrbuch*, vol. 86, 1940, pp. 112–33.

Oppel, Horst, "Die *Hamlet*-Interpretation Kierkegaards," *Shakespeare: Studien zum Werk und zur Welt des Dichters*. Heidelberg: Carl Winter Universitätsverlag 1963, pp. 133–51.

Rasmussen, Joel D.S., "William Shakespeare: Kierkegaard's Post-Romantic Reception of 'the Poet's Poet,' " in *Kierkegaard and the Renaissance and Modern Traditions*, Tome III: *Literature, Drama, Music*, ed. by Jon Stewart, Aldershot: Ashgate 2009 (*Kierkegaard Research: Sources, Reception and Resources*, vol. 5), pp. 185–214.

Rougemont, Denis de, "Kierkegaard und Hamlet," *Der Monat*, vol. 5, no. 56, 1953, pp. 115–24.

Ruoff, James E., "Kierkegaard and Shakespeare," *Comparative Literature*, vol. 20, no. 4, 1968, pp. 343–53.

Ziolkowski, Eric, *The Literary Kierkegaard*, Evanston, Illinois: Northwestern University Press 2011, pp. 183–256.

Holger the Dane:

Kierkegaard's Mention of One Heroic Legend

Robert B. Puchniak

In Frankish and Scandinavian lore, the figure of Holger the Dane (alternately, "Holger Danske" or "Ogier the Dane") was the son of Geoffrey, the first Christian king of Denmark (eighth century). Prophecy surrounded his auspicious birth, and he was destined to become the most valiant of warriors, never to be vanquished. Reared in the arts of war to be a knight without equal, Holger was surrendered as a young hostage to Charlemagne, homage due to the highest sovereign, given grudgingly by his father. Holger would become an obedient vassal who supported Charlemagne in battle, helping to preserve the Emperor under mortal threat. Bearing the royal standard, the seven-foot giant gained the loyalty of fellow soldiers, the praise of Charlemagne, and the gift of "Cortana," an enchanted sword from the fairy, Morgana. Holger's martial success would evoke the hatred and jealousy of Charlemagne's son, Charlot, who would years later cause the death of Baldwin, Holger's own son (by smashing a chess board over his head). Holger, in a fit of rage, then insulted Charlemagne, who gathered his forces to attempt the arrest of Holger, who in turn was backed by many knights. Holger, caught and bound while sleeping, suffered a long imprisonment, only to be pardoned when Charlemagne faced imminent military danger from the Saracens. Before securing Holger's assistance, Charlemagne had to acquiesce to Holger's demand that Charlot be punished. After handing over his son to Holger and expecting Charlot's death, Holger dramatically pardoned Charlemagne's son.[1] Holger first appears in the *Chanson de Roland* of the twelfth century, where he is mentioned as a trusted companion of Charles, an incomparable leader, and slayer of Saracens.[2]

The legend of Holger the Dane was further rendered in 1845 by Hans Christian Andersen.[3] In this version, Holger resides in the dark cellar of Kronenburg Castle by the Sound of Elsinore. There he sits, clad in iron and steel, head resting on his arm,

---

[1]   See Thomas Bulfinch, "The Legends of Charlemagne," in *Bullfinch's Mythology*, New York: The Modern Library 1993, pp. 837–58; Raimbert de Paris, *Le chevalrie Ogier de Danemarche*, Paris: Techener 1842; Knud Togeby, *Ogier le Dannoys: roman en prose du XVe siècle*, Copenhagen: Munksgaard 1967.

[2]   Cf. *The Song of Roland*, trans. by Glyn Burgess, New York: Penguin 1990.

[3]   Hans Christian Andersen, *Nye Eventyr*, vols. 1–2, Copenhagen: C.A. Reitzel 1844–48, vol. 1, pp. 43–52 (*ASKB* 1504–1506). See *Danish Fairy Legends and Tales*, trans. by Caroline Peachey, 3rd ed., London: Henry G. Bohn 1861, pp. 185–90.

his long beard growing into the table, as he sleeps and dreams of Denmark. Annually, on Christmas Eve an angel visits him with the news that what he has dreamt has in fact happened, then assures him that he can resume his slumber. He would be roused in outrage only if Denmark were threatened, at which time he would tear his beard from the table and strike to defend his people, coming forth to fight with strength known round the world.[4]

In Kierkegaard's works, both published and unpublished, there are scant few direct references to the "heroic legends" (or *Kjœmpehistorierne*) of Holger the Dane. Two brief meditations dating to the year 1837 reveal the quizzical amusement Kierkegaard took from mythological literature.[5] These stories, he writes, are hard to read "without smiling," for the "comical" pictures they paint. Kierkegaard notes that the story of this particular hero is remarkable for at least three reasons—one literary, one moral, and one theological: (1) The characters demonstrate "a curious naiveté" in their forgetfulness of what has recently happened in the narrative (for example, when Morgana sets a crown upon Holger's head, he forgets everything but her and her love),[6] (2) "An eccentric morality makes the heroes essentially immoral"[7] (for example, the characters place confidence in dueling to determine justice, and they show no embarrassment in fighting for an ally, even if their friend is in the wrong), and (3) There is a lingering question, about which Kierkegaard notes disagreement, regarding sin and "believing" such legends (the question being, if legendary stories are not found in Holy Scripture, should a Christian believe them?).[8]

Kierkegaard was fascinated by the richly imagined "contradiction" that such legends revealed: The way in which the warriors lived, with "great courage" and "passion for fighting" but also with some anxiety at having not only "good weapons but enchanted weapons which would give an otherwise wretched warrior the advantage over the proudest warrior."[9] In his analysis of folklore, Kierkegaard also noted that these stories are "permeated with a profound, earnest melancholy, a presentiment of the power of evil, a quiet resignation which allows every age to pay tribute to its unyielding power."[10] When it takes a long time for victory to be decided, he says further, "in this romantic life there is an irony still slumbering in and with its immediacy."[11] Mythology, according to Kierkegaard's definition, is "the compacting of eternity in the categories of time and space,"[12] that is, within myth

---

[4]   *Danish Fairy Legends and Tales*, p. 186.

[5]   *SKS* 17, 47, AA:32 / *JP* 5, 5212 and *SKS* 17, 48, AA:33 / *JP* 5, 5214. Kierkegaard would have been familiar with the tale of "Kong Olger Danskes Krønike" in *Dansk og Norsk Nationalværk, eller Almindelig ældgammel Moerskabslæsning*, vols. 1–3, ed. by Knud Lyne Rahbek, new revised and enlarged ed., Copenhagen: Hofboghandler Beekens Forlag 1828–30, vol. 1, part 2, pp. 4–5; *ASKB* 1457–1459.

[6]   *SKS* 17, 47, AA:32 / *JP* 5, 5212.

[7]   *SKS* 17, 47, AA:32 / *JP* 5, 5212.

[8]   *SKS* 17, 48, AA:33 / *JP* 5, 5214.

[9]   *SKS* 17, 44, AA:26 / *JP* 5, 5209.

[10]   *SKS* 17, 43, AA:23 / *JP* 3, 3551.

[11]   *SKS* 17, 44, AA:26 / *JP* 5, 5209.

[12]   *SKS* 18, 79–80, FF:24 / *JP* 3, 2799.

and legend one finds a conflict between some eternal ideal and its finite expression.[13] Herein lies Kierkegaard's amusement with the legendary tales of Holger Danske, and others; that these ancient stories could provide the hearer in every age a warning about danger in the world and yet express hope that evil could be overcome, if even by (comical) national heroes.

---

[13]   Cf. Gregor Malantschuk, *Kierkegaard's Thought*, ed. and trans. by Howard V. Hong and Edna H. Hong, Princeton: Princeton University Press 1971, pp. 21–5. Kierkegaard arrived at this definition in 1836–37 when he devoted himself to the study of mythologies, folk legends, and fairy tales.

Bibliography

Malantschuk, Gregor, *Kierkegaard's Thought*, ed. and trans. by Howard V. Hong and
    Edna H. Hong, Princeton: Princeton University Press 1971, pp. 21–5; pp. 147–8.
Thompson, Josiah, *Kierkegaard*, New York: Knopf 1973, pp. 57–9.

Jeppe of the Hill:

The Hedonistic Christian

Julie K. Allen

I. Introduction

There is perhaps no more iconic incarnation of the "country bumpkin" than Jeppe of the Hill, the eponymous protagonist of Ludvig Holberg's most-translated play, the comedy *Jeppe paa Bierget eller Den forvandlede Bonde* (*Jeppe of the Hill, or The Transformed Peasant*), which premiered in the fall of 1722 and was published in the first volume of his comedies in 1723. Holberg identified Jacob Bidermann's *Utopia* (1640) as his source for Jeppe's story, but several other early texts also deal with the central themes of a peasant elevated above his station and a peasant dominated by a shrewish wife, though it is unlikely that Holberg was familiar with most of them. These sources include Shakespeare's *Taming of the Shrew* and the story of Abul-Hassan in *A Thousand and One Nights*, as well as an obscure East Indian text, "The Cobbler as King," which was translated into Chinese by a Buddhist missionary, Senghuei, in the third century AD and a Polish comedy, "The Peasant as King" (1633), by Barkya.[1]

Jeppe is a drunken lout who is routinely abused by his bad-tempered wife Nille. In the opening line of the play, she declares, "I don't think there's a lazier scoundrel in the whole county than my husband!"[2] She beats him frequently with a whip she calls Master Erich, and he escapes by getting drunk whenever possible. In the first scene of the first act, Nille sends Jeppe to town with money to buy soap, but he never makes it past the inn, where he spends all the money on brandy. On his way home, Jeppe passes out in the middle of the road, where a local nobleman, Baron Nilus, finds him. The baron decides to play a joke on Jeppe by taking him home to his own house, where he awakens in a luxurious bed, dressed in fine clothing. At first, Jeppe believes himself to be dead, but the servants convince him that he is in fact the baron. Once Jeppe accepts this explanation, he begins to misuse the power his situation affords him, abusing the staff, seducing the overseer's wife, and threatening to hang

1   Ludvig Holberg, *Jeppe of the Hill and Other Comedies*, ed. by Gerald R. Argetsinger and Sven H. Rossel, Carbondale: Southern Illinois University Press 1990, p. 107. The original text of *Jeppe paa Bierget* is accessible in the new critical, annotated edition of Holberg's writings, *Ludvig Holbergs Skrifter*, at http://holbergsskrifter.dk, published digitally by the Society for Danish Language and Literature and the University of Bergen.

2   Holberg, *Jeppe of the Hill and Other Comedies*, p. 110.

every second man on the estate. He denounces the ambitions of the lower classes to upset the socioeconomic hierarchy, declaring, "When servants get more than they can eat, they get arrogant and try to put down their masters."[3] Jeppe's own tyrannical behavior amply demonstrates the truth of this accusation.

As a character, Jeppe is masterfully drawn and utterly believable, which explains why he has remained one of the most iconic figures of not only Holberg's *oeuvre*, but of the Danish theatrical tradition. In the introduction to their English translation of the play, Gerald Argetsinger and Sven Rossel explain that "dramatically, Holberg's Jeppe is a man who does not follow the patterns of any earlier works. Instead Jeppe is allowed to react—to his wife, to his baron, and to his remarkable situations. His constant drunkenness ensures that this witty and amiable peasant's reactions are honest."[4]

Thus undisguised, Jeppe shows himself to be supremely self-interested, more concerned with his own pleasure than his responsibilities, with his own well-being than that of his family, neighbors, or peers. The Danish literary critic Georg Brandes noted that Jeppe thus becomes an Everyman figure, for his character is known to all. Brandes explains, "All that we should like to know of a man when we become acquainted with him, and much more than we usually do know of men with whom we become acquainted in real life or in drama, we know of Jeppe. All our questions are answered."[5] Jeppe's fecklessness and lack of guile are amusing to watch, but they are not intended for admiration or emulation, but as a cautionary example.

Rather than fomenting revolution, Holberg's treatment of Jeppe's story ultimately reaffirms the status quo, though it also calls attention to the plight of peasants. Before Jeppe can carry out any of his despotic orders, he gets drunk again and passes out. As the baron instructs his servants to end the charade, he cautions, "We can learn from his [Jeppe's] behavior how tyrannical and arrogant such people become who are suddenly thrust from the gutter into positions of honor and nobility."[6] When Nille finds Jeppe asleep on a dung heap in his filthy peasant clothes, she beats him for drinking up the money and for claiming to have stopped in paradise on his way home. The baron then puts Jeppe on trial for the crime of impersonating a nobleman and sentences him to death by poisoning and hanging. He is drugged with a sleeping potion and hung from a gallows, where Nille first weeps over him, then beats him with her switch when he awakens and asks for brandy. The baron, pleased with the entertainment his joke has provided, sentences Jeppe to life again and compensates him for his ordeal with four rix-dollars, but cautions the audience that "peasants thrust to glory pose as much a danger as those who would, by knavery, depose one who earned greatness by industry and bravery....So leave the workmen in the fields, avoid the awful specter of elevating peasants, beating ploughshare into scepter."[7]

---

3   Ibid., p. 127.
4   Ibid., pp. 107–8.
5   Georg Brandes, *Ludvig Holberg. Et Festskrift*, Copenhagen: Gyldendal 1884, p. 182.
6   Ibid., p. 130.
7   Holberg, *Jeppe of the Hill and Other Comedies*, pp. 142–3.

II. Kierkegaard's Use of the Character Jeppe of the Hill

Although Kierkegaard lauds Holberg's comedic genius in *Jeppe of the Hill* in a journal entry,[8] Jeppe himself does not figure prominently or frequently in his works. Kierkegaard occasionally makes casual mention of elements of the play that are associated with Jeppe, such as an allusion to Nille's whip Master Erich in Judge William's monologue in volume two of *Either/Or*[9] and a passing reference to Jeppe's neighbor Moons Christophersen in Frater Taciturnus' "Letter to the Reader" in *Stages on Life's Way*.[10] At other times, he seems to be alluding to Jeppe by description rather than by name. For example, there is also a passage in "The Seducer's Diary," when Johannes is scheming about seducing Cordelia on a lonely drive through the country, when he may well be alluding to Jeppe's ignorance and alcoholism with the comment, "The peasant does not know anything; he is a clod who only knows how to drink. Yes, yes, go on drinking, my good man; you are welcome to it."[11] Similarly, in the text "The Expectancy of Eternal Salvation," which appeared in *Three Upbuilding Discourses* (1844), he describes "how terrible it must be for the drunken person to wake up suddenly in confusion of thought,"[12] which most likely refers to Jeppe's experience of awakening in Baron Nilus' bed.

When Jeppe himself appears, however, his Everyman qualities allow him to play a small but significant role in connection with Kierkegaard's critique of the decadent state of Christendom in Denmark. On these occasions, Jeppe functions as a symbol of the hedonistic Danish Christian, who eats, drinks, and makes merry, taking no thought for the morrow. His unconcern with such worldly things as money and table manners are transmuted into indifference to spiritual things, a preference for the pleasures of the pub over the treasure of the gospel truth.

Kierkegaard generally associates Jeppe with music in some way. In the first act of Holberg's play, after Jeppe has abandoned the task of buying soap for Nille and sits drinking brandy at the inn, he sings a number of bawdy songs, including a modified medieval ballad about "Little Kirsten and Sir Peder," a song about shoemakers, a drinking song based on Greek Anacreontic poetry made popular during the Renaissance, and a German student song, which also figures in Holberg's comedy *Jacob von Tyboe* (1725). In the essay "Guilty?/Not Guilty?" in *Stages on Life's Way*, Frater Taciturnus borrows the nonsense word "Peteheia" (which some translators render as "bravo") from the first song Jeppe sings and claims to have composed,[13] inserting it into a monologue about unhappy love affairs to praise the young women who "die as passionately of love as Falstaff passionately falls in the battle with Percy—and then rise up again, vigorous and nubile enough to drink to a fresh love. Peteheia!"[14]

---

8   *SKS* 27, 122–3, Papir 102:2 / *JP* 4, 4823.
9   *SKS* 3, 143 / *EO2*, 145.
10   *SKS* 6, 407 / *SLW*, 440.
11   *SKS* 2, 397 / *EO1*, 409.
12   *SKS* 5, 254 / *EUD*, 257.
13   *SKS* 6, 271 / *SLW*, 291.
14   Ibid.

    With the help of these musical referents, Kierkegaard is able to use Jeppe's dissolute, self-indulgent behavior as a symbol for the degenerate state of Christendom in Denmark in his own time. The first such usage appears in a journal entry from 1854, which condemns the debauched state of Christ's church in Denmark in the nineteenth century. Kierkegaard writes, "Protestantism, especially in Denmark, where Christendom (*sit venia verbo*) does not have the slightest remnant of a long lost similarity to Christ's Christendom, but instead exactly resembles a drinking song that Jeppe of the Hill sings: merrily, merrily, around, around."[15] In point of fact, the song to which Kierkegaard refers in this passage does not feature in the play *Jeppe paa Bierget*, but rather in Holberg's later play *Jacob von Tyboe* (1725), where it is sung by the protagonist's German valet Christoff, who is pretending to be very drunk.[16] Nevertheless, the reference to Jeppe is accurate in spirit, if not in letter, for Jeppe is a very merry, musically inclined drunk who throws responsibility to the wind in favor of the pleasures of the flesh.

    Kierkegaard repeats the same reference to Jeppe's drinking song but elaborates on its application in his so-called "attack on Christendom." In the article " 'Salt'; Because 'Christendom' is; the Decay of Christianity; 'a Christian World' Is: a Falling Away from Christianity," which appeared in the newspaper *Fædrelandet* on March 30, 1855, Kierkegaard writes:

> This has also been achieved, and best, altogether consummately, in Protestantism, especially in Denmark, in the Danish moderate convivial mediocrity. When one sees what it means to be a Christian in Denmark, who would ever dream that it should be what Christ speaks about, a cross and agony and suffering, crucifying the flesh, hating oneself, suffering for the doctrine, being salt, being sacrificed, etc. No, in Protestantism, especially in Denmark, Christianity is sung to another tune, just as Jeppe sings, merrily, merrily, around, around, around—Christianity is the enjoyment of life, reassured as neither paganism nor Judaism was, reassured by having this matter of eternity settled, settled simply in order that we should really have the desire—to enjoy this life—as well as any pagan or Jew.[17]

    In this context, Jeppe exemplifies the "moderate convivial mediocrity" that Kierkegaard so despises, for whom the enjoyment of life is paramount, regardless of the consequences. In Kierkegaard's analogy, Danish Protestants are just as oblivious to the ridiculousness of their own behavior, savoring the pleasures of life rather than suffering as befits true followers of Christ.

    Another set of references to Jeppe in Kierkegaard's work strikes a similarly musical note while further developing Kierkegaard's critique of hedonistic Danish pseudo-Christianity. In addition to the drunken Jeppe singing at the bar, Kierkegaard now also calls to mind the transformed peasant, decked out in the garb of a nobleman and drinking fine wines, who eats with his fingers, belches freely, and wipes his

---

[15]   *SKS* 26, 109, NB31:146 (my translation).

[16]   Ludvig Holberg, *Holbergs Komedier*, vols. 1–13, ed. by Julius Martensen, Copenhagen: Det Nordiske Bogforlag Ernst Bojesen 1897–1909, vol. 5, *Jacob von Tyboe, Ulysses von Ithacia*, pp. 82–4.

[17]   *SKS* 14, 173 / *M*, 42.

dripping nose on his clothes, accompanied all the while by the triumphant blast of trumpets. Despite the change in his clothing, title, and circumstances, Jeppe remains the same gluttonous boor as he had been in the inn. In an article published in the fifth issue of *The Moment*, Kierkegaard combines yet another reference to the drinking song allegedly sung by Jeppe with the phrase, "Strike up, musicians!," which evokes the scene of Jeppe impersonating the baron described above, with the musicians commemorating each drink he took. Drawing a parallel between Jeppe's failed transformation and the superficiality of the Christian character of Danish society, Kierkegaard explains:

> Christianity's idea was: to want to change everything. The result, "Christendom's" Christianity is: that everything, unconditionally everything, has remained as it was, only that everything has taken the name of "Christian"—and so (strike up, musicians!) we are living paganism, so merrily, merrily, around, around, around; or more accurately, we are living paganism refined by means of eternity and by means of having the whole thing be, after all, Christianity.[18]

Calling paganism by the name of Christianity, Kierkegaard warns, is no more effective or convincing than trying to pass Jeppe off as a nobleman.

The analogy between the superficially transformed peasant and the inadequately converted Christian is developed further in Kierkegaard's unpublished papers. In an essay titled "Sewing without Tying a Knot in the Thread (or, 'It's the Number that Matters')" (1852), which deals with the appropriate manner of preaching of the Christian gospel, he cautions against pastors accepting lavish gifts, noting:

> For my part, I would, if I could afford it, gladly throw a real party, where 10 types of wine are drunk and so forth—but one thing occupies me unceasingly. When I entered the hall with my guests to sit at table, and as I—since I would insist on chamber music—like Jeppe shouted, "Strike up the music!": then I would say very quietly to myself: God in Heaven, this is not Christendom, or I would say to the guests: my friends, allow me just one thing. In the olden days it was customary to read at table—would you object if I, instead of offering grace, just say these words: my friends, this is not Christendom.[19]

In the surrounding text, Kierkegaard explains that he does not envy others the trappings of wealth and comfort, but simply wants to make it clear that they do not belong to Christ's gospel. The reference to Jeppe serves as a reminder of the futility of trying to conflate fundamentally incompatible philosophies of life; the elegant surroundings and the festive music are no more a part of true Christianity than they were a part of Jeppe's reality. Jeppe thought himself in heaven when he awoke in the baron's bed, but Kierkegaard's conception of heaven is more subdued; rather than the endless, insatiable orgy of sensory indulgence that Jeppe seeks both in the inn and the baron's mansion, Kierkegaard describes true Christianity as a state of grace that must be earned by forsaking such pleasures and cannot be purchased with all of the merry songs, fine wines, and blaring trumpets in the world.

---

[18]   *SKS* 13, 235 / *M*, 185.
[19]   *SKS* 27, 556, Papir 451 (my translation).

Bibliography

Allen, Julie K., "Ludvig Holberg: Kierkegaard's Unacknowledged Mentor," in *Kierkegaard and the Renaissance and Modern Traditions*, Tome III, *Literature, Drama and Music*, ed. by Jon Stewart, Aldershot: Ashgate 2009 (*Kierkegaard Research: Sources, Reception and Resources*, vol. 5), pp. 77–92.

Argetsinger, Gerald R. and Sven H. Rossel, "Jeppe of the Hill," in *Jeppe of the Hill and Other Comedies by Ludvig Holberg*, ed. and trans. by Gerald R. Argetsinger and Sven H. Rossel, Carbondale: Southern Illinois University Press 1990, pp. 107–8.

Billeskov Jansen, F.J., "Holberg," in *Kierkegaard Literary Miscellany*, ed. by Niels Thulstrup and Marie Mikulová Thulstrup, Copenhagen: C.A. Reitzel 1981 (*Bibliotheca Kierkegaardiana*, vol. 9), pp. 65–82.

Niels Klim:

Project Makers in a World Upside Down

Elisabete M. de Sousa

Niels Klim is the protagonist and narrator of *Nicolai Klimii iter subterraneum* by Ludvig Holberg (1684–1754), originally published in Latin in 1741. Possibly due to its satirical content and fear of the consequences that the author might have had to endure, had the work been published in Danish, Holberg wrote it in Latin and had it published in Leipzig. However, a major goal for Holberg when writing in Latin, the scholarly *lingua franca*, was also to reach a European audience, and undoubtedly to have the work translated. Within a few years the novel was translated into Danish and several other languages. Jens Baggesen's Danish translation from 1789, *Niels Klims Reise til den underjordiske Verden*, is the edition that, most certainly, Kierkegaard was familiar with.[1] Thanks to the initial fortuitous publication in Latin, the work became widely known in Europe, and it was immediately recognized as another landmark in a series of works which since the last years of the seventeenth century had been recreating the ancient Menippean satire by means of providing modern literature with utopian worlds. The initial novel in this trend was Jonathan Swift's *Gulliver's Travels* (1726), the work that is also considered to be the most influential source for Holberg. The voyage of Niels Klim to the center of the Earth also stands as one of the first examples of a science fiction novel, coming after Johannes Kepler's *Somnium* (*The Dream*, 1634), Cyrano de Bergerac's *Comical History of the States and Empires of the Moon* (1656), and Voltaire's *Micromégas* (1752). Thus, it combines elements that are typical of utopian worlds with harsh satire of institutions and customs.

Accordingly, the reader is faced with a content that can be read as satirical of Holberg's milieus. In the work we find abundant and blunt remarks on the politics, religion, and customs of the different peoples and kingdoms where Niels Klim's adventurous travels take him; these remarks contain critical allusions to contemporary institutions. Side by side with these descriptions we find many observations of a scientific nature concerning physics, biology, fauna, and flora in those imaginary lands, as well as anatomical descriptions of their animal and tree-like inhabitants. Such commentaries go a step further than Swift's *Gulliver's Travels*, where the

---

[1]   See *Niels Klims Reise til den underjordiske Verden* in *Jens Baggesens danske Værker*, vols. 1–12, ed. by the sons of the author and C.J. Boye, Copenhagen: Andreas Seidelin 1827–32, vol. 12, pp. 173–370 (*ASKB* 1509–1520).

physical descriptions involve contrasts solely based on the size of things being very large or very small.

Holberg's observations, to a great extent, illustrate the theory that the earth was hollow. This view, which was popular in the seventeenth and eighteenth centuries, can be found in the ideas of the astronomer and mathematician Edmond Halley (1656–1742). Holberg explores this motif systematically with the literary *topos* "the world upside down." This allows the author to depict fantastic worlds as if they were real ones, where everything is out of joint, where what is praised here on earth is criticized there and vice versa. This reaches a climax in a long series of reversed roles and reserved actions, something that in the tradition of the *topos* is known as *similitudo impossibilium*.[2] On the other hand, the degree of detail implied in those descriptions brings the novel close to the imagery of cosmological myths and determines *Niels Klim* as a case of exploration narrative, a sub-genre that would soon see one of its best examples in Alexander von Humboldt's numerous books of travels.[3] The scientific descriptions of the utopian environments and their inhabitants at the center of the earth are very detailed; this contributes to underscoring the pertinence and veracity of the remarks and observations concerning the virtues and morality of the religious and political institutions and dignitaries of those utopian worlds. Moreover, educational values, standards, and expected gender roles are scrutinized, and special emphasis is given to philosophers, as we shall see. Taken all together, these aspects contribute to bring verisimilitude to those imaginary worlds; physically speaking, these are indeed upside down, but, since they are literarily developed in the model of the mentioned *topos*, they are based on completely reversed principles, resulting in a double inversion which allows Holberg's virulent satire against contemporary institutions to emerge. Indeed, the reader is invited to imagine the existence of kingdoms and lands that are described as a world upside down in terms of structure and principles of organization, which exist under the surface of the earth, that is, which occupy a reversed physical position vis-à-vis the position of the reader. Yet, the reader has to use his knowledge of the society he lives in to evaluate the degree of inversion that is depicted in those utopian societies. Thus, by means of the reflection involved in the use of the implicit comparison between the utopian worlds and the world of actuality, the reader is also invited to assess how far the political and religious principles embodied in those utopian worlds correspond to what is going on in the reader's world of actuality. This brings the reader to conclude that the political and religious institutions and dignitaries of his own society should be lampooned just like the ones found in the hollow earth. Once this process is triggered in the reader's imagination, Holberg's criticism becomes totally clear and the reader recognizes the targets of his satire.

The structure of Holberg's novel is complex, and the density of its literary construction implies that characters are intertwined with motifs; so, when Kierkegaard

---

[2]   See Ernst Robert Curtius, *European Literature and the Latin Middle Ages*, trans. by Willard R. Trask, Princeton: Princeton University Press 1953, pp. 94–8.

[3]   The first of these celebrated travel books was Alexander von Humboldt's *Le voyage aux régions equinoxiales du Nouveau Continent, fait en 1799–1804, par Alexandre de Humboldt et Aimé Bonpland*, Paris: N. Maze, Libraire 1807.

alludes or refers either to a motif or to a character, most often, a few of its characteristics are imported, and we might say that they produce a metonymical effect in the text in which they are inserted. The earliest mention, from 1838, belongs to the journals: "*Den Frisindede* is related to *Khavnsposten* the way Niels Klim's caraway pretzels are related to himself."[4] The comparison is between two liberal periodicals of Kierkegaard's day, and it implies that the former feeds itself from the content of the latter and is thus nothing but a mere subsidiary, and that both should be taken as mouthpieces of a world-view that is halfway to becoming a reversed world.

The episode that constitutes the universe of the analogy appears right in the first chapter of *Niels Klim*: while falling down into the center of the earth, Niels Klim felt hungry and, remembering that he had some caraway pretzels in his pocket, took a bite from one, but found it did not taste good. Concluding that earthly food no longer pleased him, he threw it away and, to his surprise, the pretzel started to revolve around him like a satellite around a planet.[5] Howard Hong points out that the figure of something in orbit, with Kierkegaard in the center and symbols of the heavens and of Copenhagen revolving around him,[6] was used in one of the cartoons in the *Corsair* during the infamous polemics.[7] Hong's suggestion gains plausibility, since Kierkegaard, in the accompanying text in the *Corsair*, is indeed portrayed as a *Projektmager*, a term used by Holberg, and, in turn, adopted by Kierkegaard in three different works in order to designate people who conceive schemes that in one way or the other are useless or pointless. In *Niels Klim*, the fate of being a project-maker may align the hero, for the worse, with a metaphysician and a fanatic (all three are banned from the kingdom of Potu),[8] or for the better, with the recognition of his inventiveness, even if the project he sees recognized consists in providing wigs for the all the inhabitants of the kingdom of Martinia, which is beforehand described as the paradise of project-makers, where the strangest and most incongruent projects are taken seriously.[9]

It is indeed the use of the term *Projektmager* that stands as the most relevant presence of *Niels Klim* in Kierkegaard's thought for the reasons that are here enumerated. First, in the different occurrences of this term in the works of Kierkegaard, the critical and/or satirical implications brought to the context of the work in question are consistent; moreover, the content of these works is sufficiently diversified to suggest that this term has become operative in Kierkegaard's conceptual imagery. Second, as pointed out above, this was already acknowledged during the *Corsair* polemics. Third, this is re-elaborated in *Prefaces*, the work that, on the one hand, is the utmost example of satire in Kierkegaard's production, and that, on the other hand, is the one where Holberg's presence is overwhelming, with references

---

[4]   *SKS* 18, 114, FF:207 / *KJN* 2, 106.
[5]   *Niels Klims Reise til den underjordiske Verden* in *Jens Baggesens danske Værker*, vol. 12, p. 180.
[6]   *JP* 5, Explanatory Notes, p. 493, note 479.
[7]   Meir Goldschmidt, "Den store Philosoph," *Corsairen*, no. 285, March 6, 1846, columns 8–11 (in English as "The Great Philosopher," in *COR*, Supplement, 133).
[8]   *Niels Klims Reise til den underjordiske Verden* in *Jens Baggesens danske Værker*, vol. 12, p. 285.
[9]   Ibid., p. 295.

to his plays in every chapter. Curiously enough, the first name of Notabene is the Latin name of Niels, that is, Nicolaus. In fact, from the initial author's preface to every single one of the subsequent ones, *Prefaces* makes a satire on the limits and the domains of philosophy, literature, and theology, and on the profile of their representatives who are themselves described as makers of useless, pointless, and unreliable projects. The ideas are debated in the form of a public *disputatio*, as is typical of the serious pattern of exposition present in Menippean satires. There are no limits to the subversion of arguments and transgression in behavior, and different types of discourse run in parallel. The writer and the written word live side by side with the orator and the spoken word, and fantastic and symbolic elements co-exist with real ones. All this serves the ultimate aim of the satire: to show that what is taken as truth can be demonstrated to be false. Most of these literary elements are also present in *Niels Klim*.

It is worth quoting the passages, respectively from *Philosophical Fragments*, *The Concept of Anxiety*, *Stages on Life's Way*, and *The Book on Adler*. The use of the term *Projektmager* implies more than the falsehood of a theory or science, more like the total unreliability of their proponents and the fruitlessness of their proposals. Since it is translated differently in the English translations, for the sake of clarity, the various versions quoted here are presented in italics. The first excerpt is from Climacus' *Philosophical Fragments*:

> This, as you see, is my project! But perhaps someone will say, "This is the most ludicrous of all projects, or, rather, you are the most ludicrous of all *project-cranks*, for even if someone comes up with a foolish scheme, there is always at least the truth that he is the one who came up with the scheme. But you, on the other hand, are behaving like a vagabond who charges a fee for showing an area that everyone can see.[10]

The next two come from Haufniensis' *The Concept of Anxiety*, and just as in the previous quotation, project-makers are depicted as false philosophers:

> Innocence is ignorance, but how is it lost? I do not intend to repeat all the ingenious and stupid hypotheses with which thinkers and *speculators* have encumbered the beginning of history, men who only out of curiosity were interested in the great human concern called sin, partly because I do not wish to waste the time of others in telling what I myself wasted time in learning, and partly because the whole thing lies outside of history, in the twilight where witches and *speculators* race on broomsticks and sausage-pegs.[11]

If in this first quotation, Haufniensis takes project-makers as a class of thinkers who have tried in vain to make a difference in the history of men, in the second quotation, his tone becomes fiercer and is addressed the project-maker as a kind of false prophet:

> This, of course, is entirely true, yet the confusion is that science did not energetically dismiss foolish questions but instead confirmed superstitious men in their notion that one day there would come a *project-maker* who is smart enough to come up with the

---

[10]   *SKS* 4, 129 / *PF*, 21.
[11]   *SKS* 4, 345 / *CA*, 38–9.

right answer....What the most ordinary man understands in his own way...science with the art of *speculators* has announced as a prize subject that as yet has not been answered satisfactorily....[12]

The fourth is taken from Quidam's diary in *Stages on Life's Way*, associating the project maker with daydreaming:

A year ago today. So the weather turned out fine, even clear. If one starts out early in the morning, seeking freedom and beauty, but the weather is unsettled, one sits in the carriage like a schemer, wondering whether this fickleness can possibly show a more beautiful side so it will meet with one's satisfaction.[13]

The final quotation is from *The Book on Adler*, and the inclusion of a rope also evokes the image of Niels Klim at the beginning of Holberg's story. Niels Klim falling down the cave with the hanging rope around his waist would indeed become a feature of his bodily figure in the eyes of the first inhabitants he meets, who always depicted him with the hanging rope.[14] Kierkegaard writes,

Note. Caesar tells that it was a custom among the Gauls that everyone who made a new proposal had to stand with a rope around his neck—so that they could promptly get rid of him if it did not amount to nothing. If this commendable custom were to be introduced in our day, God knows whether the country would have enough rope, since the whole population has become project planners, and yet perhaps in the first place rope would not even be needed—possibly there would be no one who would volunteer.[15]

There are two more references to Niels Klim in the works of Kierkegaard. Discovering "*à la* Niels Klim" is taken as pursuing knowledge according to aims which have been set because nothing better could be found, just as had happened to Niels Klim, who, although in the possession of a degree, could find nothing suitable to his skills in his hometown and thus dedicated himself to exploring the surrounding countryside.[16] Here is the quotation from the chapter "Reflections on Marriage" in *Stages on Life's Way*:

That the religious is a new immediacy every person easily understands who is satisfied with following the honest path of ordinary common sense. And although I imagine I have but few readers, I confess nevertheless that I do imagine my readers to be among these, since I am far from wanting to instruct the admired ones[17] who make systematic

---

[12]   *SKS* 4, 355–6 / *CA*, 50–1.
[13]   *SKS* 6, 286 / *SLW*, 308.
[14]   See *Niels Klims Reise til den underjordiske Verden* in *Jens Baggesens danske Værker*, vol. 12, pp. 294–5.
[15]   *SKS* 15, 126 / *BA*, 151.
[16]   See *Niels Klims Reise til den underjordiske Verden* in *Jens Baggesens danske Værker*, vol. 12, p. 174.
[17]   "The admired one" is Hans Lassen Martensen (1808–84); see Curtis L. Thompson, *Following the Cultured Public's Chosen One: Why Martensen Mattered to Kierkegaard*, Copenhagen: Museum Tusculanum Press 2008 (*Danish Golden Age Studies*, vol. 4), pp. 113–14.

discoveries à *la* Niels Klim, "who have left their good skin [*Skind*] in order to put on the real appearance [*virkelige Skin*]."[18]

The caraway pretzel returns in a kind of footnote to a fragment from 1849 which contains a fairly long diatribe against his brother, the Bishop Peter Christian Kierkegaard: "for such things can be repeated infinitely, and even the caraway pretzel that Niels Klim lost in his fall—of course, even that immediately assumed a posture imitating N.K."[19] Curiously enough, the fragment begins with direct allusions to two plays by Holberg, *Barselstuen* and *Ulysses von Ithacia*. Kierkegaard proceeds to denounce the unreliability of his brother as scholar, which is indeed another way of depicting him as a project-maker *à la* Klim. This passage was written three years after the *Corsair* affair, and it seems to suggest that Kierkegaard regards the world he was living in as a world upside down.

---

[18]   *SKS* 6, 152 / *SLW*, 162–3.
[19]   *SKS* 22, 418, NB14:128 / *KJN* 6, 424.

Bibliography

Undetermined.

King Lear:

Silence and the Leafage of Language

Nicholas John Chambers

The story and themes of William Shakespeare's tragedy of King Lear, though referenced rather sparsely, provide Søren Kierkegaard throughout his writings with a plentitude of emotive, profound, and overall deeply human insights to augment and illuminate his own ideas.

Shakespeare wrote *King Lear* sometime between 1605 and 1606, during the height of his genius as a tragic playwright. The play opens on a king preparing to divide his kingdom between his three daughters, Goneril, Reagan, and Cordelia. Before granting any inheritance, Lear asks each daughter what she can say to display her love for him. Both Goneril and Reagan shower their father in flowery professions and empty flattery, but when it comes Cordelia's turn, to her father's question she replies, "Nothing," saying that she loves him truly and according to her bond. Though her Father continues to insist she say more, she repeats her reply. For this, Lear repays her by disowning her and splitting her share of the kingdom between the other two. When the Earl of Kent defends Cordelia and accuses the king of madness, Lear exiles him. He then offers Cordelia, abandoned, shamed, and without dowry, to the kings of Burgundy and France. The latter recognizes Cordelia's honor in the face of Lear's injustice and takes her as his wife.

Reagan and Goneril gradually strip Lear of all the rest of his company, home, and honor, essentially sending him into exile. Lear wanders through a heath during a storm, going mad, accompanied by a fool and the Earl of Kent, who has returned in disguise to continue serving the king. Leading up to this, the king has been seeking the fool's counsel, specifically confiding in him that he fears he might lose his mind. These fears come true in his exile as he begins raving and ranting, gradually shedding all his clothing and putting on an imaginary trial for his daughters. The Earl of Gloucester (a loyal lord of the king's court) finds them holed up in a shack and urges them travel to Dover and seek safety with Cordelia, away from Lear's other daughters who plan to kill him. The whole party scatters as the daughters' men arrive. During all of this, England, fearing how France will react when Lear arrives, begins rallying troops for war to protect their newly expanded kingdom.

When Gloucester returns to his home where Goneril and her husband are staying, they interrogate him. The interrogation escalates, and they pluck out his eyes and send him out into the heath to wander. After traveling a while, he again encounters a mad Lear, roaming around on his own, dressed in flowers and weeds. Cordelia's men show up and escort Lear to her camp where he sleeps and starts to recover. When he wakes, Cordelia—who has been absent from the play for more than three acts—forgives him, and they become reconciled.

A battle ensues from the growing military tension, and Cordelia and Lear are captured. Lear embraces this fate, rejoicing simply that his daughter and he will be together, even if in prison. As they are taken away, their execution is secretly ordered by Gloucester's son, who has been manipulating Lear's older daughters. During celebration of their victory, Goneril poisons Reagan in an act of jealousy that has been escalating over the course of the play. In grief and guilt, Goneril runs away and promptly commits suicide. The Earl of Kent and the other men who are left find out about the execution order, but before they can get to the prisons, Lear appears, carrying the dead body of Cordelia. The play ends with his death as he laments his daughter's fate.[1]

I.

Kierkegaard had three different editions of Shakespeare's collected works from which he could have read *King Lear*—two in German and one in Danish.[2] The play was performed in Copenhagen for the first time in 1816, when he was only three years old, and not again until 1851. It is uncertain, however, whether or not he saw the play during his time in Berlin, or even whether it was performed. Nonetheless his familiarity with the play seems to be based primarily on the text.

Though Kierkegaard makes frequent use of Shakespeare, *King Lear* is only referenced explicitly three times in the whole of his authorship, with one additional obvious mention. In his journals and papers, there is a brief analysis of the play and one transcribed quotation from the fourth act. Though scattered and often unrelated, these references to *Lear* come together into a network of analogies that illuminate certain concepts important in Kierkegaard's work.

First, the character of Cordelia in the "Seducer's Diary" of *Either/Or* is an obvious homage to *Lear*. Johannes the Seducer himself, upon learning his target's name, draws the parallel between her and "the third of King Lear's daughters, that remarkable girl whose heart did not dwell on her lips, whose lips were silent when her heart was full."[3] The parallel between the two is based on their silence, which is already an important aesthetic theme in the preceding essays of Part One of *Either/ Or*. Silence, to the aesthetic writer, is the faithful "confidant" of suffering[4] that

---

[1]   For the sake of brevity and simplicity, the subplot surrounding the Earl of Gloucester and his sons has been glossed over. The characters involved, however, do provide enriching counterparts to Lear in his madness.

[2]   William Shakespeare, *Dramatische Werke*, vols. 1–8, trans. by Ernst Ortlepp, Stuttgart: L.F. Reiger 1838–39 (*ASKB* 1874–1881); *Shakespeare's dramatiche Werke*, vols. 1–12, trans. by August Wilhelm Schlegel and Ludwig Tieck, Berlin: G. Reimer 1839-41 (*ASKB* 1883–1888); *William Shakespeare's Dramatiske Værker*, vols. 1–9, trans. by Peter Foersom and Peter Frederik Wulff, Copenhagen: Fr. Brummer 1807-25 (*ASKB* 1889–1896).

[3]   *SKS* 2, 325 / *EOP*, 277.

[4]   *SKS* 2, 42–3 / *EOP*, 51.

preserves the purity of suffering and in the isolation of self-withdrawal is capable of making the sufferer "larger than life."[5]

A more subtle reference to *King Lear* is found in *Fear and Trembling*:

> Thanks, once again to a man who, to a person overwhelmed by life's sorrows and left behind naked, reaches out in the words, the leafage of language by which he can conceal his misery. Thanks to you, great Shakespeare, you who can say everything, everything, everything, just as it is—and yet, why did you never articulate this torment [of Abraham]? Did you perhaps reserve it for yourself, like the beloved's name that one cannot bear to have the world utter, for with his little secret that he cannot divulge the poet buys this power of the word to tell everybody else's dark secrets. A poet is not an apostle; he drives out devils only by the power of the devil.[6]

Though Johannes de silentio is talking explicitly about Shakespeare, the first sentence harkens more specifically to the fourth act of *King Lear*, in which Lear wanders through a heath clothed in flowers in a fever of sorrowful madness. Silentio praises Shakespeare and the character of Lear, but with an ironic turn that immediately reveals their inadequacy before the figure of Abraham (and the religious in general). Shakespeare's masterpiece, though it thoroughly and profoundly expresses a certain universal dimension of human existence, seems to know nothing of transcendence.

Themes tangentially introduced here are revisited more directly in Kierkegaard's later essay, "The Difference Between a Genius and an Apostle," in which Shakespeare serves as his main example of the genius type. In the present survey there is only room to point out that the genius is characterized by immanence and a lack of transcendence and thus does not relate himself to the world but in pride remains enclosed within himself.[7] It is partly on this ground that silentio accuses Shakespeare as a poet of hiding (or hiding from) the truest, deepest suffering—that of the religious hero—by using not the edifying tools of the apostle but instead the "leafage of language" to sink into the tragic.[8] In any case, Lear's verbosity is his (as well as Shakespeare's) incrimination, ironically revealing an incompleteness of human experience that is transcended and fulfilled by Abraham's (as well as Cordelia's) silent obedience.

In *The Concept of Anxiety*, the character of Lear is once again used as a picture of the utmost suffering. This time, however, the particular kind of suffering in question is repentance and thus transcends the category of the aesthetic:

> The posited sin is an unwarranted actuality. It is actuality, and it is posited by the individual as actuality in repentance, but repentance does not become the individual's freedom. Repentance is reduced to a possibility in relation to sin; in other words, repentance cannot cancel sin, it can only sorrow over it. Sin advances in its consequence;

---

[5]   *SKS* 2, 156 / *EOP*, 155.
[6]   *SKS* 4, 154–5 / *FT*, 61.
[7]   *SKS* 11, 110 / *WA*, 107.
[8]   It is perhaps significant that Shakespeare does not give Lear any monologues; such genuine reflection belongs to a higher dimension of suffering. Though Lear's insanity isolates him from the world in some sense, he still requires the external as the occasion of his despair and uses his "transparency" to hide (from) that suffering.

repentance follows it step by step, but always a moment too late. It forces itself to look at the dreadful, but like the mad King Lear (O, thou ruined masterpiece of nature) it has lost the reins of government, and it has retained only the power to grieve. At this point, anxiety is at its highest. Repentance has lost its mind, and anxiety is potentiated into repentance.[9]

Just as Lear is driven to maddening grief when he fully realizes his actions and misfortune, so also the repentant individual sorrows in hindsight over his own sin. Both are filled with the pathos of powerlessness. As will continue to become more apparent, this analogy does not necessarily classify Lear as a religious hero. Kierkegaard (through Vigilius Haufniensis) simply uses Lear's grief (a "lower" suffering of the tragic) as an analogy that can only incompletely clarify the nature of repentance (a "higher" religious suffering).

The final reference in the authorship comes from *Philosophical Fragments*, where Johannes Climacus quotes from the fourth act of the play and then jestingly calls himself out for plagiarizing.[10] The quotation comes from the mouth of Lear and has little to do with the play itself: "'Ay' and 'no' too was no good divinity."[11] Climacus simply uses this quotation in passing to talk about the paradox's relation to the understanding.

Kierkegaard's most direct interaction with the play and the character of King Lear is found in his journals:

> King Lear's fate can be accounted for as Nemesis.[12] His fault is the madness with which the play begins, of summarily requiring his children to declare the depth of their love for him. Children's love for their parents is a bottomless mystery, rooted as well in a natural relationship, and culpable to wish curiously and selfishly to dissect it, as it were, for the sake of one's own satisfaction. Such a thing is tolerable in an erotic relationship (when the lover asks the beloved how much she loves him), although even here it is pandering.[13]

This analysis has a certain consistency with the reference in *The Concept of Anxiety*, because it attributes the responsibility for Lear's downfall in some way to Lear himself. Kierkegaard claims that the most significant "madness" of Lear is found not in his raving and wandering but at the very beginning of the play in his demand for declarations of love from his daughters. This demand exhibits not love but selfishness. His descent into actual insanity is thus the just disintegration of his self under the weight of his own hubris; it is the actualization of a self-destructive pride.

Lastly, though chronologically first, in 1837, Kierkegaard wrote out a passage from *Lear* in one of the "gilt-edged documents" that Walter Lowrie uses to guide

---

[9]   *SKS* 4, 417 / *CA*, 115; the quotation in parentheses comes from Gloucester in Act IV, Scene vi, line 127.

[10]   *SKS* 4, 257 / *PF*, 53.

[11]   Shakespeare, *King Lear*, Act IV, Scene vi, lines 100–101.

[12]   In Greek mythology, Nemesis is the goddess of retribution for hubris and/or undeserved fortune.

[13]   *SKS* 20, 107, NB:169 / *KJN* 4, 107.

his biographies.[14] The quotation comes from Lear after he has been reunited with Cordelia and is so overjoyed by their reconciliation that he willingly accepts imprisonment, so long as they are together:

...So we'll live,
And pray, and sing, and tell old tales, and laugh
At gilded butterflies, and hear poor rogues
Talk of court news; and we'll talk with them too—
Who loses and who wins; who's in, who's out—
And take upon 's the mystery of things
As if we were God's spies; and we'll wear out,
In a walled prison, packs and sects of great ones
That ebb and flow by th' moon.[15]

Lowrie ties this quotation's significance to Kierkegaard's relationship with his own father, saying he read in this passage an expression of his own personal catharsis with his dead father. He even suggests that the first few lines of Lear's whole speech are omitted because they were too poignant.[16]

II.

Kierkegaard's use of *King Lear* is clearly anything but cohesive or thorough. For the most part, he uses the play and its namesake character only for analogies. Given that each reference comes to the reader from a different pseudonym, it is especially difficult to work out Kierkegaard's own reading of the play. As stated above, however, when the analogies are placed together in the scope of the authorship, one can extrapolate some helpful insights into Kierkegaard's overall understanding of tragedy as it is structured and oriented within each life stage.

More specifically, the theme of silence seems to be key in multiple distinctions, namely, between the ancient tragedy and modern tragedy and between the aesthetic hero and the religious hero. The contrast between Lear and Cordelia is instructive for Kierkegaard's understanding of the place and meaning of silence.

In his verbosity, Lear certainly possesses the "transparency"[17] of the sorrow of the ancient hero, according to the young man in *Either/Or*. More specifically, by lamenting himself as one "more sinned against than sinning,"[18] Lear sounds like the ancient tragic hero, who, in the "ambiguity of the aesthetic" suffers the sorrow of fate, in contrast to the modern tragic hero, who suffers more the pain of guilt and

---

[14]   *SKS* 27, 291, Papir 305:3. Walter Lowrie, *Kierkegaard*, New York: Oxford: Oxford University Press 1938, p. 186.
[15]   Shakespeare, *King Lear*, Act V, Scene iii, lines 11–19.
[16]   Walter Lowrie, *A Short Life of Kierkegaard*, Princeton: Princeton University Press 1942, p. 118.
[17]   *SKS* 2, 148 / *EOP*, 150.
[18]   Shakespeare, *King Lear*, Act III, Scene ii, line 60.

remorse.[19] In turn, the same aesthetic ambiguity—rather than true ethical justice—characterizes the wrath of the Greek gods. This expression of Lear is especially ironic in view of Kierkegaard's journal entry discussed above (which explicitly invokes a Greek deity), according to which Lear's fate is precisely the just result of his own actions, specifically his prideful madness and insolence toward the sacredness of love. The ironic doubling of Lear's "madness" and Kierkegaard's invocation of Nemesis demonstrate that, for him, Lear's character, expressions, suffering, and judgment all remain within the realm of the aesthetic. There is a sense, however, in which Lear's laments may be out of place, that the suffering of guilt and remorse may be more appropriate given his responsibility for his own fate.

It is thus not Lear but Cordelia who emerges as the ethical tragic hero. Her struggle, as duty, is with the "public," the "universal," while to Lear, at the beginning of the play, such orders only exist to soothe and bolster his pride. More to the present point, Cordelia's suffering does not find expression; her "heart [does] not dwell on her lips," but rather in the silent resolution of dutiful love. Her "nothing, my lord" transcends the "everything, everything, everything" of human suffering that silentio thanks Shakespeare for expressing.[20] Throughout the play, her continued silence is more terrible than any word of Lear's psychosis, because it belongs to the higher sphere of the ethical.[21] While "the totality of [Lear's] being is thoroughly exhausted by explanation and action,"[22] Cordelia's is invested in the resolution of love.

Though it is primarily focused on Hamlet and does not mention *Lear* explicitly, the discussion of the tragic hero in *Stages on Life's Way* is helpful for further classifying the characters of *King Lear* according to Kierkegaard's understanding. Here, the difference between aesthetic and religious tragedy is viewed more theatrically—that is, in terms of their effect on the spectator. In classical tragedy, the hero "expresses the regular declension of the universal for all,"[23] and the spectator "loses himself in the hero's suffering, forgetting himself in him."[24] However, "the religious man begins in another quarter; he wants to teach the listener not to fear fate, not to lose time in pity for the person who falls before fate."[25] Under the religious, the spectator is actually drawn out of the role of spectator into the realization of his or her own guilt before God. "Fear and compassion," the catharsis of which is essential to a tragedy according to Aristotle, "are to be purified of egotism, but not by becoming lost in contemplation but by finding within oneself a relationship with God."[26] In the tragic, one loses oneself in the universal, while in the religious one both loses

---

[19]   *SKS* 2, 147 / *EOP*, 147.

[20]   Stanley Stewart, "Lear in Kierkegaard," in *King Lear: New Critical Essays*, ed. by Jeffery Kahan, New York: Routledge 2008, p. 291.

[21]   *SKS* 4, 432 / *CA*, 131: "Even though the word were terrible, even though it were a Shakespeare, a Byron, or a Shelley who breaks the silence, the word always retains its redeeming power, because all the despair and all the horror of evil expressed in a word are not as terrible as silence."

[22]   Stewart, "Lear in Kierkegaard," p. 284.

[23]   *SKS* 7, 235 / *CUP1*, 259.

[24]   *SKS* 6, 425 / *SLW*, 460.

[25]   *SKS* 6, 426 / *SLW*, 462.

[26]   Ibid.

and finds oneself in God. The religious hero cannot despair over the external as Lear does, because he has lost the world in view of God and his own particularity before God. The reader will recognize that this is once again related to Kierkegaard's discussion of the difference between a genius and apostle. The qualitative difference between the two is the relation to transcendence.

All that being said, according to the criteria laid out in *Stages*, no character in *King Lear* seems to enter into the religious. The religious, like Cordelia's ethical struggle, is characterized by silence. The suffering of the religious, however, is indifferent to the external; it arises from within oneself in one's relation to God.[27] Thus, the silence of the religious is specifically precipitated by consciousness of one's own sin. Cordelia's sorrowful silence is at once a silence of duty and sorrow, but never of guilt before God. Similarly, while Lear experiences isolation from the world just as the religious hero does, his very vocal suffering is never strictly *before God*, which is the essentially religious relation. As Kierkegaard says elsewhere:

> But even Shakespeare seems to have recoiled from essentially religious collisions. Indeed, perhaps these can be expressed only in the language of the gods. And no human being can speak this language. As a Greek has already said so beautifully: From men, man learns to speak, from the gods, to be silent.[28]

In summary, silence has new significance in each sphere. To the aesthete, it is the secret of the poet, the confidant of truly profound suffering. To the ethical individual, it is the mode of ethical resolve and moral struggle. Finally, to the religious self, silence is the proper posture before the transcendent God. According to this understanding, there is no directly religious interpretation of *King Lear* and its characters, because they do not account for a sphere of true transcendence. Lear and others call out to "gods" and "Nature" only as personifications of the blind dispensation of fate.

The tragedy of *King Lear*, though not extensively treated in Kierkegaard's body of work, serves as an instrumental analogy in many texts to communicate his understanding of tragedy, suffering, and silence. The play even offers a compelling dramatic presentation of at least part of Kierkegaard's larger system of the spheres of human life. As the young man in *Either/Or* says, in Shakespeare "at least one feels that it's human beings that are talking."[29]

---

[27]   *SKS* 6, 427 / *SLW*, 463.
[28]   *SKS* 11, 238 / *SUD*, 128.
[29]   *SKS* 2, 37 / *EOP*, 48.

Bibliography

Rasmussen, Joel D.S., "William Shakespeare: Kierkegaard's Post-Romantic Reception of 'the Poet's Poet,'" in *Kierkegaard and the Renaissance and Modern Traditions*, Tome III, *Literature, Drama and Music*, ed. by Jon Stewart, Aldershot: Ashgate 2009 (*Kierkegaard Research: Sources, Reception and Resources*, vol. 5), pp. 185–213.

Ruoff, James E., "Kierkegaard and Shakespeare," in *Comparative Literature*, vol. 20, 1968, pp. 343–54.

Sløk, Johannes, *Kierkegaard og Shakespeare*, Copenhagen: Berlingske Forlag 1972.

Stewart, Stanley, "Lear in Kierkegaard," in *King Lear: New Critical Essays*, ed. by Jeffery Kahan, New York: Routledge 2008, pp. 278–96.

Loki:

Romanticism and Kierkegaard's Critique of the Aesthetic

Matthew Brake

When discussing Søren Kierkegaard's use of Loki as a literary motif, one is not left with much to work with. While there are references to Norse mythology sprinkled throughout the Kierkegaardian *corpus*, the only references found for Loki are in *The Concept of Irony*, *Either/Or*, Parts One and Two, and a few scattered references in the journals. These references do not treat Loki in any significant detail; rather, they appear to be passing illustrations Kierkegaard uses to make a larger point. In evaluating Kierkegaard's use of Loki, this article will be divided into three parts. Part I will describe the figure of Loki as well as the primary story upon which Kierkegaard draws his references. Part II will consider the surrounding cultural influences, which allowed Kierkegaard to reference Loki in such a passing way. This will involve a brief account of Kierkegaard's surrounding culture, specifically Romanticism in nineteenth-century Denmark. We will then consider the Danish cultural figures Adam Oehlenschläger and N.F.S. Grundtvig and the impact that they had upon the Danish landscape in Kierkegaard's day. Part III will examine Kierkegaard's specific references to Loki, particularly as they pertain to his use of this figure to criticize aesthetic Romanticism.

I. Loki and the Death of Balder

In Norse mythology, Loki is a trickster who lives among the gods, but he is really a descendant of giants.[1] Odin, the head of the Norse pantheon,[2] and Loki are blood brothers in the "mythic present," although the latter was "the enemy of the gods in the far mythic past," and he will revert back to being an enemy in the "mythic future" of Ragnarok, where his actions lead to the death "of the gods and the cosmos."[3] In the mythic present, Loki is depicted as an ambivalent companion of the Norse gods. On the one hand, he often accompanies the other gods on their travels, and at times, he is willing to sacrifice his reputation for the gods. On the other hand, he

---

[1]   John Lindow, *Norse Mythology: A Guide to the Gods, Heroes, Rituals, and Beliefs*, New York: Oxford University Press 2001, p. 216.
[2]   Ibid., p. 247.
[3]   Ibid., p. 219.

often causes complications for them, and many of them blame him for their troubles before actually establishing his guilt.[4]

The main story Kierkegaard draws upon in reference to Loki is the death of Balder. Balder was the most beautiful, beloved, and wise of the Norse gods.[5] In the story, Balder begins to have dreams about his death. Upon learning of his dreams, the other gods "took council and decided to seek a truce for Balder, protecting him from all dangers."[6] Once his mother Frigg obtained this protection for Balder, the other gods began to shoot at him or strike him with blows for their amusement since he could not be harmed.[7] Loki was displeased that Balder was not hurt, so disguising himself as a woman, he tricked Frigg into revealing that mistletoe was the one thing that could harm Balder. Loki obtained a branch of mistletoe and tricked the blind god Hod to throw it at Balder, which instantly killed him.[8] The gods punished Loki for his mischief by securing him to a rock. They placed a poisonous snake above Loki whose venom dripped down upon him and caused him great pain; however, Loki's wife Sigyn came and stood next to him, holding a bowl over his head. She collected the poison in the bowl, but when she emptied it, the poison dripped down on Loki once more.[9] This story plays a central role in Kierkegaard's appropriation of Loki.

II. Nationalism and Romanticism

As William McDonald notes, Romanticism seemed to be on the decline when Kierkegaard began his first authorship; however, the young Kierkegaard was greatly influenced by Romantic thought, as evidenced by his journal entries between the years 1834 and 1837. Even though the post-1837 Kierkegaard may not be considered a Romantic, he still continued to engage with Romantic thought.[10] Part of what defined the thought process of Romanticism was the "[s]pecific emphasis… given to the living sources of history within a people—myth, legend, fairy tales, folk songs—that the speculative philosophers viewed as the source of both religion and science."[11] Early Danish Romanticism specifically "sought the roots of national identity in folktales and folk music."[12] Two figures in particular who helped give prominence to Norse myth in Denmark when Romantic thought was prevalent were Adam Oehlenschläger and N.F.S. Grundtvig.

---

[4]   Ibid., p. 217.

[5]   Ibid., 65–6.

[6]   Snorri Sturluson, *The Prose Edda: Norse Mythology*, trans. by Jesse L. Byock, New York: Penguin Group 2005, p. 65.

[7]   Ibid.

[8]   Ibid., pp. 65–6.

[9]   Ibid., p. 70.

[10]   William McDonald, "Kierkegaard and Romanticism," *The Oxford Handbook of Kierkegaard*, ed. by John Lippitt and George Pattison, Oxford: Oxford University Press 2013, pp. 94–5.

[11]   Jørgen Bukdahl, *Søren Kierkegaard and the Common Man*, trans. and ed. by Bruce H. Kirmmse, Grand Rapids, Michigan: Eerdmans 2001, p. 2.

[12]   McDonald, "Kierkegaard and Romanticism," p. 96.

Oehlenschläger was one of the first Danish Romantics and a very prominent figure in bringing Norse mythology into the popular consciousness.[13] Before Oehlenschläger, Danish writers had mixed opinions about Norse mythology. There was a "prevailing negative view of Norse mythology" because "those antagonistic to the poetic use of Norse mythology [found] it impoverished and crude in comparison with the Greek," although some did take it seriously.[14] In Oehlenschläger's view, the Norse myths were special because one could find in them the hidden history of the North; therefore, Oehlenschläger believed that "Norse mythology must necessarily be intrinsically more interesting to the Northerner."[15] Oehlenschläger concluded, "the Norse myths and sagas could also serve as an inspiration for patriotism and national spirit."[16]

That Kierkegaard's world was shaped by Oehlenschläger and his employment of Norse myth is beyond doubt. As Kirmmse notes, by 1812, Oehlenschläger was considered "the unquestioned poet-king of the nation."[17] Although the quality of his poetry began to decline after 1818,[18] Kierkegaard's writings, particularly *Either/Or*, may very well be located within Oehlenschläger's Romanticism.[19] Oehlenschläger can very well be credited with being an influence on Kierkegaard's knowledge, appropriation, and use of Norse myth; however, there is one other figure who is worth considering in this regard, the Danish writer and pastor Nicolai Frederik Severin Grundtvig.

Grundtvig, unlike Oehlenschläger, is not counted as a proper Romantic, although his writings contain many Romantic ideas.[20] Flemming Lundgreen-Nielsen states that he is not classified as a Romantic due in large part to "his changing yet steadily growing sympathy for evangelical Christianity."[21] Nevertheless, Martin Arnold states that

> [N]ot even Oehlenschläger could rival the zeal and absolute conviction with which Grundtvig approached his campaign to revivify Danish culture and learning through an understanding of northern mythology: Grundtvig regarded the eddas as not only a neglected heritage, but also as a symbolic expression of the "truth" of the northern soul.

---

[13]   Kathryn Shailer-Hanson, "Adam Oehlenschläger's *Eric and Roller* and Danish Romanticism," in *Kierkegaard and His Contemporaries: The Culture of Golden Age Denmark*, ed. by Jon Stewart, New York: Walter de Gruyter 2003 (*Kierkegaard Studies Monograph Series*, vol. 10), pp. 233–5.

[14]   Ibid., pp. 237–8.

[15]   Ibid., p. 237.

[16]   Ibid.

[17]   Bruce H. Kirmmse, *Kierkegaard in Golden Age Denmark*, Bloomington and Indianapolis: Indiana University Press 1990, p. 95.

[18]   Ibid., p. 87.

[19]   David J. Gouwens, "Kierkegaard's *Either/Or*, Part One: Patterns of Interpretation," *Either/Or, Part One*, ed. by Robert Perkins, Macon, Georgia: Mercer University Press 1995 (*International Kierkegaard Commentary*, vol. 3), p. 16.

[20]   Flemming Lundgreen-Nielsen, "Grundtvig and Romanticism," in *Kierkegaard and his Contemporaries: The Culture of Golden Age Denmark*, ed. by Jon Stewart, p. 219.

[21]   Ibid.

If Oehlenschläger was the guardian of the old religion, Grundtvig was its evangelist, and he saw no contradiction between this vocation and his undeniably profound Christian faith; rather, he regarded the two as mutually stimulating or, even more than this for the dulled northern psyche, mutually essential.[22]

For Grundtvig, Norse mythology was a vehicle for pointing towards Christianity as well as for awakening national zeal.[23]

Regarding this first point, Grundtvig believed that national myths pointed the way to God and prepared a people's hearts to receive Christ.[24] Grundtvig struggled with the orthodox Lutheranism of his day, particularly its "doctrine of…the separate and nearly irreconcilable realms of the sacred and the secular, the spirit and the flesh."[25] In Nordic myth, Grundtvig found "a means of expressing both the struggle and the healing of the split in a way which did not seem possible in the context of the Christianity of his day."[26] This healing of the split ended up taking the form of Grundtvig's idea of the "human first."[27] Stephen Backhouse explains:

> Drawing from his earlier enthusiasm for Norse mythology and pagan culture, Grundtvig developed his theory that the depth and breadth of human experience need not be understood exclusively within "Christian" forms. Mankind and its cultures was a thing to be celebrated as part of God's good creation—Christianity was not an escape route but a participation in and completion of human culture. At its most basic, "human first" maintains that until one comprehends the fully human, Christianity remains alien.[28]

Nordic mythology was thus a way in which Grundtvig sought the "human first," and the "human first" was a necessary component of becoming truly Christian.

Concerning the second point, within the Norse myths, Grundtvig found unique to the Northern peoples a heroism, "which serves to describe their present character and in turn provides a clear prophetic element that suggests the people's Divine destiny."[29] The Norse myths indicated that the "Scandinavians are the sons of a great race of giants,"[30] and Grundtvig became "convinced that God had chosen the Danes for the task of returning ancient glories to the North."[31] Grundtvig believed

---

[22]   Martin Arnold, *Thor: Myth to Marvel*, New York: Continuum 2011, p. 112.

[23]   George Pattison, *Kierkegaard, Religion and the Nineteenth-Century Crisis of Culture*, New York: Cambridge University Press 2002, pp. 156–7.

[24]   Steven Borish, "N.F.S. Grundtvig as Charismatic Prophet: An Analysis of his Life and Work in the Light of Revitalization-Movement Theory," *Scandinavian Journal of Educational Research*, vol. 42, no. 3, 1998, pp. 246–7.

[25]   Martin Chase, "True at Any Time: Grundtvig's Subjective Interpretation of Nordic Myth," *Scandinavian Studies*, vol. 73, no. 4, 2001, p. 521.

[26]   Ibid., p. 521.

[27]   Stephen Backhouse, *Kierkegaard's Critique of Christian Nationalism*, New York: Oxford University Press 2011, p. 75.

[28]   Ibid.

[29]   Ibid., p. 83.

[30]   Kirmmse, *Kierkegaard in Golden Age Denmark*, p. 223.

[31]   E.F. Fain, "Nationalist Origins of the Folk High School: The Romantic Visions of N.F.S. Grundtvig," *British Journal of Educational Studies*, vol. 19, no. 1, 1971, p. 79.

this was necessary because he believed that "Denmark [had] a pre-eminent place in God's plan for history."[32] The Danes were God's chosen people, whose inheritance included the heroic spirit of the Norsemen, and because of this inheritance, they were the ultimate expression of Christianity in the present age.[33]

It should also be noted in this context that Nordic mythology was an important motif in Danish Golden Age painting. The artists from the period tried to inspire nationalism by departing from the standard neoclassical themes from Greek and Roman mythology and portraying Danish landscapes with dolmens or other elements from the Nordic past. The famous Danish painter Christoffer Wilhelm Eckersberg depicted Loki in his painting *The Death of Balder* from 1817. Balder lies dead in the foreground while Odin and the other gods look on in shock and anger. Standing behind Hod, Loki tries to slink away as he represses a smile of amusement at the scene.

III. Kierkegaard's References to Norse Mythology and Loki

Kierkegaard's references to Norse mythology, and to Loki specifically, should be seen within the cultural conversations occurring during his own day. As I have already noted, Kierkegaard lived in a Denmark whose consciousness was shaped by Oehlenschläger's Romanticism. Likewise, Kierkegaard was familiar with the writings of Grundtvig although he was "contemptuous of Grundtvig's pan-Scandinavian nationalism in which the Scandinavian peoples emerge as the new bearers of the divine message."[34] Kierkegaard himself owned three different works by Grundtvig that treat Nordic mythology.[35] Eight years before publishing *Either/Or*, Kierkegaard read the Romantic authors, some of whom "sought to preserve perfections of a golden past—even an unexperienced past, a past that never was but might, somehow mysteriously in them, be *re*born."[36] This idea of the past being reborn can be seen in Grundtvig's interpretation of Ragnorak as a sign of Danish rebirth.[37] The cultural interpretations of Norse myth in Kierkegaard's day, influenced by Romanticism and propagated by writers such as Oehlenschläger and Grundtvig, clearly played an important role in Kierkegaard's use of Norse figures such as Loki,

---

[32]   Backhouse, *Kierkegaard's Critique of Christian Nationalism*, p. 87.

[33]   Ibid., pp. 87–8.

[34]   George Pattison, *Kierkegaard and the Theology of the Nineteenth Century: The Paradox of the 'Point of Contact,'* New York: Cambridge University Press 2012, p. 179.

[35]   N.F.S. Grundtvig, *Brage-Snak om Græske og Nordiske Myther og Oldsagn for Damer og Herrer*, Copenhagen: C.A. Reitzel 1844 (*ASKB* 1548). N.F.S. Grundtvig, *Nordens Mythologie eller Udsigt over Eddalæren for dannede Mænd der ei selv ere Mythologer*, Copenhagen: J.H. Schubothes Forlag 1808 (*ASKB* 1948). N.F.S. Grundtvig, *Nordens Mythologi eller Sindbilled-Sprog historisk-poetisk udviklet og oplyst*, 2nd revised ed., Copenhagen: J.H. Schubothes Boghandling 1832 (*ASKB* 1949).

[36]   Bradley R. Dewey, "Seven Seducers: A Typology of Interpretations of the Aesthetic Stage in Kierkegaard's 'The Seducer's Diary,'" in *Either/Or, Part One*, ed. by Perkins, p. 190.

[37]   Chase, "True at Any Time: Grundtvig's Subjective Interpretation of Nordic Myth," pp. 530–2.

who would have been well known in the cultural consciousness of nineteenth-century Denmark.

Having established the cultural influences of Kierkegaard's use of Norse myth, we will now focus on Kierkegaard's appropriation of Loki within his works. We will primarily concern ourselves with the references to Loki found in *The Concept of Irony* and *Either/Or*, Parts One and Two. In an ironic twist, Kierkegaard seems to use the Norse myths, so loved by the Romantics, to refute the Romantics since all of these references to Loki appear as a critique of the aesthete.[38] Whereas the early Danish Romantics had a strong nationalist purpose in their writings, the later Romantics at the beginning of Kierkegaard's authorship were "characterized by individualism, passion, exoticism, and rebellion."[39] It is against the later Romantics that he largely directs his criticisms.[40] In what follows, we will examine Kierkegaard's use of Loki as a description of the aesthetic life. Next, we will see how the pseudonym A describes the boredom of the aesthete with an analogy of Loki. Finally, we will look at Judge William's use of Loki to critique the aesthete's understanding of love.

Kierkegaard's first use of Loki to criticize the life of the aesthetic person can be found in *The Concept of Irony*. In this instance, Kierkegaard is criticizing the ironic aesthete who creates himself poetically. As opposed to the person who recognizes what is unique in himself and guides himself toward the objective for which he was uniquely made, the aesthete recognizes no objective uniqueness; rather, the aesthete allows himself to be continually remade thereby making himself nothing.[41] The aesthete recreates himself at will and becomes "a word without meaning."[42]

As Kierkegaard continues to criticize the aesthete, he describes the aesthete's existence as being that of "contrasting moods [which] succeed one another."[43] He says:

> As the ironist poetically composes himself and his environment with the greatest possible poetic license, as he lives in this totally hypothetical and subjunctive way, his life loses all continuity. He succumbs completely to mood. His life is nothing but moods.[44]

Kierkegaard compares to Loki this succession of moods by which "an ironist who by the very duality of his existence lacked existence."[45] This analogy refers to the shifting nature of Loki's allegiances, at times aiding the gods and at other times causing them trouble.[46] Such is the nature of the aesthete's shifting moods.

According to Kierkegaard, the ironist possesses one form of continuity: boredom.[47] He describes this boredom as follows:

---

[38]   In saying this, it is important to remember that Kierkegaard associated the aesthetic with Romanticism. See McDonald, "Kierkegaard and Romanticism," p. 94.

[39]   Ibid., p. 96.

[40]   Ibid.

[41]   *SKS* 1, 316–17 / *CI*, 280–1.

[42]   *SKS* 1, 317–18 / *CI*, 282–3.

[43]   *SKS* 1, 320 / *CI*, 284.

[44]   *SKS* 1, 319 / *CI*, 284.

[45]   *SKS* 1, 321 / *CI*, 285.

[46]   See *CI*, Explanatory Notes, 547, note 96.

[47]   *SKS* 1, 321 / *CI*, 285.

Boredom, this eternity devoid of content, this salvation devoid of joy, this superficial profundity, this hungry glut. But boredom is precisely the negative unity admitted into a personal consciousness, wherein the opposites vanish.[48]

This idea of boredom defining the life of the aesthetic is picked up by A in Part One of *Either/Or*. A describes the dreadful emptiness of boredom, saying that he "[does] not even suffer pain."[49] He says:

Pain itself has lost its refreshment for me. If I were offered all the glories of the world or all the torments of the world, one would move me no more than the other; I would not turn over to the other side either to attain or to avoid. I am dying death.[50]

A compares this boredom to the pain of Loki, who experienced pain as an interruption to his boredom whenever his wife poured the poison out of the bowl.[51] A is indicating that Loki's existence was filled with less boredom than his own.

Judge William's use of Loki to critique the aesthete is a reference to the story of the death of the Norse god Balder.[52] Judge William uses this story to illustrate a weakness in the aesthete's view of love in his essay, "The Esthetic Validity of Marriage." He uses mistletoe, which was the undoing of Balder, to represent the "life principle of [the aesthete's] love."[53] The aesthete's love is defined by his moodiness. As Judge William says:

But this mistletoe is a sign of the feverish restlessness that is the life principle of your love; it cools off and heats up, is continually changing—indeed, you could simultaneously wish that the two of you might have an eternity before you and that this present instant might be the last—and therefore the death of your love is certain.[54]

The changing moods of the aesthete are again under fire here. Loki is thus appropriated, albeit implicitly, in Kierkegaard's authorship to address and critique the lack of continuity in the aesthetic life and is appropriated by Judge William to make an appeal for the ethical life.

IV. Conclusion

Kierkegaard's use of Loki in his writings can first and foremost be explained by the age in which he lived. The Romantics sought the true history of a people in mythology, and writers such as Oehlenschläger and Grundtvig played a large role in bringing Norse myth into the popular consciousness of the Danish population.

---

[48]   *SKS* 1, 320 / *CI*, 285.
[49]   *SKS* 2, 46 / *EO1*, 37.
[50]   Ibid.
[51]   Ibid. See *EO1*, Explanatory Notes, 611, note 104. In *Stages on Life's Way*, the analogy of Loki's wife emptying the bowl of poison is also used to describe the evening release of a father's depression. See *SKS* 6, 184–5 / *SLW*, 197.
[52]   See *EO2*, Explanatory Notes, 474, note 65.
[53]   *SKS* 3, 62 / *EO2*, 57.
[54]   Ibid.

Kierkegaard himself, having been interested in Romanticism prior to the beginning of his authorship, was familiar with the Romantic writers and shared their love of mythology. As Kierkegaard's first authorship began, however, he appropriated the figure of Loki, not to affirm Romantic principles, but to critique them. This is the predominant use of Loki as a literary motif in Kierkegaard's authorship.

Bibliography

Undetermined.

Lucinde:

"To live poetically is to live infinitely," or Kierkegaard's Concept of Irony as Portrayed in his Analysis of Friedrich Schlegel's Work

Fernando Manuel Ferreira da Silva

I.

Given the latest analysis of the literary and philosophical relation between Søren Kierkegaard and Friedrich Schlegel (1772–1829), one fact is certain: such a theoretical link *does indeed exist*, and Friedrich Schlegel, German philosopher, poet, and translator, and one of the great theorizers of the German Romanticism, is an author to whom the young Kierkegaard owes much of what constituted the first form of his own system of thought. Notwithstanding this fact, once confronted with the task of establishing a theoretical bridge between Kierkegaard and Schlegel, I dare say that even the unacquainted reader will stumble upon two immediate doubts. The first one is: is there a *valid*—and traceable—source of contact between both authors? —a question which, unlike the second (double) question to which it gives birth, bears no complexity. And the second question is: if that relation exists—and we have just confirmed it does—what grounds does it rely upon? This question might be reformulated to read: what use does Kierkegaard make of the character of Lucinde, especially in the scope of the development of his concept of irony/poeticity?

Kierkegaard's connection to Schlegel is rather solid and, at an ulterior level, quite visible, especially in his youth. Regardless of the fact that Kierkegaard only rarely cites Schlegel, if we consider the bulk of these citations[1] it will not be difficult to conclude that the focus of Kierkegaard's interest in Schlegel resides mainly in the latter's novel *Lucinde* (1799)[2] and, therefore, in its main topic, *irony*. But there is more than this. *Lucinde* was, as Kierkegaard says, something like "the

---

[1]   All of Kierkegaard's citations of *Lucinde* are contained in his *The Concept of Irony*, more specifically in "Friedrich Schlegel" in the chapter "Irony after Fichte": *SKS* 1, 321–34 / *CI*, 286–301.

[2]   Kierkegaard was not only the owner of Schlegel's *Collected Works* (*Friedrich Schlegel's Sämmtliche Werke*, vols. 1–10, Vienna: Jacob Mayer und Compagnie 1822–25 (*ASKB* 1816–1825)), but also acquainted with Friedrich Schleiermacher's *Vertraute Briefe über die Lucinde*.

Gospel of Young Germany,"[3] words which, to him, certainly embodied the work's true character. For *Lucinde* was, indeed, not only the result of Schlegel's previous work, but also, quite strangely, a break with his later work. It was a new kind of romance in itself (not only in its "obscene" content,[4] but also in its innovative form and disposition[5]), and, yet, it was a work whose experimental, anti-climatic (ironic) character Kierkegaard recognizes and sets in its proper position in the history of German thought, despite its singularity, despite the fact that its "ideal climate [is] nowhere to be found."[6] Kierkegaard sees it as a rather strong, though, as we shall see, in his eyes not sufficiently strong, *ironic* reaction to Kant and especially to Fichte's philosophy of the absolute "I." Herein lies the reason why Kierkegaard inscribes his own analysis of *Lucinde* precisely in his dissertation *The Concept of Irony* (1841), more specifically in the chapter "Irony after Fichte" and in the section titled "Friedrich Schlegel."

This, on the one hand, only proves that Schlegel influenced Kierkegaard at a very early stage of the development of his system of thinking—one could say even at its *very beginning*—and that the focus of that influence was precisely the topic of *irony*, which leads us to conclude that irony's ductility from work to work, from time to time, was, *per se*, one of the earliest—and strongest—motifs for Kierkegaard's reflection. One need only think of the subsequent sections, dedicated to Ludwig Tieck and Ferdinand Solger, to verify the irrefutability of this fact. On the other hand, it shows the reader that *The Concept of Irony* is not in itself—nor does its internal connection present—a mere historicization of the evolution of the concept of irony until Schlegel's *Lucinde*. Much more than that, it represents the possibility of using (Romantic) irony in choosing language as a medium of expression to defy man's—and his subjectivity's—boundaries, by striving to unite both extremes, religion and irreligiousness, spiritualization and sensuousness, language and silence, interiority and exteriority—an ambition which Kierkegaard, in *The Concept of Irony*, ultimately wishes to compare to that of Schlegel in his *Lucinde*.

As for the second question, it is more explicitly addressed in the very first pages of "Irony after Fichte," where Kierkegaard exposes his aim in presenting Schlegel's *Lucinde* as an ironic work.

Kierkegaard's intention with Schlegel's *Lucinde* is primarily to place the work in its proper position: "to form an estimate of Schlegel's efforts and those of the younger and older romantics"[7] as two separate (and extreme) views of the problem of irony. For Kierkegaard departs from the fact that Schlegel wishes to found his irony upon love (which is correct), but, in doing so, Schlegel is led to face an "ideal climate

---

3   *SKS* 1, 321 / *CI*, 286.
4   Ibid.
5   Schlegel's *Lucinde* was composed of letters, essays, confessions, diaries, and other diverse styles, all in the same novel, which, although deemed preposterous and quite confusing by Kierkegaard, seems to have been the model chosen by Kierkegaard himself in the composition of his *Either/Or.*
6   *SKS* 1, 322 / *CI*, 286.
7   *SKS* 1, 323 / *CI*, 288.

nowhere to be found"[8] caused by the bout between "moral prudery"[9] (excessive spiritualization) and an "exaggerated romanticism"[10] (excessive sensuousness)—a double path which is, of course, doubly opposed to irony, but which Schlegel nonetheless tries to trudge in all its profanity ("*profanas*"[11]). *Ironic profanity* is, therefore, the primordial character of *Lucinde*, and the way it progresses is a way of eccentricity and, yet, as is natural, a hybrid way between the two excessive ways it wishes to avoid, that being the most distinctive sign of its time, for "Those days are over and gone—those days when everything loved for love alone and for the happy lovers everything in turn was but a myth about love."[12] That is why, in this position halfway between the over-spiritualization of the world and its outcome in an "age so saturated with reflection"[13] like Kierkegaard's, "Schlegel's *Lucinde* is an attempt to suspend all ethics."[14] For, according to Kierkegaard, Schlegel's intention was to begin to refute his predecessors in the analysis of irony by inverting the axis of the problem ("the "straitjacket" of "moral prudery"[15]) by, in other words, taking the first step towards the negation of the flesh by the spirit to the negation of the spirit by the flesh.[16] The application of the intent, however, resulted, according to Kierkegaard, in Schlegel's own exaggeration of the inversion of such polarities, and in opening the way to the obscene voluptuousness, the "naked sensuousness"[17] of his posterity. Schlegel, so to speak, gave his irony too much "free rein,"[18] and that ironic exacerbation, that "brazenness"[19] that characterizes Lucinde (for Lisette, for instance, does "not live in the ordinary world but in a self-created world"[20] of irony) was, in turn, the major problem Kierkegaard's own concept of irony now faced, and the first trait of the idea Kierkegaard made of Schlegel's *Lucinde*.

Kierkegaard tries to exemplify such a striking dissonance—and the way Schlegel, according to him, unsuccessfully tries to keep his balance between both religious and irreligious extremes—in the characters of Lucius and Lisette, and the way they portray the novel's intrinsic "confusion and disorder."[21] Lucius is a character who intends to destroy order, and, in trying to do so, "abandons all understanding and lets fantasy alone prevail,"[22] but, as Kierkegaard stresses, he "is no Don Juan."[23]

---

[8]   *SKS* 1, 322 / *CI*, 286.
[9]   *SKS* 1, 322 / *CI*, 288.
[10]   Ibid.
[11]   *SKS* 1, 323 / *CI*, 288.
[12]   Ibid.
[13]   *SKS* 1, 331 / *CI*, 298.
[14]   *SKS* 1, 324 / *CI*, 289.
[15]   *SKS* 1, 323 / *CI*, 288.
[16]   *SKS* 1, 323–4 / *CI*, 289: "Christianity has set flesh and spirit at variance, and either the spirit has to negate flesh or the flesh has to negate the spirit. Romanticism wants the latter."
[17]   *SKS* 1, 325 / *CI*, 291.
[18]   *SKS* 1, 330 / *CI*, 296.
[19]   *SKS* 1, 324 / *CI*, 290.
[20]   *SKS* 1, 325 / *CI*, 290–1.
[21]   *SKS* 1, 326 / *CI*, 292.
[22]   Ibid.
[23]   *SKS* 1, 327 / *CI*, 293.

This means, of course, that Julius does not correspond to the image of the *seducer*, nor is he a symbol of Socrates' ironic *daimon*; quite on the contrary, Kierkegaard states, he is "a personality trapped in reflection,"[24] and, just like Goethe's Faust, he starts off as the image of a character who, citing Kierkegaard, indeed still lives in the "straitjacket"[25] of prudery, but who is led by that very same interior disruption to be acquainted with the "black art[s],"[26] a young man who "still raises his goblet with a certain dignity and charm, with a worldly intellectual ease,"[27] who "has had a long acquaintance with the thought of suicide,"[28] all Faustian qualities. But he does carry, despite all these traits, the symbol of a dissimulated religiousness with him. In a word, Julius' ironic effect consists of being a moral character on the verge of becoming immoral—and it is "love [which] must rescue him,"[29] something that happens when he meets "the instructor he needs in Lisette, a teacher who has long been initiated in the nocturnal mysteries of love."[30]

But who is Lisette, and what does she mean to both authors? To Schlegel, bearing in mind Julius' character, she is the necessary step towards the transition between prudery and the required level of sensuousness—in other words, *poeticity itself,* or the "catechism of love."[31] To Kierkegaard, she is *the very same*—and that is, as was said, the very root of his problem with Lucinde. To Kierkegaard, Lisette "had devoted herself totally to the service of sensuousness";[32] "mirrors reflecting her image on all sides provide the only consciousness she has left";[33] she "had no sense for anything but reality,"[34] a person thus indifferent to life, detached from it, addressing herself by the "third person,"[35] "who would write her own story as if it were that of someone else"[36]—to sum up, the very image of the absence of an appropriate climate for love (something which Kierkegaard also stresses), an "esthetic stupefaction that actually comes out in the whole of Lucinde"[37] and in which also the remainder of Julius' religious character submerges under the violence of her waves of irreligiousness. Above all, however, if there is something that emanates from the previous chapters of *The Concept of Irony*, it is that Lisette is the very image of irony in its anti-climatic, insidious, love-hate character; irony is, to Kierkegaard, what attracts Julius to Lisette, it is the preparation of the ground for a love which it will never receive, it is, in a word, the true voice of impossibility, and, as such, a pure negation which, for Schlegel is the true poetic character of Julius' union to Lisette.

24   Ibid.
25   *SKS* 1, 323 / *CI*, 288.
26   Ibid.
27   Ibid.
28   Ibid.
29   *SKS* 1, 327 / *CI*, 294.
30   *SKS* 1, 328 / *CI*, 294.
31   *SKS* 1, 325 / *CI*, 291.
32   *SKS* 1, 328 / *CI*, 294.
33   Ibid.
34   Ibid.
35   *SKS* 1, 329 / *CI*, 295.
36   Ibid.
37   *SKS* 1, 329 / *CI*, 295–6.

Therefore, it is no surprise that, to Kierkegaard, Lucinde's problem, thus so unevenly balanced between Julius and Lisette, acquires a different theoretical shape. For *Lucinde*, Kierkegaard stresses, is Schlegel's attempt to "suspend all ethics."[38] But, at the same time, the image of the boldness of its Romanticism breaks with the past, as well as sets the parameters of ironic poeticity for the future: its immediate goal is to deny the spirit and accept the flesh, and "its difference from Greek culture." Kierkegaard adds, "in its enjoyment of the flesh it also enjoys the negation of the spirit."[39] What this means, however, is that by approaching Schlegel's *Lucinde*, Kierkegaard wishes to stress that *Lucinde*—in this case, the love relation between Julius and Lisette—intends, in other words, to attain a "higher artistic sense of voluptuousness,"[40] a "naked sensuousness in which spirit is a negated element,"[41] but also "to cancel all actuality and substitute for it an actuality that is no actuality,"[42] to invert the purpose of the final remains of Socrates' tendency; in a word, it intends to refute Fichte's ironic (spiritualizing) tendency, or to sensualize what, in it, is still held in a theoretical "straitjacket."[43]

The obvious question is, therefore, none other than this: how does Schlegel do that? For that is, in fact, the most relevant part of the problem. Kierkegaard addresses it by assuming that, as opposed to Fichte's obliteration of the arbitrary "I" and concession to a deeper "I" (the absolute "I") of free rein in the resolution of the problem,[44] *Lucinde*, quite conversely, "lulls the deeper I into a somnambulant state, gives the arbitrary I free rein in ironic self-satisfaction."[45] Schlegel indeed does this as well, as we have demonstrated, by letting Julius' morality be swallowed or engulfed by Lisette's irreligiousness—by his own concept of ironic poeticity.

But this, in turn, unveils Kierkegaard's main problem with Schlegel's aspiration: for Kierkegaard, the main reason for this work's immorality, the reason for Schlegel's concession of power to a kind of irony which, it is said, satisfies itself, is that, by attaining a plane of equilibrium between subject and object, Schlegel's irony intends to proclaim itself as poetical. And what does "poetical" mean in Kierkegaard's terms? Or to ask the same question in a different way: what does the Julius' incorporation of Lisette mean to Kierkegaard? Kierkegaard proceeds to answer in this very section: poetry is "the victory over the world,"[46] the conquest of a "higher actuality,"[47] a reconciliation, but not one that "reconciles me with the actuality I am living in,"[48] rather one that sends me to another actuality altogether "by giving me another, a

---

[38]   *SKS* 1, 324 / *CI*, 289.

[39]   Ibid.

[40]   *SKS* 1, 325 / *CI*, 291.

[41]   Ibid.

[42]   *SKS* 1, 325 / *CI*, 290.

[43]   *SKS* 1, 323 / *CI*, 288.

[44]   Kierkegaard identifies the fulfillment of this evolution of the concept of irony with a "subjectivity in a still higher form," a "subjectivity raised to the second power" as proposed by Kant and decisively resumed by Fichte (*SKS* 1, 282 / *CI*, 242).

[45]   *SKS* 1, 330 / *CI*, 296.

[46]   *SKS* 1, 330 / *CI*, 297.

[47]   Ibid.

[48]   *SKS* 1, 331 / *CI*, 297.

higher and more perfect actuality."[49] Poetry, Kierkegaard says, is therefore a sort of emigration, but in such a way that the act of migrating is, as we have seen it to be in Kierkegaard's irony, a suspended, eternal, and sublime moment, forever lost and yet, absolutely infinite in itself. "To live poetically," Kierkegaard then concludes, "is to live infinitely."[50] And how does one live infinitely? In the incomprehension it emanates, that is, in that same refraction of irony where the transition is infinite, where the commerce between interior and exterior, between subject and object, between inferior and superior life are truly unending, and yet, where, as part of the refraction, one consciously—and inevitably—is in the movement of returning to oneself, towards an interiorly infinite fruition: "Only when I in my enjoying am not outside myself but am inside myself, only then is my enjoyment infinite, because it is inwardly infinite."[51] And this, of course, is something which, for Kierkegaard, was absolutely antithetical to Schlegel's conception of irony and, therefore, to his concept of interiority and exteriority, his concept of language and silence—*his concept of poetry*:

> it is easy to see that he [Schlegel] misses the highest enjoyment, the true bliss in which the subject is not dreaming but possesses himself in infinite clarity, is absolutely transparent to himself, which is possible only for the religious individual, who does not have his infinity outside himself but inside himself.[52]

II.

Let us now try to understand what leads Kierkegaard to state that, given these traits of the ironic effect, *Lucinde* is, unlike what its author intended, a profoundly non-erotic, non-poetical and, therefore, irreligious work; why, in other words, does Kierkegaard add about *Lucinde* that "it thinks it is living poetically, but I hope to show that the poetic is the very thing it misses, because true inward infinity comes only through resignation, and only this inner infinity is truly infinite and truly poetic."[53]

According to Kierkegaard, as Schlegel centers *Lucinde*'s poeticity in the "I" and gives its arbitrary dimension full rein (as inscribed in Lisette's character)—and it may be noted that, for Schlegel, the ironical doubt that enshrouds *Lucinde*, that center of hers, is of the sort of an absolute arbitrariness—the total arbitrariness of the "I," thus gained, acquires the property which we know to be Schlegel's concept of irony. Just as irony—and Schlegel knew it—is its own soil, its own land where, by momentarily dissociating from itself, it sows the seeds of its own effect, so also does the "I," by focusing itself in this *jesting* impulse of irony, view itself in the whole process and, therefore, see itself as the creator and executor of the reach, the effect and the singularity of irony. And this, according to Kierkegaard, has different consequences. Firstly, according to Schlegel's view, irony itself cannot be seen but

---

49   Ibid.
50   Ibid.
51   Ibid.
52   *SKS* 1, 331 / *CI*, 298.
53   *SKS* 1, 324 / *CI*, 289.

as an obvious repercussion of an "I" whose arbitrariness is absolute. Secondly, that the other plane, the superior life which is accessed through irony cannot be, for Schlegel—so thinks Kierkegaard—but man's extension of himself, superior, for sure—and therefore a disruption in relation to Fichte—but, however, devoid of the break or the radical change of the counter-reflection between interiority and exteriority which is the heart of Kierkegaard's proposition in *The Concept of Irony*. Thirdly, both these movements are to be seen—and Schlegel meant it so—in the aforementioned relation between Julius and Lisette, Julius being the tormented "I," the deeper "I" who seeks shelter outside of his objectivity, and Lisette the absolutely arbitrary "I," the absolute "I" *par excellence*, to use Fichte's terms, who shelters Julius by engulfing him. Instead, then, Schlegel's poetical character, Schlegel's love for the "I" (Julius + Lisette) is a unilateral refraction, a proposition of spiritualization of the arbitrary "I," which, for Kierkegaard, is so exaggerated and so inconsistent, so *arbitrary*, that it results in its sensualization (or utterly exacerbated spiritualization, which is the same) and, therefore, in its fall into the pit of irreligiousness. For this reason the special trait arises which the character of Lucinde adopts in Kierkegaard's train of thought: "The oddity about *Lucinde* and the whole trend associated with it," concludes Kierkegaard, "is that, by starting from the freedom and the constitutive authority of the I, one does not arrive at a still higher spirituality but comes only to sensuousness and consequently to its opposite."[54] Or, which is the same but in other words: "since this sensuousness is not naïve, it follows that the same arbitrariness that installed sensuousness in its presumed rights can shift over the very next instant to assert an abstract and exaggerated spirituality."[55]

This means, of course, but one thing: that, to Kierkegaard, the merit of Schlegel's poetical irony is, actually, its very defect: that, when it is placed as an axis between subjectivity and objectivity, Schlegel's irony not only shows an inescapable reverence for Fichte's doctrine, but also tries to refute the latter by *merely stating* the exterior pole of the infinite—as in *Lucinde*. By doing so, however, Schlegel's irony, so Kierkegaard thinks, returns us to our own exteriority in such an insufficient way that, if it is not we who receive ourselves there—that is, as a starting and a finishing point of irony—then we at least assume exteriority not as an exterior, but as our own interior, so that the peak of irony corresponds but to the comprehension of this same transitional movement within ourselves, and not to the real course of irony. And that is why, for Kierkegaard, Lucinde cannot live poetically: for Julius, for instance, does indeed exist for himself, but, according to Kierkegaard, he is not sufficiently *outside* Lisette's scope of ironic (and deadly) influence so that, when returning—as we always do—from the novel, we might be able to perceive the course he took as a route of the interior or, at least, as an (infinitely) interiorizing route. In a word, then, for Kierkegaard, Schlegel's irony is not sufficiently born out of nothingness, out of objectivity so that we can deem it truly ironical (poetical), or, as it is for Kierkegaard, infinitely interior: and this is the true message that Kierkegaard wants to transmit about Lucinde's character, that, according to him, "by starting from the freedom and the constitutive authority of the *I*, one does not arrive at a still higher spirituality but comes only to sensuousness and consequently

---

[54]   *SKS* 1, 334 / *CI*, 301.
[55]   Ibid.

to its opposite."[56] Much—if not everything—precedes her in this sense, and by feeling this same infinite exteriority around him, the reader loses sight of the traits which are truly interior to him. In that moment of irony, loving irony is no longer irony, and with such disappearance we, the Orpheus of this image, deplore this result, the impossibility of seeing Eurydice, the inability of living poetically. In other words, love is indeed not the center of Lucinde, as Schlegel said: but nor is Julius' and Lisette's connection "a love without any real content, and the eternity so frequently talked about is nothing but what could be called the eternal moment of enjoyment, an infinity that is no infinity and as such is unpoetic."[57]

Finally, what Kierkegaard sees as the solution for this problem, although initiated in the section "Friedrich Schlegel," only comes to life in the subsequent chapter, the last of *The Concept of Irony*, "Irony as a Controlled Element, the Truth of Irony." Kierkegaard discerned in Schlegel's *Lucinde* not so much the last stage in the development of the concept of irony, but one last—and decisive—change in *irony's contribution towards the absolute transformation of man's perception of his own image*, and that Lisette's case is the prime example of such a crucial change. This means that, to Kierkegaard, Schlegel gave, so to speak, the first impulse towards that change, not because he radically differed from Fichte, but because, due to being so close to irony's subjective zenith, he had not been able to discern it as *inhumanly* as a further spectator; that is, as we said, Schlegel's irony was not sufficiently born out of nothingness, Julius' and Lisette's love was too overpowering and sensuous to be truly ironical, when, to cite Kierkegaard, it should be a "controlled element."[58] By being born of nothingness, irony is transported to an intermediary—and confined—element which, by being situated between absence and presence, between silence and language but, above all, between nothingness and matter, *is* both and therefore is.*everything*.

Irony, then, imposes new boundaries to the exterior and the interior, to the finite and infinite, and, in doing so, irony reforms man (and his language). This singularity, one might say, is the true difference which cuts in half what Kierkegaard calls repetition. For this "totality-view of the world"[59]—of irony's world—he adds, is about as much as irony allows man to perceive in her. Irony is, in a word, man's best—and yet most difficult—possibility of speaking to the world. It is the "dialectic of life,"[60] but, because it thus breaks with the regular order of things, it is held in a voice quite other than the one we so far used to speak about our condition in the world. Irony's voice, as with any "controlled" element, no longer consists of sounds, tones, and inflections, it has no deixis, no context whatsoever: it is genuinely poetical, it lives poetically, and therefore, in conclusion, it has no subject or object: irony's voice is the inspiration of a new reality, no longer a negative or a positive one, but, indeed, a true one: "Irony limits, finitizes, and circumscribes and thereby yields truth, actuality, content; it disciplines and punishes and thereby yields balance and consistency."[61]

---

[56]   Ibid.
[57]   *SKS* 1, 333 / *CI*, 300.
[58]   *SKS* 1, 352 / *CI*, 324.
[59]   *SKS* 1, 353 / *CI*, 325.
[60]   *SKS* 1, 355 / *CI*, 327.
[61]   *SKS* 1, 355 / *CI*, 326.

Bibliography

Behler, Ernst, "Kierkegaard's The Concept of Irony with Constant Reference to Romanticism," in *Kierkegaard Revisited*, ed. by Niels Jørgen Cappelørn and Jon Stewart, Berlin and New York: Walter de Gruyter 1997 (*Kierkegaard Studies Monograph Series*, vol. 1), pp. 13–32.

— *Ironie und literarische Moderne*, Paderborn: Ferdinand Schöningh 1997, pp. 157–81.

Dierkes, Hans, "Friedrich Schlegels *Lucinde*, Schleiermacher und Kierkegaard," *Deutsche Vierteljahrsschrift für Literaturwissenschaft und Geistesgeschichte*, vol. 57, no. 3 1983, pp. 431–49.

Kinter, Achim, "Friedrich Schlegels Lucinde," in his *Rezeption und Existenz. Untersuchungen zu Sören Kierkegaards Entweder-Oder*, Frankfurt am Main: Peter Lang 1991 (*Texte und Untersuchungen zur Germanistik und Skandinavistik*, vol. 26), pp. 65–6.

Mininger, J.D., "The Insistence of Desire: Paul de Man on Kierkegaard on German Romanticism," in *Kierkegaard Studies Yearbook*, 2009, pp. 167–84.

Pattison, George, "Friedrich Schlegels Lucinde: A Case Study in the Relation of Religion to Romanticism," *Scottish Journal of Theology*, vol. 38, 1986, pp. 545–64.

— "A Literary Scandal," in his *Kierkegaard, Religion and the Nineteenth-Century Crisis of Culture*, Cambridge: Cambridge University Press 2002, pp. 116–36.

Perkins, Robert L., "Three Critiques of Schlegel's Lucinde," in *The Nature and Pursuit of Love: The Philosophy of Irving Singer*, ed. by David Goicoechea, Amherst, New York: Prometheus Books 1995, pp. 149–66.

Rasmussen, Joel D. S., "The Imaginative Anticipation of the Eternal," in his *Between Irony and Witness: Kierkegaard's Poetics of Faith, Hope and Love*, New York and London: T&T Clark 2005, pp. 15–54.

Söderquist, K. Brian, "Friedrich Schlegel: On Ironic Communication, Subjectivity and Selfhood," in *Kierkegaard and His German Contemporaries*, Tome III, *Literature and Aesthetics*, ed. by Jon Stewart, Aldershot: Ashgate 2008 (*Kierkegaard Research: Sources, Reception and Resources*, vol. 6), pp. 185–233.

Lady Macbeth:

The Viscera of Conscience

Malgorzata Grzegorzewska

I. Shakespeare's Lady Macbeth

Shakespeare is known to have based the plot of his *Tragedy of Macbeth* on the Holinshed chronicles, but there is little doubt that the historical Macbeth, notwithstanding Holinshed's hypothetical claim that this "valiant gentleman…if he had not been somewhat cruell of nature, might have been thought most woorthie of the government of a realme,"[1] had little to do with Shakespeare's villainous usurper. "Shakespeare deals freely with his source," asserted Frank Kermode, trying to explain the relationship of the dramatic fiction of *Macbeth* to Holinshed's narrative and pointing to the fact that the protagonist's image is "blackened" in the play.[2] Hardly anyone today, however, would be concerned by the question of historical accuracy. Instead, we all agree that historical narrative is always subject to manipulation, always written from somebody's partial perspective, always burdened with vested interests.

So although *Macbeth* is not a "history play" in the strict sense of this term (not only because Shakespeare did not follow Holinshed's Chronicle in every detail, but also because the play does not represent English history), Jan Kott's essays included in the volume entitled *Shakespeare Our Contemporary*[3] and the following wave of New Historical and Cultural Materialism revisions of the playwright's work have resulted in a number of critical readings and stage adaptations which encourage us to view "the Scottish play" primarily through the lenses of politics and history.[4] On the one hand, critics imply that Shakespeare was directly engaged in Jacobean court propaganda (either as a piece of straightforward royalist support or as a tacit critique of James' politics, cleverly masked as a political encomium); on the other

---

[1]   *Holinshed's Chronicle as Used in Shakespeare's Plays*, ed. by Alladryce Nicoll and Josephine Nicoll, London: Dent 1969, p. 207.

[2]   Frank Kermode, "Introduction" to Macbeth, in *The Riverside Shakespeare*, ed. by G. Blakemore Evans, Boston: Houghton Mifflin 1974, p. 1308.

[3]   Jan Kott, *Shakespeare Our Contemporary*, trans. by Bolesław Taborski, Methuen: London 1964.

[4]   Cf. Jonathan Goldberg, "Speculations: *Macbeth* and Source," in *Shakespeare Reproduced*, ed. by Jean E. Howard and Marion F. O'Connor, London and New York: Methuen 1978, pp. 242–64.

hand, theater directors have presented Macbeth as "our contemporary," involved in the military conflicts of the Balkan wars, in Africa, and in the Middle East. Those who still choose to focus on the question of the protagonist's inevitable descent into the hell of eternal perdition present this motif from the historically and culturally specific perspective of English Renaissance Calvinism.[5]

The second most popular issue currently brought up in the context of "the Scottish tragedy," no doubt for good reasons, is gender. In the predominantly masculine world of *Macbeth*, where war and the struggle for power paint the backdrop of the Macbeths' demonic descent into bloody red, Lady Macbeth appears as a woman of outstanding strength and fearlessness, although in the end she also proves genuinely fragile. The most persistent and forceful of Shakespeare's female characters, she incorporates the wildness and unruliness of Tamora, the Queen of the Goths from *Titus Andronicus*; the seductiveness and articulateness of Cleopatra, the Queen of Egypt; and the imperious authority of Volumnia, the mother of Coriolanus. Most often portrayed as a dangerous temptress, the theatrical Lady Macbeth frequently appears on stage in a crimson dress and red high-heeled shoes. Roman Polański's decision to cast in this role a young actress with an almost angelic face and to explore a little further the motif of the couple's conjugal affection was a praiseworthy departure from this convention.[6] More commonly, it is stressed that Macbeth's wife draws her strength from her uncanny association with the witches—the odd, androgynous creatures whose unexpected appearance on the moorlands of Scotland sows the seed of Macbeth's undoing.

In this respect, Shakespeare does agree with Holinshed, who explains that "the words of the three weird sisters…greatlie incouraged him [Macbeth] herevnto [to usurp the kingdom by force],"[7] as soon as Duncan appointed his elder son, Malcolm, whom he had by the daughter of Siward, the earl of Northumberland, his successor in the realm. Needless to say, the decision stifled Macbeth's budding hopes, fostered by the witches, but what the playwright does not include in his account is Holinshed's idea that these expectations were not necessarily sinful in their origin, since "where, by the old lawes of the realme, the ordinance was, that if he that should succeed were not of able age to take the charge vpon himself, he that was next of blood vnto him, should be admitted."[8] As for the final outcome of the witches' temptation, however, both Shakespeare and Holinshed place the blame unanimously on Lady Macbeth. Holinshed writes in this context that "specially [Macbeth's] wife lay sore upon him to attempt the thing, as she was verie ambitious, burning in vnquenchable desire to bear the name of the queen."[9]

Lust for power need not have been the historical Lady Macbeth's, or as she was also called Queen Gruoch's, sole or strongest motive in this case; motherly care for her son and the painful experience of the violent struggle for power, which had

[5]	John Stachniewski, "Calvinist Psychology in *Macbeth*," *Shakespeare Studies*, vol. 20, 1988, pp. 169–89.
[6]	*Macbeth*, directed by Roman Polański (1971).
[7]	*Holinshed's Chronicle as Used in Shakespeare's Plays*, p. 211.
[8]	Ibid.
[9]	Ibid.

affected her family even before she married Macbeth, and perhaps also fear or desire for revenge, would provide other powerful incentives to act. Gruoch, like Macbeth, was a descendant of an old Gaelic family, the daughter of King Kenneth III. Her first husband, Gill Coemgain, with whom she had a son, Lulach, was burnt alive in a hall with fifty other men in 1032; the following year her only brother was killed by the successor of Kenneth III, Malcolm II. Let us hear Holinshed speak: "Malcolme had two daughters, the one of which was Beatrice [Bethoc] being giuen in marriage vnto one Abbanath Crinen, an man of great nobility, and thane of the Isles and west part of Scotland, bare of that marriage the foresaid Duncane; the other called Doada."[10] Thus, Malcolm II ordered the murder of the grandson of Kenneth III, Gruoch's only brother, in order to ensure that his daughter Bethroc's son, Duncan, could inherit the throne after his death. Macbeth, Gruoch's second husband and Lulach's stepfather, was the son of Malcolm's second daughter, Doada, married to Sinnell, thane of Glamis. Yet the provisions undertaken by the historical Lady Macbeth to protect her son by her first marriage, Lulach, failed to do him any good at all. Although he was crowned the king of Scotland immediately after Macbeth's death, a year later he, too, was killed by Duncan's son, who then became Malcolm III.[11]

We shall not find in Shakespeare's play any hint of Lady Macbeth's turbulent life, nor shall we be introduced to the long history of family feuding that finally led to Macbeth's apparently quite efficient reign. But a brief look at the historical accounts helps us solve one of the basic conundrums of Shakespeare criticism. The perennial question, "How many children did Lady Macbeth have?" returns now and again, usually only as a playful pretext for more serious divagations concerning the heroine's femininity.[12] It is often invoked in the context of her most chilling confessions, as when, having read the letter from her husband, she prays to the dark spirits to endow her with the courage to assist her husband in the crime:

> Come, you spirits
> That tend on mortal thoughts, unsex me here,
> And fill me from the crown to the toe top-full
> Of direst cruelty. Make thick my blood,
> Stop up th'access and passage to remorse,
> That no compunctions visiting of nature
> Shake my fell purpose, nor keep pace between
> Th' effect and it. Come to my woman's breasts,
> And take my milk for gall, you murd'ring ministers…[13]

---

[10]   Ibid., p. 207.

[11]   Anna Cetera, "Komentarz" [Critical Commentary] to William Shakespeare, *Makbet*, trans. by Piotr Kamiński, Warsaw: WAB 2011, p. 210.

[12]   See, for instance, William Empson, "Macbeth," *Essays on Shakespeare*, ed. by David Pirie, Cambridge: Cambridge University Press 1986, pp. 137–57.

[13]   William Shakespeare, *The Tragedy of Macbeth*, in *The Oxford Shakespeare: The Complete Works*, ed. by Stanley Wells and Gary Taylor, Oxford: Clarendon Press 1986, Act 1, Scene 5.39–47. All further quotations from *Macbeth* refer to this edition.

In a similar vein, she persuades Macbeth, who is afraid of the consequences of the deed of murder:

> I have given suck, and know
> How tender 'tis to love the babe that milks me.
> I would, while it was smiling in my face,
> Have plucked my nipple from his boneless gums
> And dashed the brains out, had I so sworn
> As you have done to this.[14]

Macbeth's response to this again brings to the fore the question of progeny, although it is also marked with the ironic equivocation characteristic of many of his utterances:

> Bring forth men-children only,
> For thy undaunted mettle should compose
> Nothing but males.[15]

This passage is usually disambiguated by rendering the phrase "compose nothing but males" as the repetition of "bring me male children only"; but such an interpretation, although correct, misses the ingenious pun on male/mail or maille, chainmail, a type of armor consisting of small metal rings linked together. This second meaning is certainly in line with Macbeth's commitment to war and his conviction that his wife is a trustworthy companion in martial endeavors. Furthermore, it once again associates Lady Macbeth with the masculine, warlike, and ultimately destructive aspect of existence (marked also by the recurring references to blood and gall), rather than with its feminine, domestic, procreative, and nurturing side (symbolized by milk).

In fact, however, the world of *Macbeth* is a world where oppositions are not so much toppled, as disrupted. The play refers to clear-cut gender stereotypes (masculinity denotes courage, daring, warlike ambition, and bloodshed; femininity is associated with feeding, caring, tenderness, milk) only in order to subvert them and abolish the difference between the husband and wife; and to make them truly one person who falls into the trap set by the "Enemy of Mankind."[16]

II. Kierkegaard's Appropriations of Shakespeare

Simon Palfery is surely right when he says that the philosopher's way of reading had little to do with our history-oriented and overtly impersonal modes of textual analysis: "Kierkegaard wasn't interested in historical differences between mid-

---

[14]   Shakespeare, *The Tragedy of Macbeth*, Act 1, Scene 7.54–9.

[15]   Ibid., Act 1, Scene 7.72–4.

[16]   Hecate also called Antania, translated as "Enemy of mankind," is a Greek goddess who in Shakespeare's play reveals the reason for the downfall of Macbeth. "Security is mortal's chiefest enemy" (Act 5, Scene 5.32–3), proclaims Hecate, signaling that Macbeth's belief in being untouchable would later ruin him.

nineteenth century Copenhagen and Jacobean England (and still less eleventh-century Scotland). Kierkegaard is interested only in 'subjective truth, the truth of appropriation': his reading always obeys this injunction."[17] In a similar vein Joel D.S. Rasmussen has argued that Kierkegaard's texts "appropriate quotations and characters in order to illustrate, extend, and explore categories more apposite to Kierkegaard's writings than to Shakespeare's own."[18] Rasmussen points also to the fact that Kierkegaard dealt mostly with Shakespeare as mediated through his nineteenth-century German reception, which likewise took great liberties with the original plays; yet he stresses at the same time the major difference between these two kinds of critical appropriation:

> Yet, if the German-language lectures and treatises on Shakespeare that proliferated during the generations prior to Kierkegaard aimed primarily to understand some theme or another in Shakespeare's plays, then the appropriation of Shakespeare by Kierkegaard tends more often to supplement the Kierkegaardian text itself.[19]

On the other hand, though, Rasmussen reminds us of some "notable exceptions" to this overall pattern: "For sometimes Kierkegaard's pseudonyms offer penetrating interpretations of key Shakespearean *dramatis personae*."[20] In the rest of this section I shall argue that, scarce—and seemingly also inaccurate—though Kierkegaard's allusions to the character of Lady Macbeth may appear to us, they no doubt belong to this latter category in Rasmussen's description.

Indeed, in the case of the Scottish tragedy, we may say that Kierkegaard's imaginative appropriation provides us with an insight into the underlying structure, the metaphysical core of Shakespeare's play. Following the astute suggestion made by Simon Palfrey in his interpretation of Kierkegaard's understanding of *Macbeth*, one might call this "still point" of the tragedy the breathless (and therefore also speechless and incapable of prayer) "self of a determinist."[21] Furthermore, the

---

[17]   Simon Palfrey, "Macbeth and Kierkegaard," in *Macbeth and His Afterlife: An Annual Survey of Shakespeare Studies and Reception*, ed. by Peter Holland, Cambridge: Cambridge University Press 2004 (*Shakespeare Survey*, vol. 57), p. 96.

[18]   Joel D. S. Rasmussen, "William Shakespeare: Kierkegaard's Post-Romantic Reception of the 'Poet's Poet,'" *Kierkegaard and the Renaissance and Modern Traditions*, Tome III, *Literature, Drama and Music*, ed. by Jon Stewart, Aldershot: Ashgate 2009 (*Kierkegaard Research: Sources, Reception and Resources*, vol. 5), p. 191.

[19]   Ibid., pp. 191–2.

[20]   Ibid., p. 192.

[21]   Palfrey, "Macbeth and Kierkegaard," p. 111. Palfrey reads *Macbeth* from the perspective of the following important passage about the junction of possibility and necessity from *The Sickness unto Death*: "Personhood is a synthesis of possibility and necessity....The self of the determinist cannot breathe, for it is impossible to breathe necessity exclusively, because that would utterly suffocate a person's self....Therefore the fatalist's worship of God is at most an interjection, and essentially it is a muteness, a mute capitulation: he is unable to pray....Nevertheless, possibility alone or necessity alone can no more be the condition for the breathing of a prayer than oxygen alone or nitrogen alone can be that for breathing...if there is nothing but necessity, man is essentially as inarticulate as the animals" (*SKS* 11, 156 / *SUD*, 40–1).

Kierkegaardian perspective allows us better to understand Macbeth's closing soliloquy about the meaninglessness of human existence: "a tale / Told by an idiot, full of sound and fury, / Signifying nothing."[22] Both Macbeth and his wife truly become desperate fatalists in the course of the play, even if in the beginning they still reside in the realm of perilous, yet not hopeless possibility. As Palfrey explains, "possibility" in Kierkegaard's sense of the word, which translates so well into Shakespeare's *Macbeth*,

> is never safely grounded, never without some latent power ignition: anything might fall or return; if there has been a leap one way, there might always be a recursive leap in the opposite direction. This means, for one thing, that he cannot dismiss criminality as the contemptible "fate" of some "criminal."[23]

And indeed, any honest reader of *Macbeth* must bear this in mind, instead of safely watching from a distance the fate of the Macbeths, which indeed becomes inevitable only because they freely accept the (apparent) inevitability of the prophecy.

Far more interested in the knowledge of the self than the objective knowledge of the world, the philosopher thus advocated a very peculiar strategy for approaching the works of the poet: "Tear away every covering in your brain, expose the viscera of feeling and then read Shakespeare."[24] Needless to say, this was not a call for a "Romantic," starry-eyed Shakespeare removed from the constraints of historical contingency and material reality. On the contrary, Kierkegaard speaks here about a reading that permits words to become incarnate, no longer abstractions born in the brain, but embodied in a lived sensation of pain, loss, and despair. The reader is literally anatomized, made to impersonate both the bloody captain whom we meet in the first act of the play, and Macduff ripped out of his mother's womb; as if the secret of Macbeth's tragic fall had to be ripped out by violence from the drawn and quartered body of human sensation, very precisely from "the viscera of feeling" that are mercilessly exposed in the process of torturous reading.

Perhaps the best-known passage in Kierkegaard's works relating to William Shakespeare comes from *Fear and Trembling*. It is there that Johannes de silentio ponders the reasons for the single most important omission in the playwright's portrayal of human passions:

> Thanks, once again thanks, to a man who, to a person overwhelmed by life's sorrows and left behind naked, reaches out the words, the leafage of language by which he can conceal his misery. Thanks to you, great Shakespeare, you who can say everything, everything, everything just as it is—and yet, why did you never articulate this torment? Did you perhaps reserve it for yourself, like the beloved's name that one cannot bear to have the world utter, for with his little secret that he cannot divulge the poet buys this power of the word to tell everybody else's dark secrets. A poet is not an apostle; he drives out devils only by the power of the devil.[25]

---

[22]   Shakespeare, *The Tragedy of Macbeth*, Act 5, Scene 5.25–6.
[23]   Palfrey, "Macbeth and Kierkegaard," p. 98.
[24]   *SKS* 11, 238 / *SUD*, 127.
[25]   *SKS* 4, 154–5 / *FT*, 61.

This might have been a declaration of profound gratitude and appreciation for the poet's efforts, referring the reader to Christ's parable of the Good Samaritan who brought relief to a traveler cruelly beaten on the way down from Jerusalem to Jericho by highway robbers and left suffering and naked. The passage might serve as an apology for poetry, had it not, on second thoughts, turned into a serious challenge raised against someone who trades with impunity in "everybody else's dark secrets" and instead of true comfort offers only the thin leafage, a fig-leaf indeed, of language by which the sufferer "may conceal"—only conceal, we should add!—"his misery." Surely then, poets cannot bring true relief to humankind overwhelmed by sin. "A poet is not an apostle," as Kierkegaard himself asserted, let alone a Savior who can deliver man from evil.

On the other hand, the Danish philosopher frequently assumed the role of a poet who "sees experience as a thing mediated almost entirely through varieties of screen, mask, indirection, and ventriloquism."[26] Literary allusions, poet's fables, borrowed words, and purloined identities are very frequent in the first part of his *Concluding Unscientific Postscript*. There is a crucial moment when he explains the difference between the possibility of dialectical mediation between opposites and the need for a radical decision involving a leap over a chasm which becomes infinitely wide in the eye, indeed in the imagination of the beholder, and compares the imagined difficulty of making the decision with the thoroughly subjective, intensely hyperbolical, and therefore genuine acuity of Lady Macbeth's "passion," which "makes the blood spot so immensely large that the ocean cannot wash it away."[27]

This reference convinces us that Kierkegaard dealt with his literary sources almost as "freely" as Shakespeare transformed Holinshed's Chronicle. The comparison he forges conflates Macbeth's speech delivered just after the murder:

> What hands are here? Ha! They pluck out mine eyes.
> Will all great Neptune's ocean wash this blood
> Clean from my hand? *No, this my hand will rather*
> *The multitudinous seas incarnadine,*
> Making the green one red[28]

with Lady Macbeth's sleep-walking confession:

> *Out, damned spot; out I say.* One, two,—why then, 'tis time to do it. Hell is murky. Fie, my lord, fie, a soldier and afeared? What need we fear who knows it when none can call our power to account? Yet who would have thought the old man had so much blood in him.[29]

It is patently obvious, then, that in his pursuit of the demonic in Shakespeare's gloomiest tragedy, Kierkegaard misquoted the play and mixed up the speeches of its protagonists. At the same time, it might be argued that Kierkegaard's "slip of the

---

26   Palfrey, "Macbeth and Kierkegaard," p. 98.

27   *SKS* 7, 97 / *CUP1*, 99.

28   Shakespeare, *The Tragedy of Macbeth*, Act 2, Scene 2.57–61. Emphasis added.

29   Ibid., Act 5, Scene 1.33–8. Emphasis added.

pen" in fact pointed to his deeper, intuitive understanding of Shakespeare's original design: to show the prodigious union of crime and devastating solidarity of guilt that binds the murderous couple together more strongly than their original love.

That the Danish philosopher was not a careless reader, but a farsighted interpreter of Shakespeare's play can be confirmed by his other appropriation of exactly the same motif, that is, the image of Lady Macbeth who cannot wash her hands even with the water of multitudinous seas, in a journal entry from 1850. It is worth recalling at length:

> In *Dogmatiske Oplysninger* Martensen complains that Stilling mixes in things with "unwashed hands," and therefore one cannot get involved with him.
>
> From the essentially Christian point of view, this should not be disturbing, because, after all Christ (who, by the way, this elegant preacher who continually brings Christianity back to external elegance) himself declares that whether or not one eats with unwashed hands is of no consequence. How natural for Christ to make this appraisal, he who was concerned with the very opposite, that a Lady Macbeth, for example, can wash her hands from morning until night—use the ocean to wash them—and they still do not get clean, or that Pilate also washed his hands, presumably not to crucify the truth with "unwashed hands."[30]

For the sake of clarity it should be said that in the beginning of this passage Kierkegaard makes a reference to his friend Peter Michael Stilling (1812–69), the author of *Modern Atheism, or the Consequences of the so-called Neo-Hegelianism*, who became acquainted with Hegelian philosophy through Kierkegaard's most fierce opponent, Hans Lassen Martensen. In 1837–38 Stilling attended Martensen's lectures on speculative dogmatics, and it was there that he became acquainted with Hegel's ideas, but "later [he] became estranged from both Hegelianism and Martensen" and—for a time at least—joined Kierkegaard's camp.[31]

---

[30]   *SKS* 23, 333-4, NB19:7 / *JP* 5, 6635. Palfrey lists two other references to Lady Macbeth in Kierkegaard's incidental writings: "a journal entry of 1843 has him suggest that Lady Macbeth's 'remorseful conscience' would have been more effectively presented if she 'never dared relax in sleep for fear of betraying herself.' Another entry from 1845 again extemporizes a different Lady Macbeth, one who 'does not dare sleep' and who curses both her 'excruciating wakefulness' and her need for sleep," Palfrey, "Macbeth and Kierkegaard," p. 100 (see *SKS* 18, 159, JJ:61 / *JP* 4, 3972. *SKS* 18, 254–5, JJ:347 / *JP* 4, 3973). I refrain, however, from discussing this apparent contradiction. Suffice it to say that the exact character of Lady Macbeth's demonic despair preoccupied him greatly and served as a springboard for a variety of reflections on the guilt-ridden sleeplessness that at least in one instance he attributes to Macbeth's partner in crime and culpability alike.

[31]   Istvan Czako, "Feuerbach: A Malicious Demon in the Service of Christianity," in *Kierkegaard and his German Contemporaries*, Tome I, *Philosophy*, ed. by Jon Stewart, Aldershot: Ashgate 2007 (*Kierkegaard Research: Sources, Reception and Resources*, vol. 6), p. 33. Carl Henrik Koch reminds us that Kierkegaard once called Stilling a "thinker skating on such a thin ice" which allowed him to entertain an idea of "a current." Koch explains in this context that Kierkegaard used this metaphor to suggest that he was among the few who understood that "in Christianity God demands sacrifice and suffering from the human being, that is, the imitation of Christ." That would certainly suggest that he saw Stilling as his possible successor. The critic immediately adds, however, that Stilling's career did not develop

What is really interesting in this passage, apart from the fact that it allows us to savor the climate of the intellectual debates of nineteenth-century Copenhagen, is once again Kierkegaard's ingenuous (and this time also very consistent) appropriation of the character of Lady Macbeth. As in the case of Pontius Pilate, we are made to believe, the mere act of washing one's hands does not absolve the sinner of his guilt. What matters is inward cleanness, which Lady Macbeth can no more regain after the murder than Pontius Pilate can retain after the unjust verdict sentencing truth, or rather Truth Incarnate, to death. So instead of conflating two characters (Lady Macbeth and Macbeth), as in the previous case, Kierkegaard here builds a three-level metaphor, which allows him not only to compromise his enemy, Martensen, but also to examine still more penetratingly the "viscera" of the criminal's conscience, which indeed, have nothing to do with the outward righteousness of the hypocrite. Lady Macbeth's futile efforts to be rid of the spots of blood that are objectively invisible, because they are only conceived in her guilt-ridden and delirious consciousness, in effect become here the key to understanding Pilate's double error of judgment: concerning both the (innocent) accused and the (guilty) judge who boasts of clean hands. In fact, Lady Macbeth in her madness comes to understand what Pilate does not yet know: that every crime is inwardly "red-handed."

---

according to Kierkegaard's favorable prognosis, for "Stilling never made it further than being a possibility." Carl Henrik Koch, "Peter Michael Stilling: As Successor? 'Undeniably a Possibility,' " in *Kierkegaard and His Danish Contemporaries*, Tome I, *Philosophy, Politics and Social Theory*, ed. by Jon Stewart, Aldershot: Ashgate 2009 (*Kierkegaard Research: Sources, Reception and Resources*, vol. 7), p. 289). Having rejected, under the influence of Kierkegaard, "scholarly" theology of Martensen's kind, Stilling also seems to have rejected faith (ibid., p. 290), and distanced himself both from biblical faith and Kierkegaard (ibid., p. 298).

Bibliography

Cheung, King-kok, "Shakespeare and Kierkegaard: 'Dread in *Macbeth*,' " *Shakespeare Quarterly*, vol. 35, 1984, pp. 430–9.

Palfrey, Simon, "Macbeth and Kierkegaard," in *Macbeth and His Afterlife: An Annual Survey of Shakespeare Studies and Reception*, ed. by Peter Holland, Cambridge: Cambridge University Press 2004 (*Shakespeare Survey*, vol. 57), pp. 96–111.

Sløk, Johannes, *Shakespeare og Kierkegaard*, Copenhagen: Berlingske 1972, p. 103; p. 117.

Margarete:

The Feminine Face of Faust

Antonella Fimiani

The brief essay "Silhouettes" is dedicated to the literary figure of Margarete. This essay can be found in *Either/Or*, Part One, and was published in 1843. In Kierkegaard's journals and notebooks significant reflection on this figure can be dated to the period prior to the publication of *Either/Or*. Decidedly of Goethean inspiration, the image of Margarete is intimately connected with that of the seducer, Faust. In "Silhouettes," the pseudonymous author chooses to place the character alongside Elvira and Marie Beaumarchais, partners of Don Giovanni and Clavigo respectively. The trait which unites the three women is the fact that they are victims of seducers without scruples who seduced and then abandoned them. Margarete is the unhappy companion of Faust, victim of the demonic desire he incarnates. She belongs to the aesthetic stage, and her character should be read and interpreted in the context of aesthetic seduction. The aesthetic theory of the feminine takes form in her. This theory has its roots in the particular way in which the seducer conceives relationships with the opposite sex and more generally with the "other." The objectives of the present article are to reconstruct the literary inspiration of the feminine figure as well as to analyze the theoretical value of this figure in the context of the aesthetic stage.

I. Historical and Literary Background

The tragedy of Margarete plays a central role in Goethe's *Faust*. Her character is dealt with in *Faust. Eine Tragödie*, published in 1808.[1] In *Faust. Der Tragödie zweyter Theil*,[2] which was published posthumously in 1832, around 30 years after the first part, there is no trace of Margarete until right at the end when she appears as a spirit guide to help the main character ascend to heaven. The story of Gretchen is a tragedy within a tragedy, a masterpiece within another masterpiece. It was a story that had occupied Goethe from the time of *Urfaust* (1775), which was the beginning

---

[1]   Johann Wolfgang von Goethe, *Faust. Eine Tragödie*, Tübingen: J.G. Cotta 1808.

[2]   Johann Wolfgang von Goethe, *Faust. Der Tragödie zweyter Theil in fünf Acten*, in *Goethe's Werke. Vollständige Ausgabe letzter Hand*, vols. 1–40, Stuttgart and Tübingen: J.G. Cotta 1827–30 and *Goethe's nachgelassene Werke*, vols. 41–55, Stuttgart and Tübingen: J.G. Cotta 1832–33 (*ASKB* 1641–1668), vol. 41 (vol. 1 in *Goethe's nachgelassene Werke*). See also Johann Wolfgang von Goethe, *Faust, erster Theil* and *Faust, zweyter Theil*, in *Goethe's Werke. Vollständige Ausgabe letzter Hand*, vol. 12.

of the gestation period of *Faust*, the foundations of which were laid at a young age during the prolific five years from 1770 to 1775.

The *Gretchen-Handlung* was first drafted in this youthful piece of work, which assumes tones of extreme violence and immediacy, which are then notably toned down in the later version. A young woman, a member of the *petite bourgeoisie*, falls victim to a supposed knight, who, after having seduced her, proceeds to abandon her. The consequences of their relationship prove fatal: the death of her mother, the murder of her brother at the hands of Faust himself, the murder of the baby resulting from their illicit relationship, and finally, the death of Margarete herself. Margarete is a murderess, an infanticide to be more precise. She has blood on her hands after killing her son to hide her sinful relationship from the world. She is a victim of her own passions, but also a victim of masculine desire and crushing societal pressures.

Her story in reality is not particularly original.[3] Even without taking into consideration the legends of Saint Margaret of Cortona and of Saint Margaret of Antioch—other martyrs to overbearing masculine desire, of which Goethe was no doubt aware at the time of writing Faust—it is not difficult to find similar figures who came before her. In the cultural climate of the 1700s, the seduction of a young and innocent member of the middle class by a member of the nobility was the subject of innumerable literary works (one need only think of Richardson or Lessing), and it is also a popular theme in earlier literary history. Even the most brutal aspects of the tragedy, such as the murder of Margarete's baby son and her subsequent sentencing to death are nothing new. Gretchen preceded and inspired the main character of Heinrich Leopold Wagner's (1747–79) drama *Die Kindermörderin* (1776) as well as the main character of the poem *Des Pfarrers Tochter von Taubenhain* (1781) written by Gottfried August Bürger (1747–94).

The cases of infanticide in the poetry of *Sturm und Drang* refer to real and frequent cases in society at the time. Indeed, in 1780 a contest was announced for the study of the best method of reducing this phenomenon without encouraging libertine behavior. The most famous case was that of Susanna Margaretha Brandt (1746–72), who was sentenced to death for infanticide in Frankfurt in 1772.[4] The debate about the law which punished infanticide with death was of considerable interest to intellectuals of the time, and the young Goethe followed this particular case with great interest, doubtless drawing inspiration from it for the final tragedy of Gretchen. The theme of infanticide took on a role of clear social importance during the period of *Sturm und Drang*. Together with fratricide, this crime presupposes the violation of one of the most sacred of religious laws of the 1700s—filial obedience.

The theme of the unmarried mother exalts the Rousseauian rights of the heart. By claiming the right to choose the man to whom they wish to belong, such women in literature violate the principle of filial obedience, and their parents are also judged to be guilty of having pushed the young women into free love by denying them the permission that they had requested. In the doubly tragic case of Margarete, the young mother not only commits infanticide but also accidentally commits matricide.

---

[3]   For this connection see Sten Bodvar Liljegren, *The English Sources of Goethe's Gretchen Tragedy*, Lund: C.W.K. Gleerup 1937, pp. 25–33.
[4]   Ibid.

The theme of disobedience is thus reinforced by the relationship established between disobedience and matricide.

The figure of Margarete does not appear in the original legend of Faust as handed down in the first *Faust-Buch* of Johann Spies (1540–1623), *Historia von D. Johann Fausten* published in 1587, from which Goethe originally got his inspiration. In the original legend, Faust is involved with Greek Elena, lives with her, and has a child. In 1674, Nicolas Pfitzer's rewriting of the myth introduces the idea of a beautiful but poor girl's love—a timid introduction to the theme, which would become central to Goethe's literary work. There is no trace of the girl in *The Tragical History of Doctor Faustus* (1589) by Christopher Marlowe (1564–93) nor in *Johann Faust* (1775) by Paul Weidmann (1744–1801). Margarete is therefore the exclusive intellectual property of the German genius, and around her image there is a clear convergence of both literary and autobiographical themes.

The abandonment of a beloved woman is a frequent theme in Goethean literature, and it is possible to see in the character of Margarete a part of Goethe's own history.[5] The gestation period of Faust took place during the peak of a wonderful and incredibly prolific period of poetry (1770–75),[6] which gave birth to numerous works such as *Götz von Berlichingen* (1773), *Clavigo* (1774), *Stella* (1816), and *Die Leiden des Jungen Werthers* (1773), where the themes of abandonment and class contrast in the relationship between the sexes were central.

The *Gretchen-Handlung* is a *Sturm und Drang* tragedy about insurmountable social barriers. That much is obvious from "A Street,"[7] the very first scene in which the lovers meet. Margarete immediately refuses to be referred to as "young lady"[8] (*Fräulein*), a title attributed solely to young noblewomen and used by Faust in an attempt to get closer to her. Gretchen is not poor but belongs to the *petite bourgeoisie* and, as such, love between the two is socially unacceptable, and both of them are well aware of this. In an attempt to get closer to his prey, Faust pretends to be unaware of the social *impasse*, despite the fact that he betrays himself with the familiar personal pronoun with which he addresses the victim from the very beginning. The knight has no desire to marry the victim since his sole objective is possession of her. His love is willing to go to the lengths of making a pact with the devil, and the help of Mephistopheles reveals itself to be of fundamental importance to the success of his mission.

Faust is not, however, an ordinary seducer, and the tale is destined to go well beyond that of Clavigo, Marie of Weisslingen, and Adelheid. Faust is the incarnation of modern humanity, a humanity in the grip of infinite, limitless desire, the image of eighteenth-century thought turned in on itself with the arrogant presumption of being the absolute truth. In the darkness of his study full of dusty books during the

---

[5]   Nicholas Boyle, *Goethe: The Poet and the Age*, vols. 1–2, Oxford: Clarendon Press 1997, vol. 1, pp. 100–103.

[6]   Ibid., pp. 107–25; pp. 152–78; pp. 212–29.

[7]   See Goethe, *Faust. Erster Theil*, in *Goethe's Werke*, vol. 12, p. 126. (English translation: *Faust I & II*, trans. and ed. by Stuart Atkins, in *Goethe's Collected Works*, vols. 1–12, ed. by Victor Lange et al., Princeton: Princeton University Press 1994ff., vol. 2, p. 67.)

[8]   Ibid.

scene entitled "Night,"[9] Faust attempts suicide after the realization of the sterility of his knowledge. He wants the infinite and is unsatisfied and anxious due to his inability to act within the constraints of reality and accept its limits. This is the incarnation of an infinite *Streben*, which produces no action because it is destined to wander aimlessly. What does the knight ask for in his pact with the devil? Faust has an abstract, infinite desire for infinity:

> And what have you to give, poor devil!
> Has any human spirit and its aspirations
> ever been understood by such as you?
> Of course you've food that cannot satisfy,
> gold that, when held, will liquify
> quicksilverlike as it turns red,
> games at which none can ever win,
> a girl who, even in my arms, will with her eyes
> pledge her affections to another,
> the godlike satisfaction of great honor
> that like a meteor is gone at once.
> Show me the fruit that, still unplucked, will rot
> and trees that leaf each day anew.[10]

Love is the projection of this desire, and the woman for him is the idealized image of his desire for the infinite.

In the scene entitled "Witch's Kitchen," a magic mirror reflects, for the first time, "a form whose beauty is divine,"[11] with which the knight will fall hopelessly in love: a face with no identity, a form onto which the seducer projects his insatiable desire. Whether the face belongs to Margaret or to Elena is of little importance. The woman who the seducer is on the hunt for is an idea of femininity, an idol. Woman is not an end to man in this sense but merely a means to be used in the search for pleasure. Margaret is merely an object of veneration.[12] In her, the image of the woman-doll typical of rococo art takes form, and it is against this form that Goethe lets loose his Stürmerian darts. When Faust meets her, he is deeply fascinated. Gretchen represents, in his eyes, that "small world" which he cannot seem to succeed in being a part of. She is of an immediacy, which grounds; she is a "cottage," a limitation, a root.[13] She is the living incarnation of "humility" and of

---

9   Goethe, *Faust. Erster Theil*, in *Goethe's Werke*, vol. 12, p. 27. (*Faust I & II*, in *Goethe's Collected Works and Papers*, vol. 2, p. 13.)

10   Goethe, *Faust. Erster Theil*, in *Goethe's Werke*, vol. 12, p. 81. (*Faust I & II*, in *Goethe's Collected Works and Papers*, vol. 2, pp. 43–4).

11   Goethe, *Faust. Erster Theil*, in *Goethe's Werke*, vol. 12, p. 116. (*Faust I & II*, in *Goethe's Collected Works and Papers*, vol. 2, p. 62).

12   Goethe, *Faust. Erster Theil*, in *Goethe's Werke*, vol. 12, p. 174. (*Faust I & II*, in *Goethe's Collected Works and Papers*, vol. 2, p. 90).

13   Goethe, *Faust. Erster Theil*, in *Goethe's Werke*, vol. 12, p. 131. (*Faust I & II*, in *Goethe's Collected Works and Papers*, vol. 2, p. 69).

"innocence."[14] She is the very image of a "nature" which is missing from his soul, worn down as it is from abstract reflection. In the scene entitled "Evening"[15] the set depicts the clean and orderly room of the girl which both excites and terrifies the seducer. The peace inspired by that small room is both an escape from a race without end and a jail cell, which imprisons and limits research.

Margarete is the incarnation of a nature which brings the knight back down to earth, and he both needs this and is horrified by it. If masculinity is the reaching of the spirit towards infinity, the *Streben* of ceaseless research, then femininity is a reminder of the immediacy of earth, a oneness with nature. Here the idea of the duality of masculine and feminine principles, which is present in all of Goethe's work, takes form, inspired by the theory of the sexes of the time.[16]

The story of the two lovers is only a part of the tragedy of social barriers, and the latter is composed of the drama of conflicting visions of the world and divergent religious beliefs. In "Martha's Garden,"[17] the famous scene of the "catechization," two completely incompatible visions of the world become clear. Margarete immediately realizes that there is something strange about her handsome knight. She declares: "there is a hitch in it, / since you don't hold to Christianity."[18] With all her candor, the clear line separating the two lovers is not lost on the girl. During his demonic research, Faust had repudiated God, and with God the world. For Margarete, things could not be more different. Her faith is a deep and immediate, and she is the priestess of a religion founded on the inviolable purity and dignity of the human soul. She is both strong and fragile at once, almost defenseless in her sensitivity and yet sustained by an indestructible moral awareness. In this, her character embodies a further conflict, which manifests itself between passion and religion. This is a conflict that will lead to her death but does not have the strength to corrupt her underlying morality.

In the final scene, "Prison,"[19] the emotional intensity of the character erupts with full force. Margarete has at this point been condemned to death by decapitation for the murder of her child. With the help of Mephistopheles, Faust races to free her. Although half mad and tormented by her feelings of guilt, the woman firmly refuses to follow her diabolical lover: "We'll meet again, / but not at a wedding dance."[20]

---

[14]   Goethe, *Faust. Erster Theil*, in *Goethe's Werke*, vol. 12, p. 152. (*Faust I & II*, in *Goethe's Collected Works and Papers*, vol. 2, p. 79).

[15]   Goethe, *Faust. Erster Theil*, in *Goethe's Werke*, vol. 12, p. 130. (*Faust I & II*, in *Goethe's Collected Works and Papers*, vol. 2, p. 69).

[16]   For the connection between Goethe's *Faust* and patriarchal culture see James Simpson, *Goethe and Patriarchy: Faust and the Fates of Desire*, Oxford: Legenda 1998, pp. 101–2; p. 228.

[17]   Goethe, *Faust. Erster Theil*, in *Goethe's Werke*, vol. 12, p. 170. (*Faust I & II*, in *Goethe's Collected Works and Papers*, vol. 2, p. 88).

[18]   Goethe, *Faust. Erster Theil*, in *Goethe's Werke*, vol. 12, p. 172. (*Faust I & II*, in *Goethe's Collected Works and Papers*, vol. 2, p. 89).

[19]   Goethe, *Faust. Erster Theil*, in *Goethe's Werke*, vol. 12, p. 224. (*Faust I & II*, in *Goethe's Collected Works and Papers*, vol. 2, p. 114).

[20]   Goethe, *Faust. Erster Theil*, in *Goethe's Werke*, vol. 12, p. 233. (*Faust I & II*, in *Goethe's Collected Works and Papers*, vol. 2, p. 118).

This is prophetic, a feeling with no need for moral precepts. In her the voice of the heart is the sign of morality, which leads her to naturally accept the need for sacrifice. Margaret is at once "judged" and "saved."[21] Like Ottilie or Iphigenia, she is the Goethan image of the eternal feminine, the spirit and nature, which take the form of a feeling which embraces all of humanity, a redemptive and irresistible force. The figure of Gretchen plays a central role in the catharsis of Faust. Her presence causes the drama in the first place but is also necessary as a way for the seducer to find himself once more. The last words with which this first part closes are spoken by a voice which echoes over the whole scene before disappearing. It is probable that this voice belongs to Margarete. "Heinrich! Heinrich!,"[22] she cries, calling to Faust with his given name and thus underlining the indissoluble link between her and the protagonist.

II. Kierkegaard's Margarete

Kierkegaard's reflection on the figure of Margarete can be traced back to his early years. It goes hand in hand with his reflections on Faust, the first evidence of which are notes in his journals and notebooks dating back to 1835. Kierkegaard's Gretchen is openly declared to be a product of Goethe's character, and he is said to be fundamentally inspired by her. For Kierkegaard, the character becomes an object of interest in the period which is most heavily influenced by Goethe's work, of which *Either/Or* is the most important milestone.[23] The young Kierkegaard found himself caught up in the Goethe fever which swept Denmark immediately after the poet's death.[24] In particular, in *Either/Or* there exists a particular predilection for explicitly recycled female figures. In addition to a 55-volume edition of *Goethe's Werke*,[25] published between 1827 and 1833, Kierkegaard's personal library contained a good number of relevant works. Concerning Margarete, one work, which stands out is the essay "Gretchen im *Faust*" by Heinrich Theodor Rötscher (1802–71) printed in the second volume of his *Die Kunst der dramatischen Darstellung*, published between 1841 and 1846.[26]

---

[21]   Goethe, *Faust. Erster Theil*, in *Goethe's Werke*, vol. 12, p. 234 *(Faust I & II*, in *Goethe's Collected Works and Papers*, vol. 2, p. 119).

[22]   Ibid.

[23]   Jon Stewart and Katalin Nun, "Goethe: A German Classic Through the Filter of the Danish Golden Age," in *Kierkegaard and His German Contemporaries*, Tome III, *Literature and Aesthetics*, ed. by Jon Stewart, Aldershot: Ashgate 2008, pp. 71–5.

[24]   See Henning Fenger, *Kierkegaard: The Myths and their Origins*, trans. by George C. Schoolfield, New Haven and London: Yale University Press 1980, pp. 81–8. See also Louis Bobé, "Goethe og Danmark," *Gads Danske Magazin*, vol. 20, 1926, pp. 288–302; Georg Brandes, "Goethe og Danmark," in his *Mennesker og Værker*, Copenhagen: Gyldendalske Boghandels Forlag 1883, pp. 1–79.

[25]   *Goethe's Werke. Vollständige Ausgabe letzter Hand* and *Goethe's nachgelassene Werke (ASKB* 1641–1668).

[26]   Heinrich Theodor Rötscher, "Gretchen im *Faust*," in his *Die Kunst der dramatischen Darstellung. In ihrem organischen Zusammenhange wissenschaftlich entwickelt*, vols. 1–3, Berlin: Wilhelm Thome 1841–46, vol. 2, pp. 270–97 *(ASKB* 1391 and 1802–1803).

An initial reflection on the character can be dated back to 1836. In the pages of his *Journal BB*,[27] Kierkegaard lingers on the criticism concerning Goethe's *Faust* in Ernst Schubarth's work, *Ueber Goethe's Faust*.[28] Schubarth's work appears in the long list of literature on Faust compiled by the author in that period.[29] Kierkegaard is particularly attracted to Schubarth's thoughts concerning the "catechization" scene. The philosopher highlights how the critical evaluation is particularly concerned with the differing religious natures of the two lovers; a difference rooted in the differing religious needs of the two sexes—the male more individual and the female more general. In his journal on September 9, 1839 there is a return to the feminine character in literature, which makes explicit reference to a passage of Faust, which Kierkegaard reads in keeping with his own personal experience: "As motto for my childhood I know nothing better than the words from Goethe's Faust '*Halb Kinderspiele, Halb Gott im Herzen!*' "[30] The same quotation appears in 1843 at the beginning of his main reflection on Margarete, the essay "Silhouettes" of *Either/Or*,[31] published in the same year. Kierkegaard's Margarete is "betrothed to sorrow,"[32] tied in an almost sisterly relationship to other misfortunate women: Marie Beaumarchais and Donna Elvira.

"Silhouettes" is dedicated to Donna Elvira, Marie Beaumarchais, and Margarete. The link between the three women is that of the tragic destiny of being seduced and abandoned. They are lovers and victims of deceit in love by the famous seducers Clavigo, Don Giovanni, and Faust. Their love is absolute and all-consuming, a love which they endure rather than fully experience first-hand. It is this love which condemns them to play out the hopeless role of prey. Not dissimilar to that of their partners, their existence is doomed to be one of desperation. "Seducing all the maidens means for the man the same as for a woman—to let herself be seduced once and for all, heart and soul, and then to hate—or, if you please, to love her seducer with an energy that no married woman has."[33] Seducer and seduced have in common the same attitude: that of placing at the center of their lives not themselves but an external reality which they always end up being at the mercy of. Both are victims of a finiteness rendered absolute by the seducer's search for pleasure and by the seduced's totalizing conception of a romantic relationship. The "reflective sorrow"[34] remains the only faithful companion of the young woman. This is unleashed by the abandonment, an external event, a deception about which her cognition agonizes. Deception is always something of a paradox in love, underlines aesthete A. It forces the lover into the agonizing contradiction which is the rational knowledge of the guilt of the loved one, without the ability to react by stopping an emotion which has very little to do with rationality. Despite the fact that they are well aware of the

---

[27]   *SKS* 17, 76–89, BB:7 / *KJN* 1,70–83.
[28]   Carl Ernst Schubarth, *Ueber Goethe's Faust. Vorlesungen*, Berlin: Enslin 1830 (*ASKB* U 96).
[29]   *SKS* 17, 92–104, BB:12 / *KJN* 1, 85–96.
[30]   *SKS* 18, 60, EE:177 / *KJN* 2, 55.
[31]   *SKS* 2, 200 / *EO1*, 204.
[32]   *SKS* 2, 213 / *EO1*, 214.
[33]   *SKS* 2, 193 / *EO1*, 196–7.
[34]   *SKS* 2, 167 / *EO1*, 171.

negativity of those hurting them, the "betrothed to sorrow" are condemned to live with the agony of knowing that those they continue to love are imposters. Their "reflective sorrow" is borne of such contradiction and is fed by the worm of doubt, which gives no peace and which slowly eats away at their spirit. Their pain is hidden in the depths of their souls, invisible to the outside world. The feeling is intensified by the impossibility of it being alleviated by any single, precise thing. The ambiguity finds no remedy and is fed by doubt and paradox.

The only thing to unite the three figures is their pain, aesthete A realizes immediately, because Margarete is neither an Elvira nor a Marie:

> At first glance, it might seem that the only difference between Elvira and Margarete was the difference between two different individualities who have experienced the same thing. But the difference is far more essential and yet is due not so much to the difference in the two feminine natures as to the essential difference between a Don Juan and Faust.[35]

The abyss separating Elvira from Margarete cannot be reduced to the mere fact that the first is a noblewoman and the second "a little middle-class girl."[36] The difference between them cannot be found in their single, female individualities but in the *desire* of the seducers:

> From the very start, there must be a difference between an Elvira and a Margarete, since a girl who is to make an impression on a Faust must be essentially different from a girl who makes an impression on a Don Juan. Yes, even if I supposed that it was the same girl who engaged the attention of both, it would be something different that appealed to each of them.[37]

The *silhouettes* do not have an autonomous life and are the projection of masculine desire, the desire which permeates all of *Either/Or* and which sees female subjectivity as being produced by the narcissistic eyes of the seducers.

The difference between the seduced and abandoned can be found not in them but in their seducers or more precisely in the manner in which they are desired. Faust's desire is fundamentally different from that of Don Giovanni:

> Faust is admittedly a reproduction of Don Juan, but his being a reproduction is precisely what makes him essentially different from him, even in the stage of life in which he can be called a Don Juan, for to reproduce another stage does not mean only to become that but to become that with all the elements of the preceding stage in it.[38]

Faust desires the same thing as Don Giovanni, but "in a different way. But in order for him to be able to desire it in a different way, it also must be present in a different way."[39] Goethe's seducer is a demon but is "superior."[40] "Sensuousness

---

[35]   *SKS* 2, 200 / *EO1*, 205.
[36]   *SKS* 2, 203 / *EO1*, 208.
[37]   *SKS* 2, 201 / *EO1*, 205.
[38]   Ibid.
[39]   *SKS* 2, 201 / *EO1*, 205–6.
[40]   *SKS* 2, 201 / *EO1*, 206.

does not acquire importance for him until he has lost a whole previous world, but the consciousness of this loss is not blotted out; it is always present, and therefore he seeks in the sensuous not so much pleasure as distraction."[41] Faust is the incarnation of the first aesthetic image of the "reflective" seducer, in whom the consciousness of his seduction has reached a level alien to the immediacy of Don Giovanni. He has *chosen* pleasure as a last and extreme distraction from the agony of his soul tortured by his thoughts. He wishes to survive the nihilism which has caused him to see reality as senseless. Margarete is, in his eyes, an "island of peace in the calm ocean,"[42] a restorative for him against desperation. The seducer does not love her because, for him, love, as with all other finite aspects of the world, is no longer real or consistent. His is a feverish desire, and that which he desires so is her "immediacy of the spirit,"[43] the "pure, undisturbed, rich, immediate joy of a feminine soul,"[44] which is missing from his own soul, emptied by his reflections. "Just as ghosts in the underworld, when a living being fell into their hands, sucked his blood and lived as long as this blood warmed and nourished them, so Faust seeks an immediate life whereby he will be rejuvenated and strengthened."[45] Feminine subjectivity assumes the form of the serene and immediate existence of a young soul free of reflections. Margarete is pure and what her seducer desires in her is her "innocence and childlikeness."[46]

With this, Kierkegaard recaptures the traits of Goethe's version of the character. More than the mere physical innocence of virginity, Margarete's innocence is, for Kierkegaard's seducer, a kind of spiritual candor, belonging to spirit alone and which substantiates itself in ignorance of her own sexuality.[47] Simplicity, by contrast, is intended as lack of formal education, the aim of which is to cause reflection, and the lack of which is indispensible in order to preserve innocence from the criticism of one's own conscience. Grete is "a silly poor young thing," as Goethe has her say,[48] "a girl one could almost be tempted to call insignificant."[49] The candor of her existence is contaminated by her meeting with her seducer who, in the act of seducing her, rips apart the veil of immediacy and leaves her open to reflection. After being abandoned, Margaret is no longer the same since she is reborn into a new existence dominated by a knowledge that before was unknown to her. The maiden is reborn with her seducer because she owes this knowledge to him, and she could not separate herself from him if she wanted to, because he has become, in a sense, her creator. This is the *impasse* of her desperation. "But what can more truthfully be called a woman's life than her love?"[50] The destiny of the woman is to be found in the tragic fact of her

41   Ibid.
42   *SKS* 2, 202 / *EO1*, 207.
43   *SKS* 2, 201 / *EO1*, 206.
44   *SKS* 2, 202 / *EO1*, 207.
45   *SKS* 2, 201 / *EO1*, 206.
46   *SKS* 2, 202 / *EO1*, 207.
47   *SKS* 4, 341–7 / *CA*, 35–41.
48   Goethe, *Faust. Erster Theil*, in *Goethe's Werke. Vollständige Ausgabe letzter Hand*, vol. 12, p. 160. (*Faust I & II*, in *Goethe's Collected Works and Papers*, vol. 2, p. 83.)
49   *SKS* 2, 203 / *EO1*, 208.
50   *SKS* 2, 169 / *EO1*, 172.

belonging to the man. Johannes comments cruelly in his diary: "she first becomes free [*fri*] through man and therefore we say 'to propose' [*at frie*], and therefore man proposes. If he proposes properly, there can be no question of any choice."[51]

Between the pages of "The Seducer's Diary" an *aesthetic theory of femininity*[52] takes form and this permeates the whole of *Either/Or*. Margarete is one of the first significant examples of this theory. It is important at this point to make a brief aside on the aesthetic conception of the feminine in order better to reconstruct the theoretical role of Grete in the Kierkegaardian *corpus*. What role does woman have for the aesthete? The answer to this question can be found in some of Johannes' fundamental expressions, which constitute the theoretical foundations of the aesthetic vision of the opposite sex:

> It can give me joy, it can joy my heart, to imagine the sun of womanhood sending out its rays in an infinite multiplicity, radiating into a confusion of languages, where each woman has a little share of the whole kingdom of womanhood, yet in such a way that the remainder found in her harmoniously forms around this point. In this sense, womanly beauty is infinitely divisible. But the specific share of beauty must be harmoniously controlled, for otherwise it has a disturbing effect, and one comes to think that nature intended something with this girl, but that nothing ever came of it....Every particular point has its little share and yet is complete in itself, happy, joyous, beautiful.[53]

Femininity is therefore a sort of Platonic sun of infinite size and is for this reason infinitely divisible. Its light radiates from its multiple parts, infusing them with its beauty. The finite can therefore contain only a part of this reality, and each part is different. In each woman there is present only a single aspect of the idea, although it

---

[51]   *SKS* 2, 418 / *EO1*, 431.

[52]   For this connection see Antonella Fimiani, *Sentieri del desiderio. Femminile e alterità in Søren Kierkegaard*, Soveria Mannelli: Rubbettino 2010, pp. 23–67; Céline Léon, *The Neither/Nor of Second Sex: Kierkegaard on Women, Sexual Difference, and Sexual Relations*, Macon, Georgia: Mercer University Press 2008, pp. 15–72; Guillermine de Lacoste, "The Dialectic of Real Erotic and of Eroticism in Kierkegaard's Seducer's Diary," *Kierkegaardiana*, vol. 22, 2002, pp. 125–35; Wanda Warren Berry, "The Heterosexual Imagination and Aesthetic Existence in Kierkegaard's *Either/Or*, Part I," in *Feminist Interpretations of Søren Kierkegaard*, ed. by Céline Léon and Sylvia Walsh, University Park, Pennsylvania: Pennsylvania State University Press 1997, pp. 25–49; Vincent McCarthy, "Narcissism and Desire in Kierkegaard's *Either/Or*, Part One," in *Either/Or, Part One*, ed. by Robert L. Perkins, Macon, Georgia: Mercer University 2004 (*International Kierkegaard Commentary*, vol. 3), pp. 51–72; Sylvia Walsh, *Living Poetically: Kierkegaard's Existential Aesthetics*, University Park, Pennsylvania: Pennsylvania State University Press 1994, pp. 63–98; Simonella Davini, "La maschera estetica del seduttore," in *Maschere kierkegaardiane*, ed. by Leonardo Amoroso, Turin: Rosemberg & Sellier 1990, pp. 105–98; Carla Benedetti, "Il femminile e l'infinito temporale," in *Il Centauro*, vol. 5, 1982, pp. 184–7; Kristine Nordentoft, "Erotic Love," in *Kierkegaard's Classical Inspiration*, ed. by Niels Thulstrup and Marie Mikulová Thulstrup, Copenhagen: C.A. Reitzel 1980 (*Bibliotheca Kierkegaardiana*, vol. 14), pp. 87–99; Giovanni Velocci, *La donna in Kierkegaard*, L'Aquila: L.U. Japadre Editore 1980, pp. 89–99; Silviane Agacinski, *Aparté. Conceptions et morts de Sören Kierkegaard*, Paris: Aubier-Flammarion 1977, pp. 152–63.

[53]   *SKS* 2, 416 / *EO1*, 428.

is in harmony with her existential concretion. Every woman possesses but a fragment of an infinite, intangible, and indefinable idea. What the seducer is in fact looking for in a woman is the infinite image of femininity. The *imago* is the reflection of her subjectivity of which the opposite sex reveals itself to be only a temporary means of manifestation. Once a woman has been possessed, she loses her perfume since the abstract idea of her is bound to shatter under the force of temporal finiteness. Seductive love becomes a kind of game of mirrors.

The choice of Kierkegaard to recast the scene of Faust's first meeting his beloved reflected in a mirror, described by Goethe in the "Witch's Kitchen,"[54] is not by chance. As it was for Goethe, for Kierkegaard the mirror is a symbol of the narcissistic reflection of the seducer himself. Like Narcissus, Faust sees not Margarete in the reflected image, but himself and his own infinite subjectivity. In "The Seducer's Diary," the mirror is once more intermediary in the first meeting between Johannes and Cordelia.[55] Seduction of the opposite sex is compromised at its very core by a powerful narcissistic transfiguration. Woman is aesthetically defined as "being-for-other"[56] (*Væren for Andet*), the profound sense of which is her extinguishing herself in man. The essence of woman is "devotedness"[57] (*Hengivelse*), an alienated and alienating dedication. "Pure virginity"[58] is its *proprium* as a candor, which is spiritual open-endedness and absolute lack of form. The seducer desires this immediacy because he can transfigure himself freely in it. Between man and woman is an ontological difference, an insurmountable distance, which allows for no possibility of an authentic relationship. Woman is "substance"[59] (*Substans*), intimately linked to the immediacy of nature, and man on the opposite end of the spectrum is "reflection"[60] (*Reflexion*), condemned to the abstraction of spirit. Their heterogeneity prevents them from being able to relate to one another.

In Margarete, Faust desires the immediacy he does not possess; he hungers after her sensually, and his objective is the physical possession of her innocence. For this reason he resorts to the strength of his spiritual superiority. If Don Giovanni wins over Elvira with the "seductive talent"[61] of his desire alone, Faust puts a genuine plan for seduction into action, and at the heart of it are mystification and lies. Because it is more elaborate, Faust's seduction is far more destructive than Don Giovanni's. Kierkegaard reinterprets the fundamental scene of the "catechization" in the footsteps of Goethe as being a profound vision of the world characterizing the lovers. "Faust readily perceives that Margarete's entire significance hinges on her innocent simplicity. If this is taken from her, she is nothing in herself, nothing to him. This, then, must be preserved."[62] Desiring in her the immediate faith, which is

---

[54]   Goethe, *Faust. Erster Theil*, in *Goethe's Werke. Vollständige Ausgabe letzter Hand*, vol. 12, p. 116. (*Faust I & II*, in *Goethe's Collected Works and Papers*, vol. 2, p. 62.)

[55]   *SKS* 2, 305 / *EO1*, 315.

[56]   *SKS* 2, 136 / *EO1*, 430.

[57]   *SKS* 2, 376 / *EO1*, 388.

[58]   *SKS* 2, 418 / *EO1*, 430.

[59]   *SKS* 2, 419 / *EO1*, 431.

[60]   Ibid.

[61]   *SKS* 2, 205 / *EO1*, 210.

[62]   *SKS* 2, 204 / *EO1*, 209.

missing from his soul, tortured as it is by the worm of reflection, the seducer cannot be content with merely ripping her faith from her with a simple revelation of doubt. What renders the victim desirable is her immediacy, and this must be preserved at all costs through deception and dissimulation:

> So now he finds his joy in enriching her with the opulent content of a way of looking at things; he takes out all the finery of immediate faith and finds joy in embellishing her with it, for it is very becoming to her, and she thereby becomes more beautiful in his eyes. In doing so, he has the added advantage that her soul attaches itself ever more tightly to his. She really does not understand him at all; like a child she attaches herself tightly to him; what for him is doubt is unswerving truth for her.[63]

The objective of the seducer is to build up the faith of the victim to such a point that it is damaged at its very foundations, to place himself in the role of God as her singular and progressive object of devotion. Conquered by his intellectual superiority, the prey slowly but surely comes to belong to him to the point that she gives him everything, including her faith. She "disappears in Faust"[64] not so much because she loves him with all of her being but because she has placed all of her "life force"[65] in him, and it is with him that she is tragically born.

After being abandoned, she condemns a man who has become her very creator, the origin of her thoughts.[66] Margarete *cannot* stop wanting her killer because their relationship has been transformed by the link between creator and created:

> God in heaven, forgive me for loving a human being more than I loved you, and yet I still do it; I know that it is a new sin that I speak this way to you. O Eternal Love, let your mercy hold me, do not thrust me away; give him back to me, incline his heart to me again; have mercy on me, God of mercy, that I pray this way again![67]

This is the echo of the Goethean conflict between passion and religion, an ambiguity, which, according to the philosopher, can have no trace of redemption. Kierkegaard's Margarete is destined to succumb because in her there is no sign whatsoever of autonomous individuality. Her conflict is apparent because it finds its roots in an ontological subordination, which from the very beginning marks her with her fatal destiny.

The destiny of Kierkegaard's Margarete is written in the aesthetic way in which her seducer views relations with the opposite sex: a false relationship, in which the woman is no more than the reproduction of a narcissistic subjectivity, which knows no alterity. The words of the protagonist spoken at the end of the work are explicit:

> Can the clay pot be presumptuous toward the potter? What was I? Nothing! Clay in his hands, a rib from which he formed me! What was I? A poor insignificant plant, and he stooped down to me; he lovingly raised me; he was my all, my god, the origin

---

63   Ibid.
64   *SKS* 2, 205 / *EO1*, 210.
65   *SKS* 2, 207 / *EO1*, 212.
66   *SKS* 2, 208 / *EO1*, 213.
67   Ibid.

of my thoughts, the food of my soul....And I am a mother! A living being demands nourishment from me. Can the hungry satisfy the hungry, the feeble from thirst refresh the thirsty? Shall I become a murderer, then? O Faust, come back; save the child in the womb even if you do not want to save the mother![68]

The aesthetic vision of the feminine is inserted in the context of a more ample criticism of the Romantics and their way of looking at the relationship between the sexes, the most eloquent example of which for Kierkegaard was *Lucinde*.[69] *Either/Or* doubtless evidences the distance he took from this viewpoint, a distance which, as Kierkegaard explains in *The Concept of Irony*, goes hand-in-hand with a condemnation of free love unfettered by social ties, a central theme in the Romantic period.[70] The use of Goethe's female character can be read in the light of this criticism. The theme of *Die Wahlverwandtschaften* (1809), a Goethean masterpiece which caused scandal by suggesting the idea of an emotion based on natural attraction capable of surpassing and upsetting bourgeois conventions, cannot be excluded from this criticism.[71] Borrowed in the most part from Romantic writers, the female characters of *Either/Or* must be looked at in the light of this criticism.

Kierkegaard's Margarete reveals itself to be a sort of caricature of Goethe's character, created with the sole aim of demonstrating the most extreme consequences of a Romantic sentiment, of which the philosopher could see the limits and contradictions. This appears evident when we compare the two characters. Goethe's Margarete undoubtedly has a complex, articulated structure, which is revealed in the final part of the piece. This complexity has not been passed down to Kierkegaard's version, and it is here that the philosopher chose to distance himself from Goethe: in the way in which the female character confronts her destiny. Goethe's character has the strength to oppose her killer, to choose not to follow him from prison. The heroine accepts that she must pay for her sins, and in her there is a moral autonomy which serves to elevate and redeem her. Kierkegaard's Gretchen is turned in on herself, marked by her destiny and with no chance of redemption. This is not only because she belongs to the aesthetic stage but because her character depends on the male character from the very beginning, ontologically subsumed by male domination, with no right of appeal.

---

[68]   *SKS* 2, 208 / *EO1*, 213–14.
[69]   *SKS* 1, 321–4 / *CI*, 286–301.
[70]   *SKS* 1, 321–52 / *CI*, 286–323.
[71]   *SKS* 1, 352–7 / *CI*, 323–9.

Bibliography

Agacinski, Silviane, *Aparté. Conceptions et morts de Sören Kierkegaard*, Paris: Aubier-Flammarion 1977, pp. 152–63.

Benedetti, Carla, "Il femminile e l'infinito temporale," *Il Centauro*, vol. 5, 1982, pp. 184–7.

Bobé, Louis, "Goethe og Danmark," *Gads Danske Magazin*, vol. 20, 1926, pp. 288–302.

Boyle, Nicholas, *Goethe: The Poet and the Age*, vols. 1–2, Oxford: Clarendon Press 1997, vol. 1, pp. 25–33; pp. 89–229.

Brandes, Georg, "Goethe og Danmark," in his *Mennesker og Værker*, Copenhagen: Gyldendalske Boghandels Forlag 1883, pp. 1–79.

Davini, Simonella, "La maschera estetica del seduttore," in *Maschere kierkegaardiane*, ed. by Leonardo Amoroso, Turin: Rosemberg & Sellier 1990, pp. 105–98.

Fenger, Henning, *Kierkegaard: The Myths and their Origins*, trans. by George C. Schoolfield, New Haven and London: Yale University Press 1980, pp. 81–8.

Fimiani, Antonella, *Sentieri del desiderio. Femminile e alterità in Søren Kierkegaard*, Soveria Mannelli: Rubbettino 2010, pp. 23–67.

Lacoste, Guillermine de, "The Dialectic of Real Erotic and of Eroticism in Kierkegaard's Seducer's Diary," *Kierkegaardiana*, vol. 22, 2002, pp. 125–35.

Léon, Céline, *The Neither/Nor of Second Sex: Kierkegaard on Women, Sexual Difference, and Sexual Relations*, Macon, Georgia: Mercer University Press 2008, pp. 44–51.

McCarthy, Vincent, "Narcissism and Desire in Kierkegaard's *Either/Or*, Part One," in *Either/Or, Part One*, ed. by Robert L. Perkins, Macon, Georgia: Mercer University 2004 (*International Kierkegaard Commentary*, vol. 3), pp. 51–72.

Nordentoft, Kristine, "Erotic Love," in *Kierkegaard's Classical Inspiration*, ed. by Niels Thulstrup and Marie Mikulová Thulstrup, Copenhagen: C.A. Reitzel 1980 (*Bibliotheca Kierkegaardiana*, vol. 14), pp. 87–99.

Simpson, James, *Goethe and Patriarchy: Faust and the Fates of Desire*, Oxford: Legenda 1998, pp. 101–2; p. 228.

Stewart, Jon and Katalin Nun, "Goethe: A German Classic Through the Filter of the Danish Golden Age," in *Kierkegaard and His German Contemporaries*, Tome III, *Literature and Aesthetics*, ed. by Jon Stewart, Aldershot: Ashgate 2008 (*Kierkegaard Research: Sources, Reception and Resources*, vol. 6), pp. 72–3.

Velocci, Giovanni, *La donna in Kierkegaard*, L'Aquila: L.U. Japadre editore 1980, pp. 89–99.

Walsh, Sylvia, *Living Poetically: Kierkegaard's Existential Aesthetics*, University Park, Pennsylvania: Pennsylvania State University Press 1994, pp. 63–98.

Warren Berry, Wanda, "The Heterosexual Imagination and Aesthetic Existence in Kierkegaard's *Either/Or*, Part I," in *Feminist Interpretations of Søren Kierkegaard*, ed. by Céline Léon and Sylvia Walsh, University Park, Pennsylvania: Pennsylvania State University Press 1997, pp. 25–49.

The Master-Thief:

A One-Man Army against the Established Order

F. Nassim Bravo Jordan

During the winter of 1834–35 Kierkegaard wrote on some loose papers some thoughts about a figure that he called the "master-thief (*mestertyv*)." Apparently he intended to write a drama or novel on the topic and declared his surprise that no one before had ever embarked on such a work, inasmuch as the theme, according to his own view, was very suitable for "dramatic treatment."[1] Although he only dedicated seven brief entries to the idea, it seems that this was Kierkegaard's very first literary enterprise and, even if the master-thief figure only appeared explicitly in these notes, the motif of the noble-hearted outlaw, a sort of one-man army against the corrupted established order, misunderstood and outlawed by society, was one that would reappear in one way or another throughout the rest of Kierkegaard's writing career. It could even be argued that Kierkegaard personally assumed that role himself, as if he was prophesying what would become of him in the years to come.

The idea, however, was not new. As Kierkegaard himself underscores, "almost every country has had the idea of such a thief."[2] Thus the master-thief is a figure of lore, a popular ideal, and Kierkegaard tried to collect information from several sources in order to create his own hero. He had literature about the topic at his disposal, and in the entries he explicitly mentions six famous, real-life thieves that he probably took as models for his project. Three of them were contemporary Danish criminals (Frederiksen, Mikkelsen, and Kagerup), and it is likely that Kierkegaard was familiar with them. It also helped that when he lived in the family house at Nytorv, he was neighbor to the courthouse, so he could not easily avoid seeing the prisoners brought to trial. The other three thieves came respectively from Germany (Forster), France (Cartouche), and Italy (Fra Diavolo).

I. The Master-Thieves

A. Morten Frederiksen

Morten Johan Frederiksen was indeed referred to as the "infamous master-thief." He is one of the three famous Danish criminals mentioned in the entries about the

---

[1]   *SKS* 27, 118, Papir 97:1 / *JP* 5, 5061.

[2]   Ibid.

master-thief project. Kierkegaard probably got to know about him from the work *Den berygtede Mestertyv og Rasphuusfange Morten Frederiksens sandfærdige Levnetshistorie*, based on criminal records,[3] and from a lecture given by P.L. Benzon on February 11, 1826 in front of the Student Union and later published in 1827.[4]

Frederiksen had a difficult childhood, as he became an orphan at a very young age. A man of restless spirit, he traveled a lot both in Denmark and abroad, and was arrested several times on various charges (mainly theft and, after he had joined the army, desertion) in Denmark, Sweden, and Germany. However, he was a resourceful man, and he always managed to flee, even though once in Roskilde he was chained to the ground. This happened in 1812. After several attempts to escape, the guards of Roskilde prison decided that Frederiksen had to be chained. But then, on November 23, 1812, Frederiksen fashioned a leg out of cloth and straw, which was chained by the deceived guards instead of the real leg, and thus he could escape. It seems that the anecdote was well known, as Kierkegaard alludes to it several times in other texts, most notably in *Prefaces*, where the pseudonym Nicolaus Notabene recalls Frederiksen's trick to escape prison and suggests it could be a nice way to elude literary reviewers.[5] Finally, after "many odd adventures,"[6] Frederiksen was caught and imprisoned in the Citadel of Copenhagen, where he remained for the rest of his life.

Besides the entries on the master-thief project, Kierkegaard mentions Frederiksen elsewhere in his writings, either referring to the aforementioned escape from Roskilde prison or comparing the thief's famous sagacity with the falsity in Christendom.[7]

B. Peder Mikkelsen

Peder Mikkelsen (1762–1809), who was also nicknamed "master-thief," became fairly well known in the cultural circles of Copenhagen when in 1800 the painter Nicolai Abildgaard (1743–1809) made a drawing of the thief with hands and feet in chains.[8] Like Morten Frederiksen, Mikkelsen was an orphan from a very young age. When he was young he lived as a beggar and was then employed by a farmer.

---

[3]   Cf. *Den berygtede Mestertyv og Rasphuusfange Morten Frederiksens sandfærdige Levnetshistorie; hvorledes han nemlig, efter at have taget Tjeneste ved det Militaire, flere Gange blev afstraffet som Tyv og Deserteur baade her i Danmark og i Udlandet; hvorledes han herpaa blev hensat i* Slaveriet *og senere i* Rasphuset, *hvorfra han brød ud, for at begaae nye Forbrydelser, indtil han endelig efter mangfoldige sælsomme Eventyr blev hensat i Citadellet,* Copenhagen: no year (ca. 1820), pp. 14ff.

[4]   Cf. P.L. Benzon, "Kort Omrids af Morten Frederiksens Levnetsløb," in *Criminalhistorier uddragne af Danske Justits-Acter,* Copenhagen: Andreas Seidelin 1827, pp. 46–60.

[5]   Cf. *SKS* 4, 482 / *P,* 18. See also *SKS* 24, 502, NB25:86; *SKS* 26, 399, NB35:40 / *JP* 1, 603. In this last entry, Kierkegaard tells the same anecdote but refers to Peder Mikkelsen as the author of the feat. He probably confused the names of the two famous thieves.

[6]   See note 3.

[7]   Cf. *SKS* 26, 137, NB32:28 / *JP* 1, 408; *SKS* 26, 137, NB32:29; *SKS* 27, 570–3, Papir 458 / *JP* 3, 2543. See also note 5 above.

[8]   *Mestertyven Per Mikkelsen,* 1800.

During this period he learned the blacksmith trade, but in spite of this he decided to pursue a criminal career. He was charged with theft in both Denmark and Germany. He managed to escape twice from prison, once from his imprisonment in Spandau and another time from Copenhagen. He was arrested again in 1802, and from that year to his death in 1809 he remained in jail.

Kierkegaard probably read about Mikkelsen from a work edited by T.P. Hansen, *Archiv for danske og norske Criminalhistorier*,[9] although there was no copy of this text in his personal library. It is interesting that Kierkegaard attributes to Mikkelsen the personality of a Robin Hood, "stealing from the rich to help the poor,"[10] as this trait is nowhere to be found in the work mentioned above. However, Mikkelsen was a popular figure, and so perhaps this magnanimity came from oral tradition. After the master-thief entries, Kierkegaard mentions Mikkelsen once in his *Journal NB35* in reference to the said escape from Roskilde prison, here wrongly attributed to Mikkelsen.[11]

C. Kagerup

The third Danish criminal mentioned by Kierkegaard is Søren Andersen Kagerup (1811–32). Unlike the other two "master-thieves," Kagerup was only imprisoned once and subsequently executed. The son of divorced parents, Kagerup had to take care of himself from his early days, working in the service of several farmers. When he turned eighteen he committed a careless robbery but managed to get away with it unpunished. Nevertheless, since he could not stop boasting about the stolen money, he was eventually arrested. As Kierkegaard writes in one entry from September of 1834,[12] he openly admitted his crime and accepted his sentence, a harsh one, for he was imprisoned for life. From Kierkegaard's point of view, Kagerup represented the thief who, although fighting for a lofty ideal, admits his faults and thus acknowledges the reality of the established order.

Kagerup had an impetuous and unruly character, and he could not get along well with the other prisoners. On one occasion, an inmate called Johannes Davidsen was brutally attacked. Another convict, named Morten Christiansen, accused Kagerup of taking part in the assault. As a result of this accusation, Kagerup became furious and murdered Christiansen. He was sentenced to death and executed in 1832.

It was probably thanks to a series of articles published by the pastor Carl Holger Visby (1801–71) that Kierkegaard learned of the story of Kagerup.[13] Kierkegaard

---

[9]   Cf. *Archiv for danske og norske Criminalhistorier, eller mærkværdige Domfældtes Levnet, Forbrydelser og Straf*, ed. by T.P. Hansen, Copenhagen: [published by the editor] 1834, pp. 55ff.

[10]   *SKS* 27, 118, Papir 97:1 / *JP* 5, 5061.

[11]   See note 5 above.

[12]   Cf. *SKS* 27, 119, Papir 97:2 / *JP* 5, 5062.

[13]   Cf. C.H. Visby, "Psychologiske Bemærkninger over den, med Øxen henrettede, Morder Søren Andersen Kagerup," in *Borgervennen*, nos. 20–24, 1832. See also *Archiv for danske og norske Criminalhistorier*, ed. by T.P. Hansen, pp. 220ff.

was acquainted with Visby and thought highly of him.[14] The pastor also wrote a prayerbook for the prisoners at the penal institution[15] and purportedly even held an interview with Kagerup, from which he deduced that a remarkable feature in the prisoner's character was an astounding indifference for life. Kagerup does not appear again in Kierkegaard's authorship.

D. Forster

Johann Paul Forster (1791–?) was a German thief and murderer. Born in a religiously oriented family near Munich, Forster, who as a young man was called "good little Paul," worked as a gardener before joining the army. He started his criminal career with petty robberies when he was still a gardener, but it is said that his crimes became increasingly serious. When he was in the army, he deserted several times, probably because he wanted to spend time with his girlfriend, Margareta Preiss. In 1816, when he was twenty-four and still in the army, he was accused of theft and indiscipline, and sentenced to prison for three and a half years, but was released before time. Soon after, he committed a brutal double murder, killing the owner of a store and his maid. Apparently, Forster wanted to get money in order to get married to Margareta, a gesture that Kierkegaard mentions in his notes.[16] Indeed, Kierkegaard sketches the "romantic quality" and the "warm affection for the opposite sex" of his imagined master-thief from the figure of Forster.[17]

Regarding the figure of Forster, Kierkegaard quotes in his notes a work by Anselm von Feuerbach, *Aktenmässige Darstellung merkwürdiger Verbrechen*.[18] Forster is not mentioned again in Kierkegaard's writings.

E. Cartouche

The real name of this brigand was Louis Dominique Garthausen (1693–1721), but he was also known as L.D. Bourguignon or simply as Cartouche, his well-known nickname. He was a famous French criminal and underworld leader during the Regency. At the beginning of his criminal career, Cartouche became the leader of a band of thieves in Normandy in northern France, which then achieved notoriety for terrorizing the roads between Versailles and Paris. His band grew larger and larger, and charges of theft and murder against him accumulated quickly, turning him into one of the most wanted criminals in France. Cartouche was also famous for his seductive and roguish personality. He was eventually arrested on October 14, 1721, denounced by a member of his band, Gruthus. Cartouche confessed all his crimes, and during a long session of eighteen hours he revealed the names of all the members

---

[14]   Cf. Bruce H. Kirmmse, *Encounters with Kierkegaard: A Life as Seen by his Contemporaries*, Princeton: Princeton University Press 1996, p. 13; p. 91.

[15]   Cf. ibid., p. 68.

[16]   Cf. *SKS* 27, 118, Papir 97:1 / *JP* 5, 5061.

[17]   Ibid.

[18]   Cf. Anselm von Feuerbach, *Aktenmässige Darstellung merkwürdiger Verbrechen*, vols. 1–2, Giessen: Heyer 1828–29, vol. 2, pp. 123ff. Cf. *SKS* 27, 118, Papir 97:1 / *JP* 5, 5061.

of his band. Even so he was sentenced to death, tortured, and finally broken on the wheel.

Kierkegaard refers to this thief as an example of the master-thief's humor, alluding to an anecdote where Cartouche goes to the authorities to claim the reward placed on his head.[19] Kierkegaard does not mention him again in his writings.

F. Fra Diavolo

Fra Diavolo (literally Brother Devil) was the nickname of Michael Pezza (1771–1806), a renowned Italian brigand and rebel against the French occupation of Naples. Many stories are told about Pezza. It is said that in 1797 he got involved with a woman who already had a lover. One night, his rival and another man assaulted Pezza, but he managed to defeat them and kill them both. He tried to escape, but was caught by the authorities. However, since his crime was committed in self-defense, the sentence of imprisonment was commuted to military service. Afterwards, when the Neapolitan army was defeated by the French, Pezza managed to flee and started to organize local resistance, thus acquiring fame in the eyes of the French troops of being a brigand. He became then the leader of a small band of irregulars based around Naples, and used his men to raid French outposts. It was during this period that he got the nickname Fra Diavolo.

Years later, during the Napoleonic occupation of Italy, he continued to fight in Calabria as a guerrilla leader. Fra Diavolo was finally defeated in 1806, and he was captured soon after. In November of the same year, Pezza was tried for banditry, whereupon he was sentenced to death and hanged in Naples.

In this case, Kierkegaard's source was not historical. He might have heard of Fra Diavolo for the first time from the opera by Daniel François Esprit Auber (1782–1871), *Fra Diavolo eller Værtshuset i Terracina* (*Fra Diavolo, ou L'hôtellerie de Terracine*),[20] with lyrics by the French poet Eugène Scribe (1791–1861). The opera was first performed at the Royal Theater of Copenhagen on May 19, 1831. Another performance was staged on January 29; Kierkegaard wrote three entries about the master-thief on the same day.[21] We must take into account that the young Kierkegaard was a regular at the opera house, and that he was at the time deeply interested in the work of Scribe, perhaps due to the early influence of Johan Ludvig Heiberg (1791–1860), who translated several vaudevilles by the French author into Danish. Moreover, *Fra Diavolo* was performed at the Royal Theater several times during the 1834–35 season, the same period of the master-thief entries, and so it is likely that Kierkegaard saw at least one of the performances.

---

[19]   Cf. *Den Franske Ertzspidsbube Cartouche og hans Kamraters Levnets-Beskrivelse. Uddragen af Proces-Acterne og andre særdeeles Efterretninger*, Copenhagen: L.N. Svare 1759. Cf. *SKS* 27, 120, Papir 97:4 / *JP* 5, 5073.

[20]   Cf. *Fra Diavolo eller Værtshuset i Terracina. Syngespil i 3 Akter af E. Scribe; oversat til Aubers Musik af Th. Overskou* (*Det kongelige Theaters Repertoire*, no. 37, Copenhagen 1831).

[21]   *SKS* 27, 119, Papir 97:3 / *JP* 5, 5072; *SKS* 27, 120, Papir 97:4 / *JP* 5, 5073; *SKS* 27, 120, Papir 97:5 / *JP* 5, 5074.

The opera is only loosely based on Pezza's life. Written by the Frenchman Scribe, the piece presents Fra Diavolo as a mere bandit. In any case, Kierkegaard accentuated the social element of the Italian "robber,"[22] and this is accurate, since Fra Diavolo was first and foremost a social fighter and a man of the people. Although Kierkegaard does not refer explicitly to Fra Diavolo again after the notes on the master-thief, he quotes a passage of the aforementioned opera in his *Journal JJ*.[23]

II. The Master-Thief Project

As we have said, Kierkegaard sketched his project on the master-thief in seven entries written on loose papers. The first entry is dated on September 12, 1834, and the last one on March 15, 1835. Just before he started working with this idea, Kierkegaard was still immersed in his theological studies at the University of Copenhagen. He attended Sibbern's course on the philosophy of Christianity a few months before (winter semester, November 1833–April 1834), and the entries written before the master-thief's notes are concerned with theological themes, especially that of predestination. It is difficult to say why Kierkegaard suddenly became interested in the more aesthetic topic of the master-thief, but perhaps it had something to do with the performance of the aforementioned opera, *Fra Diavolo*, which he probably saw at the Royal Theater.

In any case, it is clear that there was something about criminal life that was strongly appealing to him. What captivated him was not so much the perspective of breaking the law as the notion of a segregated man who holds an elevated ideal and clandestinely opposes the established order. A sign of this is that even after he abruptly discontinued his notes on the master-thief, Kierkegaard became increasingly interested in the more aristocratic characters of Don Juan, Faust, and the Wandering Jew, figures who also represented isolation from the established order and a desire to go beyond the conventional through seduction, doubt, or despair. It is not for us to say if Kierkegaard himself felt this kind of isolation at the time, but it is obvious that the idea was constantly present in his mind and notes.

The title of "master-thief" was of course not an original one. Both Morten Frederiksen and Peder Mikkelsen were honored with the nickname, and Kierkegaard doubtless took it from them. But unlike these thieves, who were in fact genuine crooks, Kierkegaard chose to highlight the more romantic features of clandestine life. It is interesting that although for the most part Kierkegaard possessed and read serious literature based on actual criminal records about the abovementioned thieves, he decided to create his character by focusing on local lore. He claims that the idea of the master-thief actually belongs to the sphere of popular belief, and that within this sphere the traits of the various real-life thieves tended to mix with each other. In the first master-thief entry of September 12, he writes:

---

[22]   Cf. *SKS* 27, 123, Papir 103 / *JP* 5, 5081.
[23]   Cf. *SKS* 18, 171, JJ:98 / *KJN* 2, 158: "That I will not do, I will not, I will not, no, no." Cf. *Fra Diavolo*, Act 1, Scene 3.

This shows that men have imagined a certain ideal of a thief with some broad general features which have then been attributed to this or that actual thief. We must especially bear in mind that wickedness, a propensity for stealing, etc. were not considered to be the one and only core of the idea. On the contrary, the master-thief has also been thought of as one endowed with natural goodness, kindness, charitableness, together with extraordinary bearing, cunning, ingenuity, one who really does not steal just to steal, that is, in order to get hold of another person's possessions, but for some other reason.[24]

The master-thief is therefore not a regular outlaw. It must be said that the romantic image that Kierkegaard presented in his notes resembled more a figure like Robin Hood than the actual thieves he was purportedly taking as a source of inspiration. The master-thief steals from the rich in order to help the poor; he has of course a lover (like Forster) who "walks by his side like a guardian angel"[25] and is a source of solace amid the general misunderstanding he suffers. Since he is a noble-hearted man, he must necessarily despise the other thieves, inferior and vicious, with whom he is forced to collaborate. He only tolerates their wicked company because he needs them to accomplish his ideal.[26] Even if he opposes the system, he does not deny his crimes and openly accepts his just punishment (like Kagerup), for he is against corruption of the established order, not against the reality of the state as a whole. Like a Socrates, he mocks and hoodwinks authority only as a way to denounce its injustice.[27] The master-thief is himself a satire of the established order, and therefore he must be "well-equipped with a very good sense of humor."[28] Kierkegaard also imagines his master-thief as someone who comes from the lower classes of society.[29]

In his relations to others, the master-thief tries to dissuade them from pursuing the same crooked lifestyle he must lead. It is only his ideal that allows him to endure his criminal existence.[30] Besides his lover, the master-thief has also a dear friend who is not a thief, and "an old mother whom he loves dearly and she him."[31]

As we can see, the main feature of the master-thief is his belief in an "ideal," the one trait that distinguishes him from all the other thieves who steal out of selfishness and vice. Kierkegaard does not further describe what this ideal is about, and so we must suppose that the importance of the ideal is not so much its content as the power and subjective nature of its conviction. As a consequence, in the last master-thief entry Kierkegaard parts with the model of the "Italian robber" (probably Fra Diavolo), whose social character did not fit well with the image of the loner that Kierkegaard had for his own hero. As he explains, "in the master-thief something far deeper is operative, a touch of melancholy, an encapsulation within himself, a dim view of life-relationships, an inner dissatisfaction."[32] These were the last

---

[24] *SKS* 27, 118, Papir 97:1 / *JP* 5, 5061.
[25] Ibid.
[26] Ibid.; see also *SKS* 27, 120, Papir 97:5 / *JP* 5, 5074.
[27] Cf. *SKS* 27, 119, Papir 97:2 / *JP* 5, 5062.
[28] Cf. *SKS* 27, 119, Papir 97:3 / *JP* 5, 5072.
[29] Ibid.
[30] Cf. *SKS* 27, 120, Papir 97:5 / *JP* 5, 5074.
[31] Ibid.
[32] *SKS* 27, 123, Papir 103 / *JP* 5, 5081.

words written about the master-thief literary project. They reflect quite well what Kierkegaard had in mind.

III. The Idea for Which I am Willing to Live and Die

The notion of having an ideal for which one could risk everything, as occurred with the fictitious master-thief, had a personal interest for Kierkegaard. The last entry on the master-thief project was dated, as we have said, March 15, 1835. A month and a half later, Kierkegaard went on a leisure trip to Gilleleje in northern Zealand. It was during this summer that he wrote in his *Journal AA* the well-known draft of the letter addressed to paleontologist Peter Wilhelm Lund, who was at the time living in Brazil. In this letter we read:

> Our early youth is like a flower at dawn, cupping a lovely dewdrop, reflecting pensively and harmoniously its surroundings. But soon the sun rises over the horizon and the dewdrop evaporates; with it vanish life's dream, and now the question is (to use once again a flower metaphor) whether one is able, like the oleander, to produce by his own effort a drop that can stand as the fruit of his life. This requires, above all, that a person find the soil where he really belongs, but that is not always so easy to discover. In this respect there are fortunate temperaments so decisively oriented in a particular direction that they go steadily along the path once assigned to them without ever entertaining the thought that perhaps they should really be taking another path. There are others who let themselves be so completely directed by their environment that they never become clear about what they are really working toward. Just as the former class has its internal categorical imperative, so the latter has an external categorical imperative. But how few are in the former class, and to the latter I do not wish to belong.[33]

What matters most for the young Kierkegaard is to find his own path in life, a path that, he underscores, must come from within as a sort of "internal categorical imperative." It is the kind of conviction the master-thief had, but now Kierkegaard is talking about himself. What follows is one of the most famous passages in Kierkegaard's authorship:

> What I really need is to get clear about *what I am to do*, not what I must know, except insofar as knowledge must precede every act. What matters is to find my purpose, to see what it really is that God wills that I shall do; the crucial thing is to find a truth that is truth *for me*, to find *the idea for which I am willing to live and die*.[34]

The essential element here is this "idea." As happened with the master-thief notes, he does not describe the nature of the truth of this idea; he only stresses the fact that its truth must be a "truth for me."

It is difficult to say whether or not Kierkegaard found his idea at the time, but it seems that he thought that a good way to look for it was through the vantage point of an outsider such as the master-thief. Now, in Gilleleje, he apparently realized that this was a mistake:

---

[33]   *SKS* 17, 18–19, AA:12 / *KJN* 1, 14.
[34]   *SKS* 17, 24, AA:12 / *KJN* 1, 19.

But to find that idea, or more properly to find myself, it is no use my plunging still further into the world. And that is exactly what I did before, which is why I had thought it would be a good idea to throw myself into *jurisprudence*, to be able to sharpen my mind on life's many complications. Here a whole mass of details offered itself for me to lose myself in; from the given facts I could perhaps fashion a totality, an organism, of the life of thieves, pursue it in all its darker aspects (here, too, a certain community spirit is highly remarkable).[35]

It looks as if the previous passage is an allusion to his earlier master-thief project. Maybe the point of view of the criminal offered a wider picture of what was going wrong with reality, but it did not necessarily provide the right clues for discovering one's own ideal. As Kierkegaard suggests, this cannot be found outside in the "world." In any case, he found no answer in the figure of the master-thief, and perhaps that is why he abandoned the project. A couple of years later, in 1837, Kierkegaard recalled in his *Journal BB* these juvenile and fruitless efforts:

> I still remember how I felt when a few years ago, in my youthful, romantic enthusiasm for a master-thief, I said he was merely misusing his talents, that such a man could no doubt change, and my father very earnestly said: "These are crimes that can be fought only with the constant help of God." I hurried to my room and looked at myself in the mirror.[36]

Kierkegaard had moved on. He continued to look for his idea, but the master-thief as such dropped out of his authorship. Nevertheless he lingered under the shadow of those other great outsiders that haunted his imagination: Faust, Don Quixote, the Romantic ironist Johannes the Seducer, even Abraham. It could be argued that the master-thief played only a minor role in Kierkegaard's vast writing career and that he was merely the subject of a juvenile literary exercise. In the big picture, however, I think it is apparent that the figure of the noble outlaw decisively shaped the path that Kierkegaard would follow in the years to come.

---

[35]   *SKS* 17, 25, AA:12 / *KJN* 1, 20.
[36]   *SKS* 17, 134–5, BB:42 / *KJN* 1, 128.

Bibliography

Fenger, Henning, " 'Mestertyven'. Kierkegaards første dramatiske forsøg," in *Edda*, no. 71, 1971, pp. 331–9.

Greenway, John L., "Kierkegaardian Doubles in Crime and Punishment," *Orbis Litterarum*, vol. 33, no. 1, 1978, p. 47.

Hall, Amy Laura, *Kierkegaard and the Treachery of Love*, Cambridge: Cambridge University Press 2002, pp. 108–9.

Hannay, Alastair, *Kierkegaard: A Biography*, Cambridge and New York: Cambridge University Press 2001, p. 53; p. 58; p. 298.

Jandrup, Sara Katrine, "The Master Thief, Alias S. Kierkegaard, and his Robbery of the Truth," *Søren Kierkegaard Newsletter*, no. 43, 2002, pp. 7–11.

Malantschuk, Gregor, *Kierkegaard's Thought*, trans. by Howard V. Hong and Edna H. Hong, Princeton: Princeton University Press 1971, p. 27.

Mooney, Edward, *On Søren Kierkegaard: Dialogue, Polemics, Lost Intimacy and Time*, Aldershot: Ashgate 2007, pp. 3–4; pp. 10–11.

Mephistopheles:

Demonic Seducer, Musician, Philosopher, and Humorist

Will Williams

Mephistopheles is the term for the demon or devil found in the Faust tradition, going back to its origins in the sixteenth century. Kierkegaard's writing on the figure, then, at times touches upon the conception of the Devil in Christian theology, but often his observations about Mephistopheles are confined to the demonic literary figure and cannot necessarily be applied directly to traditional Christian conceptions of the Devil. For example, in one journal entry Kierkegaard quotes Goethe's Mephistopheles, despite his demonic identity, and seems to approve of his words as a patient reminder of the existence of eternity and God.[1]

I. Sources

The most fundamental influence on Kierkegaard's conception of Mephistopheles is the broad Faust tradition, well known among Europeans of the time. For example, Kierkegaard made several notes on one old chapbook,[2] including one where he comments on how amusingly naïve the Faust legend can appear to the modern reader, who expects to find Faust seeking absolute mastery over nature but instead finds him dealing with Mephistopheles to get out of scrapes and to acquire money.[3] He finds Mephistopheles' supernatural aiding of Faust in these petty concerns to be equally amusing.[4]

While the medieval Faust legend, with its various sources and variations, is the most foundational for Kierkegaard's conception of Mephistopheles, *Faust:*

---

[1]   *SKS* 20, 124, NB:214.b / *JP* 4, 5011. Cf. *Goethe's Werke. Vollständige Ausgabe letzter Hand*, vols. 1–60, Stuttgart, Tübingen: J.G. Cotta 1828–33; *ASKB* 1641–1668 (vols. 1–50), vol. 12, p. 113; Johann Wolfgang von Goethe, *Faust: A Tragedy*, trans. by Walter Arndt, ed. by Cyrus Hamlin, New York: W.W. Norton 2001, Part I, lines 2370–3.

[2]   *Pap.* I C 107–11 / *JP* 5, 5168–72. Cf. *SKS* 2, 94–5 / *EO1*, 89–91. The citation of the referenced chapbook is as follows: *Den i den gandske Verden bekiendte Ertz-Sort-Kunstner og Trold-Karl Doctor Johan Faust, og Hans med Dievelen oprettede Forbund, Forundringsfulde Levnet og skrækkelige Endeligt*, Copenhagen: n.d. (*ASKB* U 35).

[3]   *Pap.* I C 109 / *JP* 5, 5170.

[4]   *Pap.* I C 110 / *JP* 5, 5171.

A Tragedy by Johann Wolfgang von Goethe (1749–1832) is nevertheless the single most important influence. Published in 1808, with the final revised version only appearing in 1832 after the author's death, Goethe's *Faust* was the dominant version of the Faust story during Kierkegaard's lifetime.[5] Even when Kierkegaard reflects on other accounts, he implicitly considers them in relation to Goethe's version.

One commentator on Goethe's *Faust* who provoked Kierkegaard's thinking about Mephistopheles is Karl Ernst Schubarth (1796–1861) in his work *Ueber Goethe's Faust*.[6] Kierkegaard is interested in Schubarth's comments, although he is not always in agreement with them nor even always understanding of them, as he himself admits. He is particularly provoked by Schubarth's "theory of the Devil," which he refers to in critical ways throughout his notes on the work.[7] As Kierkegaard presents it, Schubarth characterizes the Devil as not necessarily seeking Faust's destruction. In fact, Schubarth thinks the Devil may truly wish for the good or, at least, wants to chasten the exaggeration and eccentricity he finds in Faust.[8] In this way, Schubarth presents the Devil as being more or less in harmony with the purposes of God as an agent rather than as an opponent. Kierkegaard has many reservations about this theory. For one thing, he is not convinced that it is in accord with Goethe's own view of Mephistopheles.[9] For another, Kierkegaard is concerned that such a characterization "either makes the Devil into Our Lord or Our Lord into the Devil."[10] Kierkegaard points out that even if God does use worldly evil for divine purposes, this is not equivalent to saying that the Devil is a knowing collaborator with the plans of God.[11] At the end of his notes on Schubarth, Kierkegaard considers the idea that Goethe's portrayal of Mephistopheles resembles the portrayal of Satan in the Book of Job. He concludes that it is not very "devilish" for the Devil to have "undertaken to be provost in the divine court," particularly when, as Schubarth suggests, this provost "thinks well of mankind."[12] Schubarth's influence on Kierkegaard's thoughts about Mephistopheles, then, appears to be primarily negative.

Another significant version of the Faust story that influences Kierkegaard's understanding of Mephistopheles is *Faust* by Lenau,[13] which was a pseudonym for Nicolaus Franz Niembsch Edler von Strehlenau (1802–50). Kierkegaard may have been directed to considering Lenau's *Faust* by reading a review written by Hans

---

[5]   *Goethe's Werke*, vol. 12, *Faust. Eine Tragödie*.
[6]   Karl Ernst Schubarth, *Ueber Goethe's Faust*, Berlin: Enslin 1830 (*ASKB* U 96).
[7]   *SKS* 17, 76–89, BB:7 / *KJN* 1, 70–83.
[8]   Kierkegaard identifies the Devil's attempt to restrain and satirize excessiveness as "irony" (*SKS* 17, 78, BB:7 / *KJN* 1, 71. Cf. *SKS* 17, 106, BB:14 / *KJN* 1, 98). His most concentrated reflection on Schubarth's theory of the Devil is found at *SKS* 17, 78–9, BB:7.c / *KJN* 1, 72.
[9]   *SKS* 17, 78, BB:7 / *KJN* 1, 71–2.
[10] *SKS* 17, 78–9, BB:7.c / *KJN* 1, 72.
[11] *SKS* 17, 79, BB:7.c / *KJN* 1, 72.
[12] *SKS* 17, 89, BB:7 / *KJN* 1, 83.
[13] Nicolaus Lenau, *Faust. Ein Gedicht*, Stuttgart and Tübingen: J.G. Cotta 1836.

Lassen Martensen (1808–84).[14] Kierkegaard's interest in Lenau's *Faust* centers on two elements. First, Lenau has Faust commit suicide at the end, which Kierkegaard thinks is a mishandling of the character, believing that Goethe understands the matter better.[15] Second, in the scene "*Der Tanz,*"[16] Mephistopheles himself is the one who strikes up the music by grabbing a fiddle so that Faust may dance seductively with a beautiful woman.[17]

Finally, Kierkegaard's imagination about Mephistopheles was captured in a single moment from a ballet version of the Faust story by Antoine August Bournonville (1805–79).[18] Bournonville was a Danish choreographer and ballet master who was permanently employed by the Danish Royal Theater starting in 1830. He would perform in his own ballets, and he danced in *Faust* as well. Initially, he danced the part of Faust himself, but Bournonville danced as Mephistopheles from June 10, 1842.[19] When Bournonville made his entrance on stage as Mephistopheles, he performed a striking leap that stayed with Kierkegaard as a suitable illustration that the demonic is, as he says, "the sudden."[20] Bournonville's performance, then, links the character of Mephistopheles to demonic suddenness and to the concept of the leap for Kierkegaard.[21]

II. Mephistopheles as Demonic

There is a certain ambiguity regarding Mephistopheles as to whether he is the Devil proper or only one of the Devil's demonic minions sent to do his bidding with Faust. The same ambiguity is found within Goethe's account. There, Mephistopheles is

---

[14] *SKS* 17, 49, AA:38 / *KJN* 1, 43. The German version of Martensen's piece was published under a pseudonym: Johannes M.......n, *Ueber Lenau's Faust*, Stuttgart: J.G. Cotta 1836. Martensen's review also appeared in Danish in *Perseus, Journal for den speculative Idee*, ed. by Johan Ludvig Heiberg, no. 1, Copenhagen: C.A. Reitzel 1837, *ASKB* 569), pp. 91–164. Kierkegaard's awareness of Martensen's pseudonym from the German version (*SKS* 17, 49, AA:38 / *KJN* 1, 43) and the inclusion of the Danish version in his auction catalogue (*ASKB* 569) suggests that he was familiar with both versions. Given the Faustian subject matter, one wonders whether Kierkegaard's own pseudonym, "Johannes Mephistopheles" (*SKS* 18, 199, JJ:183 / *KJN* 2, 183), is not intended in part as a lampooning of Martensen's "Johannes M.......n."

[15] *SKS* 17, 49, AA:38 / *KJN* 1, 43; *SKS* 17, 51, AA:44 / *KJN* 1, 44; cf. *SKS* 17, 80, BB:7 / *KJN* 1, 73.

[16] Lenau, *Faust*, pp. 46–51.

[17] *SKS* 17, 91, BB:11.a / *KJN* 1, 84; *SKS* 17, 244, DD:69 / *KJN* 1, 235; *SKS* 18, 83, FF:38 / *KJN* 2, 76. Kierkegaard is confident that Martensen has missed the significance of Mephistopheles' being the one who strikes up the music (*SKS* 18, 83, FF:38 / *KJN* 2, 76).

[18] Antoine August Bournonville, *Faust. Original romantisk Ballet i tre Akter*, Copenhagen: J.H. Schubothe 1832.

[19] See *SKS* K18, 273.

[20] *SKS* 18, 172, JJ:104 / *KJN* 2, 160.

[21] *SKS* 4, 432–3 / *CA*, 131–2. Cf. *SKS* 4, 135–6 / *FT*, 40–1.

referred to as the "Devil"[22] and "Satan"[23] but, on the other hand, is only cousin to the old serpent[24] and is generally characterized more as a roguish[25] libertine than as a truly evil and sinister force.[26]

Unsurprisingly, Kierkegaard uses Mephistopheles as a convenient illustration of the demonic. One of the central qualities of the demonic is that it knows the good but actively resists it. The demonic is oppositional in its orientation,[27] defending itself against repentance and grace "just as the good defends itself against temptation."[28] Consequently, Kierkegaard's pseudonym Anti-Climacus approves of the assertion by Goethe's Mephistopheles that nothing is more miserable than a despairing devil since such despair expresses its weakness in being open to repentance and grace.[29] Additionally, in one undeveloped writing project, Kierkegaard considered writing an extension of the seduction of Cordelia from *Either/Or*, Part One,[30] called "An Essay in the Demonic" by Johannes Mephistopheles.[31] In this piece, Johannes Mephistopheles expresses regret that Victor Eremita has left off pursuing his excellent ideas about seduction and has become "edifying" instead, demonstrating Mephistopheles' demonic dedication to seduction.[32] Because of this oppositional quality of the demonic, such a one will also exhibit a "brooding, inclosing reserve."[33]

Other qualities of the demonic associated with Mephistopheles are "the sudden,"[34] discussed above in relation to Bournonville, and a preternatural connection to music and dance, discussed both above in relation to Lenau and immediately below.[35] Faust—presumably due in part to the influence from Mephistopheles—is also said to be demonic.[36]

---

[22]   *Goethe's Werke*, vol. 12, p. 23; Goethe, *Faust*, Part I, line 353.
[23]   *Goethe's Werke*, vol. 12, p. 120; Goethe, *Faust*, Part I, line 2504.
[24]   *Goethe's Werke*, vol. 12, p. 23; Goethe, *Faust*, Part I, line 335.
[25]   The Lord expresses that he does not abominate Mephistopheles and considers him to be a mere "rogue" (*Goethe's Werke*, vol. 12, p. 23; Goethe, *Faust*, Part I, lines 336–43).
[26]   It should be noted that in his discussions of Mephistopheles, Kierkegaard frequently uses the name "Mephistopheles" interchangeably with "Mephisto" and "the Devil."
[27]   In one well-known description, Goethe characterizes Mephistopheles as "the spirit which eternally denies" (*Goethe's Werke*, vol. 12, p. 67; Goethe, *Faust*, Part I, line 1338).
[28]   *SKS* 11, 221 / *SUD*, 109.
[29]   Ibid. Cf. *Goethe's Werke*, vol. 12, p. 167; Goethe, *Faust*, Part I, lines 3372–3.
[30]   *SKS* 2, 291–432 / *EO1*, 301–445.
[31]   *SKS* 18, 199, JJ:183 / *KJN* 2, 183–4.
[32]   Ibid.
[33]   *SKS* 4, 432–3 / *CA*, 131–2. Cf. *SKS* 11, 221–2 / *SUD*, 109–10. *SKS* 6, 215 / *SLW*, 230 expresses a similar point, although without explicit relation to Mephistopheles.
[34]   *SKS* 18, 172, JJ:104 / *KJN* 2, 160; *SKS* 4, 432–3 / *CA*, 131–2. Cf. *SKS* 4, 135–6 / *FT*, 40–1.
[35]   *SKS* 17, 91, BB:11.a / *KJN* 1, 84; *SKS* 17, 244, DD:69 / *KJN* 1, 235.
[36]   *SKS* 2, 201 / *EO1*, 206.

III. Mephistopheles as Seducer and Musician

Perhaps the most consistent association that Kierkegaard makes with the character of Mephistopheles is with his role as a seducer. For Kierkegaard, the connection between Mephistopheles and sensuous erotic seduction comes most centrally from the "Witch's Kitchen" scene in Part I of Goethe's *Faust*.[37] There, through dark magic, Faust is made to see the beautiful Gretchen in a mirror, which incites his sensuous desire for her.[38] Kierkegaard is familiar with the scene[39] and therefore understands Mephistopheles as a kind of demonic matchmaker.[40] Erotic temptation is a profitable means of seducing one toward evil, and this insight leads Kierkegaard to consider naming his own demonic seducer Johannes Mephistopheles.[41] If Mephistopheles' role is to tempt, then erotic temptation will surely be one of the primary means.

Because of the aesthetic immediacy of music, Kierkegaard also thinks of music in relation to the sensuous and to seduction. For example, Don Juan, set to music in *Don Giovanni* by Wolfgang Amadeus Mozart (1756–91), becomes a powerful illustration for Kierkegaard of the link between seduction and music.[42] Extending the association to the seducer Mephistopheles, it is not surprising to see Kierkegaard comparing Don Juan and Mephistopheles as prime illustrations of the musical, the sensuous, and seduction.[43] Notably, in the context of the musical, it is not Goethe's but Lenau's Mephistopheles that Kierkegaard first thinks of, for it is Lenau who has Mephistopheles strike up the music, giving Faust the courage and the sensuous environment in which to seduce a woman.

Since the Faust story is a folk tradition, Kierkegaard connects the image of Lenau's Mephistopheles striking up the music to various folk stories of supernatural creatures either playing or dancing to music.[44] Specifically, Lenau's Mephistopheles is cited in relation to a folk story from *Irische Elfenmärchen* where a demonic changeling is said to have the supernatural power of compelling others to dance

---

[37]   *Goethe's Werke*, vol. 12, pp. 112–25; Goethe, *Faust*, Part I, lines 2337–2604.

[38]   In Kierkegaard's interpretation, Gretchen is tempting for Faust precisely because she is innocent, humble, and pure, which he is not. The attraction, then, is fundamentally spiritual, but he makes clear that this gets received by Faust in a sensuous way (*SKS* 2, 202–3 / *EO1*, 207). The end of the Witch's Kitchen scene also alludes to Helen of Troy (*Goethe's Werke*, vol. 12, p. 125; Goethe, *Faust*, Part I, line 2604), whom Faust also seeks to seduce later in the play. This one scene, then, anticipates Faust's two major romantic interests in the play.

[39]   *SKS* 2, 202–3 / *EO1*, 207; *SKS* 4, 198 / *FT*, 109. Cf. *Goethe's Werke*, vol. 12, pp. 116–17; Goethe, *Faust*, Part I, lines 2429–40. Note that Gretchen is called "Margarete" by Kierkegaard. Goethe's text uses both versions of her name.

[40]   *SKS* 2, 339–40 / *EO1*, 350.

[41]   *SKS* 18, 199, JJ:183 / *KJN* 2, 183.

[42]   *SKS* 17, 113–17, BB:24 / *KJN* 1, 107–11; *SKS* 2, 53–136 / *EO1*, 45–135.

[43]   *SKS* 17, 91, BB:11.a / *KJN* 1, 84; *SKS* 17, 244, DD:69 / *KJN* 1, 235; *SKS* 18, 83, FF:38 / *KJN* 2, 76; *SKS* 18, 199, JJ:183 / *KJN* 2, 183–4. Cf. *SKS* 2, 202–3 / *EO1*, 207; *SKS* 17, 49, AA:38 / *KJN* 1, 43.

[44]   *SKS* 17, 244, DD:69 / *KJN* 1, 235.

when he plays the pipes.[45] This is a less obviously erotic form of seduction than the scene from Lenau, but the music is still supernaturally seductive in a menacing and sensuous way.

IV. Mephistopheles and the Philosophical Seductions of Doubt

Kierkegaard believes that one quality of a specifically Goethian Mephistopheles is that he educates.[46] In relation to this, Kierkegaard alludes to the scene where Mephistopheles, disguised as Faust, leads a new student to cynical conclusions about the curriculum, thus preventing education from being an upbuilding experience for him.[47]

Mephistopheles' "education" leads Faust astray as well. As Kierkegaard narrates it, Faust

> gave himself to the Devil for the express purpose of becoming enlightened, which formerly he was not. And it was just because he gave himself to the Devil that his doubt increased (just as a sick man falling into the hands of a quack is likely to get even worse). For although Mephistopheles admittedly let him look through his spectacles into the hidden secrets of man and of the world, Faust was unable to refrain from harboring doubts about him; intellectually he could never enlighten him about the deepest things. His guiding idea of course prevented him from ever turning to God....[48]

Mephistopheles does educate Faust, after a fashion, but this education only manages to magnify Faust's doubts rather than quelling them. Faust emerges as worse off than before he was "enlightened." If Faust is the "personification of doubt,"[49] then Mephistopheles surely deserves some credit for magnifying that doubt in him through his demonic education.

Mephistopheles' endorsement of reason has its supporters. For example, immediately prior to the scene where he cynically educates the young student, Mephistopheles has a short soliloquy where he suggests that those who spurn reason and science will inevitably fall under the power of the Devil.[50] Mephistopheles' soliloquy is happily endorsed by Georg Wilhelm Friedrich Hegel (1770–1831), who

---

[45]   *SKS* 17, 91, BB:11.a / *KJN* 1, 84; *SKS* 17, 244, DD:69 / *KJN* 1, 235. Cf. *Irische Elfenmärchen*, trans. by the Brothers Grimm, Leipzig: Friedrich Fleischer 1826 (*ASKB* 1423), pp. 25–35; Thomas Crofton Croker, *Fairy Legends and Traditions of the South of Ireland*, London: Thomas Davison, Whitefriars 1825, pp. 47–64.

[46]   *SKS* 27, 148, Papir 180 / *JP* 5, 5160; *SKS* 27, 148, Papir 181 / *JP* 2, 1457.

[47]   *SKS* 27, 148, Papir 181 / *JP* 2, 1457. Cf. *Goethe's Werke*, vol. 12, p. 88–95; Goethe, *Faust*, Part I, lines 1868–2050.

[48]   *SKS* 17, 19, AA:12 / *KJN* 1, 14–15.

[49]   *SKS* 17, 19, AA:12 / *KJN* 1, 14. Cf. *SKS* 2, 201–5 / *EO1*, 206–10; *SKS* 4, 195–9 / *FT*, 107–10.

[50]   *Goethe's Werke*, vol. 12, pp. 87–8; Goethe, *Faust*, Part I, lines 1851–67. For a more pessimistic take from Mephistopheles on the power of reason, see *SKS* 1, 19n / *EPW*, 63n. Cf. *Goethe's Werke*, vol. 12, p. 92; Goethe *Faust*, Part I, lines 1976–7.

uses Mephistopheles' authority in defense of his own project of reason.[51] Schubarth's commentary, as Kierkegaard reports, also shows support for Mephistopheles' endorsement of reason in this soliloquy.[52] Kierkegaard, though, is less sanguine about Mephistopheles' endorsement of reason, noting, "But it must be pointed out that, first, we must know in what sense Mephisto praises reason, since it could also be understood as not being in harmony with God...."[53] Reason is not an infallible and unqualified good for Kierkegaard, even if there is much that may be very good in it, because it can be used for unholy ends. Both Faust and the young student, for example, cannot be said to have been improved through their exposure to Mephistopheles' education. Thus, while Kierkegaard was both comfortable with and proficient in his own use of rational argumentation, reason has a certain ambiguous standing for him since it may be rallied to the purposes of a Mephistopheles.[54]

V. Mephistopheles as Humorous

Kierkegaard noticed that Mephistopheles—particularly in Goethe's presentation[55]— had the capacity for generating amusement. Nevertheless, whatever amusement Kierkegaard detects in Mephistopheles, he continues to read the character in light of earnest concerns for morality and theology and does not permit himself to be carried away aesthetically by laughter. For example, Kierkegaard notes the absurdity of Mephistopheles' initial appearance to Faust in the form of a little black dog, but he takes the occasion to reflect on the dog as a perversion of the virtue of faithfulness. That is, although he is an evil spirit, Mephistopheles continues to abide by the side of Faust in a form of canine fidelity.[56] Again, Kierkegaard associates the humorous idea

---

[51]   G.W.F. Hegel, *Elements of the Philosophy of Right*, ed. by Allen W. Wood, trans. by H.B. Nisbet, Cambridge: Cambridge University Press 2012, Preface, p. 16. Cf. G.W.F. Hegel, *Phenomenology of Spirit*, trans. by A.V. Miller, Oxford: Clarendon Press 1977, pp. 217–18.

[52]   *SKS* 17, 78–9, BB:7.c / *KJN* 1, 72.

[53]   *SKS* 17, 78, BB:7.c / *KJN* 1, 72.

[54]   In a journal entry written soon after his proposal to write an essay as Johannes Mephistopheles, Kierkegaard says, "It is and remains a thought one cannot dismiss without further ado—namely, how far reason should be regarded as temptation in relation to faith, how far reason is sinful, how far this—that truth and reason agree—is again an object of faith" (*SKS* 18, 202, JJ:193 / *KJN* 2, 186). To speak more precisely, this passage indicates that Kierkegaard's specific concern is perhaps not with reason as such but with the temptation for one to trust one's own reasoning over and against one's faith. It may be the temptation of intellectual pride that is the more precise concern. The suggestion here is that faith must be more fundamental for existing human beings since even to believe that truth and reason agree must itself be an article of faith.

[55]   That he at times finds Mephistopheles' relationship to Faust to be humorous in the folk legends is more of a reflection of his estimation of the humorousness of the conceptions of the folk legends themselves, not an evaluation that they intended to portray Mephistopheles humorously (*Pap.* I C 109 / *JP* 5, 5170).

[56]   *SKS* 19, 93, Not2:3 / *JP* 5, 5086. It was Goethe who introduced the concept of Mephistopheles appearing in the form of a black poodle, though Kierkegaard's entry appears to attribute this to the Faust folk legends. There is, however, some precedence in the folk

of leading someone by the nose with Goethe's *Faust*. For example, he remarks on the irony involved in Faust's leading his students by the nose[57] and alludes to the scene in Auerbach's Cellar where Mephistopheles tricks the angry and intoxicated students into grabbing one another by the nose, thinking that they are about to slice off a fresh bunch of grapes.[58] Further, he alludes to humorous stories of Mephistopheles himself being led off by the nose.[59] This theme is more than comic amusement for Kierkegaard, however, for it naturally connects to reflection on such Faustian themes as seduction and leading others into doubt. Whatever amusement may surround Mephistopheles' antics, earnest matters of morality and theology lie nearby.

While he recognizes the amusement that Mephistopheles brings, Kierkegaard shows concern in reflecting on the degree to which it is appropriate for Faust to find Mephistopheles to be humorous upon their first encounter.[60] Some of this concern must be understood in relation to Kierkegaard's specific conception of the idea of "humor," which is never mere amoral amusement for him.[61] Is it morally problematic to find humor in the demon?[62] After all, as Kierkegaard suggests in one note, someone of Mephistophelean character would be perfectly willing to mock the Christian.[63]

The question of humor and Mephistopheles is also raised in another way. Schubarth's commentary on Goethe's *Faust* reflects on the humor there, and

---

legends for Faust's having a spirit familiar in the form of a black dog, so perhaps it is this precedence to which Kierkegaard alludes. It may be that the dog Mephistopheles is to be understood as a replacement companion for Faust's assistant Wagner, who discovers the black dog with Faust but then leaves them (Cf. *SKS* 17, 98, BB:12 / *KJN* 1, 91).

[57]   *SKS* 27, 146–8, Papir 180 / *JP* 5, 5160.

[58]   *SKS* 14, 16 / *EPW*, 11. Cf. *Goethe's Werke*, vol. 12, pp. 105–11; Goethe, *Faust*, Part I, lines 2245–336. See also *SKS* 6, 30 / *SLW*, 25.

[59]   *SKS* 27, 154, Papir 202.

[60]   *SKS* 27, 146, Papir 180 / *JP* 5, 5160. Much of this entry shows Kierkegaard's reflection on Goethe's *Faust* in relation to concepts of irony and humor.

[61]   While there is not space here for a full discussion of these concepts, one should remember that Kierkegaard's pseudonym Johannes Climacus locates both irony and humor as essentially belonging to the transition points between his famous stages of existence (*SKS* 7, 455 / *CUP1*, 501–2). "Humor" is located between ethical existence and religious existence, so Kierkegaard's narration of something as "humorous" should never be understood as altogether divorced from ethics and religiousness. There is always some earnestness behind both ironic and humorous play. As Climacus puts it, "Remember that you are ethically responsible for your use of the comic" (*SKS* 7, 471n / *CUP1*, 519n). E.g., *SKS* 21, 294, NB10:70 / *JP* 2, 1761; *SKS* 22, 416, NB14:126 / *JP* 2, 1763.

[62]   *SKS* 27, 146, Papir 180 / *JP* 5, 5160. It is not entirely clear where the absolute heart of Kierkegaard's question lies. Is Kierkegaard asking for the sake of the character Faust, who might be morally compromised by finding humor in Mephistopheles? Is he asking for the sake of the audience, inquiring into the moral propriety of an audience being exposed to a humorously portrayed demon? Is he questioning Goethe's moral and artistic sensibilities in his decision to portray Mephistopheles as humorous?

[63]   *SKS* 20, 266, NB3:40 / *KJN* 4, 266–7. The passage imagines a demon becoming a priest, not to seduce people away from the faith so much as to mock it.

Kierkegaard reads these observations carefully.[64] Here, humor is defined as the bringing into relation of two things such that their obvious differences disappear. This gives rise to an intuitive perspective that is able to view things with the insight of the higher element, in light of which the normally understood differences have receded. Schubarth uses the example of standing on a high mountain and surveying the valley down below.[65] The suggestion is that since this humor requires a certain breadth of view and a certain familiarity with a diversity of elements, it reaches a level of development in modernity unknown to the classical world.[66] Mephistopheles, whose magic and longevity has granted him a familiarity—and sometimes even boredom—with the diversity of the world, presumably therefore has a well-developed humorousness.[67] Kierkegaard, for whom the truly humorous must be in relation to Christian religiousness,[68] is thus brought to ask to what degree it is appropriate for Goethe to locate humorousness in the character of the demonic Mephistopheles. A provisional answer may be found in Kierkegaard's remark that the Devil has a "grandiose yet not omniscient standpoint."[69] His humor may be vast relative to humans like Faust, but it remains incomplete from a divine standpoint.

VI. Conclusion

The character of Mephistopheles provides Kierkegaard with a literary avenue to broach questions of morality, theology, and metaphysics with his audience, perhaps while avoiding some of the didactic overtones that would come with a sermon about the Devil. For the aesthetically inclined reader of Kierkegaard, Mephistopheles is an amusing and intriguing figure, especially when presented by someone with the literary skills and cultural prowess of Goethe. Kierkegaard captures that literary and cultural interest in Mephistopheles to use for his own various philosophical purposes. If Mephistopheles is widely recognized as a seducer, then Kierkegaard can use him to draw attention to his own reflections about the nature of seduction.

Despite his humor, Mephistopheles is far from harmless, and, perhaps due to the aesthetic strains in his own personality, Kierkegaard is very aware of the seductive and corruptive power of such a figure. Mephistopheles is seductive, but he is also

---

[64]   *SKS* 17, 88–9, BB:7 / *KJN* 1, 81–2.

[65]   *SKS* 17, 88, BB:7 / *KJN* 1, 81–2. This metaphor of standing on the mountain indicates that the following passage has Schubarth in mind, although he is not cited: "*What is the nature of Goethe's irony and humor*—it is like thunder and lightning viewed by someone who is on a mountain and elevated above it—he has *outlived* them, to that extent it is more than classical (romantic-classical)" (*SKS* 27, 146, Papir 180 / *JP* 5, 5160).

[66]   *SKS* 17, 88, BB:7 / *KJN* 1, 82. Cf. *SKS* 27, 146, Papir 180 / *JP* 5, 5160; *SKS* 17, 216, DD:6.a / *KJN* 1, 208; *Pap.* I C 109 / *JP* 5, 5170. For the related discussion of how views of the Devil in modernity compare to those of the Middle Ages, see for example, *SKS* 17, 105–6, BB:14 / *KJN* 1, 98; *SKS* 27, 173, Papir 249.

[67]   If so, then in this way Goethe's Mephistopheles may be seen as a particularly modern character.

[68]   E.g., *SKS* 17, 214, DD:3 / *KJN* 1, 206; *SKS* 17, 216–18, DD:6 / *KJN* 1, 208–10.

[69]   *SKS* 17, 79, BB:7.c / *KJN* 1, 72.

corrupting. He is musical, but his music is contrary to the harmonies of God. He is philosophical and educating, but he leads one only deeper into doubt. He is humorous, but his antics, at base, are deadly serious in their intent. In short, the figure of Mephistopheles is very culturally sophisticated, but he is no less harmful for that. Rather, his sophistication and demonic wisdom grant him a dark authority that he uses to lead people astray.

Seduction comes in many types and may be erotic, aesthetic, or intellectual. Through Mephistopheles, Kierkegaard can broach the theologically and morally serious topic of corruption through seduction, whatever its form, but in an indirect and literarily polished way. Perhaps there may have been sophisticated members of the Danish culture whom Kierkegaard believed would not take seriously direct instruction about the nature of evil but who would pay attention to the figure of Mephistopheles, especially given Goethe's cultural cachet. Even otherwise unreflective attendees of opera or ballet would be familiar with the moral issues that Mephistopheles raises and might, like Kierkegaard, have been captured by some element of Mephistopheles' portrayal on stage, such as his sudden and alarming leap. Discussing the figure would be a convenient and valuable means of entering into a morally earnest conversation.

It is characteristic of Kierkegaard that he does not puritanically refuse to deal with the character Mephistopheles but, rather, handles him deliberately and carefully for the sake of his own philosophical purposes. Kierkegaard does not try to shield his readers from Mephistophelean seduction by refusing to address it but, instead, deliberately draws their attention to the seduction—in whatever form it manifests itself—in order that they might not be lead away by the seduction thoughtlessly. In Mephistopheles, Kierkegaard gives seduction a face and a personality, which can be exteriorized in one's mind and therefore dealt with in a morally reflective way that is conducive to subjective development. The hope is that Kierkegaard's readers would not succumb to seduction unawares and so, like Faust overcome with erotic obsession, end up "worn out in madness, fear and trembling."[70]

---

[70]   *Goethe's Werke*, vol. 12, p. 164; Goethe, *Faust*, Part I, line 3302.

Bibliography

Roos, Carl, *Kierkegaard og Goethe*, Copenhagen: Gad 1955, p. 148; p. 156.

Minerva:

Kierkegaard's Use of a Greek Motif

Anne Louise Nielsen

With Pallas Athena as example, Minerva was adopted as an Etruscan martial goddess and as a patron of the Sabinian town Orvinium at a time when there were flourishing Etruscan commercial relations with Greece.[1] As early as the sixth century BC Etruscan amphora depict the myth found in Hesiod about the birth of Pallas Athena from the head of Zeus. The story is that Zeus had a splitting headache, and so the god and blacksmith Vulcan opened his head with a stroke of an axe, whereupon Pallas Athena sprang out, fully armed with shield and lance.

From the early dynastic period Minerva had an influence in Rome, and together with Jupiter and Juno she made up the so-called Capitoline triad, all connected to the Capitoline temple. This triad followed the Greek triad consisting of Pallas Athena, Zeus, and Hera, and Minerva was depicted as Pallas Athena with armor and aegis, owl and olive. She was blended with the Italian goddess of skilled trade, and her first temple on the Aventine hill was established around the third century BC. In Rome she was also celebrated as a goddess of music and medicine but not as a patron of the town since Jupiter and Juno already assumed this role. In her later Roman development she was celebrated as a martial goddess, often associated with the ruling emperors; the emperor Domitian (51–96) especially stressed her importance.

Minerva's owl held different meanings in antiquity; not only did the owl symbolize wisdom and intelligence, but it was also associated with the proclamation of birth or luck, connected to magic, and it was even feared as a bird of evil omen and death.

I.

It was the philosopher G.W.F. Hegel (1770–1831) above all who made the symbol of Minerva's owl famous by comparing philosophy with the activity of the owl at dusk in the *Philosophy of Right* (1820): "When philosophy paints its grey in grey, then has a shape of life grown old. By philosophy's grey in grey it cannot be rejuvenated but only understood. The owl of Minerva spreads its wings only with the falling of

---

[1]   See *Der Neue Pauly, Enzyklopädie der Antike*, vols. 1–16, ed. by Hubert Cancik and Helmuth Schneider, Stuttgart: Verlag J.B. Metzler 2000, vol. 8, pp. 211–16.

the dusk."[2] The meaning of the quotation is a bit obscure; Hegel seeks to state that philosophy is incapable of catching the color of life in life's own vividness, so it can only seek to understand life *after* life has shown itself and grown old. This is not a resigning attitude, however; on the contrary it makes up Hegel's main thesis: only reality grasped in concepts is actual reality.

Hegel hereby warns against empty talk about ideas, moral talk, and prophecy and instead presents philosophy as "its own time apprehended in thoughts."[3] The *Philosophy of Right* is Hegel's attempt to grasp the rational concept of the state, not to construct it. Only that which is already in experience can be made conscious; that is, philosophy transports the substance of the objective world into the intellectual realm.

The *Philosophy of Right* is connected to the *Lectures on the Philosophy of History* in the sense that it stresses that philosophy first begins with "the grey" of reality—for example, Greek philosophy culminated only with the fall of the Roman Empire. Therefore, philosophy is the highest stage of the spirit, and it completes history as a syllogism as it draws the end from the prevailing assumptions of history and turns it into a birth of something new. The image of the owl points to the fact that philosophy comes from the end of the old world in order to intensify the conscious inner life as a reflected search for a new world. This idea is connected to Hegel's inaugural Berlin lectures in which he stresses "the spirit of youth"[4] and "the dawn of a genuine spirit"[5] that possesses the courage to demand the truth—so the night flight of the owl is related to the morning cockcrow.

II.

Kierkegaard was inspired by the original myth (probably through P.F.A. Nitsch's *Neues mythologisches Wörterbuch* that was in his possession)[6] and clearly also by the Hegelian use of the myth for describing the *Zeitgeist*. However, he refers to the motif "Minerva" only five times (excluding a letter addressed to him in which the concept appears), and the usage can roughly be divided into two different meanings: (a) "Minerva" used in its mythical meaning in relation to the birth of Minerva, namely, as a symbol of something born complete and perfect, and (b) "Minerva" used in connection with the owl in order to characterize the *Zeitgeist*. More precisely, the motif is used to treat the relationship between Christianity and science in a manner parallel to Hegel's description of the role of philosophy.

---

[2]   *Hegel's Philosophy of Right*, trans. by T.M. Knox, Oxford: Clarendon Press 1942, p. 13.

[3]   Ibid., p. 11.

[4]   See *Hegels Vorreden mit Kommentar zur Einführung in seine Philosophie*, ed. by Erwin Metzke, Heidelberg: F.H. Kerle Verlag 1949, p. 284.

[5]   Ibid.

[6]   See Paul Friedrich Achat Nitsch, *Neues mythologisches Wörterbuch für studirende Jünglinge, angehende Künstler und jeden Gebildeten überhaupt*, 2nd revised edition by Friedrich Gotthilf Klopfer, vols. 1–2, Leipzig and Soran: Friedrich Fleischer 1821, vol. 2, p. 251 (*ASKB* 1944–1945).

The word "Minerva" occurs respectively in *The Concept of Irony*, in *Either/Or*, in the Journals *AA* and *DD*, in Letter 68, and in *Notebook NB15*. These six usages will now be examined more closely.

III.

In *The Concept of Irony* Kierkegaard plays on the mythical meaning of "Minerva" as he describes Julius, the protagonist in Friedrich Schlegel's novel *Lucinde* (1799), by contrasting him with Don Juan. Julius has a personality "caught in reflection" that slowly develops, whereas Don Juan has no past, no line of development, but he steps forward, as a fully armed Minerva, being fully developed as a character.[7]

In *Either/Or*, Part One, the seducer in "The Seducer's Diary" uses the mythical meaning of "Minerva" in depicting the young girl whom he wants to seduce as a Minerva who, completely developed, springs out of the head of Jupiter. The point of the comparison is that the young girl, in contrast to the young boy who slowly develops, suddenly wakes up after an unending dream, symbolizing her getting married after a long, dreaming youth. In this way "she is born twice," or "she is finally born as she marries."[8]

In a footnote to the journal entry AA:12 from 1835 Kierkegaard refers to the mythical "Minerva." This journal can be divided into a first part, drawn up as a letter presumably for the natural scientist P.W. Lund, and a second part that contains different notes. The content concerns Kierkegaard's reflections regarding his own education and personal development, and a philosophical reflection concerning the relationship between Christianity and philosophy. More precisely, Kierkegaard reflects upon human reason and states that a philosopher always has his own subjectivity at stake in his work. This statement functions as a demarcation from Hegel, who presents his philosophy as "objective knowledge." To give an example of subjectivity, Kierkegaard emphasizes that the act of cracking a joke is part of the author's or the philosopher's personality and natural life style; the springing joke alludes to the springing Minerva. This is also proven by the natural blush, which follows or is "born" with the joke.[9] Instead of letting this joke be a kind of lyrical philosophical thought, the discipline of philosophy has a tendency to treat the joke as "a flower" (symbolizing a philosophical idea) that is to be picked and sacredly saved for later use.

In the journal entry DD:78 from 1837 Kierkegaard uses the motif of "Minerva" in order to refer to the *Zeitgeist*. *Journal DD* contains a longer part, which is the actual journal with 207 notes, and a shorter part that contains a sketch for a student drama. The content of the entries is quite varied, but some main themes are historical subjects concerning the church and dogmas, a theme concerning fairy tales and legends, reflections about irony and humor, and private religious reflections. In DD:78 Kierkegaard uses the symbol of Minerva in order to state what his own time lacks, namely, the ability to understand "the idea." Instead the course of the

---

[7]   *SKS* 1, 327 / *CI*, 293.
[8]   *SKS* 2, 321 / *EO1*, 332.
[9]   *SKS* 17, 30n, AA:12 / *KJN* 1, 20n.

understanding runs like this: at first a couple of people grasp the idea, in the same way, just as disciples of Copernicus existed before Copernicus himself entered the stage. But none of the disciples are able to handle the idea, and in the end they all go crazy. Then "a great spirit" like Copernicus conceives the idea and presents it in public, but he is misunderstood by his own time. The final consequence is that the idea changes into a commonplace; that is, Minerva does not spring from the head of Jupiter, but she "blows up his head, wanders restlessly around and ends up in an asylum," as it is put.[10]

In Letter 68 (from 1850) the motif of "Minerva" is applied in its mythical meaning by Kierkegaard's personal doctor, Oluf Lundt Bang (1788–1877), who in poetical rhymes expresses his gratitude to Kierkegaard for a gift copy of *Practice in Christianity*, published the same day as the letter is dated. Bang later became a professor in medicine, and in this connection the concept of Minerva is applied in Bang's referring to his own doctor's ring that is decorated with the head of Minerva, the goddess of wisdom, carrying a wreath. His reflection is that, despite the fact that he carries this worthy ring, he has not fully entered the inner sanctum of wisdom.[11]

In the journal entry NB15:103 (from 1850) Kierkegaard uses the motif of "Minerva" in order to characterize the *Zeitgeist*. He presents Christian culture as a degenerated culture since its original message has lost its radicalism. He emphasizes the degraded Christ as a role model and in several disputes rebukes his contemporaries who feel that Christians are superior to others. Entry 103 deals with "science" (Hegelian philosophy) as the most praised concept of the time. This entry is the most direct play on the Hegelian quotation concerning Minerva; but Kierkegaard turns it around and lets religion be what is current or contemporary, while science arrives too late. In this way, he is able to cast out his contemporaries' horoscope, as it is worded, namely, by discovering how they understand science in the ethical-religious sphere. So Kierkegaard's claim, referring also to Johannes Climacus, is that it is a complete illusion to turn Christianity into science.[12]

To summarize, Minerva is the Roman parallel to Pallas Athena, the goddess of wisdom, born fully developed from the head of Jupiter, and with the owl as her attribute, symbolizing intelligence, death, and birth. The modern use of the myth is framed above all by Hegel's comparison of the act of philosophy with the activity at dusk of Minerva's owl. Hegel stresses that philosophy as a conceptual discipline presupposes experience and always arrives late. However, in describing a completed world that, however, begins to decline, philosophy also grasps the new world. Kierkegaard takes up this comparison, and the concept appears six times in his writings with mainly two meanings: one plays on the whole myth of Minerva, and one refers specifically to Minerva's owl and the Hegelian usage of the concept, describing the *Zeitgeist*. In this connection the journal entry NB15:103 is the most direct play on the Hegelian quotation.

---

[10]   *SKS* 17, 147, DD:78 / *KJN* 1, 238.
[11]   *SKS* 28, 115, Brev 68 / *LD*, 362, Letter 267.
[12]   *SKS* 23, 73, NB15:103 / *KJN* 7, 70-2.

Bibliography

Undetermined.

Münchhausen:

Charlatan or Sublime Artist

Anders Rendtorff Klitgaard

When Søren Kierkegaard mentions Münchhausen, he is thinking of the literary figure popularized by the German poet Gottfried August Bürger (1747–94). Münchhausen is a teller of tall tales featuring himself as an ingenious soldier and huntsman; these tales are showcases for his cleverness, courage, and strength. Boastful and improbable, the stories are absurd exaggerations typically defying physical laws. Indeed, they were designed to amuse rather than to be believed. The Münchhausen stories spring from a well of European folk tales that predate Bürger by centuries.[1] Genealogically as well as conceptually, the figure of Münchhausen is at home only in a fictional universe. Even so, for the popularization they received in the late eighteenth century the stories are indebted to a real historical person, namely, Karl Friedrich Hieronymus Freiherr von Münchhausen (1720–97) in whose name they were published. A member of a North German noble family, he had traveled extensively in his youth; and as an officer in the Russian army, he had taken part in campaigns against the Turks. Like his eponymous literary figure, the historical Münchhausen is said to have enjoyed entertaining his guests at his estate in Bodenwerder by boasting of his adventures. But the real Münchhausen never published his stories, and only two or three of these are known to us.[2] However, seventeen stories attributed to him were published between 1781 and 1783 in *Vade Mecum für lustige Leute*.[3] An

I would like to express my gratitude to Münchhausen specialist Bernhard Wiebel for sending me scans of books from his Münchhausen collection, and for his friendly communication about all things concerning Münchhausen; to Dr. Eva-Maria Jansson, Research Librarian and Project Manager, Danish Books (1701–1900) on Demand, from the Royal Library in Copenhagen, for going the extra mile in making available to me in electronic form rare *Münchhausen* books and related materials; and to Dr. Niels Jørgen Cappelørn, Professor at the Søren Kierkegaard Research Centre, for general advice on the subject of Kierkegaard's sources.

[1]   Carl Müller-Fraureuth, *Die deutschen Lügendichtungen bis auf Münchhausen*, Hildesheim: Georg Olms Verlagsbuchhandlung 1965, pp. 81–4.

[2]   Even scholarly literature has a tendency to read the literary fictions published in his name into the historical Münchhausen. I am grateful to Münchhausen specialist Bernhard Wiebel for pointing out to me just how little is in fact known. In Zürich, Switzerland, Wiebel has established a private Münchhausen research library holding 3,550 items.

[3]   [Anonymous], "M-h-s-nsche Geschichten," *Vade Mecum für lustige Leute: enthaltend eine Sammlung angenehmer Scherze witziger Einfälle und spaßhafter kurzer Historien aus den besten Schriftstellern zusammengetragen*, Achter Theil, Berlin: August Mylius Buchhändler

expanded English translation appeared in 1785 as *Baron Münchhausen's Narrative of his Marvellous Travels and Campaigns in Russia*.[4] This edition was published by the German writer and scientist Rudolf Erich Raspe (1736–94), who may also have been responsible for the publications in *Vade Mecum*. The question is disputed. A second edition of the English version forms the basis for Bürger's expanded translation back into German as *Wunderbare Reisen zu Wasser und Lande, Feldzüge und lustige Abentheuer des Freyherrn von Münchhausen*.[5] Bürger's *Münchhausen* is the most popular and famous version. Subsequent variations on the theme have given rise to still more stories. A famous later adaptation of the Münchhausen motif is that of Karl Leberecht Immermann, published 1838–39 as *Münchhausen. Eine Geschichte in Arabesken*.[6]

I. Sources

Kierkegaard's conception of Münchhausen is remarkably simple. The Münchhausen stories to which he refers are just two, possibly three, in number, in addition to which comes the overall impression of Münchhausen as a liar, braggart, fantasist, and so on. The stories are the bog/pigtail incident and the tale of Münchhausen's dog wearing its legs down by running. In addition, Kierkegaard may be said to allude to the story of Münchhausen's dog eating its master's stomach. There are no explicit references in the Kierkegaard *corpus* to the literary basis for Kierkegaard's acquaintance with Münchhausen. A Danish translation was published by Schiøtz in 1799 in Copenhagen,[7] which contains most of the material to which Kierkegaard

---

in der Brüderstraße 1781, pp. 92–101. [Anonymous], "M-h-s-nsche Geschichten," *Vade Mecum für lustige Leute: enthaltend eine Sammlung angenehmer Scherze witziger Einfälle und spaßhafter kurzer Historien aus den besten Schriftstellern zusammengetragen*, Neunter Theil, Berlin: August Mylius Buchhändler in der Brüderstraße 1783, pp. 76–9, pp. 96–103.

[4]   Rudolf Erich Raspe [Anonymous], *Baron Münchhausen's Narrative of his Marvellous Travels and Campaigns in Russia. Humbly Dedicated and Recommended to Country Gentlemen; and, If They Please, To Be Repeated as Their Own, After a Hunt at Horse Races, in Watering-Places, and Other Such Polite Assemblies; Round the Bottle and Fire-Side*, Oxford: Smith 1786. (This book was published in December 1785, although the frontispiece says 1786.)

[5]   Gottfried August Bürger [Anonymous], *Wunderbare Reisen zu Wasser und Lande, Feldzüge und lustige Abentheuer des Freyherrn von Münchhausen, wie er dieselben bey der Flasche im Cirkel seiner Freunde selbst zu erzählen pflegt*, London [sc. Göttingen]: Johann Christian Dieterich 1786.

[6]   Karl Leberecht Immermann, *Münchhausen. Eine Geschichte in Arabesken*, Düsseldorf: J.E. Schaub 1838–39. Henry Garland and Mary Garland, *The Oxford Companion to German Literature*, Oxford: Oxford University Press 1997, p. 604. Bernhard Wiebel, "Zeittafel—Raspe, Regenten und Revolutionen," *Der Münchhausen-Autor Rudolf Erich Raspe: Wissenschaft—Kunst—Abenteuer*, ed. by Andrea Linnebach, Kassel: Euregioverlag 2005, pp. 28–31.

[7]   [Anonymous], *En meget løierlig og forunderlig Historie, hvorledes den vidtberømte Friherre von Münchhausen paa sine Reiser i Luften, Skove og Udørkener haver kiempet ikke allene imod de vilde Dyr men og imod Ild, Luft og Vand, og dog altid kommen vel derfra*

refers. Details that Kierkegaard attributes to Münchhausen but cannot be traced back to this source are likely the result of his own creative exuberance. Bursting with the artist's drive to invent and to alter, Kierkegaard had a natural impulse to revise his sources, a point that can be easily proved from examples where these are known, such as his reworking of Genesis 22 into *Fear and Trembling*. Kierkegaard is nothing if not an extreme case of what Harold Bloom has called a strong misreader; indeed, Bloom relies in part on Kierkegaard for his conceptualization of misreading, also called misprision.[8] Schiøtz is a short but sufficient source and hence illustrative of how little Kierkegaard needed. In 1834 an expanded version was published in Roskilde by Andreas Carl Hanson.[9] The Hanson edition contains the third story mentioned above to which Kierkegaard may or may not allude. Regrettably, it is not possible to establish which source Kierkegaard was working from—it could be either one of these, or it could be a third source. One such might be the *Münchhausen* published in 1800 by F.L. Fabricius.[10] It too has the third story of debatable relevance.[11] Hanson writes in his Preface that he is working from "the Danish translation" alongside German editions, since complete German editions were slow in coming. What these editions were he does not say, and there were at least two Danish translations at his point of writing. The Münchhausen literature is riddled with uncertainty, and Bernhard Wiebel puts it succinctly when he quips that "there is no original Münchhausen—because an older one always turns up!"[12] More than one hundred precursors to and sources for the first published editions are known to exist, some of which can be traced back to the Middle Ages.[13]

One does well to remember the folkloristic roots of this motif. Kierkegaard may have known a Danish translation, or he may have read it in German. He refers to Bürger's *Lenore*, a Gothic poem published in 1774, but nowhere in the *corpus* is Bürger a byword for Münchhausen. Nor are there any references to Raspe or Immermann.

---

formedelst sin Snildhed og Manddoms Gierninger og store Bedrifter. Samt Spøgelse-Historier. Skreven til Nytte og Fornøielse, samt til Tidsfordriv, meget fornøielig at læse for dem som gierne vil lee, Copenhagen: Schiøtz 1799.

[8]   Harold Bloom, *A Map of Misreading*, Oxford: Oxford University Press 1980 [1975], pp. 56–7: "I turn to Kierkegaard as the great theorist of the Scene of Instruction, particularly in his brilliantly polemical text, the *Philosophical Fragments* (1844). The title page of this short book asks the splendid triple question...his triple question is perfectly applicable to the secular paradox of poetic incarnation and poetic influence. For the anxiety of influence stems from the ephebe's assertion of an eternal, divinating consciousness that nevertheless took its historical point of departure in an intra-textual encounter, and most crucially in the interpretative moment or act of misprision contained in that encounter."

[9]   *Baron von Münchhausens vidunderlige Reiser, Feldttog og Hændelser, fortalte af ham selv*, ed. by Andreas Carl Hanson, Roskilde: J.D.C. Hanson 1834.

[10]   *Baron von Münchhausens Reiser og Eventyrer*, vols. 1–3, trans. by F.L. Fabricius, Copenhagen: M. Sibberns Forlag 1800.

[11]   Ibid., vol. 2, pp. 5–7.

[12]   The remark was made in private conversation.

[13]   Bernhard Wiebel, "Münchhausen—das Märchen vom Lügenbaron: Über die anspruchsvolle Aufgabe, sowohl literarische Figur als auch literarische Gattung zu sein," in *Hören, Lesen, Sehen, Spüren. Märchenrezeption im europäischen Vergleich*, ed. by Regina Bendix and Ulrich Marzolph, Baltmannsweiler: Schneider Verlag Hohengehren 2008, p. 53.

A certain expression is of significance since it derives from the different versions of
Münchhausen, namely "floating in the air" (*svævende i Luften*). Kierkegaard uses
this phrase when referring to the bog/pigtail story, and the expression is found in
both Schiøtz and Hanson (verbatim) and in Bürger's original (*schwebend in der
Luft*).[14] Fabricius renders the same story, but has a printing error here—*Svævende
i Luf[de]*.[15] Kierkegaard calls Münchhausen's dog *en Mønde*, a greyhound, while
Schiøtz, Fabricius and Hanson refer to it as *en Vindspiller* and *en Vindspiller-
Hund*—Bürger has *ein Windspiel*. All four words are synonyms, however, although
Vindspiller, *Vindspiller-Hund*, and *Windspiel* may suggest a smallish greyhound.
As we shall see below, Kierkegaard seems to introduce somersaults into the bog/
pigtail story of his own accord, but since Münchhausen's hyperboles are already
physical in nature, this imaginative addition is in line with the motif and may be
said to grow organically out of it. Hence, it hardly requires a source of its own. Even
so, a somersault—in the context of a horse race in London—is mentioned in the
collection by Nyegaard.[16] But this book will not do as the sole source since it lacks
the two or three stories to which Kierkegaard refers.

II. Occurrences

There are a total of fourteen explicit references to Münchhausen in Kierkegaard's
corpus, and with two exceptions they all fall within his published writings—from *The
Concept of Irony* (1841) to *The Moment* (1855). When the name is invoked, it is chiefly
for its negative connotations, meaning a fantasist or someone prone to boasting, lying,
or deceiving. However, in two instances the reference is given in a positive sense.

Proceeding chronologically, the first occurrence dates back to April 1836 and so
forms part of the journals and papers. The note is so short that it is worth quoting
in full: "There are metaphysicians of a certain kind who, when they are not able to
proceed any farther, take themselves by the scruff of the neck, like Münchausen, and
thus acquire something *a priori*."[17] The context is a satirical jab at philosophers who
substitute fantasy for thought, thus relieving themselves of what Georg Wilhelm
Friedrich Hegel had called the "strenuous effort of the notion."[18] Or must we
count Hegel among these "metaphysicians of a certain kind"? He certainly later
became an object of unbridled ridicule on the same grounds, that is, by reminding
Kierkegaard of Münchhausen. Obviously, the note itself cannot settle this question.

---

[14]   [Bürger], *Wunderbare Reisen zu Wasser und Lande, Feldzüge und lustige Abentheuer
des Freyherrn von Münchhausen, wie er dieselben bey der Flasche im Cirkel seiner Freunde
selbst zu erzählen pflegt*, p. 54.

[15]   *Baron von Münchhausens Reiser og Eventyrer*, vol. 1, trans. by F.L. Fabricius, p. 42.

[16]   *Lystigt Post- og Reise-Vademecum: muntre Reisende helliget af Monsieur
Heemkengryper, forhenværende Kammertjener hos Hr. von Münchhausen, og udgivet af hans
skoggerleende Arvinger*, trans. by H. Nyegaard, Copenhagen: M.J. Sebbelom 1802, p. 12.

[17]   *SKS* 27, 87, Papir 41 / *JP* 3, 3249.

[18]   Georg Wilhelm Friedrich Hegel, "Vorrede," *Phänomenologie des Geistes*, Bamberg:
Goebhardt 1807, p. lxxi: "Anstrengung des Begriffs." ("Preface," *Phenomenology of Spirit*,
trans. by A.V. Miller, Oxford: Oxford University Press 1977, p. 35.)

The connotations to Münchhausen—or "Münchausen," as the name is here spelled with a single "h"—may be thought of as neutral, in so far as he, unlike a philosopher, can take himself by the scruff of the neck without denigration, being merely a figure of literary jest. Even so, the contextual criticism may be said to rub off on Münchhausen, making him the image of a knave. Kierkegaard is not the first to appreciate the link between Münchhausen and philosophy. Decades earlier Madame de Staël had made the same observation with regard to Johann Gottlieb Fichte's concept of the "I," much to the dismay of the transcendental idealist. Kierkegaard has in mind the bog/pigtail episode, while Madame de Staël is thinking of a different story: "…when he [Münchhausen] arrived once on the banks of a vast river, where there was neither bridge nor ferry, nor even a poor boat or raft, he was at first quite confounded, quite in despair, until at last, his wits coming to his assistance, he took a good hold of his own sleeve and jumped himself over to the other side."[19] Madame de Staël's story may be perceived as a variation on the bog/pigtail story, since they both share the same structure: the predicament being a crossing and the solution Münchhausen's becoming the source of his own kinetic energy. The common trope can be regarded as a special case of the divine *creatio ex nihilo*, here as a *creatio energiae cineticae ex nihilo*, a creation of kinetic energy from nothing.

The second occurrence is in *The Concept of Irony*. "Münchhausen" is here synonymous with *poetic license* and as such the word bears positive connotations. The context is a contrast between Friedrich von Schlegel and Ludwig Tieck, in which Kierkegaard states: "Schlegel didacticizes; he turns directly against actuality. This is not the case with Tieck, who indulges in a poetic abandon [*hengiver sig til en poetisk Overgivenhed*], but he maintains this in its indifference toward actuality."[20] Kierkegaard clearly prefers Tieck and even defends him against Hegel, supporting the view that Hegel was unable to appreciate Tieck's irony. The expression of the original, *poetisk Overgivenhed*, translated as "poetic abandon," is important because, not only is it repeated with just a sentence in between, but the prefix *over* is reiterated in *overvættes* just as the corresponding adverb, *oven*, recurs in *aldeles oven ud*.[21] The upward movement of *over* underscores the positive connotations pertaining to Tieck's irony and so to Münchhausen, since we conceive of "over" and "up" as happy orientational metaphors.[22] What Oscar Wilde half a century later would celebrate as

---

[19]   Abel Stevens, *Madame de Staël: A Study of her Life and Times*, vols. 1–2, New York: Harper & Brothers 1881, vol. 2, p. 27.

[20]   *SKS* 1, 335 / *CI*, 301–2. The expression *poetisk Overgivenhed* is emphasized in the original.

[21]   The original reads: "*At en saadan poetisk Overgivenhed, der i et overvættes ironisk Hopsasa er aldeles oven ud, har sin Gyldighed, vil vist Ingen nægte*" (*SKS* 1, 335). The Hong translation reads: "Surely no one will deny that such a poetic abandon that is utterly inordinate in its excessively ironic capering has its validity" (*CI*, 302). Although "poetic abandon" is a correct translation, "poetic overflow" has the advantage of remaining within the metaphor of *over and above*, which is so dominant in the original.

[22]   Cf. George Lakoff and Mark Johnson, "Orientational Metaphors," in *Metaphors We Live By*, Chicago: University of Chicago Press 1981, pp. 14–16: "Orientational metaphors give a concept a spacial orientation…Happy is up; sad is down…health and life are up; sickness and

art for art's sake—"[a]ll art is quite useless"[23]—is here foreshadowed in Kierkegaard's tribute to Tieck: such poetry as Tieck represents is alien to actuality (*Virkeligheden*) since its native soil is the infinite realm of pure poetry. Once it enters into a relationship with actuality, it loses its innocence—and "[t]hen it is no longer the poetic license that like Münchhausen collars itself and in this way, without any footing, floating in the air, makes one somersault stranger than another."[24] The expression "floating in the air" stems from the adventure in which Münchhausen attempts to cross a bog or mire (*Morast*). Jumping on horseback across a bog, Münchhausen midway realizes that his run-up has been insufficient—and so he floats back through the air to the bank whence he came to try to attempt the crossing a second time. But, alas, the second attempt also proves unsuccessful, and so Münchhausen, atop his horse, sinks up to his neck in the bog. However, being the very image of self-reliance, Münchhausen soon finds a solution. He manages to drag not only himself but also his horse out of the bog—by pulling his own pigtail! If we imagine Münchhausen the way he is often portrayed—wearing a wig—the feat hardly becomes less astonishing. As is evident, Kierkegaard (or possibly an unknown source) has conflated the first attempt's floating back through the air with the second attempt's gravity-defying rescue, which is the climax of the story, on top of which he has added the somersaults. Even despite this imprecision and embellishment, Kierkegaard is in tune with the logic of Münchhausen, here seen as *that which grants poetic license.*

The third occurrence is found in *Repetition* (1843). Münchhausen is now synonymous with *aesthetic perfection—sublime artistic talent and performance.* The context is the accolades lavished on Friedrich Beckmann (1803–66), an actor who, according to Kierkegaard, is a comic genius. Interestingly, the expression from before reoccurs, albeit this time as *one* adverb—*ovenud* rather than *oven ud*—the meaning, however, remains the same, literally "over the top." The original reads: "*Han [Beckmann] er nu aldeles ovenud,*"[25] which in the Hongs' translation is rendered, "He is now completely beside himself."[26] The rather more felicitous original thus explodes in exaltation, its metaphor moving along a vertical axis going upward as opposed to the horizontal axis of the translation. Indeed, the expression "to be beside oneself" is used with negative connotations more often than not. Beckmann is "beside himself" or, better, "over the top," because the art of comedy that he communicates is too large to be confined within the human frame or language. At this sublime juncture, where art transcends the human sphere, there is nothing left for the artist to do but *like Münchhausen* "to take himself by the scruff of the neck…and cavort in crazy capers."[27] Having reached this summit, we must now leave behind the positive interpretations of Münchhausen since the remaining eleven are all negative.

---

death are down…More is up; less is down…High status is up; low status is down…Good is up; bad is down…Virtue is up; depravity is down."

[23]   Oscar Wilde, "The Preface," in *The Picture of Dorian Gray* in *Collins Complete Works of Oscar Wilde*, centenary edition, Glasgow: HarperCollins 1999, p. 17.

[24]   *SKS* 1, 335 / *CI*, 302.

[25]   *SKS* 4, 38.

[26]   *R*, 164.

[27]   *SKS* 4, 39 / *R*, 164.

Published on the very same day as *Repetition* (October 16, 1843), *Fear and Trembling* nevertheless takes a diametrically opposite stand. The name being employed generically as a noun, "a Münchhausen," it is contrasted with a "tried and tested person."[28] The context is one of Faustian doubt, and so Münchhausen is viewed from Faust's perspective, that old "apostate of the spirit."[29] Faust may be a demonic figure, but he is spiritually profound and thus immune to being deceived by a *superficial charlatan*, which is what Münchhausen signifies in this context.

The fifth occurrence is in *Philosophical Fragments* (1844). Münchhausen is here contrasted with "good, honest people." Again the name is employed with the distance of making the proper name a noun—"a Münchhausen"[30]—and in the context it means *a person one should not believe*: a liar, deceiver, or charlatan.

Stages on Life's Way (1845) has three occurrences, the first of which is enclosed in a mid-sentence parenthesis: "(so it is only very young apprentices or Münchhausens who carry on about making conquests)."[31] Yet again the proper name is used as a noun, as evidenced by the plural. "Münchhausen" here means *a braggart*. In the second occurrence "Münchhausen" plays a rather more prominent role: "It has been correctly observed that reflection cannot be exhausted, that it is infinite. Quite right—it can be exhausted in reflection no more than someone, be he ever so hungry, can eat his own stomach, and thus one dares to look upon anyone who says he has done this, be he a systematic hero or a newsboy, as a Münchhausen."[32] Once more Münchhausen equals a braggart or a liar, but what is striking is the match between Kierkegaard's satirical hyperbole and the humor of Münchhausen—they are kindred spirits. Incidentally, Immermann's *Münchhausen* has been called "a satire of the aristocracy."[33] It is telling of the seminal strength of the Münchhausen motif that Kierkegaard, rather than quoting an actual Münchhausen story, is here inventing his own. However "disrespectful" such creative engagement with tradition may seem, what he effectively accomplishes is to capture the spirit of it, and in so doing he continues the tradition. There is in neither Bürger nor Schiøtz a story about Münchhausen, or anyone else, eating his own stomach; however, Hanson's Danish translation, which incorporates stories that were in circulation prior to Raspe and Bürger,[34] comes close to doing so. In Hanson, we find the story of the time when

---

[28]   *SKS* 4, 197 / *FT*, 109.

[29]   *SKS* 4, 196 / *FT*, 107.

[30]   *SKS* 4, 300 / *PF*, 103.

[31]   *SKS* 6, 139 / *SLW*, 148.

[32]   *SKS* 6, 151 / *SLW*, 161–2.

[33]   Siegfried Kohlhammer, "Der 'Münchhausen'-Roman 1. Die irreale Existenz des Vergangenen: die Satire auf den Adel," in his *Resignation und Revolte. Immermanns "Münchhausen": Satire und Zeitroman der Restaurationsepoche*, Stuttgart: J.B. Metzlersche Verlagsbuchhandlung 1973, pp. 42–83.

[34]   "Regarding the tone of the tales," Hanson writes, "I have maintained that of the older editions." Hanson, *Baron von Münchhausens vidunderlige Reiser, Feldttog og Hændelser, fortalte af ham selv*, p. vii. What these editions are, he does not say. However, he dates the Münchhausen tradition back to the *Mendacia ridicula* in the third volume of the *Deliciae academicae* by Johan Peter Lange from 1665. Hanson, *Baron von Münchhausens vidunderlige Reiser, Feldttog og Hændelser, fortalte af ham selv*, pp. v–vi.

Münchhausen's dog ate up its master's stomach. Fortunately for Münchhausen, he soon found a replacement in a pig's stomach, a trade, however, not without impact on his character.[35] The story of Münchhausen pulling himself out of a bog is said to be the most famous of all.[36] If this story is taken as paradigmatic, Kierkegaard may be said to be closer to the spirit of Münchhausen than is Hanson, given the fact that Kierkegaard incorporates a self-referential element. While Hanson lets Münchhausen's dog eat the stomach of another,[37] Kierkegaard envisions the scenario of an individual eating his own stomach. We hereby witness the paradoxical structure of the Münchhausen tradition: the lie or the poetic revision comes closer to the core of the tradition than does the loyal follower of the same. A similar paradoxical structure is arguably at stake when engaging with the writings of Harold Bloom, whose poetic theory turns on the notion of misreading. The work being perceivable only through the lens of misreading, there is, as it were, no inside to it, merely an outside: "Only when we are outside Bloom are we inside."[38] The fact that the tales of Münchhausen are legion is therefore not a sign of corruption of the original motif, but, on the contrary, evidence of loyalty to the spirit of a tradition that cannot be adhered to without creativity. The third occurrence of Münchhausen in *Stages on Life's Way* is satirical since it mocks the Hegelian dictum that "the outer is the inner and the inner the outer" (in Kierkegaard's rendering). It is a satire that harks back to the irony imparted by the opening lines of the Preface to *Either/Or*. Such beliefs, it is said, are "the inventions of Münchhausens who have no understanding whatever of the religious."[39] Münchhausen thus becomes a byword not just for a Hegelian but also for *a profane Hegelian*.

The next four occurrences are from the *Concluding Unscientific Postscript* (1846). The context of the first pokes fun at Hegel's school of thought in mock veneration for "the enormous power" of speculation, which in aloof objective grandeur has left behind all that is subjective and humane. As so often in Kierkegaard, the irony is aimed at the Hegelian notion of "going further," which here amounts to "ceasing to be what one was, a true feat *à la* Münchhausen."[40] Münchhausen hereby becomes shorthand for *what is humanly impossible*. The second occurrence within this work continues this train of thought—"a Münchhausen" is a caricature of the thinker who

---

[35]   Hanson, *Baron von Münchhausens vidunderlige Reiser, Feldttog og Hændelser, fortalte af ham selv*, pp. 80–3.

[36]   Bernhard Wiebel, "Münchhausens Zopf und die Dialektik der Aufklärung," in *Europa in der Frühen Neuzeit*, vols. 1–7, ed. by Erich Donnert, Cologne: Böhlau Verlag 1997–2008, vol. 3 (*Aufbruch zur Moderne*), p. 779.

[37]   Hanson relies upon an unacknowledged source for this story, namely, Heinrich Theodor Ludwig Schnorr's *Wunderbare Reisen zu Wasser und Lande, und lustige Abentheuer des Freyherrn von Münchhausen, wie er dieselben bey der Flasche Wein im Zirkel seiner Freunde selbst zu erzählen pflegt*, vols. 1–4, Copenhagen [Stendal]: Franzen und Grosse 1795, vol. 2, pp. 3–5.

[38]   Anders H. Klitgaard, "Bloom, Kierkegaard, and the Problem of Misreading," *The Salt Companion to Harold Bloom*, ed. by Graham Allen and Roy Sellars, Cambridge: Salt 2007, p. 292.

[39]   *SKS* 6, 396 / *SLW*, 428.

[40]   *SKS* 7, 56 / *CUP1*, 52.

has forgotten that he is existing, whereby "he makes an attempt to cease to be a human being, to become a book or an objective something that only a Münchhausen can become."[41] Emblem of the fantastical, Münchhausen is here the speculative philosopher lost in thought, in short: *a Hegelian*. The third occurrence is found in the context of discussing Gotthold Ephraim Lessing on the subject of transition. The process of association that ends in Münchhausen takes its point of departure in Kierkegaard's musing upon the word "leap" as used by Lessing: "Perhaps that word 'leap' is only a stylistic turn. Perhaps that is why the metaphor is expanded for the imagination by adding the predicate *breit* [broad]."[42] By way of Lady Macbeth's tremendous sense of guilt that "makes the blood spot so immensely large that the ocean cannot wash it away,"[43] Kierkegaard accuses Lessing of being a rogue, "for surely he has, if anything, with the utmost earnestness made the ditch broad."[44] The humor of the passage turns on the premise that the leap, the ditch, and the broadness of it, are all enclosed within a mental or metaphorical sphere. Kierkegaard's attack on Lessing—presumably somewhat tongue-in-cheek if one is to go by the zest with which it develops—therefore reaches its mock indignant climax, thus: "is that not just like making fun of people! Yet, as is well known, with regard to the leap it is also possible to make fun of people in a more popular manner: one closes one's eyes, grabs oneself by the neck *à la* Münchhausen, and then—then one stands on the other side, on that other side of sound common sense in the promised land of the system."[45] Whether the ditch is broad or narrow is really immaterial when it comes to making or not making the leap. This qualitative, as opposed to quantitative, concern is Kierkegaard's serious contention underlying the jest. The fourth and last occurrence in the *Concluding Unscientific Postscript* is another triumph for Kierkegaardian wit, and as per usual it is leveled at Hegelians and assistant professors with their "ludicrous sullenness and paragraph-pomposity."[46] The satire revolves around the dichotomy between a sense for the comic and the world of spirit, on the one hand, and, on the other, a self-importance that is in fact just a cloak for stupidity. Humor is thus an ally to spirit and intelligence. Unfortunately for Münchhausen he gets grouped with the poseurs since their claims to achievements in matters of the spirit are lies.

The thirteenth and penultimate occurrence is from the journals and papers dated November 1854. The context is a most interesting meditation upon the difficult task of relating objectively to one's own subjectivity. It starts off in profound misanthropy, going through a celebration of Socrates—subsequent to which follows a discussion of the nature of God's being—and culminating in the shortcomings of humans in contrast to divine perfection, and all within the short space of a one-page column. Kierkegaard's point of departure is the belief that "The majority of men are truncated *I*'s; what was structured by nature as the possibility of being sharpened to

---

41   *SKS* 7, 91–2 / *CUP1*, 93.
42   *SKS* 7, 97 / *CUP1*, 98.
43   *SKS* 7, 97 / *CUP1*, 99.
44   Ibid.
45   Ibid.
46   *SKS* 7, 256 / *CUP1*, 281.

an *I* is quickly truncated to a third person."[47] Or, is this statement really his starting point—perhaps he really begins his trajectory from within the story to which he alludes? In the margin of the page Kierkegaard has entered: "Like Münchhausen's dog, a greyhound that wore down its legs and became a dachshund."[48] Thus, we must ask, does Kierkegaard recall the Münchhausen story starting from thoughts already formed in his mind; or is it rather the other way around, that the Münchhausen story exerts a formative power over his thinking? The wording is rather striking. What the translation renders as "truncated" is *afstumpede* in the original, meaning— when applied to people—emotionally stunted or callous, a strong word indeed. A similar sinister ring pertains to "sharpened" (*tilspidses*) when applied to a man. One wonders if it is not the virtues of the polemicist, epitomized by pen and intellect, that have been transposed, so as to become a general ideal held up for the masses, a displaced ideal of which they fall short. The opening words—"The majority of men are truncated *I*'s"—read like a grave and effete echo of the flamboyant statement, "I…proceed from the basic principle that all people are boring," with which the "Rotation of Crops" had opened almost twelve years before.[49] And if the "Rotation of Crops" may be regarded as a Wildean precursor, then so may an element in this meditation. For just as the disenchanted Wilde would write in *De Profundis*, in stark violation of those Kierkegaardian categories that must be kept apart, "I see a far more intimate and immediate connection between the true life of Christ and the true life of the artist.…Christ's place indeed is with the poets,"[50] so too does Kierkegaard here begin a conflation of the aesthetic and the ethico-religious: "He [Socrates] is subjectivity raised to the second power; his relationship is one of objectivity *just like that of a true poet in relation to his poetic production*; with this objectivity he relates to his own subjectivity."[51] The chapter on interpretation will elaborate further on this autopoietic theme.

The last occurrence refers to the same Münchhausen story and is found in *The Moment*. The context is again satirical, this time acidic, and the assault aimed at the clergy. The genre is said to be "*A Kind of Short Story*,"[52] and at the center of attention we find the young theological graduate Ludvig From. The story, entitled " 'First *the Kingdom of God*,' "[53] derives its vitriolic power from an obvious confusion of categories: the infinite passion with which one should seek always first and foremost the Kingdom of God has spilled into the world, making the young Ludvig look equally ludicrous and profane. When religious passion for the unconditioned is extended to the prosaic world, so as to fathom even monetary affairs with religious fervor, then not only does it make a mockery of God and his church, but people go astray and lose their ways in the world. And this is where Münchhausen comes in,

---

47   *SKS* 26, 265, NB33:23 / *JP* 4, 4571.
48   Ibid. The allusion of the journal entry and the note giving the explicit reference are counted as one occurrence.
49   *SKS* 2, 275 / *EO1*, 285.
50   Wilde, *De Profundis*, in *Collins Complete Works of Oscar Wilde*, p. 1027.
51   *SKS* 26, 265, NB33:23 / *JP* 4, 4571. Emphasis added.
52   *SKS* 13, 290 / *M*, 233.
53   Ibid.

for poor Ludvig has sought so "unconditionally"—not God's Kingdom, alas—but a royal livelihood as a pastor. He has therefore been running around so tirelessly that "one of his acquaintances, who has not seen him the last few years, is amazed to discover that he has become smaller; perhaps the explanation is that the same thing happened to him that happened to Münchhausen's dog, which was a greyhound but because of much running became a dachshund."[54] Whereas Kierkegaard used to mock his opponents by likening them to Münchhausen, they are now compared to Münchhausen's dog. With "dog" and "cur" being traditional terms of abuse, the increase in insult and degradation is probably a sign of Kierkegaard's bitterness during his attack on the church. Münchhausen's dog may be regarded as a synecdoche for Münchhausen.

A note on the translation: "dachshund" is a translation of *Grævling*, which means a badger. The comprehensive *Dictionary of the Danish Language: Historical Dictionary 1700–1950* gives two possible meanings for *grævling*, the second being *grævlingehund*, that is, dachshund,[55] but here reference is made to Kierkegaard and two other sources, Kierkegaard being the oldest. Justifying rendering Kierkegaard's *Grævling* as "dachshund" with reference to this dictionary is therefore circular reasoning. However, *Dachs* in German displays the same ambiguity, meaning both badger (strictly speaking) and dachshund (informally). So the Hong translation seems indeed a sensible reading of Kierkegaard, but let us for a moment consider the prospect of rendering Münchhausen's greyhound literally as a badger, corresponding to Kierkegaard's original. Bürger has "I could use it only as a dachshund" ("*ich es...nur noch als Dachssucher gebrauchen konnte*"),[56] with which Schiøtz[57] and Hanson[58] roughly correspond. Kierkegaard is thus alone in portraying Münchhausen's dog as ending up as a badger. Three possibilities lie open: ellipsis, hyperbole and metonymy. (1) Ellipsis: When Kierkegaard says *Grævling* it is intended as a short form of "*grævlingehund*" (corresponding to the Hong translation). (2) Hyperbole: Kierkegaard has taken the already absurd metamorphosis even further. (3) Metonymy: Instead of recounting the conclusion of the story, Kierkegaard uses *Grævling* as a shorthand substitute intended to cover this part of the narrative. The point to opening up the perspective so as to include the possibility for hyperbole and

---

[54]   *SKS* 13, 290–1 / *M*, 233.

[55]   *Ordbog over det danske Sprog*, vols. 1–28, published by the Society for Danish Language and Literature, Copenhagen: Gyldendal 1918–56, vol. 7, p. 253.

[56]   [Bürger], *Wunderbare Reisen zu Wasser und Lande, Feldzüge und lustige Abentheuer des Freyherrn von Münchhausen, wie er dieselben bey der Flasche im Cirkel seiner Freunde selbst zu erzählen pflegt*, p. 31.

[57]   [Schiøtz], *En meget løierlig og forunderlig Historie, hvorledes den vidtberømte Friherre von Münchhausen paa sine Reiser i Luften, Skove og Udørkener haver kiempet ikke allene imod de vilde Dyr men og imod Ild, Luft og Vand, og dog altid kommen vel derfra formedelst sin Snildhed og Manddoms Gierninger og store Bedrifter. Samt Spøgelse-Historier. Skreven til Nytte og Fornøielse, samt til Tidsfordriv, meget fornøielig at læse for dem som gierne vil lee*, p. 30.

[58]   Hanson, *Baron von Münchhausens vidunderlige Reiser, Feldttog og Hændelser, fortalte af ham selv*, p. 17.

metonymy is to consider that the story may have taken on a tropological life of its own in Kierkegaard's creative mind.

III. Interpretation

"Bifrontal," to use Kierkegaard's own term for the subjectively existing thinker and his existence-situation,[59] is a word that aptly applies to Münchhausen— for Münchhausen is nothing if not two-faced for Kierkegaard. But whereas the subjectively existing thinker is bifrontal because he must straddle the infinite and the finite, Münchhausen is bifrontal due to being the equivocal object of esteem and dismissal. While there is productive tension in the existential challenge facing the individual, the ambivalence invested in Münchhausen may not be equally constructive. At first glance, it would seem as if Kierkegaard has not cared enough for this motif to elevate it to a level of conceptual consistency. However, a critical approach will argue that, although this may be true, the motif is in fact so close to him that it makes sense to *identify* Kierkegaard with certain aspects of it.

Let us revisit the second occurrence of "Münchhausen," the earliest published use, the context being the celebration of Tieck in *The Concept of Irony*. The sentence in which Kierkegaard refers to Münchhausen is so long that the Hongs' translation divides it up into two. The original has "Münchhausen" appear in a sentence that ends as follows (quoting from the Hong translation): "[i]t is no longer poetry's pantheistic infinity, but it is the finite subject, who applies the ironic lever in order to tip all existence out of its fixed consolidation."[60] What is no longer thus superbly poetic is Tieck when he has given up his Münchhausen-like poetic abandon. Tieck's irony therefore spans a continuum going from "poetry's pantheistic infinity" "in its indifference towards actuality" to applying "the ironic lever in order to tip all existence out of its fixed consolidation."[61] In this manner Tieck's happy aestheticism slides into an ironic battle against existence, a battle that begins where Münchhausen ends. Münchhausen is therefore closely associated with existence—contextually within a single sentence—even as he is pitched against it. Two years after this, in the "Rotation of Crops," Kierkegaard would write about "the Archimedean point with which one lifts the whole world."[62] This *tour de force* of aestheticism, a splendid precursor to Oscar Wilde's decadent Lord Henry,[63] is easily a candidate for being the

---

[59]   *SKS* 7, 88 / *CUP1*, 89.

[60]   *SKS* 1, 335 / *CI*, 302.

[61]   Notice how this latter expression echoes Hamlet's "The time is out of joint. O cursed spite, / That ever I was born to set it right." William Shakespeare, *Hamlet* in *The Arden Shakespeare*, ed. by Harold Jenkins, Walton-on-Thames: Nelson 1997, Act I, Scene v, p. 228. The German translation reads: "*Die Zeit ist aus den Fugen; Schmach und Gram, / Daß ich zur Welt, sie einzurichten, kam!*" William Shakespeare, *Shakespeare's dramatische Werke*, trans. by August Wilhelm von Schlegel and Ludwig Tieck, vols. 1–12, Berlin: G. Reimer 1839–41, vol. 6, p. 36.

[62]   *SKS* 2, 284 / *EO1*, 295.

[63]   A character in Oscar Wilde's *The Picture of Dorian Gray* and a champion of aestheticism.

apex of Kierkegaardian comedy and may be characterized by the same expression Kierkegaard had used for Tieck: "the ironic lever" that seeks to "tip all existence out of its fixed consolidation." It is significant that this Archimedean point is said to ensure the "complete suspension" (*den fuldkomne Svæven*)[64] since this expression harks back to Münchhausen's "*Schwebend in der Luft.*" Now, it may be argued that *Either/ Or*, Part One, to which the "Rotation of the Crops" belongs, gives us the aesthetic Kierkegaard and therefore not the real serious message Kierkegaard hopes to convey. The motif of the Archimedean point, however, is fairly widespread in Kierkegaard and reoccurs, among other places, in Judge William's ethical discourse, the "Balance Between the Esthetic and the Ethical in the Development of the Personality," in *Either/ Or*, Part Two: "When the personality is the absolute, then it is itself the Archimedean point from which one can lift the world."[65] This optimistic formulation, echoing Fichte, succinctly captures the notion in its positive aspect. In other places the hope of finding the Archimedean point is ruled out, upon which dejection ensues. In either case, the Archimedean point is a place beyond the world. But if Münchhausen is a gesture in this direction, he is a figure of transcendence. Let us take a structural approach to him. For Theodor Adorno the bog/pigtail incident signifies the ability to be "at every moment both within things and outside them,"[66] while for Arthur Schopenhauer the same story is indicative of a "*petitio principii,*"[67] the logical error of presupposing what is to be proved. Had Schopenhauer taken Adorno's view, he could have welcomed Münchhausen as an emblem of his philosophy, for even in the very chapter that equates Münchhausen with the fallacy of begging the question,[68] he once again stresses his philosophical point of departure in representation, that is, that which subsumes both object and subject. Man, in Schopenhauer's philosophy, is barred from ever acquainting himself with the noumenal object, the thing-in-itself, and as such he is on the outside. But as man himself is one of the objects he desires to know about, a possibility for penetrating the world of phenomena suddenly appears, placing man on the inside of the noumenon: "a subterranean passage, a secret alliance, which as if by treachery, places us all at once in the fortress that could not be taken by attack from without. Precisely as such, the *thing-in-itself* can come into consciousness only quite directly, namely by *it itself being conscious of itself.*"[69] But, like Kierkegaard, Schopenhauer shies away from embracing Münchhausen as an

---

[64]   *SKS* 2, 284 / *EO1*, 295.

[65]   *SKS* 3, 253 / *EO2*, 265.

[66]   Theodor W. Adorno, "Zur Moral des Denkens," in his *Minima Moralia. Reflexionen aus dem beschädigten Leben*, Frankfurt am Main: Suhrkamp 1980 [1951], (§ 46) p. 82. "On the Morality of Thinking," in his *Minima Moralia: Reflections on a Damaged Life*, trans. by E.F.N. Jephcott, London: Verso 2005, (§ 46) p. 74.

[67]   Arthur Schopenhauer, *Die Welt als Wille und Vorstellung*, Leipzig: F.A. Brockhaus 1819, p. 40. Arthur Schopenhauer, *The World as Will and Representation*, vol. 1, trans. by E.F.J. Payne, New York: Dover Publications 1969 [1859], p. 27.

[68]   Schopenhauer, *Die Welt als Wille und Vorstellung*, pp. 37–51; *The World as Will and Representation*, vol. 1, pp. 25–35.

[69]   Arthur Schopenhauer, *Die Welt als Wille und Vorstellung*, vol. 2, Leipzig: Brockhaus 1844, pp. 198–9. Arthur Schopenhauer, *The World as Will and Representation*, vol. 2, trans. by E.F.J. Payne, New York: Dover Publications 1969 [1859], p. 195.

emblem of his philosophy, thus perpetuating a phobic tradition that possibly began in Fichte's anxiety when confronted with Madame de Staël.

There is something circular about Münchhausen, to be sure—epitomized in the gesture whereby he grabs hold of his own pigtail—but is it necessarily a vicious circle? If we view Münchhausen as a uroboros, the snake or dragon biting its own tail, interesting perspectives appear. In *Alchemical Studies* Carl Gustav Jung writes: "In Horapollo the uroboros is the hieroglyph of eternity. For the alchemists the self-devouring dragon was hermaphroditic because it begot and gave birth to itself."[70] This is a paradox, admittedly, but a positive one. We find the same uroboric and hermaphroditic motif in Kierkegaard too, even in connection with the structure of being simultaneously inside and outside. The following compressed quotation, with emphasis added, spans less than a page in the original as in the Hong translation:

> The phrase γνῶθι σεαυτόν [know yourself] is a stock phrase, and in it has been perceived the goal of all a person's striving. And this is entirely proper, but yet it is just as certain that *it cannot be the goal if it is not also the beginning*....When the individual knows himself, he is not finished; but this knowing is very productive, and from this knowing emerges the authentic individual. If I wanted to be clever, I could say here that *the individual knows himself in a way similar to the way Adam knew Eve, as it says in the Old Testament. Through the individual's intercourse with himself the individual is made pregnant by himself and gives birth to himself*....Only *within* himself does the individual have the objective toward which he is to strive, and yet he has this objective *outside* himself as he strives toward it....That is why the ethical life has this duplexity, in which *the individual has himself outside himself within himself*.[71]

The quotation above is again taken from the "Balance Between the Esthetic and the Ethical in the Development of the Personality," a seminal existentialist text which introduces the notion of choosing oneself (alternatively formulated as receiving oneself), but the uroboric motif recurs even on a global scale in Kierkegaard, namely, within the authorship as a whole. In *On My Work as an Author*, Kierkegaard recounts how he prefers to relate to his authorship as a humble reader notwithstanding the fact that he himself is the author.[72] To be simultaneously the giver and the receiver marks a uroboric structure, and it is arguably no mere coincidence that Kierkegaard considered publishing *The Point of View for My Work as an Author* under the pseudonym of A-O.[73] If we take this name to mean *alpha* and *omega*, the first and

---

[70]   Carl Gustav Jung, *Studien über alchemistische Vorstellungen*, in *Gesammelte Werke*, vols. 1–17, ed. by Lilly Jung-Merker and Elisabeth Rüf, Olten: Walter-Verlag 1958–78, vol. 13, p. 279. *Alchemical Studies*, in *Collected Works*, vols. 1–20, ed. by Herbert Read et al., trans. by R.F.C. Hull, Princeton: Princeton University Press 1953–92, vol. 13, p. 259.

[71]   *SKS* 3, 246–7 / *EO2*, 258–9.

[72]   *SKS* 13, 19 / *PV*, 12: "I regard myself rather as a *reader* of the books, not as the *author*."

[73]   Joakim Garff, *SAK: Søren Aabye Kierkegaard, en Biografi*, Copenhagen: Gad 2000, p. 484. *Søren Kierkegaard: A Biography*, trans. by Bruce H. Kirmmse, Princeton: Princeton University Press 2005, p. 559.

the last letter in the Greek alphabet, we hereby have another name for the uroboros.[74] It is, however, questionable if this was a conscious consideration on Kierkegaard's part, for as Joakim Garff has so wonderfully demonstrated in elaborate detail,[75] Kierkegaard struggled to understand the sense of attenuated autonomy he felt when looking back on his authorship. Hence, he admitted Governance a part in it. But once one understands that Kierkegaard's authorship originated in part from the depths of his unconscious mind—corresponding to the symbol of the uroboros—so as to be not the sole product of consciousness or ego, the puzzles he experienced can be explained. Rather than seeing Kierkegaard's contemplating the possibility of issuing *The Point of View for My Work as an Author* under the guise of A-O as evidence of his playing a "rhetorical game"[76] with the reader, it now becomes possible to appreciate that his sense of elusiveness was genuine and A-O probably intended as an honest trope for what to him was *the real writer*. Münchhausen pulled himself out of a bog, and Kierkegaard elevated himself by means of his own edification. Kierkegaard, however, did not appreciate this resemblance; indeed, his ambivalence towards Münchhausen may be said to be indicative of the extent to which aspects of his work as an author remained opaque to him.

---

[74]   Carl Gustav Jung, *Mysterium Coniunctionis*, in *Gesammelte Werke*, vol. 14:2, p. 56; *Mysterium Coniunctionis*, in *Collected Works*, vol. 14, p. 307.

[75]   Joakim Garff, *"Den Søvnløse": Kierkegaard læst æstetisk/biografisk*, Copenhagen: C. A. Reitzels Forlag 1995, pp. 298–330. Garff, *SAK: Søren Aabye Kierkegaard, en Biografi*, pp. 476–86; *Søren Kierkegaard: A Biography*, pp. 550–62.

[76]   Garff, *SAK: Søren Aabye Kierkegaard, en Biografi*, p. 485; *Søren Kierkegaard: A Biography*, p. 560.

Bibliography

Hannay, Alastair, *Kierkegaard: A Biography*, Cambridge: Cambridge University Press 2001, p. 66, p. 294, p. 410.

Kampmann Walther, Bo, "Web of Shudders: Sublimity in Søren Kierkegaard's *Fear and Trembling*," *Modern Language Notes*, vol. 112, no. 5, 1997, p. 753–85; see p. 756.

Watzlawick, Paul, "Münchhausen's Pigtail and Wittgenstein's Ladder: On the Problem of Self-Reference" in his *Münchhausen's Pigtail or Psychotherapy & "Reality": Essays and Lectures*, New York and London: W.W. Norton 1990, pp. 179–206; see p. 189.

Nemesis:

From the Ancient Goddess to a Modern Concept

Laura Liva

I. Restoring the Balance

Among the many personifications of metaphysical necessity in Greek mythology (Moirae, Ananke, Tyche or Fortune), Nemesis was the one that most specifically represents revenge. The word "nemesis" stems from the verb "nemo" (νέμω), which means "deal out, dispense, distribute." This etymology emphasizes the idea of compensation (retribution, payback)[1] that characterizes this concept. As a goddess, Nemesis expresses the envy of the gods, and her task is related to the manifestation or the result of this envy. It is a figure that represents the wrath of the gods and, as a consequence, their vengeance upon mortals. More specifically, she was charged with exacting divine punishment for human hubris, the arrogance of human beings who consider themselves equal to the gods, thus not respecting the limits imposed on them. Nemesis is thus the righteous wrath directed against mortals who violated the order of nature, disregarding its rules.[2]

Nemesis acts in three different situations: first, she harasses people who have too much luck; second, she pursues those who have acted unjustly; third, she punishes those whose sin is arrogance or hubris.[3] In each of these cases, a balance has been disturbed, namely, the law that governs the relationships between gods and mortals, and Nemesis intervenes to restore the order of the cosmos. As a deity, she personifies punishment (and the sense of justice implied therein), but as a concept it could be defined as natural law.[4]

As Søren Holm points out, the concept that revolves around Nemesis is a rather complicated matter in the Greek world-view: "It is nothing, if not ambiguous."[5] And

---

[1]   For a detailed account of the etymology of the term "nemesis," see Søren Holm, *Græciteten*, Copenhagen: Munksgaard 1964 (*Søren Kierkegaard Selskabets Populære Skrifter*, vol. 11), p. 78.

[2]   Cf. Karl Kerényi, *The Gods of the Greeks*, London: Thames and Hudson 1951, Part I, Chapter VI, § 6, p. 96. Kerényi writes that Nemesis resembles the Furies—goddesses of anger and revenge, who have the specific task of punishing matricides—although Nemesis was always present every time the natural law, the law of coexistence between man and gods, was violated (ibid., p. 97).

[3]   See Holm, *Græciteten*, pp. 79–80.

[4]   Ibid., pp. 78–9.

[5]   Ibid., p. 79.

Laura Liva

like many other Greek myths, the variations are innumerable. The poet Hesiod,[6] the historian Herodotus and the tragedians Aeschylus, Sophocles, and Euripides, all knew this figure, and all refer to her in their works.[7]

In the *Iliad*, Nemesis is not yet personified as a goddess, but Homer uses the word "nemesis" to express an abstract concept. As Kierkegaard's Danish contemporary Johan Ludvig Heiberg puts it: "The concept of Nemesis comes forth most purely, albeit most abstractly, in Homer, *Iliad*, III, 156, for here nemesis is not a personal being, but only the expression of a concept."[8] Hesiod's *Theogony*, however, tells the story of her origin from her mother, Night.[9] Heiberg writes, "In Hesiod Nemesis is a goddess whose concept is firmly fixed....[She is] a daughter of the Night, and accordingly her development from Tyche or blind contingency, the development of the rational from the irrational, is compared with the progression of the light forms of day from the bosom of Night."[10]

If nemesis is still an abstract concept for Homer, for Pindar and the tragedians she acquires the definite character of the bearer of doom, and the bestower of misfortunes upon happy souls who experience a beatitude equal to that of the gods. Her charge is to protect the order and the balance of the universe, assigning to every man his fate, that is, assigning happiness or misery according to justice and merit, while restoring the moral order whenever it has been violated.

II. Nemesis in Kierkegaard's Time

The concept of nemesis was still used in ordinary language in Kierkegaard's day. Kierkegaard knew of the figure of Nemesis from his personal study of Greek mythology, but a likely source was the treatise by his contemporary Johan Ludvig Heiberg: "Nemesis: A Popular Philosophical Introduction."[11] Unlike Kierkegaard,

---

[6]   "The earliest literary references to an actual goddess Nemesis occur in Hesiod where she, along with Aidos, is said to have forsaken the realm of interhuman relations at the onset of the Iron Age (*Opera et Dies*, 197), and where she is seen as the daughter of Nyx (*Theogonia*, 223)" (Michael B. Hornum, *Nemesis, the Roman State and the Games*, Leiden: Brill 1993, p. 6). Cf. Hesiod, *The Works and Days*, in *The Works of Hesiod, Callimachus, and Theognis*, trans. by John Banks, London: Henry G. Bohn 1856, pp. 85–6.

[7]   For a detailed account, see Holm, *Græciteten*, pp. 80–9.

[8]   Johan Ludvig Heiberg, "Nemesis. Et popular-philosophisk Forsøg," *Kjøbenhavns flyvende Post*, no. 41, May 21, 1827, pp. 175–6. (English translation: "Nemesis: A Popular Philosophical Investigation," in *Heiberg's Contingency Regarded from the Point of View of Logic and Other Texts*, ed. and trans. by Jon Stewart, Copenhagen: Museum Tusculanum Press 2008 (*Texts from Golden Age Denmark*, vol. 4), p. 108.) Cf. Heiberg, "Nemesis: A Popular Philosophical Investigation," pp. 108–9 and Holm, *Græciteten*, p. 79.

[9]   Hesiod, *Theogony*, 223, in *The Works of Hesiod, Callimachus, and Theognis*, p. 13: "Then bare pernicious Night Nemesis also, a woe to mortal men."

[10]   Heiberg, "Nemesis: A Popular Philosophical Investigation," p. 109.

[11]   This essay was published in four parts in *Kjøbenhavns flyvende Post* between May 21 and June 4, 1827. (See Jon Stewart, "Introduction: Hegel and Heiberg's Philosophical Works," in *Heiberg's Contingency Regarded from the Point of View of Logic and Other Texts*, pp. 16–21.

who never fully explains his understanding of nemesis, Heiberg published an entire treatise dedicated to this concept. He writes that his aim is to "show how great the scope of this concept is in a way that demonstrates that even today a nemesis is still constantly assumed in every contingency, if not as a personal being, then as a representation which contains truth."[12] Ultimately, Heiberg's purpose is to demonstrate how the concept is "grounded in the nature of contingency and can be deduced philosophically from it."[13] Even though Heiberg traces the origins of the concept of nemesis to Greek mythology, he explicitly deprives the notion of any moral connotation (thus rejecting the original idea of the punishment of hubris). Unlike Dike (Justice) and Adrastea (another personification of necessity), Nemesis "*is the rational...in what is contingent...*[S]he expresses unconscious reason, the objectified subjectivity, the justice which can rule over what is still regarded as contingent."[14] Heiberg continues by examining the similarities between this and other divinities that represent some form of necessary justice. Although all these other figures all have a moral connotation in one way or another, Heiberg insists that properly understood, there is no moral aspect to the figure of Nemesis.[15]

We are not sure if Kierkegaard read Heiberg's work on Nemesis,[16] and their respective understandings of the concept are quite different, as we will see. However, their common interest in this mythological figure is useful in understanding why a concept of pagan origins was still of great importance at that time.

III. Kierkegaard's Use of Nemesis: Individual Nemesis

Kierkegaard's use of the concept of nemesis is rather sporadic. In most cases, he understands nemesis in its classical sense as an event that can be regarded as an act of compensatory justice. There are, however, a few important exceptions. As a matter of fact, nemesis is a term always used in an aesthetic/pagan context, that is, it

---

[12] Heiberg, "Nemesis: A Popular Philosophical Investigation," p. 103.

[13] Ibid.

[14] Ibid., p. 108.

[15] Meïr Goldschmidt responded to Heiberg in his book *Memories and Results of Life*, of which the second part was entirely dedicated to this concept (Meïr Goldschmidt, *Livs Erindringer og Resultater*, vols. 1–2, Copenhagen: Gyldendal 1877, vol. 2, pp. 45–7). As Bruce Kirmmse points out, "in the latter part of his life, Goldschmidt became obsessed with the idea that our lives are ruled by 'Nemesis,' by which he meant a sort of cosmic justice. He traced the origins of this idea to ancient Egypt, corresponded on the subject with learned men, and dedicated the second volume of his memoirs, significantly entitled *Livs Erindringer og Resultater* [Memories and Results of my Life], to propagating his rediscovery of the Nemesis theory as his life's greatest 'result' " (*Encounters with Kierkegaard: A Life as Seen by His Contemporaries*, ed. by Bruce H. Kirmmse, trans. by Bruce H. Kirmmse and Virginia R. Laursen, Princeton: Princeton University Press 1996, p. 292). In general, however, Goldschmidt "rejects Heiberg's claim that nemesis is not a moral concept"(Stewart, "Introduction: Hegel and Heiberg's Philosophical Works," p. 21).

[16] Stewart, "Introduction: Hegel and Heiberg's Philosophical Works," p. 21: "Although there are several allusions to the concept of nemesis in Kierkegaard's works, there is no clear evidence that he read Heiberg's treatise."

always represents a "lower" concept of expiation for one's finite guilt, as opposed to the Christian concept of absolute guilt.

We find nemesis named, for example, in Quidam's "Guilty?/Not Guilty?," and it is highlighted by Frater Taciturnus in his "Letter to the Reader." Here Taciturnus explains:

> The demonic in Quidam of the construction is this, that he is unable to take himself back in repentance, that at the extreme point he becomes suspended in a dialectical relation to actuality…Juno, as is known, sent a gadfly to torment Latona so she could not give birth; similarly a girl's actuality is a gadfly, a "perhaps" that teases him, a nemesis of actuality, an envy of life that will not let him slip out and thereby absolutely into the religious.[17]

In this cryptic passage, the protagonist of the book, Quidam, is said not to be able to find himself because he is unable to develop a dialectical relation with actuality. That is, Quidam has lost touch with the factical context in which he lives, and is thus on his way toward "infinite" categories (such as religious life). Yet as a counterbalance to his lack of actuality, the girl's actuality is a nemesis for him, a force that tries to drag him into actuality and away from the religious. Here, then, we see nemesis used to represent the necessity of facticity in the balance of the human person that Kierkegaard discusses so often in other contexts. But in this case, nemesis is an expression of necessity from a purely aesthetic/pagan point of view, in contrast with the Christian world-view.

Nemesis understood as revenge in the strongest sense appears in one of Kierkegaard's discussions of Don Giovanni. In Paper 186, Don Giovanni's nemesis is embodied in the Commander. In this aesthetic context, nemesis acquires a moral connotation as a punishment for Don Giovanni's wrongdoings. Against this ominous figure stands the figure of Elvira (who "is not really a character"[18]), who opens to the seducer the possibility of escaping punishment. Through Elvira "we see the finger of God, providence, which in a way mitigates the impression of the all too vindictive nemesis in the Commander."[19] If Elvira's almost transparent, angelic figure represents the hand of God, it is only through her that Don Giovanni can save himself from damnation.

In Kierkegaard's discussions of nemesis, literary examples prevail: we find King Lear,[20] whose tragic fate is explained as a "nemesis" (he is punished for demanding the impossible: he demands that his daughters prove their love for him). The same goes for *Faust*, where nemesis punishes Faust's hubristic desire for knowledge. It shows up in the balance of his nature,[21] which is characterized by the contrast between life and knowledge. His striving for knowledge "has caused him to seize upon magic," because "he has sensed that the knowledge possessed by his contemporaries will not satisfy him." But the problem with magic is that "it seeks

---

17   *SKS* 6, 413 / *SLW*, 447.
18   *SKS* 27, 150, Papir 186 / *JP* 3, 2785.
19   Ibid.
20   *SKS* 20, 107, NB:169 / *KJN* 4, 107.
21   *SKS* 17, 79, BB:7 / *KJN* 1, 72.

truth for an inferior purpose" and will eventually lead to Faust's downfall.[22] Here, nemesis is used to describe the other side of the dialectic of the ideal and actual. Faust wants to disappear into ideality, but nemesis demands actuality.

IV. Nemesis in History

Rarely does Kierkegaard thematize the meaning of nemesis, or explain in detail the role and significance of this concept in a broader sense, that is, when nemesis represents a balance that must be restored to the cosmos as a whole.

A first example of using the concept of nemesis without explaining it is found in *The Concept of Irony*, where Kierkegaard draws a comparison between Socrates and nemesis on the issue of human destiny. Socrates acts as a nemesis towards his contemporaries; his role is not to save the world but to judge it: "What Nemesis had previously been in relation to the great and outstanding, was now completely and profoundly accomplished by Socrates' ironic activity in relation to humanity as such."[23] Here Kierkegaard recovers the original meaning of nemesis, that is, the punishment of hubris. Socrates is a nemesis to his contemporaries, who hubristically think they know something when they are truly ignorant. His nemesis-like wisdom is "knowledge of the negativity of all finite content."[24] Kierkegaard refers to the negative role of Socrates/nemesis, "punishing" those who think they know the truth by taking it away from them.

In the *Concluding Unscientific Postscript* Kierkegaard analyzes the concept of nemesis more extensively: Nemesis, as the aesthetic-metaphysical concept of natural necessity, is a lower, external form of justice. In the religious sphere, total guilt is the highest form of justice or "satisfaction," which is an internal category. In contrast to this highest form, there are two lower forms of satisfaction. On the one hand, there is civil punishment, on the other hand, the aesthetic-metaphysical concept of nemesis:

> The civil concept of punishment is a lower satisfaction. This concept corresponds to this or that guilt and therefore is altogether outside the totality-category. The esthetic-metaphysical concept of Nemesis is a lower satisfaction. Nemesis is externally dialectical, is the consistency of externality or natural justice. The esthetic is unopened inwardness; therefore that which is or is to be inwardness must manifest itself externally.[25]

---

[22]   *SKS* 17, 76–7, BB:7 / *KJN* 1, 70: "He then shows how a *conflict between life and knowledge* has taken root in Faust's consciousness, which has caused him to seize upon magic, which precisely on account of the good-humored side it gives life has something very enticing about it. By broadening knowledge, magic would secure riches, all kinds of enhanced pleasure in living, long life, etc. Magic is therefore not objectionable in itself, since it strives for knowledge; it is objectionable because it seeks truth for an inferior purpose. Faust's scientific side had received a severe setback in that conflict, but an *impatience* connected to his tantalized striving for knowledge also arose—he wanted to embrace everything."

[23]   *SKS* 1, 221 / *CI*, 173, translation modified.

[24]   Ibid.

[25]   *SKS* 7, 492 / *CUP1*, 541.

At this point, Kierkegaard adds the example of another mythological figure, the Furies, who "were visible, but their very visibility made the inwardness less terrible and because of their visibility a boundary was established for them."[26] Their limits were the doors of the temple,[27] that according to Kierkegaard, represents the inner life, and the Furies are the "commensurability between the outer and the inner, whereby the guilt-consciousness is finitized, and satisfaction consists in death, and everything ends in the sad exaltation that is death's mitigation."[28] Like "natural justice" represented by nemesis, all self-inflicted penance (for example, the medieval cloister movement) "is a lower satisfaction, not only because it is self-inflicted, but because even the most enthusiastic penance makes guilt finite by making it commensurable, whereas its merit is inwardly to discover guilt that evades the attention not only of the police but even of Nemesis."[29] The natural justice represented by nemesis is a lower satisfaction because it makes inwardness commensurable, that is, it finitizes guilt, turning it into a relative concept.

V. Nemesis and the Irony of Fate: Ironic Contradiction

Another example is taken from an episode of Goethe's *Faust*. In an early note, Papir 196 from 1836, Kierkegaard writes: "Does not some of what I have called irony approach what the Greeks called Nemesis—for example, the overrating of an individual the very moment he feels most distressed about some guilt."[30] As an example of this irony Kierkegaard mentions the episode in Goethe's work precisely because here we see the tension between two opposites, a contrast between two contrary feelings: he is guilty, and he knows it, but at the same time he is admired by the people around him because they cannot see it; his inner condemnation is counterbalanced by a paradoxical external admiration.

There are other examples of irony being compared to nemesis. In another journal entry from 1836,[31] Kierkegaard makes the observation that in mythological tales something good is counterbalanced by something tragic, which implies that there is a balance in the world that must be maintained:

> In order to extort some gift from a troll it was only a matter of intruding when the troll wanted to descend. But the really remarkable thing is the nemesis that was likely to follow when someone became involved with them, for how often we hear of someone's having gotten the good sword, the bow, the arrow, etc., he asked for, and yet there usually was a little "but" that went with it in that he often thereby became an instrument in the hands of fate to wipe out his own family etc., how many tragic consequences resulted

---

26   Ibid.

27   See, for example, Aeschylus, *Eumenides*, in *Tragedies and Fragments*, trans. by Edward H. Plumptre, Boston: D.C. Heath & Co. Publishers 1906.

28   *SKS* 7, 492 / *CUP1*, 542.

29   *SKS* 7, 492 / *CUP1*, 541–2.

30   *SKS* 27, 153, Papir 196 / *JP* 2, 1678.

31   *SKS* 27, 132, Papir 134 / *JP* 5, 5133.

from the minor circumstance that this sword once drawn cannot be put in its sheath unless it has been dipped in warm human blood.[32]

Kierkegaard uses in his own way the concept of nemesis as he does with all other figures from Greek mythology, in order to emphasize the contrast with the Christian point of view. This is evident especially in the *Postscript*, but if we look at other examples, Kierkegaard refers to nemesis always in an aesthetic context (Quidam, Faust, Don Giovanni, Johannes the Seducer).[33]

Nemesis is always present in a purely aesthetic-literary context: a punishment, a kind of law of retaliation in order to maintain a visible cosmic balance. Despite the fact that nemesis has a necessary character, it is not the same as Fate. While Fate is the "unity of necessity and the accidental,"[34] nemesis lacks the accidental element, for it is a necessary reaction to restore a balance that has been disturbed.

---

[32]   Ibid., translation modified.
[33]   Cf. *SKS* 2, 391–2 / *EO1*, 404.
[34]   *SKS* 4, 400 / *CA*, 97.

Bibliography

Drachmann, Anders Bjørn, "Skyld og Nemesis hos Æschylus," in his *Udvalgte Afhandlinger*, Copenhagen and Kristiania: Gyldendal 1911, pp. 9–37; see pp. 9–14.

Gredal Jensen, Finn, "Herodotus: Traces of *The Histories* in Kierkegaard's Writings," in *Kierkegaard and the Greek World*, Tome II, *Aristotle and Other Greek Authors*, ed. by Jon Stewart and Katalin Nun, Aldershot: Ashgate 2010 (*Kierkegaard Research: Sources, Reception and Resources*, vol. 2), pp. 247–62.

Holm, Søren, *Græciteten*, Copenhagen: Munksgaard 1964 (*Søren Kierkegaard Selskabets Populære Skrifter*, vol. 11), pp. 79–84.

Stewart, Jon, "Introduction: Hegel and Heiberg's Philosophical Works," in *Heiberg's Contingency Regarded from the Point of View of Logic and Other Texts*, ed. and trans. by Jon Stewart, Copenhagen: Museum Tusculanum Press 2008 (*Texts from Golden Age Denmark*, vol. 4), p. 21.

Vorobyova, Nataliya, "Heiberg and Kierkegaard: Playing with Nemesis," in *Johan Ludvig Heiberg: Philosopher, Littérateur, Dramaturge, and Political Thinker*, ed. by Jon Stewart, Copenhagen: Museum Tusculanum Press 2008 (*Danish Golden Age Studies*, vol. 5), pp. 165–91.

Nero:

Insatiable Sensualist

Sean Anthony Turchin

Lucius Domitius Ahenobarbus (Nero) was born on December 15, AD 37 in Antium, near Rome. His father, Gnaeus, had died in AD 39 when Nero was only two. But since Nero's mother, Agrippina the younger (the great granddaughter of Caesar Augustus), had been exiled that same year by Caligula, Nero's maternal uncle, Nero was sent to live with his aunt.

When the Emperor Caligula and his family were murdered in AD 41, Nero's great uncle, Tiberius Claudius Caesar Augustus Germanicus (Claudius) became Roman Emperor from AD 41 to 54. Claudius then brought Nero's mother back from exile in AD 49 and married her.[1] He then adopted Nero in AD 50 whose name was changed from Lucius to Nero Claudius Caesar Drusus Germanicus.[2] Most ancient sources tell us that Claudius was later murdered by his wife, Nero's mother Agrippina.[3] With Claudius' death in AD 54, Nero took the throne, taking the name Nero Claudius Caesar Augustus Germanicus. Nero's infamy as a Roman Emperor rests in his noted treachery; he is reported to have murdered both his mother and his stepbrother, Britannicus, the natural son of the late emperor Claudius.[4]

Later, Nero would divorce his wife Octavia, the emperor's daughter, in order to marry another woman, named Poppaea. He would later have Octavia brutally murdered as well.[5] But what he is most known for is both his burning of Rome in AD 64 and his brutality towards the Christians whom he used as human torches to light up his gardens at night.[6] In the end, with the threat of insurrection at the hands of his

---

[1]   Plutarch, *The Lives of the Noble Grecians and Romans*, ed. by Robert Maynard Hutchins, Chicago: William Benton 1952 (*Great Books of the Western World, Encyclopedia Britannica*), p. 779.

[2]   Ibid., p. 779. See also P. Cornelius Tacitus, *The Annals and The Histories*, trans. by Alfred John Church and William Jackson Brodribb, Chicago: William Benton 1952 (*Great Books of the Western World, Encyclopedia Britannica*), Book XII, no. 26, p. 115.

[3]   Tacitus, *The Annals*, Book XII, no. 66, p. 125.

[4]   Tacitus, *The Annals*, Book, XIII, nos. 15–16, p. 129; XIV, nos. 8–9, p. 143; Plutarch, *Lives*, p. 779; Philostratus the Elder, *Life and Times of Apollonius of Tyana*, trans. by Charles P. Eells, Stanford: Stanford University Press 1923, Book IV, no. 38, p. 114.

[5]   Tacitus, *The Annals*, Book XIV, no. 60, p. 64.

[6]   Ibid., Book XV, no. 38, p. 44.

general Vindex, Nero committed suicide on June 9 of that same year, thus ending the Julian Claudian Dynasty.[7]

Concerning possible sources for Kierkegaard's knowledge of Nero, the Roman historians Tacitus, Philostratus the Elder, and Suetonius are most likely. With regard to Tacitus, Kierkegaard owned four different editions of his works.[8] With regard to Suetonius, his edition of the Danish translation *Tolv første romerske Keiseres Levnetsbeskrivelse* appears in the auction catalogue of his library.[9] Another possible source from which Kierkegaard read of Nero is the German translation of Philostratus' *Leben des Apollonius von Tyana*.[10]

Kierkegaard's discussions of Nero are found in a few entries in his journals and papers as well as in *Either/Or*, where Nero is mentioned most. Concerning his journals and papers, in an entry dating from 1844, Kierkegaard writes, "to speak ill of it [the absolute method] was the prime philosophical high-treason against Hegel. In the same way Nero was incensed at the guard, not because he incited rebellion, not because he said he was a bad emperor, but because he said Nero was a bad zither player."[11]

Kierkegaard's use of Nero here is strikingly similar to Philostratus the Elder's *Life and Times of Apollonius of Tyana*, which Kierkegaard owned. In this work, Philostratus mentions how Vindex, the general of the forces of Gaul who later began an insurrection against Nero, said "that Nero was nothing of a singer and yet was a better singer than he was an emperor."[12] Interestingly, Kierkegaard notes the same incident from the same source earlier sometime between the years 1842 to 1843. He writes: "What embittered Nero most of all was that he had said that Nero was anything but a zither player and was more of a zither player than he was a king. Nero was offended that Vindex regarded him as a bad zither player."[13]

The final entry concerning Nero in Kierkegaard's journals and papers was written in 1854 towards the end of Kierkegaard's life. In this entry, Kierkegaard seemingly notes what is most remembered about Nero, namely, how he used the early Christians as night torches to light his roads and gardens.[14] Discussing the

[7]   Plutarch, *The Lives of the Noble Grecians and Romans*, p. 860.
[8]   *C. Cornelii Taciti Opera ex recensione Ernestiana*, ed. by Immanuel Bekker, Berlin: G. Reimer 1825 (*ASKB* 1282); *Des C. Cornelius Tacitus Sämmtliche Werke*, vols. 1–3, trans. by Johann Samuel Müller, Hamburg: Johann Carl Bohn 1765–66 (*ASKB* 1283–1285); *Cajus Cornelius Tacitus*, vols. 1–3, trans. and ed. by Jacob Baden, vols. 1–3, Copenhagen: trykt hos Morten Hallager 1773–97 (*ASKB* 1286–1288); *Dialog om Talerne eller om Aarsagerne til Veltalenhedens Fordærvelse*, trans. by Jacob Baden, Copenhagen: Johan Frederik Schultz 1802 (*ASKB* 1289).
[9]   [Suetonius], *Tolv første romerske Keiseres Levnetsbeskrivelse*, trans. and ed. by Jacob Baden, Copenhagen: Joh. Fred. Schultz 1802 (*ASKB* 1281).
[10]   [Philostratus], *Flavius Philostratus, des Aeltern, Werke*, vols. 1–5, trans. by Hofrath Friedrich Jakobs zu Gotha, Stuttgart: Metzler 1819–32, vol. 5, *Leben des Apollonius von Tyana*. See *JP* 2, note 342, p. 581.
[11]   *Pap* V B 41 / *JP* 2, 1606.
[12]   Philostratus the Elder, *Life and Times of Apollonius of Tyana*, Book V, no. 10, p. 125.
[13]   *SKS* 18, 150, JJ:25 / *JP* 4, 4105.
[14]   See Tacitus, *The Annals and The Histories*, The Annals, Book XV, nos. 43–51, p. 168.

nature of the relation between Christianity and how it affects the Christian in terms of "fire" which purifies, Kierkegaard states, "As gold is purified in fire, in the same way the Christian is purified….Thus there was a demonic ingenuity in the most horribly shocking atrocity perpetuated on some of the first Christians—burning them as torches along the road."[15] But whereas these entries reveal Kierkegaard's historical awareness of those events that surrounded the infamous Nero, it is in *Either/Or* where Kierkegaard offers more of a character sketch of him.

Prefacing his use of Nero as an example of one who represents a life of insatiable desire, Kierkegaard is thankful that one rarely witnesses such a life.[16] In his opinion, such a life would be a "terrible spectacle" to observe.[17] Nevertheless, Kierkegaard wishes to offer an example of where such a life leads an individual, and his example of such an individual is Nero. It is Nero, Kierkegaard states, "before whom a whole world bowed, who was perpetually surrounded by a countless host of the accommodating messengers of desire."[18]

In Kierkegaard's account, Nero's life, as one of excessive sensuality, had to no limits in acquiring pleasure. Such a desire for pleasure is exemplified in Kierkegaard's mentioning of Nero's burning of Rome which was a product of the emperor's quest for excitement.[19] Likely drawing on Suetonius' account of the "Trojan conflagration," Kierkegaard recalls Nero's role in burning Rome "in order to get an idea of the conflagration of Troy."[20]

According to Kierkegaard, Nero's unquenchable hunger for pleasure is one not directly derived from the want of pleasure itself but rather from depression.[21] Although a person cannot be blamed for being sad, one can be blamed, according to Kierkegaard, for being depressed.[22] And so how depression relates to an insatiable desire for pleasure is what Kierkegaard begins to explore with Nero serving as the subject of investigation. Thinking of Nero, Kierkegaard states, "I picture, then, that imperial sensualist…he sets out to satisfy his appetites."[23]

In capturing the nature of the sensual life, Kierkegaard imagines an old man who, being passed the prime of life has not learned from life. This individual continues in the futile quest for pleasure, unreflective in his existence. As such, this individual is comparable to children or young men who have not been able to be reflective enough to comprehend the sheer waste of such a life.[24] This being the case, the sensualist "snatches at pleasure; all the ingenuity of the world must devise new pleasures for him, because only in the moment of pleasure does he find rest, and when that is over, he yawns in sluggishness."[25]

---

[15]   *SKS* 26, 210; NB32:122 / *JP* 4, 4355.
[16]   *SKS* 3, 178 / *EO2*, 184.
[17]   Ibid.
[18]   *SKS* 3, 179 / *EO2*, 184.
[19]   *SKS* 3, 181 / *EO2*, 187.
[20]   *SKS* 3, 179 / *EO2*, 184.
[21]   *SKS* 3, 180 / *EO2*, 185.
[22]   Ibid.
[23]   *SKS* 3, 180 / *EO2*, 185–6.
[24]   *SKS* 3, 180 / *EO2*, 186.
[25]   Ibid.

In conclusion, Nero serves Kierkegaard as a portrait of one whose life is utterly wasted and selfishly situated in order to feed the desires of their own appetite, even to the detriment of others. Although Kierkegaard's conception of Nero appears historical, it is not so much the events of Nero's life and actions that capture Kierkegaard's imagination but rather the personality of Nero himself. For Kierkegaard, Nero's personality reflects one who is indeed prone to melancholy, a sort of sadness that finds diversion in indulging an unquenchable appetite for pleasure. This is a sad individual whose life never gets beyond the immediate to that of a more developed and reflective way of living.

This is Kierkegaard's Nero: an individual consumed with anxiety who has not grasped that there is no ultimate pleasure through which the individual can finally come to rest. No matter what this person does in order to quench their hunger for pleasure, the hunger itself evolves to require a higher form of satisfaction for which none can be found. Kierkegaard questions "whether this was the case with Nero."[26] But whether or not Nero was himself the epitome of boundless desire is second in importance to what he represents in this sketch; he is depression, one who knows not why he is sad and thus endlessly seeks pleasurable diversions to ease his anxiety.[27]

[26]   *SKS* 3, 182 / *EO2*, 187.
[27]   *SKS* 3, 180 / *EO2*, 185; *SKS* 3, 183 / *EO2*, 189.

Bibliography

Gulmann, Sebastian Høeg, "Suetonius: Exemplars of Truth and Madness: Kierkegaard's Proverbial Uses of Suetonius' *Lives*," in *Kierkegaard and the Roman World*, ed. by Jon Stewart, Aldershot: Ashgate 2009 (*Kierkegaard Research: Sources, Reception and Resources*, vol. 3), pp. 126–41.

Stewart, Jon, "Tacitus: Christianity as *odium generis humani*," in *Kierkegaard and the Roman World*, ed. by Jon Stewart, Aldershot: Ashgate 2009 (*Kierkegaard Research: Sources, Reception and Resources*, vol. 3), pp. 147–61.

Papageno:

An Aesthetic Awakening of the Ethics of Desire

Karen Hiles and Marcia Morgan

In early October 1791, Wolfgang Amadeus Mozart (1756–91) attended a performance of his new opera, *Die Zauberflöte* (*The Magic Flute*), at Vienna's Freihaustheater auf der Wieden. In a letter to his wife, Mozart explained that he had run into an acquaintance at the theater:

> [name crossed out] had a box today.—[he] applauded *everything*, but he, the know-all, revealed himself to be such a thoroughgoing *Bavarian* that I couldn't stay, otherwise I'd have ended up calling him an ass;—unfortunately I was there at the start of the 2nd act, in other words, during a solemn scene. —He laughed at everything; to begin with I was patient enough to draw his attention to some of the speeches, but—he just laughed at everything as before—it got too much for me—I called him *Papageno* and left—but I don't think the fool understood me.[1]

Mozart scoffs at the enthusiastic yet unserious audience member. In calling him a "Papageno," the composer connects him to the convivial yet simple-minded character on stage and dismisses him for his ignorance and lack of curiosity. In Mozart's estimation, neither the spectator nor Papageno demonstrated sufficient desire for understanding and enlightenment.

As Jessica Waldoff points out, however, Mozart's use of "Papageno" here does not correspond entirely to the presentation of the character within *The Magic Flute*, "where Papageno is rewarded despite his shortcomings and where his resistance to enlightenment is mitigated by the fact that it does not seem to be a requirement for happiness."[2] Indeed, the character is more complex than he first seems, and a half-century later Kierkegaard analyzes the figure of Papageno at length, paying more serious attention to the opera and to Papageno than did Mozart's acquaintance. After briefly outlining the dramatic and musical characterization of Papageno in *The Magic Flute* and sketching the conditions of Kierkegaard's reception of the opera,

---

[1]   *The Letters of Mozart*, ed. by Cliff Eisen, trans. by Stewart Spencer, New York: Penguin 2006, pp. 564–5. Letter of October 8–9, 1791.

[2]   Jessica Waldoff, *Recognition in Mozart's Operas*, Oxford: Oxford University Press 2006, p. 310.

this article explores Kierkegaard's use of Papageno as a mythic figure within his theory of the musical-erotic.[3]

The Magic Flute tells the story of a young prince's quest for enlightenment, as he (Tamino) must choose between evil and darkness (in the form of the Queen of the Night) and goodness and light (in the form of Sarastro). The libretto and the score are filled with references to Freemasonry, and the opera has often been interpreted as a metaphor for, in Rose Rosengard Subotnik's formulation, "a conception of a humanity bound by universal principles."[4] At the beginning of the two-act opera, Tamino befriends Papageno, a simple bird catcher who provides comic relief throughout much of the work and who comes to serve as both his sidekick and foil.[5] Papageno ultimately pairs off with his Papagena, just as Tamino finds the princess Pamina. Whereas the latter characters sing in a more lyrical, elevated style, Papageno's music is mostly folk-like, cheerful, and lively, though as Peter Branscombe points out, the role is not purely comic in its action or in its music. A deeper, melancholy side of Papageno emerges occasionally (for example, during his suicide attempt in Act 2) as well as in several other passages where his music turns to minor keys, moving Branscombe to suggest that perhaps Papageno "is a less simple fellow than Tamino."[6]

Though he is important for much of the opera's action and participates in several ensembles, Papageno's main numbers consist of three solo arias and two duets (one with Pamina and the other with his future wife, Papagena). In his introductory number, "Der Vogelfänger" ("The Birdcatcher"), Papageno sings, "I am the bird-catcher, always lively, merry, hopsassa!"[7] This G-Major song presents a happy, twittering, (and for Subotnik) "prereflective, preconscious" character at peace within

[3]   Kierkegaard's discussion of Mozart's operas had very little influence on Mozart studies up until the mid-twentieth century, when scholars began considering the first translations from the Danish. John Daverio cites Alfred Einstein's *Mozart: His Character, His Work* (New York: Oxford University Press 1945) as one of the first biographies to mention Kierkegaard's work. See John Daverio, "Mozart in the Nineteenth Century," in *The Cambridge Companion to Mozart*, ed. by Simon P. Keefe, Cambridge: Cambridge University Press 2003, pp. 171–84; p. 261, note 8.

[4]   Rose Rosengard Subotnik, "Whose *Magic Flute*? Intimations of Reality at the Gates of the Enlightenment," in her *Deconstructive Variations: Music and Reason in Western Society*, Minneapolis: University of Minnesota Press 1996, pp. 1–38; p. 3. For a comprehensive introduction to the opera, see Peter Branscombe, *W.A. Mozart: Die Zauberflöte*, Cambridge: Cambridge University Press 1991 (*Cambridge Opera Handbooks*).

[5]   For a brief summary of the figure of the bird-man in European literature, see Branscombe, *W.A. Mozart: Die Zauberflöte*, pp. 98–101.

[6]   Ibid., p. 128.

[7]   Act 1, Scene 2: "*Der Vogelfänger bin ich ja, stets lustig, heißa, hopsassa!*" For the score with German text, see Wolfgang Amadeus Mozart, *Die Zauberflöte*, Serie II: Bühnenwerke, Werkgruppe 5, Band 19, ed. by Gernot Gruber and Alfred Orel, Kassel: Bärenreiter 1970. A digitized version of this critical edition is available online from the *Neue Mozart Ausgabe* (NMA) website at www.nma.at. Translations from the German are by Karen Hiles and scene numbers are taken from the NMA edition.

a clear and simple musical world free of surprises and complications.[8] Between each strophe of his strophic song, he sounds his panpipes in a rising five-note scale— a motif that he will carry with him throughout the opera and which here acts as both a musical question and its answer, compounding the sense of cyclicity in the song.[9] The panpipes, the musical repetition, and the lyrics' expression of a totality set off from the world, all place this song within the pastoral tradition.[10]

Just after "Der Vogelfänger," Tamino asks Papageno which land they are in, and Papageno can only reply, "I can answer that no better than I can tell you how I came into the world,"[11] a response perfectly in line with the naïveté and blissful ignorance of his entrance song. But Papageno will not remain in this idyllic state for long. By Act 2, Papageno's awareness is growing: at one point he laments, "If only I knew where I was! …Now I can't go forwards or back"[12]—a pronouncement that not only speaks to his journey through new lands with Tamino, but also to his journey through new levels of consciousness, from which there is no going back.

Papageno eventually encounters Pamina, and together they momentarily step out of the opera's hierarchy of couples to sing a non-love duet about the nobility and power of love ("Bei Männern"). Pamina begins the duet by adopting Papageno's simple musical style: here a serene, lilting rhythm again evokes the pastoral mode and eventually becomes almost hymn-like. They join together to sing, "[Love's] high purpose shows clearly / that nothing is nobler than woman and man. / Man and woman…reach toward godliness."[13] The ordinary Papageno joins the noble Pamina; one will achieve enlightenment by the end of the opera and the other will not.[14] In joining Pamina with Papageno rather than Tamino, the duet evokes a spiritual rather than erotic love.[15] Indeed, the end of the song gestures toward that "high purpose" as Pamina's ornate melody twice reaches upward before the final phrase comes to

---

[8]   This discussion of "Der Vogelfänger" draws on Subotnik's analysis. See Subotnik, *Deconstructive Variations: Music and Reason in Western Society*, pp. 2–6.

[9]   Strophic form is the simplest of song forms, in which the melody repeats for each new strophe of text.

[10]   On the concept of repetition in the characterization of Papageno, see Hayoung Heidi Lee, "Papageno Redux: Repetition and the Rewriting of Character in Sequels to *Die Zauberflöte*," *Opera Quarterly*, vol. 28, nos. 1–2, 2012, pp. 72–82. Lee makes passing reference to Kierkegaard on p. 74 within a brief summary of past critical readings of Papageno's repetitions.

[11]   Act 1, Scene 2: "*Das kann ich dir ebensowenig beantworten, als ich weiß, wie ich auf die Welt gekommen bin.*"

[12]   Act 2, Scene 22: "*Wenn ich nur wenigstens wüßte, wo ich wäre…Nun kann ich weder zurück, noch vorwärts.*"

[13]   Act 1, Scene 14: "*Ihr hoher Zweck zeigt deutlich an: / nichts Edlers sei, als Weib und Mann…./ Mann und Weib…/ reichen an die Gottheit an.*"

[14]   Waldoff, *Recognition in Mozart's Operas*, p. 37.

[15]   Nicholas Till reads this duet as the celebration of marriage as "a symbolic union, a consummation of the desired reunion of all the wrongly separated elements of life: matter and spirit, masculine and feminine, God and the world, Christ and his Church." Nicholas Till, *Mozart and the Enlightenment: Truth, Virtue and Beauty in Mozart's Operas*, London: W.W. Norton 1992, p. 285.

a close.[16] This duet may be contrasted with Papageno's duet at the end of the opera with a different partner (Papagena), in which he sings of a simpler, earthly happiness to music of a much less elevated style.[17]

As the opera progresses, Papageno begins to fall away from the difficult path toward godliness and reverts to dreams of wine, women, and song rather than knowledge or enlightenment. Whereas Tamino, when questioned by Sarastro's priests in Act 2, explains that he seeks friendship and love, Papageno answers, "Fighting is not my thing. I also don't ask for wisdom. I am a child of nature, satisfied with sleep, food, and wine."[18] Left alone onstage he sings his second solo aria wishing for a wife while accompanying himself on his magic bells (a Glockenspiel in the orchestra). "Ein Mädchen oder Weibchen" is again strophic in form, this time set in the pastoral key of F Major: "Oh how a gentle little dove / would be bliss for me! / Then food and drink would taste wonderful, / then I could compare myself with princes."[19] The penultimate line presents a new urgency: "If no one will grant me love, then I must be consumed by flames!"[20] An old woman suddenly appears and asks for his hand, but Papageno hesitates. She transforms into the lovely Papagena, and Papageno is pronounced unworthy of her. But his desire is inflamed, and he answers, "I'd just as soon let the earth swallow me up as back down now!"[21] before promptly falling through a trapdoor.

As Tamino and Pamina prepare to undergo their final trials on the path to enlightenment, Papageno is back in the garden and back in G major, playing his panpipe and desperately calling for Papagena in his third solo aria ("Papagena"). Not finding her, he despairs: where his first song moved at a pleasant, steady tempo, his music here is rushed and despondent. His earlier major-key ascending panpipe motive is now heard in the violins, descending through a minor scale. "I'm tired of my life!" he declares as he prepares to hang himself. "Good night, you black world!"[22] He is reminded to play his magic bells and Papagena appears, ushering in their exuberant love duet ("Pa-pa-pa-pa-pa-pa") constructed around a proliferation of pattersong syllables as they look forward to their projected proliferation of Papagenos and Papagenas.[23]

Ultimately, Papageno chooses to remain unenlightened and yet is welcome to remain with Papagena in Sarastro's realm. By contrast, the Queen of the Night

---

[16]   In this respect, Mozart's alteration of Schikaneder's original text from "reach toward the gods" to "reach toward godliness" (from "*Götter*" to "*Gottheit*") is significant, as Till explains. Till, *Mozart and the Enlightenment*, p. 285.

[17]   Waldoff, *Recognition in Mozart's Operas*, p. 37.

[18]   Act 2, Scene 3: "*Kämpfen ist meine Sache nicht. —Ich verlang' auch im Grunde gar keine Weisheit. Ich bin so ein Naturmensch, der sich mit Schlaf, Speise und Trank begnügt.*"

[19]   Act 2, Scene 23: "*O so ein sanftes Täubchen / wär' Seligkeit für mich! / Dann schmeckte mir Trinken und Essen, / dann könnt' ich mit Fürsten mich messen....*"

[20]   Act 2, Scene 23: "*Wird keine mir Liebe gewähren, / so muß mich die Flamme verzehren!*"

[21]   Act 2, Scene 25: "*Eh' ich mich zurückziehe, soll die Erde mich verschlingen.*"

[22]   Act 2, Scene 29: "*Müde bin ich meines Lebens!...Gute Nacht, du schwarze Welt!*"

[23]   Pattersong is a technique of rapid-fire text setting in opera, used especially for servant characters, which creates the comic effect of "patter."

and her Three Ladies are banished: their hostility to enlightenment is far more threatening than Papageno's ambivalence.[24] In Waldoff's reading, Papageno, "though unenlightened, might be understood to represent a necessary part of an enlightened universe: the commoner whose lot is improved by the betterment of society as a whole."[25] And though Papageno fails to reach enlightenment, he is changed by the journey.

The role of Papageno was originated by Emanuel Schikaneder, Mozart's collaborator on *The Magic Flute* and also the owner, manager, and one of the stars of the Theater auf der Wieden. Schikaneder's range was broad: he was well regarded in both comic and serious roles (Mozart saw him play Hamlet) and was also a singer, librettist, composer, director, and producer. His theater, located in the suburbs of Vienna and patronized by a broad cross-section of social classes, specialized in *Zauberoper* ("magic opera"): pieces demanding marvelous stage effects such as flying machines, elaborate lighting, thunder, fires, waterfalls, and trapdoors (all of which are used to good effect in *The Magic Flute*).[26]

In its plot and stage effects, then, *The Magic Flute* is unlike most of Mozart's other operas (which were commissioned by other theaters) but nevertheless shares with them a portrayal of individuals searching for emotional fulfillment.[27] The opera also represents a particularly Viennese type of hybrid. With its "combination of moral earnestness, comedy, and farce," according to Daniel Heartz, "*The Magic Flute* could have happened only at Vienna, where it crowned a century of German popular theater and a decade of Josephinian Enlightenment."[28] The opera was an immediate success at the premiere on September 30, 1791; over the course of the 1790s it reached most other European capitals, whether in the original German (sometimes clumsily adapted) or in translation. German versions had begun spreading from Vienna into other German-speaking areas in 1793 and translations to the local vernacular were popular elsewhere: the opera was first heard in Copenhagen in Danish in 1816.[29]

The crucial years for Kierkegaard's exposure to Mozart's operas begin with the 1831–32 season and conclude around 1844–45.[30] The experience of opera-going during this era stands in marked contrast to the wealth of music and ease of access

---

[24]   Jessica Waldoff, "*Die Zauberflöte*," in *The Cambridge Mozart Encyclopedia*, ed. by Cliff Eisen and Simon P. Keefe, Cambridge: Cambridge University Press 2006, pp. 540–53, see p. 550.

[25]   Waldoff, *Recognition in Mozart's Operas*, p. 41.

[26]   Waldoff, "*Die Zauberflöte*," p. 541.

[27]   Ibid., p. 540.

[28]   Daniel Heartz, "La Clemenza di Sarastro: Masonic Beneficence in the Last Operas," in *Mozart's Operas*, ed. by Thomas Bauman, Berkeley: University of California Press 1990, pp. 254–75, see p. 266.

[29]   Branscombe, *W.A. Mozart: Die Zauberflöte*, pp. 160–3.

[30]   An account of Kierkegaard's exposure to *The Magic Flute* is presented within a broader discussion of nineteenth-century reception in Copenhagen of Mozart's operas in Elisabete de Sousa's article, "Wolfgang Amadeus Mozart: The Love for Music and the Music of Love," in *Kierkegaard and the Renaissance and Modern Traditions*, Tome III, *Literature, Drama and Music*, ed. by Jon Stewart, Aldershot: Ashgate 2009 (*Kierkegaard Research: Sources, Reception and Resources*, vol. 5), pp. 137–67.

enjoyed by opera-goers today. For one thing, repeated exposure to any one work in its entirety would have been unlikely, even for those living in capital cities. In this era before recordings, therefore, one cannot underestimate the importance to opera reception of popular excerpts arranged for voice and piano in domestic performance. Secondly, only a subsection of Mozart's major efforts in the genre circulated as part of the repertory at this time. Nevertheless, Kierkegaard was able to attend performances in Copenhagen of *The Marriage of Figaro* (Vienna, 1786), *Don Giovanni* (Prague, 1787), and *The Magic Flute* (Vienna, 1791), all of which appeared repeatedly in multiple seasons.[31] With three theaters—the Royal Theater (enlarged in 1773), the Court Theater (renovated 1842), and the Vesterbro Nye or "New" Theater (built in 1834)—Copenhagen's opera life was vibrant and diverse; Mozart's operas appeared alongside works from the various subgenres that dominated programs in the early decades of the nineteenth century, including the Italian *bel canto* repertory, French *opéra comique*, and grand opera.

The most important difference in early nineteenth-century reception, however, was that Mozart's operas were nearly always presented in radically transformed versions: even when staged, they were often sung in translation and in adaptations of varying quality in order to appeal to local audiences and fit local dramatic traditions. Although in some cases, visiting troupes made more "authentic" performances possible,[32] Kierkegaard is likely to have attended performances that varied considerably from both the premiere versions and the versions familiar to us today. His declaration in response to a performance of *The Magic Flute* exemplifies this aspect of nineteenth-century reception: "the spoken lines, *which are either Schikaneder's or the Danish translator's*, are generally so lunatic and foolish that it is almost incomprehensible how Mozart has brought as much out of them as he has done."[33] That he attended opera performances frequently, however, is evident from his fascinating account in *Either/Or* of different vantage points in the theater: "I have sat close to the front; I have moved back more and more; I have sought a remote corner in the theater in order to be able to hide myself completely in this music."[34] It would seem that although the performances he viewed were a long way from the premieres overseen by Mozart, he immersed himself in Copenhagen's rich operatic offerings.

Kierkegaard's references to Papageno appear in volume one of *Either/Or*, specifically in the essay titled "The Immediate Erotic Stages or the Musical-Erotic,"[35] and in a journal entry relevant to "The Immediate Erotic Stages." The first volume of *Either/Or* comprises Kierkegaard's writings on the aesthetic realm of existence *per se*, although there are aesthetic dimensions in other of Kierkegaard's literary

---

[31]   Ibid., p. 142.

[32]   For example, an Italian company performed regularly at the Court Theater from 1842 to 1854 in a season that ran from November to April. See Claus Røllum-Larsen, "Copenhagen," *The New Grove Dictionary of Opera*, vols. 1–4, ed. by Stanley Sadie, London: Macmillan 1992, vol. 1, pp. 941–2.

[33]   Emphasis added. *SKS* 2, 89 / *EO1*, 83–4.

[34]   *SKS* 2, 122 / *EO1*, 120.

[35]   *SKS* 2, 53–136 / *EO1*, 47–135.

creations. Under many layers of pseudonyms in *Either/Or*, Kierkegaard delivers his musings on what is, in his judgment, the ideal musical creation. According to the author of "The Musical-Erotic," the pseudonym identified simply as "A," music is the most immediate form of sensuous existence.

The reader becomes privy to a direct statement from Kierkegaard on music through a journal reference to Homer, which can serve as a point of departure for Papageno's context for Kierkegaard's philosophy *in toto*. In the journal entry Kierkegaard writes: "What Homer says of music is true: οἷον ἀκούομεν οὐδέ τι ἴδμεν [we only hear, we know nothing]. *Iliad*, II, 486. One hears it, but one does not know, does not understand it."[36] For Kierkegaard music is perceived only sensuously and not grasped through any act of conscious understanding. The extent to which this musical ideal can be captured concretely by one specific opera is the task to be determined in "The Immediate Erotic Stages." Ultimately, A regards Mozart's *Don Giovanni* as the winner, since that musical piece fulfills the ideal of "that happy Greek view of the world that calls the world a κόσμος [cosmos],"[37] in which matter (the drama of the seducer, Don Juan, expressed through the dramaturgical play of *Don Giovanni*) meets its perfect form (Mozart's musical composition). This is to finalize A's goal of "uniting what belongs together,"[38] as dictated by the pinnacle of classical, idealist aesthetics.[39] To A's assessment the character of Don Giovanni is the supreme manifestation of the "champagne"[40] immediacy of music because the content of Don Giovanni's seductions dissolves effortlessly and effervescently into the form of Mozart's composition.

To this extent the Page from *The Marriage of Figaro* and Papageno from *The Magic Flute* provide "stages on the way" to the culmination of the musical perfection embodied by *Don Giovanni*. The three stages of the musical erotic mirror the trajectory of the three stages or spheres in Kierkegaard's *corpus*. This is important to consider for further contextualization of Papageno, for he represents the ethical moment, albeit one embedded in the immediacy of the aesthetic realm. Noteworthy is that A's interest in Papageno, and each of the three Mozart characters for that matter, lies in the perspective of the mythical nature of the respective characters, and not as a precise match to the way in which Mozart represents them through the operatic work. Within this mythical nature is a striving for enlightenment, which, however, falls short of any robust notion of a rational, autonomous-self. Hence, in some measure A's interpretation of Papageno suits the musicological renderings that regard the latter as a common, simple, even unenlightened man, although there are also important contrasts since A is not concerned to meet the operatic form with any exactness of representation.

Internal to the first manifestation of Kierkegaard's *oeuvre*, depicted in the aesthetic realm in volume one of *Either/Or*, the Page whiles away in the locomotion

---

[36]   *Pap.* IV A 222 / *JP* 1, 147.

[37]   *SKS* 2, 55 / *EO1*, 47.

[38]   Ibid.

[39]   For the quintessential characterization of this aesthetics see G.W.F. Hegel, *Aesthetics*, vols. 1–2, trans. by T.M. Knox, Oxford: Oxford University Press 1998 [1975].

[40]   *SKS* 2, 136 / *EO1*, 134.

of "dreaming," Papageno contemplates the activity of "seeking" and "discovering," and Don Giovanni thrives in the enjoyment of "desiring" *par excellence*. The three Mozartian characters represent three stages of desire in A's analysis. Within the "musical," the first moment of immediate form-taking for A, Papageno stands for the ethical questioning of what one desires. For this reason he is too complicated for A. As Elisabete de Sousa has documented, Papageno has a "complex dramaturgical context," which precludes A's satisfaction with him as the musical.[41]

In "The Immediate Erotic Stages" several appropriations of Hegel's dialectic are readily apparent and have a direct bearing on A's analysis. For example, the plant metaphor, well-known from the Preface to Hegel's *Phenomenology of Spirit*,[42] is conspicuously developed, whether as direct quotation or parody, through A's appropriation of both German Idealism and Romanticism.[43] Following the plant metaphor, in contrast to the Page's comfortable stability in his home setting of abstract desire, Papageno's "longing tears itself loose from the soil and takes to wandering,"[44] moving him away from a position as a firmly situated aesthete. Papageno loosens himself from the organic oneness of "being-there" with the ground in which he was naturally located, and through his own *sittliche* (ethical) restlessness positions himself upright, taking a stance through contemplation of his actions.[45] As A romanticizes further, "Just as the plant's life is confined to the soil, so the first stage [that of the Page] is captivated in substantial longing."[46] But in the next stage: "In Papageno, desire aims at discoveries. This urge to discover is the pulsation in it, its liveliness. It does not find the proper object of this exploration, but it discovered the multiplicity in seeking therein the object that it wants to discover."[47]

Papageno's self-dislocation mimics—at a basic and superficial level—the ethical move of later Kierkegaardian literary creations, Judge William of *Either/Or*, Part Two most prominently among them; these are individuals who choose themselves as ethical beings. Since Papageno appears in the aesthetic sphere, he does not become an ethical figure. But his character signifies the first yearning toward an ethical positioning of the self, albeit through an immediate and sensuously experiential form: music and desire in the face of ever-changing objects of seduction grapple with intimations of their own normative credibility. It is the ethical admixture within Papageno's aesthetic that makes his character, his music, and finally *The Magic Flute* itself "unmusical." A testifies: "Ethically qualified love or marital love is set

---

[41]   Sousa, "Wolfgang Amadeus Mozart: The Love for Music and the Music of Love," p. 153.

[42]   G.W.F. Hegel, *Phenomenology of Spirit*, trans. by A.V. Miller, Oxford: Oxford University Press 1977, p. 2.

[43]   See Marcia Morgan Vahrmeyer, "The Role of Music in Schleiermacher's and Kierkegaard's Writings," in *Schleiermacher und Kierkegaard. Subjektivität und Wahrheit*, ed. by Niels Jørgen Cappelørn et al., Berlin and New York: Walter de Gruyter 2006 (*Kierkegaard Studies Monograph Series*, vol. 11), pp. 93–106.

[44]   *SKS* 2, 86 / *EO1*, 80.

[45]   *Sittlichkeit* (here in the form of the adjective *sittlich*) refers to Hegel's notion of ethicality or ethical life, based on the German *Sitte* (in English: "customs" or "norms").

[46]   *SKS* 2, 86 / *EO1*, 80.

[47]   Ibid.

as the goal of the action, and therein lies the play's basic defect, for whatever that is, ecclesiastically or secularly speaking, one thing it is not, it is not musical—indeed it is absolutely unmusical."[48] One exception to this, as Tschuggnall has commented, takes place in Papageno's opening aria; this can be considered "musical" to A.[49]

Papageno "overcomes all kinds of obstacles to gain his ideal partner for marriage,"[50] thus suspending his own desire at crucial junctures. Whereas the Page is content to find pleasure in the longing for an ever-revolving series of objects, which are not enjoyed as conquests but offer pleasure solely through the loftiness of the abstract possibility of their seduction, Papageno fixates on only one object (much like Judge William of *Either/Or*, Part Two chooses to marry his "first love") and through this focus fractures the object of his fixation into a multiplicity. A compares Papageno's process of discovery to an earthquake,

> [which] splits the desire from its object infinitely for a moment; but just as the moving principle shows itself for a moment as disuniting, so it manifests itself in turn as wanting to unite the separated. The result of the separation is that desire is torn out of its substantial repose in itself, and as a consequence of this, the object no longer falls under the rubric of substantiality but splits up into a multiplicity.[51]

What once appeared for Papageno as a unitary object, the woman of his affection, has now, upon the recognition of the tendency toward consciousness—an ethical awakening internal to an aesthetic experience of desiring—become divided upon itself.

Through the introduction of an ethical questioning of seduction a visual element enters into Papageno's musical field, described alternatively as the eye of the soul, an internal tendency toward consciousness, and a process of awakening. All of this muddles the crystal clarity of the dreamlike sensate experience characterized by the Page. Giovanni, by comparison, has no qualms about the acts of his conquests; indeed the latter identifies himself with an aestheticized religiosity about his character as a seducer and takes full delight in it. Giovanni is not yet as reflective as the Johannes of the "Diary of a Seducer," which closes *Either/Or*, Part One; but Giovanni thrives

---

[48]   *SKS* 2, 88 / *EO1*, 83. In the sentence just before this one, "A" explains that the problem in *The Magic Flute* "is that the whole piece tends toward consciousness, and as a consequence the actual tendency of the piece is to annul the music, and yet it is supposed to be an opera." What stands as a fault for "A" (the dramatization of consciousness) is lauded as a central theme in recent musicological readings of the opera as an allegory of Enlightenment in which the protagonists seek "knowledge *of* the self and *for* the self," in Jessica Waldoff's words. Waldoff, *Recognition in Mozart's Operas*, p. 20. See also Till, *Mozart and the Enlightenment*, p. 285.

[49]   Peter Tschuggnall, *Søren Kierkegaards Mozart Rezeption. Analyse einer philosophisch-literarischen Deutung von Musik im Kontext des Zusammenspiels der Künste*, Frankfurt am Main: Peter Lang 1982 (*Europaische Hochschuleschriften*, vol. 364), pp. 121–5.

[50]   Sousa, "Wolfgang Amadeus Mozart: The Love for Music and the Music of Love," p. 153.

[51]   *SKS* 2, 86 / *EO1*, 80.

on his activity as a superficial womanizer. In this sense A does not regard Giovanni as the fullest manifestation of a seducer, but only as an individual who desires: "[Don Giovanni] does not seduce. He desires, and this desire acts seductively."[52] If Don Giovanni is desiring *only*, according to A, Papageno is not desiring enough.

---

[52]   *SKS* 2, 102 / *EO1*, 99.

Bibliography

Dunning, Stephen, "The Dialectic of Contradiction in Kierkegaard's Aesthetic Stage," *Journal of the American Academy of Religion*, vol. 49, no. 3, 1981, pp. 383–408.

Görner, Rüdiger, "*Die Zauberflöte* in Kierkegaards *Entweder-oder*," *Mozart-Jahrbuch*, 1980, pp. 247–57.

Honolka, Kurt, *Papageno: Emanuel Schikaneder, Man of the Theater in Mozart's Time*, trans. by Jane Mary Wilde, Portland: Amadeus Press 1990, p. 106.

Kost, Otto-Hubert, *Von der Möglichkeit. Das Phänomen des selbstschöpferischen Möglichkeit in seinen kosmogonischen, mythisch-personifizierten und denkerisch-künsterlischen Realisierung als divergenz-theologisches Problem*, Göttingen: Vanderhoeck & Ruprecht 1978, p. 72; p. 79.

Petersen, Nils Holger, "Frihed og Form hos Mozart," *Transfiguration. Nordisk Tidsskrift for Kunst og Kristendom*, vol. 1, no. 1, 1999, pp. 117–39.

Pieper, Annemarie, *Søren Kierkegaard*, Munich: C.H. Beck 2000, p. 64.

Schellong, Dieter, "Annäherungen an Mozart. Ein Beitrag zum Verhältnis von weltanschaulicher und praktischer Interpretation," *Anstösse. Materialien für Theorie und Praxis*, vol. 27, no. 1, 1980, pp. 10–34.

Sousa, Elisabete M. de, "Wolfgang Amadeus Mozart: The Love for Music and the Music of Love," in *Kierkegaard and the Renaissance and Modern Traditions*, ed. by Jon Stewart, Aldershot: Ashgate 2009 (*Kierkegaard Research: Sources, Reception and Resources*, vol. 5), pp. 137–67.

Subotnik, Rose Rosengard, "Whose *Magic Flute*? Intimations of Reality at the Gates of the Enlightenment," in her *Deconstructive Variations: Music and Reason in Western Society*, Minneapolis: University of Minnesota Press 1996, pp. 1–38, see pp. 3–5.

Till, Nicholas, *Mozart and the Enlightenment: Truth, Virtue and Beauty in Mozart's Operas*, London: W.W. Norton 1992, p. 285.

Tschuggnall, Peter, "Papageno contra Tamino: Mozarts Mysterienspiel *Die Zauberflöte* in der eigenwilligen Deutung Søren Kierkegaards," in *Welttheater, Mysterienspiel, Rituelles Theater: "Vom Himmel durch die Welt zur Hölle";— Gesammelte Vorträge des Salzburger Symposions 1991*, ed. by Jürgen Kühnel, Ulrich Müller, Oswald Panagl, Peter Csobádi, Gernot Gruber, and Franz Viktor Spechtler, Anif-Salzburg: Müller-Speiser 1992, pp. 243–50.

— *Søren Kierkegaards Mozart Rezeption. Analyse einer philosophisch-literarischen Deutung von Musik im Kontext des Zusammenspiels der Künste*, Frankfurt am Main et al.: Peter Lang 1982 (*Europaische Hochschuleschriften*, vol. 364), pp. 121–5.

Per Degn:

Towards Kierkegaard's Genealogy of the Morals of the Servitors of the State Church

Gabriel Guedes Rossatti

I. Introduction: Per Degn as Holberg's Deacon

Per Degn, or rather "Deacon Per" (the Danish word *degn*, coming from the Greek διάκονος, meaning "server" or "helper," which has its exact equivalent in English as *deacon*) is one of the characters portrayed in Ludvig Holberg's (1684–1754) play entitled *Erasmus Montanus or Rasmus Berg*. This work was presumably written in 1723 and first published in 1731 but only performed for the first time in Danish in 1747.[1] (Prior to its first Danish performance the play had been performed in Hamburg in 1742.) There are many possible reasons that would explain the delay in its performance. Perhaps it was due to the fact that Holberg, while producing and publishing a play which contains an overt criticism of empty scholarship, was a prominent member of the University of Copenhagen and he feared the work would alienate his fellow scholars. Or perhaps its performance was delayed because its subject matter or theme, formalistic learning versus useful *dannelse*, did not appeal to a broader audience. This comedy was never a success in Holberg's lifetime, or for that matter in the rest of the eighteenth century, and had to wait until the Golden Age to enjoy a wider recognition. Holberg occupied the chair of metaphysics (from 1717 to 1720), then was the chair of Latin oratory (from 1720 to 1730), and then assumed the chair of history (from 1730 onwards). In 1735 he became the rector of the university for one year (1735–36) and from 1737 to 1751 was its bursar.[2] "Deacon Per," while being a secondary character in *Erasmus Montanus*, is a vehicle for a satire on the emptiness and pretentiousness of knowledge, specifically *scholastic* knowledge, based on Latin, the *learned* language of the time. Apart from this characteristic, Per Degn is also a man who, according to Christian Molbech's definition of "deacon," is

---

[1]   This information can be found in Ludvig Holberg, *Jeppe of the Hill and Other Comedies*, trans. and ed. by Gerald S. Argetsinger and Sven H. Rossel, Carbondale and Edwardsville: Southern Illinois University Press 1990, p. 147. The original text of *Erasmus Montanus* is accessible in the new critical, annotated edition of Holberg's writings, *Ludvig Holbergs Skrifter*, at http://holbergsskrifter.dk, published digitally by the Society for Danish Language and Literature and the University of Bergen.

[2]   See Sven H. Rossel, "Holberg and His Times," in Ludvig Holberg, *Jeppe of the Hill and Other Comedies*, pp. xiii–xxiii.

a "servitor of the Church," understood as one who sings and generally helps priests in the service of God,[3] and as such Holberg also aimed at revealing through this character the concrete power of the knowledge of the members of the upper classes over the uneducated peasants in a vastly rural Denmark. This latter aspect, as will be seen, could not fail to attract Kierkegaard's attention, since his father was of humble origin, being originally a peasant from Jutland. As his polemical career unfolded, he sided more and more with the "common man," to the detriment of the bourgeois upper classes, which were composed of many members, or rather *servitors* (such as his own brother, the pastor Peter Christian Kierkegaard) of the State Church.[4]

All of this is to say that Per Degn, precisely on account of the fact that he represents a middle point between secular and religious affairs, embodies *power* in a play whose main character, Rasmus Berg, is one of the two sons of a couple of simple, uneducated peasants.[5] After having finished his studies in Copenhagen, the latter goes back home, supposedly for a short time; however, Berg, now demanding that everyone call him "Monsieur Montanus,"[6] has become arrogant with his recently acquired knowledge. He says, I cannot "talk much with my poor parents; they're simple folks and don't know much more than their childhood catechism, so their association doesn't provide much comfort....I can't live without disputations!"[7] So he seeks to dispute in Latin with the deacon of the village, Per, an older man who supposedly had acquired some learning while Berg was still in his infancy. But it becomes clear that Per's knowledge of Latin, about which he boasts, is very poor and can only impress ignorant people.

However, more than being a mere sham in scholarly matters, Per Degn really seems to be a forerunner of Kierkegaard's late notion of what being a priest was about.[8] In this sense, a brief monologue by Per deserves to be quoted at length since it gives a very good idea of how he himself understood his own calling:

> PER: [*Alone.*] To tell the truth, I'm not very anxious for Rasmus Berg to get home. It's not because I'm afraid of his education; after all, I was already an old student when he was still a schoolboy....I only became a deacon, but I'm content so long as I get my daily bread and understand my duties. I've been improving my income a lot and live better than any of my predecessors, so those who follow me won't curse me in my grave. People think there's nothing to being a deacon; yeah, sure! Believe me, the deacon's calling is very difficult when you must carry it far enough to provide for you. Before my

³   Christian Molbech, *Dansk Ordbog indeholdende det danske Sprogs Stammeord*, vols. 1–2, Copenhagen: Gyldendal 1855, vol. 1, p. 161.
⁴   Regarding Kierkegaard's form of "populism" and the criticism of the State Church that it implies, see Jørgen Bukdhal, *Søren Kierkegaard and The Common Man*, trans. by Bruce Kirmmse, Grand Rapids, Michigan: Eerdmans 2001.
⁵   On this character, see more specifically Julie Allen, "Erasmus Montanus: The Tragi-Comic Victim of the Crowd," in *Kierkegaard's Literary Figures and Motifs*, Tome I, *Agamemnon to Elvira*, ed. by Jon Stewart and Katalin Nun, Aldershot: Ashgate 2014 (*Kierkegaard Research: Sources, Reception and Resources*, vol. 16), pp. 201–8.
⁶   Ludvig Holberg, *Erasmus Montanus or Rasmus Berg*, in *Jeppe of the Hill and Other Comedies*, p. 159 (Act II, Scene 2).
⁷   Ibid., p. 158 (Act II, Scene 1).
⁸   In this sense, see *SKS* 13, 383 / *M*, 321.

time, people here in town thought one funeral hymn was as good as the other, but I've carried it so far that I can say to a peasant, "Which hymn do you want? This one costs so much and that one so much." It's the same with tossing soil on the deceased, "Do you want fine sand or plain old dirt?" There are other considerations that my predecessor, Deacon Christoffer, never even heard of! But he wasn't learned. I can't understand how that man ever became a deacon. But he was a deacon accordingly. Latin helps a man a lot in all of his business. I would't do without my Latin, not for a hundred rix-dollars! It's already benefited me in my calling more than a hundred rix-dollars, yes and a hundred more.[9]

Holberg's Per Degn already pointed to those dubious characters who, over a century later, Johannes Climacus would allude to when in the *Concluding Unscientific Postscript* he mentions those "pastors [who] turn their clerical robes inside out so that they might almost look like professors' gowns."[10] So now it remains to be seen how Kierkegaard appropriated this character throughout his career.

II. Per Degn as Kierkegaard's Prototypical Deacon

Kierkegaard, who throughout his life seems to have written the deacon's name exclusively as "Peer" (and not "Per"), owned the Høpffner edition of 1788, in which Holberg's plays are presented in seven tomes.[11] Per Degn is mentioned 19 times, with 5 of these appearing in his published writings from the so-called "first authorship," that is, the works published up until the *Concluding Unscientific Postscript*. He is mentioned once in an unpublished work (namely, *The Book on Adler*). Finally there are 13 private annotations, which in a sense take up from where the public appearances of "the deacon" had been interrupted, since they start in 1845 and eventually come to an end in 1854. This pattern shows that Kierkegaard had a lifelong interest in the character of Per Degn. I will argue that this figure was appropriated by him with different intentions as his career unfolded; consequently, the best way to understand Kierkegaard's ongoing interest in this character is to follow a diachronic analysis of his engagement with Holberg's deacon.

Kierkegaard's very first mention of Per Degn occurs in *The Concept of Irony* and more particularly in a footnote in which Socrates, as portrayed in Aristophanes' play *The Clouds*, is compared with Per Degn for "his linguistic hairsplitting."[12] In *Repetition*, Per Degn is mentioned once in passing in a letter by the "young man"

---

[9]   Holberg, *Erasmus Montanus or Rasmus Berg*, in *Jeppe of the Hill and Other Comedies*, pp. 152–3 (Act I, Scene 3).
[10]   *SKS* 7, 167 / *CUP1*, 181. In this sense, see also Kierkegaard's sketch from 1848–49 (and in which Per Degn is mentioned) entitled " 'The Preacher' and the Schoolteacher," in *SKS* 27, 465–8, Papir 391 / *JP* 3, 3138.
[11]   Ludvig Holberg, *Den Danske Skue-Plads, deelt udi 7 Tomer*, Parts 1–7 in 2 volumes, Copenhagen: J.J. Høpffner [1788] (*ASKB* 1566–1567). This edition of the comedies was the third reprint of *Den Danske Skue-Plads*, which had originally appeared in tomes 1–5, 1731, and tomes 6–7, 1753–4.
[12]   *SKS* 1, 201n / *CI*, 151n.

to Constantin Constantius.[13] In *Stages on Life's Way*, and more particularly in the diary written by Quidam, one sees Per Degn being engaged by the latter in that he, justifying his stance as a "scoundrel," confesses that "[i]f one just says something silly and drinks *dus* with humanity *en masse*, then one comes to be, like Per Degn, loved and esteemed by the whole congregation."[14] This reading of Per Degn, which downplays his faulty or nonexistent Latin in favor of his social hypocrisy, seems to mark the beginning of Kierkegaard's later polemical views on this character. In the *Concluding Unscientific Postscript*, however, two different passages mention very briefly Per Degn, but neither of these problematizes the character.[15] Thus, however brief the allusions to this character in the published writings may be, they seem to retain a common understanding of Per Degn fundamentally as a poor scholar.

However, this interpretation radically changed in Kierkegaard's so-called "second authorship," that is, the one that began after the infamous *Corsair* affair and which led him to a greater socio-political awareness. This is something which was attested by Kierkegaard himself in the following words: "As author I have gotten a new string on my instrument and have been made capable of producing notes that I never would have dreamed of otherwise….I have come to 'actuality' in the stricter sense of the term."[16]

Now, Kierkegaard's first mention of Per Degn in his private annotations seems to have occurred in 1845. Here Kierkegaard compares a priest's lack of knowledge of the litany which he had witnessed in a service he had (supposedly) recently attended to Per Degn's lack of knowledge of the Greek litany, since the latter, in Holberg's play, is portrayed as saying that "twenty years ago I could stand on one foot and read the entire Litany in Greek. I can still remember the very last word: Amen."[17] In 1849, this aspect of Holberg's character would be taken up again in another entry.[18] Later in this same year, though, Kierkegaard indirectly associated Per Degn in an entry entitled "The Status of Prof. Martensen" with none other than Hans Lassen Martensen, the future bishop of Zealand.[19] In 1851, he compared the latter's predecessor, that is, Bishop Mynster,[20] as well as the Pope, to Per Degn.[21] In 1854, he makes "Dr. Rudelbach" the target of the comparison.[22] This, then, shows that Kierkegaard started to problematize the character much more in terms of Per Degn's role as a *deacon* than in terms of his role as a *scholar*, as had been the case in his published writings.

[13] See *SKS* 4, 71 / *R*, 203.
[14] See *SKS* 6, 316 / *SLW*, 340.
[15] See *SKS* 7, 66 / *CUP1*, 64; *SKS* 7, 181 / *CUP1*, 198.
[16] *SKS* 22, 390, NB14:77 / *KJN* 6, 394.
[17] See *SKS* 27, 333, Papir 322 / *JP* 3, 3471. See Holberg, *Erasmus Montanus or Rasmus Berg*, in *Jeppe of the Hill and Other Comedies*, p. 155 (Act I, Scene 4).
[18] See *SKS* 22, 52, NB11:91 / *KJN* 6, 48.
[19] See *SKS* 22, 325ff., NB13:86 / *KJN* 6, 329ff.
[20] See *SKS* 24, 307–8, NB23:209.
[21] See *SKS* 24, 396–7, NB24:120 / *JP* 3, 2539.
[22] See *SKS* 26, 262–3, NB33:20 / *JP* 4, 3869. It should also be mentioned that in the unpublished work, *The Book on Adler* Kierkegaard had also drawn a comparison between Per Degn and Adler; see *SKS* 15, 242 / *BA*, 296.

That Kierkegaard more and more linked the figure of Per Degn not only to the Danish clergy specifically, but to the clergy generally is better seen in an entry from 1854 entitled "The Priest," in which one reads:

> As in so much of what Peer Degn said, there is something typical in these lines also: "If you want fine sand, it will cost so much; if you want coarse sand, it will cost so much."
>
> Basically, this explains the existence of the entire clerical officialdom.
>
> In vain does God have it proclaimed that he is love, that everyone, unconditionally everyone, is able to address him directly, that God is very glad to have him do it.
>
> In vain. This is too high for man; he cannot get it into his head; dares not believe it. Then "the priest" comes to his aid and sets things right, satisfies man's deep need to be fooled—Peer Degn was very accomplished in this. "The priest" introduces gradations, a whole cast of officials—and everywhere there is money to be paid.[23]

This passage was Kierkegaard's last reference to Per Degn. It synthesizes his "late" reading of the figure, which accords perfectly with his attack on the amalgam between the state and the church. In this sense, then, the apparently harmless deacon Per seems to function as an invaluable mark in terms of Kierkegaard's problematization of the genealogy of the morals of the servitors of the State Church, for, as seen, Holberg's character "Per Degn" ends up not only representing, but also, as Kierkegaard himself put it, *explaining* nothing more and nothing less than "the existence of the *entire* clerical officialdom."

---

[23]   *SKS* 26, 318, NB34:7 / *JP* 3, 3185.

Bibliography

Watkin, Julia, "Holberg, Ludvig" in her *Historical Dictionary of Kierkegaard's Philosophy*, Lanham: Scarecrow Press 2001, pp. 121–2.

Prometheus:

Thief, Creator, and Icon of Pain

Markus Pohlmeyer

I. Myth

Prometheus/Προμηθεύς—son of the Titan Iapetus, father of Deukalion, according to a specific reading of the tradition—is one of the most prominent figures of Greek mythology. This myth with its variety of elements had a significant impact on world literature, the arts and even film under different aspects, for example, the revolt against the gods, the creation of man or the archetype of the ingenious artist.[1] The Prometheus myth passes through different metamorphoses. A negative figure in the beginning, Prometheus is increasingly represented in a tragic and at the same time more positive way in the course of reception. Finally, the famous dictum in Karl Marx's doctoral thesis praises him as follows: "*Prometheus ist der vornehmste Heilige und Märtyrer im philosophischen Kalender.*"[2]

The first literary evidence for the Prometheus myth can be found in Hesiod's hexameter poetry in the *Theogony* and *Works and Days*, though interestingly enough not in Homer's works. In the *Theogony,* the narration of the myth starts with Prometheus' punishment:

> And with painful fetters he [sc. Zeus] bound shifty-planning Prometheus, with distressful bonds, driving them through the middle of a pillar; and he set upon him a long-winged eagle which ate his immortal liver, but this grew again on all sides at night just as much as the long-winged bird would eat during the whole day.[3]

Subsequently Hercules delivers Prometheus from his ordeal. The reason for the punishment is that Prometheus, cunning and seeking to deceive, betrayed the

---

[1]   For more details see Philipp Theisohn, "Prometheus," in *Der Neue Pauly. Enzyklopädie der Antike, Supplemente*, vols. 1–14, ed. by Manfred Landfester and Helmuth Schneider, trans. by Regina Spöttl, Stuttgart and Weimar: J.B. Metzler 2004-, vol. 5, *Mythenrezeption. Die antike Mythologie in Literatur, Musik und Kunst von den Anfängen bis zur Gegenwart*, ed. by Maria Moog-Grünewald, pp. 605–21.

[2]   Karl Marx, *Doktordissertation (1841)*, 2nd ed., ed. by Georg Mende and Ernst Günther Schmidt, Jena: Friedrich-Schiller-Universität, n.d. (*Jenaer Reden und Schriften*), p. 25.

[3]   Hesiod, *Theogony*, verses 521–5, in Hesiod, *Theogony, Works and Days, Testimonia*, ed. and trans. by Glenn W. Most, reprinted and corrected ed., Cambridge, Massachusetts and London: Harvard University Press 2010 (*Loeb Classical Library*), p. 45.

gods during a sacrifice and even stole fire for mankind. In revenge, Zeus makes Hephaestus fashion a virgin who is then endowed with great beauty by Athena. This virgin was to be the ancestress of all women and the source of all evil for men, both for the wed and the unwed. The intentions of the myth are manifold here. With a sequence of etiologies, sacrificial rites, the use of fire, and the origin of women are to be explained. And Zeus appears as the sovereign guarantor of order.

In his later work *Works and Days*, Hesiod varies and amends the Prometheus myth. The robbery of the fire is immediately followed by the creation of a girl made out of clay: "and the messenger of the gods placed a voice in her and named this woman Pandora (All-Gift), since all those who have their mansions on Olympus had given her a gift—a woe for men who live on bread."[4] Then Zeus sent Pandora to Epimetheus, Prometheus' brother: "And Epimetheus did not consider that Prometheus had told him never to accept a gift from Olympian Zeus, but to send it back again, lest something evil happen to mortals; it was only after he accepted her, when he already had the evil, that he understood."[5] Hesiod skillfully plays with the etymology revealed by the name itself, which means "pre-thinker" (derived from προ- and the stem μηθ-/μαθ-).[6] *Epimetheus* would then consequently mean "after-thinker"—also perceived as someone who is left behind with nothing, just as in Hesiod's myth. For Epimetheus' acting was not without serious consequences: previously mankind had lived in a kind of Golden Age, "[b]ut the woman removed the great lid from the storage jar[7] with her hands and scattered all its contents abroad—she wrought baneful evils for human beings. Only Anticipation [hope][8] remained...and did not fly out."[9]

The misogynic tendency is maintained, and in spite of his care for mankind Prometheus remains the point of departure of a negative turnaround. While the legitimacy of Prometheus' acting remains questionable in Hesiod, Aeschylus in his

---

[4]   Hesiod, *Works and Days* in Hesiod, *Theogony, Works and Days, Testimonia*, verses 79–82; ibid., p. 93.

[5]   Ibid., verses 85–9; p. 93.

[6]   See the article "Prometheus," in *Der Neue Pauly. Enzyklopädie der Antike*, vols. 1–16, ed. by Hubert Cancik and Helmuth Schneider, Stuttgart and Weimar: J.B. Metzler 1996–2003, vol. 10, p. 402: "*P[rometheus] ist genuin griech[isch] und bedeutet soviel wie 'der Vorbedenker' aus προ- und μηθ-/μαθ- (aus idg. *mendh-/*men-, 'denken')*."

[7]   Pandora's famous box is due to a translation error by Erasmus of Rotterdam. See Immanuel Musäus, *Der Pandoramythos bei Hesiod und seine Rezeption bei Erasmus von Rotterdam*, Göttingen: Vandenhoeck & Ruprecht 2004, pp. 179–82. A resumption of the Pandora myth can be found in Kierkegaard's work "In vino veritas" from *Stages on Life's Way*. See *SKS* 6, 73–4 / *SLW*, 74.

[8]   I would prefer the more traditional translation of the Greek ἐλπίς as "hope." Cf. also *Hesiod and Theognis*, trans. by Dorothea Wender, London: Penguin 1973, p. 62.

[9]   Hesiod, *Works and Days*, verses 94–8, in Hesiod, *Theogony, Works and Days, Testimonia*, p. 95. Otto Schönberger refers to many illogical passages of the story, for example, that Pandora herself is evil incarnate; see Hesiod, *Werke und Tage*, trans. and ed. by Otto Schönberger, Stuttgart: Philipp Reclam jun. 2011, pp. 68–9.

drama *Prometheus Bound,* whose authenticity is still under debate,[10] reinterprets the myth along with apologetic tendencies, as pointed out by Philipp Theisohn.[11] Zeus is now negatively described as a tyrant: "In return mankind owes everything to P[rometheus]; he does not yet act in a literal but already in a metaphorical sense as a demiurge. He not only brings fire, but also the arts…and—most important—'blind hope' which he plants into the hearts of mankind."[12]

Plato's version of the myth in his dialogue *Protagoras* assigns a central function to Epimetheus. Although the gods entrusted both brothers with the endowment of all mortal races, Epimetheus takes over the allocation of abilities—and at first not at all unskillfully:

> To some creatures he attributed strength without swiftness, the weaker ones he endowed with speed….Now Thinxtoolate wasn't all that smart, and before he knew it he'd used up all the available abilities on the non-reasoning animals. That meant he still had human beings on his hands, with no embellishments at all. And he simply didn't know what to do with them. And while he sat there with no idea what to do, along came Thinxahead…. Now it was Thinxahead who didn't know what to do: he couldn't come up with any way for human beings to survive, so he stole: he stole the technical ingenuity that belonged to Hephaestus and Athena, along with fire….By that means human beings at least acquired the kind of intelligence they needed to remain alive, but what they didn't have was civic and ethical intelligence.[13]

There is only a minor reference to the fact that *Prometheus/Thinxahead* was punished for this theft. However, the nature of the punishment is not mentioned since it is traditionally considered well known. In addition, Zeus thus appears in a more favorable light. It is Zeus who, with Hermes as a mediator, conveys to mankind the concept of justice as the basis of all political communal life. Justice is *the* gift equally bestowed on all human beings.[14] Based on Plato, the further development of the myth can be outlined as follows:

> The image of the founder of culture is continuously coming to the fore and is later on—as e.g. in Aristophanes's *Birds,* in Philemon and Menander and finally in Ovid's *Metamorphoses*[15]—logically exaggerated in Prometheus's transfiguration as the creator of mankind. More and more, P[rometheus] advances to an allegory of a certain anthropological finding which declares *téchnē* the centre of human existence and whose manifestation is sophism.[16]

---

[10]   See Robert Bees, *Zur Datierung des Prometheus Desmotes,* Stuttgart: Teubner 1993 (*Beiträge zur Altertumskunde,* vol. 38).

[11]   Theisohn, "Prometheus," p. 606.

[12]   Ibid.

[13]   Plato, *Protagoras,* 320d–321d, in Plato, *Protagoras and Meno,* trans. by Adam Beresford, London: Penguin 2005, see pp. 20–1.

[14]   Ibid., 322c–d.

[15]   Ovid, *Metamorphoses,* Book 1, verses 78–83 and 390.

[16]   Theison, "Prometheus," p. 606 (trans. by Regina Spöttl).

II. Kierkegaard's Sources

The impressive workload of Greek literature that the pupil Kierkegaard had already to cope with included selections from Homer, Plato (*Crito, Euthyphro*), Xenophon, Herodotus, and the Gospel of John.[17] The works of Aeschylus, however, were presumably not among these works: "Apparently, Kierkegaard was not familiar with Greek tragedy from his time at the Borgerdyd School....We cannot even be certain if at any time later he read Aeschylus in Greek. At the time of his death, Kierkegaard's library contained only German and Danish translations: in German, the second edition of Johann Gustav Droysen's (1808–84) *Des Aischylos Werke* (Berlin 1842)."[18] The following passage of Droysen's translation makes clear that Kierkegaard knows this very well because he—or his pseudonym—in *Either/Or* inverts the sense of Aeschylus[19] provokingly:

> *Chor*: Du bist doch weitergegangen, als du sagst?
> *Prometheus*: Ich nahm's den Menschen, ihr Geschickt vorauszusehen.
> *Chor*: Sag, welch Mittel fandest du für dieses Gift?
> *Prometheus*: Der blinden Hoffnung gab ich Raum in ihrer Brust.[20]

Kierkegaard read Hesiod in the original texts but also through Plato's works. Nicolae Irina concludes:

> Kierkegaard was acquainted with ancient Greek texts in general, and he was familiar with many of Hesiod's theogonic tenets in particular. Nevertheless, direct references in Kierkegaard's writings to Hesiod and his works are scarce....In fact, there are some editorial notes that offer some direct references to Hesiod, but only by the way of quotations from Plato's dialogues. These notes illustrate how Kierkegaard, while reading Plato, had the opportunity to consider Hesiod's thought.[21]

---

[17]   See, for instance, *Encounters with Kierkegaard: A Life as Seen by His Contemporaries*, ed. by Bruce H. Kirmmse, Princeton: Princeton University Press 1996, p. 16; p. 273.

[18]   Finn Gredal Jensen, "Aeschylus: Kierkegaard and Early Greek Tragedy," in *Kierkegaard and the Greek World*, Tome II, *Aristotle and Other Greek Authors*, ed. by Jon Stewart and Katalin Nun, Aldershot: Ashgate 2010 (*Kierkegaard Research: Sources, Reception and Resources*, vol. 2), p. 222.

[19]   See below Section III, B. Aeschylus.

[20]   See Aischylos, *Tragödien*, nach der Übersetzung von Johann Gustav Droysen (Berlin 1832), Frankfurt am Main: Fischer 2008, p. 263. See also *Aeschylus: Prometheus Bound...*, trans. by Philip Vellacott, London: Penguin 1961, p. 28: "Chorus: Did your offence perhaps go further than you have said? Prometheus: Yes: I caused men no longer to foresee their death. Chorus: What cure did you discover for their misery? Prometheus: I planted firmly in their hearts blind hopefulness."

[21]   Nicolae Irina, "Hesiod: Kierkegaard and the Greek Gods," in *Kierkegaard and the Greek World*, Tome II, *Aristotle and Other Greek Authors*, p. 264. None of Hesiod's works are mentioned in the *The Auction Catalogue of Kierkegaard's Library*.

Kierkegaard also owned a translation of Plato's works by Schleiermacher.[22] As further sources for the myth, Kierkegaard most likely made use of the comprehensive dictionary published by Nitsch[23] and the less elaborated dictionary published by Vollmer.[24] Of further importance is the fact that both Vollmer and Nitsch use the German term *Adler* ("eagle") in their dictionaries.[25]

Traces of Kierkegaard's reception of the Prometheus myth in the works of ancient theologians—such as Tertullian[26] and Augustine[27]—as well as in the Renaissance, for example, in Boccaccio,[28] are seemingly not to be found in his works. Only Kierkegaard's explicit reference to the preface of Shelley's verse drama *Prometheus Unbound* of 1820[29] allows a glimpse of the Romantic reception of the subject matter:

> The only imaginary being resembling in any degree Prometheus, is Satan; and Prometheus is, in my judgment, a more poetical character than Satan....Prometheus is, as it were, the type of the highest perfection of moral and intellectual nature, impelled by the purest and the truest motives to the best and noblest ends.[30]

Kierkegaard was able to read Shelley's *Prometheus Unbound* by means of a German translation.[31]

---

[22]   See Katalin Nun, "Cumulative Plato Bibliography," in *Kierkegaard and the Greek World*, Tome I, *Socrates and Plato*, ed. by Jon Stewart and Katalin Nun, Aldershot: Ashgate 2010 (*Kierkegaard Research: Sources, Reception and Resources*, vol. 2), p. 147.

[23]   Paul Friedrich Achatus Nitsch, *Neues mythologisches Wörterbuch für studirende Jünglinge, angehende Künstler und jeden Gebildeten überhaupt*, vols. 1–2, ed. by Friedrich Gotthilf Klopfer, 2nd ed., Leipzig and Sorau: Fleischer 1821 [1793] (*ASKB* 1944–1945).

[24]   Wilhelm Vollmer, *Vollständiges Wörterbuch der Mythologie aller Nationen. Eine gedrängte Zusammenstellung des Wissenswürdigen aus der Fabel- und Götterlehre aller Völker der alten und neuen Welt. In einem Bande mit einem englischen Stahlstich und 129 Tafeln*, Stuttgart: Hoffmann 1836 (*ASKB* 1942–1943).

[25]   See below Section III, A. Hesiod.

[26]   Tertullian, *Apologetikum/Verteidigung des Christentums*, lateinisch und deutsch, ed. and trans. by Carl Becker, 4th ed., Munich: Kösel-Verlag 1992, p. 120 [cap. 18]: "*...praedicarent deum unicum esse...hic enim est verus Prometheus....*"

[27]   See Augustine, *Civitas Dei*, chapter 18, 8.

[28]   See Boccaccio, *Genealogiae Deorum Gentilium*, 4, 44.

[29]   *SKS* 18, 228, JJ:280 / *KJN* 2, 209.

[30]   See Percy Bysshe Shelley, "Preface," in *The Complete Poetical Works of Shelley*, ed. by Thomas Hutchinson, Oxford: Oxford University Press 1952, p. 205.

[31]   See *Percy Bysshe Shelleys Poetische Werke in einem Band*, trans. by Julius Seybt, Leipzig: Wilhelm Engelmann 1844 (*ASKB* 1898). See also Bartholomew Ryan, "Percy Bysshe Shelley: Anxious Journeys, the Demonic and 'Breaking the Silence,'" in *Kierkegaard and the Renaissance and Modern Traditions*, Tome III, *Literature, Drama and Music*, ed. by Jon Stewart, Aldershot: Ashgate 2009 (*Kierkegaard Research: Sources, Reception and Resources*, vol. 5), pp. 215–24.

III. Prometheus in Kierkegaard's Works

Prometheus is mentioned explicitly six times in Kierkegaard's printed works and five times in his journals, notebooks, and published papers, whereas *Don Juan* is mentioned 110 times in the first category and a further 18 times in the second. This fact may be an argument for the marginality of the Prometheus myth in Kierkegaard's works. However, it is no indicator of its relevance in the respective textual passages, as will be shown below. My thesis is that several passages where Kierkegaard alludes to aspects of the Prometheus myth mirror the context of the respective source. By adhering to this pattern, the texts will be presented and briefly commented upon below.

A. Hesiod

How dreadful boredom is—how dreadfully boring; I know no stronger expression, no truer one, for like is recognized only by like. Would that there were a loftier, stronger expression, for then there would still be one movement. I lie prostrate, inert; the only thing I see is emptiness, the only thing I live on is emptiness, the only thing I move in is emptiness. I do not even suffer pain. The vulture pecked continually at Prometheus' liver; the poison dripped down continually on Loki; it was at least an interruption, even though monotonous. Pain itself has lost its refreshment for me. If I were offered all the glories of the world or all torments of the world, one would move me no more than the other: I would not turn over to the other side either to attain or to avoid. I am dying death.[32]

In this excerpt from the "Diapsalmata," the drastic and almost eternal punishment of Prometheus mentioned in Hesiod is quoted and at the same time de-potentiated in a kind of mirror inversion in the face of vacuousness and doubt.[33] Gredal Jensen assumes that Kierkegaard might have remembered the myth wrong and that he therefore confused the term "vulture" (*grib*) with "eagle" (*ørn*).[34] However, I consider it more likely that Kierkegaard follows a tradition of Danish literature. As described in the *Ordbog over det danske Sprog* the word *grib* is sometimes used in connection with the Prometheus myth, for example, also in Carsten Hauch (1790–1872).[35] Furthermore, due to a homophony, the word *grib* could have coincided with (1) the medieval Danish term *gryp* for a mythical creature—see the ballad *Harpens Kraft*—and (2) with the originally Middle High German term *grîf(e)*, handed down to Middle Low German, which is the generic name and umbrella term for birds of prey, including eagles.

---

[32]   *SKS* 2, 46 / *EO1*, 37. Kierkegaard uses a wonderful *figura etymologica*: *Jeg døer Døden*.

[33]   See also Gredal Jensen, "Aeschylus: Kierkegaard and Early Greek Tragedy," pp. 228–9. The translation problem concerning the term *Gribben* ("vulture") is also discussed here. Both Vollmer and Nitsch use the German term *Adler* (*eagle*) in their dictionaries.

[34]   Ibid., p. 229.

[35]   *Ordbog over det danske Sprog*, published by the Society for Danish Language and Literature, vols. 1–28, Copenhagen: Gyldendalske Boghandel/Nordisk Forlag 1919–56, vol. 7, column 66.

In *Repetition*, the metaphor of the bound Prometheus whose liver is hacked to pieces by a vulture/eagle is repeated as a comparison in order to illustrate the state the young man puts his beloved in with his love strategy.[36] *Stages on Life's Way* focuses only on Prometheus' shackling and this micro-element of the myth is then transferred to the lonely imprisonment in temporality—paradoxically as a result of an eternal resolve.[37] *The Sickness unto Death* presents an ensemble of concepts of the self and forms of desperation derived from it.[38] For an acting self that conceives itself as autonomous—and thus not related to God, the necessary foundation of the self—earnestness thus turns out to be just a feigned gesture, similar to Prometheus who only stole the fire from Zeus without being its inventor. This unessential act of theft reflects Hesiod's negative interpretation of the Prometheus figure as deceiver and thief:

> This is a simulated earnestness. Like Prometheus stealing fire from the gods, this is stealing from God the thought—which is earnestness—that God pays attention to one; instead, the self in despair is satisfied with paying attention to itself, which is supposed to bestow infinite interest and significance upon his enterprises, but it is precisely this that makes them imaginary constructions.[39]

In the *Journal AA*, Prometheus' punishment is cited in a literary context. Kierkegaard refers to a review of Lenau's *Faust* by Martensen and criticizes Faust's suicide—contrary to Goethe's drama: "Despair is Romantic—not punishment as in case of Prometheus."[40] Maybe this short passage can be interpreted as a key to the perception of the Prometheus myth in Kierkegaard's work: *Faust* is an idea and *Don Juan* collides with the world. Prometheus, however, is not Romantic; despair is Romantic. Prometheus was just punished—and thereby his literary potential seems to be exhausted:

> When an ironist laughs at a humorist's witticisms and fancies, it is like the vulture tearing at Prometheus' liver, for the humorist's fancies are not the darlings of caprice but the sons of pain; with every one of them goes a little piece of his innermost viscera, and it is the emaciated ironist who is in need of the despairing depth of the humorist.[41]

The mention of Prometheus in the *Journal DD* is also made in an aesthetic context in order to underpin the difference between a humorist and an ironist in a kind of asymmetrical relationship. Just like the eagle feeding on Prometheus' liver, the "meagre" ironist lives on the entrails of the humorist whose aesthetic activity thus

---

[36]   *SKS* 4, 18 / *R*, 141.

[37]   *SKS* 6, 106 / *SLW*, 111.

[38]   See Markus Pohlmeyer, "*Die Krankheit zum Tode*—Aporien des Selbstbewusstseins. Fichte, Kierkegaard und Dieter Henrich," in *Existenz und Reflexion. Aktuelle Aspekte der Kierkegaard-Rezeption*, ed. by Matthias Bauer and Markus Pohlmeyer, Hamburg: Igel Verlag 2012 (*Schriften der Georg-Brandes-Gesellschaft*, vol. 1), pp. 168–98.

[39]   *SKS* 11, 182 / *SUD*, 68–9.

[40]   *SKS* 17, 49, AA: 38 / *KJN* 1, 43.

[41]   *SKS* 17, 243, DD:68 / *KJN* 1, 234.

virtually gains an existential momentum: metaphorically seen, he pays for humor with his life:

> Paganism is the sensuous, the full development of the sensuous life—its punishment, therefore, as we see in Prometheus, is that the liver is pecked [by a vulture] and continually grows [again], the continually awakening and yet never satisfied desire— Christianity is the *cerebral*, therefore Golgotha is called *the place of the skulls*.[42]

The aspect of Prometheus' suffering in this passage illustrates the distinction between paganism and Christianity. Metaphorically seen, paganism and Christianity represent the juxtaposition of passion and spirituality. The use of Prometheus' punishment alludes to unredeemed paganism and to passion or desire, never coming to a rest, growing back again and again painfully. In addition, paganism is passively chained to its passions, just as Prometheus is chained to the Caucasus. In contrast, the spirituality of Christianity appears to be active and redeeming. Nevertheless, the evidence for this thesis is quite disturbing: Kierkegaard boldly transcends the literal meaning of Golgatha—place of the skulls—as a place of the epiphany of the spirit.

B. Aeschylus

> It is indeed beautiful to see a person put out to sea with the fair wind of hope; one may utilize the chance to let oneself be towed along, but one ought never have it on board one's craft, least of all as pilot, for it is an untrustworthy shipmaster. For this reason, too, hope was one of Prometheus' dubious gifts; instead of giving human beings the foreknowledge of the immortals, he gave them hope.[43]

This passage taken from *Either/Or*, Part One alludes to the Prometheus drama by Aeschylus. While in Hesiod hope dwells in Pandora's jar, Prometheus himself passes on this gift to mankind in Aeschylus. In this passage hope is, however, reinterpreted as an anti-gift, almost accusatorily, by skillfully playing with the Greek etymology of *Prometheus/Thinxahead*: *forudvidenhed* (foreknowledge) would have been by far the better gift.

C. Plato

> Thus your scorn is not directed against people but against existence, where it happens that in the scheme of things not everybody has money. "Prometheus and Epimetheus," you say, "were undeniably very wise [*klog*], but still it is unconceivable that whereas they otherwise equipped human beings so gloriously, it did not occur to them to give them money also."[44]

By adding Epimetheus, this quotation from *Either/Or*, Part Two unambiguously refers to Plato's *Protagoras*. The point is what both brothers have given to mankind.

---

[42] *SKS* 27, 213, Papir 259:1 / *JP* 3, 3059.
[43] *SKS* 2, 282 / *EO1*, 292–3.
[44] *SKS* 3, 264–5 / *EO2*, 279.

However, within the framework of a fictitious dialogue, it is critically remarked that they forgot money. Considering that mankind received σοφία/τέχνη and justice from Prometheus and Zeus, this sounds by all means appropriate albeit ironic—above all in a *city of merchants*. In the course of the history of reception, the combination of Prometheus and Epimetheus developed into an epistemic, even psychological figure of thought, as it was adapted, for example, in "The Crisis and a Crisis in the Life of an Actress."[45] In *The Concept of Anxiety*, Vigilius Haufniensis alludes to Plato's *Protagoras* only in a footnote.[46] Even if these two passages refer to the pair of brothers as creators of culture, it is—in the Platonic sense—Hermes rather than Epimetheus who asks Zeus how justice should be allocated to mankind. This misunderstanding can also be found in a marginal note where justice is replaced by the category of the ethical—and Hermes/Zeus by Prometheus.[47]

D. Shelley

Another—indirectly accessible—theological context of the Prometheus myth in Kierkegaard can be found in his concise analysis of Percy Bysshe Shelley's *Prometheus Rebound*:

> Shelley remarks that the idea of Prometheus seems to him far more beautiful than the idea of the Devil because Prometheus is pure and lofty, not corrupted and corrupting like Satan. This is true, but there is an entirely different problem: vis-à-vis God to think an idea as justified as the idea of Prometheus. Satan is indeed great, but his corruptedness is precisely what makes it possible to think of him together with God.[48]

This is an example of how the ancient myth interferes with Christian philosophy in the history of reception. Although Kierkegaard underpins Shelley's poetic interpretation, he shies away from the theological implications and even interprets Shelley's choice in a virtually mirror-inverted way as a mishap (*ulykke*). According to the Christian conception of the world, God and Satan are antagonists complementing each other dualistically. However, in Shelley's preface Prometheus is compared to Satan and thus becomes an alternative ideal figure,[49] the great sufferer, tormented by Zeus' injustice, and this illustrates the two aspects of Marx's dictum: the most eminent saint and martyr.

IV. Interpretation

In its history of reception, the figure of Prometheus combines quite varying aesthetic discourses critical of religion. Goethe writes, *"Der Aufrührer Prometheus ist die*

---

45   *SKS* 14, 104–25 / *C*, 301–25. See also Carl Gustav Carus, *Psyche. Zur Entwicklungsgeschichte der Seele* [2ⁿᵈ edition of 1860], with an introduction to the new edition by Friedrich Arnold, Darmstadt: Wissenschaftliche Buchgesellschaft 1975, p. 31.
46   *SKS* 4, 408n / *CA*, 106n.
47   *SKS* 27, 394, Papir 365:7 / *JP* 1, 649.
48   *SKS* 18, 228, JJ:280 / *KJN* 2, 209.
49   See Shelley, "Preface," p. 205.

beliebteste mythologische Figur der Geniezeit."[50] The motif of the ingenious creator/
artist and rebel against the gods was translated by Goethe into his powerful poem
Prometheus and the drama of the same name. The poem became famous and notorious
after its publication by Friedrich Heinrich Jacobi in the year 1785 in his work *Über
die Lehre des Spinoza in Briefen an den Herrn Moses Mendelssohn.* Jacobi alleged
that Lessing, during a conversation with him and after having read *Prometheus*,
had called himself a Spinozist. Under certain circumstances this statement could
have been interpreted as atheism and was thus highly volatile. Jacobi's course of
action triggered the so-called Pantheism Controversy. It is also to be noted that
the authenticity of Jacobi's dialogue with Lessing is controversial and that Goethe
had not authorized the publication of his poem.[51] At least within the context of the
Prometheus quotations dealt with in this article, Kierkegaard apparently does not
refer to this poem, which, as Goethe put it, became the *Zündkraut einer Explosion.*[52]
Nevertheless, the poem was present in the aesthetical discourse of Copenhagen.
This is underpinned, for example, by Hans Lassen Martensen's Hegelian oriented
interpretation.[53]

Kierkegaard knows the central ancient sources of the Prometheus myth although
he sometimes confuses the actors. In the few passages of his monumental work
where Prometheus is mentioned, the intention of Hesiod, Plato, and Aeschylus is
still recognizable. In his printed publications, Kierkegaard focuses first and foremost
on the aspect of suffering and only secondly on the role of a creator of culture.
The important subsidiary theme of Pandora is hardly to be found. In Kierkegaard's
journals, papers, and notebooks Prometheus is explicitly cited in literary, aesthetical,
ethical, and even theological contexts, that is, he is dealt with in wider contents.
Nevertheless, these few and quite reductionistic quotations do not provide a
thoroughly developed picture of the Prometheus myth or even of a mythopoeia in
Kierkegaard's reception. The quotations are rather like the pieces of a mosaic meant
to bring light to or to obscure a certain mood or thought. Sometimes Prometheus
just serves as part of a comparison. Now and then, however, Kierkegaard changes
some aspects and sticks to them. Thus he draws on the long tradition of creatively
handling this myth.

Kierkegaard does not take up the idea of Prometheus as the creator of humankind.
One reason could be the fact that the establishment of a *second creator* along with
the Christian Creator God would have been problematic. Aspects of the myth that
are critical of religion, for example, Prometheus as a rebel against Zeus, presented
in Goethe's *Sturm und Drang* poem, also go unmentioned. It is only the concise
analysis of Shelley's "Preface" which allows a glimpse of the theological potential

---

[50]   Johann Wolfgang von Goethe, *Gedichte 1756–1799*, ed. by Karl Eibl, Berlin:
Deutscher Klassiker Verlag 2010, p. 925.
[51]   See also Inge Wild, "Prometheus, 'Jünglingsgrillen' oder 'Zündkraut einer
Explosion'?," in *Interpretationen. Gedichte von Johann Wolfgang Goethe*, ed. by Bernd
Witte, Stuttgart: Philipp Reclam jun. 2009, pp. 43–61.
[52]   See Goethe, *Gedichte 1756–1799*, p. 922.
[53]   Hans Lassen Martensen, "Review of the *Introductory Lecture to the Logic Course*,"
in *Heiberg's Introductory Lecture to the Logic Course and Other Texts*, ed. and trans. by Jon
Stewart, Copenhagen: C.A. Reitzel 2007 (*Texts from Golden Age Denmark*, vol. 3), pp. 84–5.

and aesthetic provocations immanent in this myth. It seems that Kierkegaard—with Promethean foresight—had no intention of opening Pandora's religious-philosophical jar.

Bibliography

Gredal Jensen, Finn, "Aeschylus: Kierkegaard and Early Greek Tragedy," in *Kierkegaard and the Greek World*, Tome II, *Aristotle and Other Greek Authors*, ed. by Jon Stewart and Katalin Nun, Aldershot: Ashgate 2010 (*Kierkegaard Research: Sources, Reception and Resources*, vol. 2), pp. 211–34; especially pp. 228–30.

Irina, Nicolae, "Hesiod: Kierkegaard and the Greek Gods," in *Kierkegaard and the Greek World*, Tome II, *Aristotle and Other Greek Authors*, ed. by Jon Stewart and Katalin Nun, Aldershot: Ashgate 2010 (*Kierkegaard Research: Sources, Reception and Resources*, vol. 2), pp. 263–9; especially p. 264.

Richard III:

The Prototype of the Demonic

Nataliya Vorobyova Jørgensen

What do most people know about King Richard III? If you ask a random passerby in the street, one of the many things that people might be familiar with is the fact of Richard's deformity. He was a hunchback with withered arm, and his mind and character were as wicked and deformed as his body. We owe such common knowledge to William Shakespeare and one of his best historical plays entitled the *Tragedy of Richard III*. Only the recent discovery of the king's remnants under a parking lot in Leicester revived public interest in the historical figure, who represents the most talked about monarch in British history. There are, in fact, two very different Richards: the first one is the real historical figure and the second one—the protagonist of Shakespeare's play. For the purpose of this particular article, there is a need to have a closer look at the latter, for there is no doubt that Kierkegaard used Shakespeare's character and completely neglected the possibility of the existence of a "good" King Richard.[1]

Many contemporary theatrical interpretations focus on the struggle for power in the play. Yet, what is really interesting in Shakespeare is more general; in his texts historical details should rather be treated as a façade for the presentation of the psychologically complex portraits of some significant *dramatis personae*. Critics, however, invariably argue for the historicity of Shakespeare's plays in general and *Richard III* in particular. Shakespeare did not invent the way the former English king was presented. His primary sources for this play were two English chronicles: one by Edward Hall (1497–1547) and Holinshed's Chronicle (first edition 1577).[2] These sources provide

---

[1]   An interesting study by the English historian Jeremy Potter provides an insightful view of the real figure behind the numerous myths about King Richard. See Jeremy Potter, *Good King Richard? An Account of Richard III and his Reputation*, London: Constable 1983.

[2]   Even though these two chronicles have been identified as the main sources of the play, it has been pointed out that all of the possible sources were interconnected: "The English *History* was first published when William Rustell, More's nephew, bought out the works in 1557 (the Latin edition was published in Louvain in 1565). However, a version of More, supplemented by Vergil, had already appeared in Richard Grafton's edition to Harding's *Chronicle* (1543) and had been incorporated, nearly verbatim, along with materials for Commines, into Edward Hall's *Union* (1548). Another version of More, incorporating the material added to Hall, went into Holinshed's *Chronicle* (1577, 1587). More materials were invoked by sixteenth-century humanists and inspired literary works such as *The Mirror for Magistrates* (1559–1610), Thomas Legge's Latin university drama *Richardus Tertius* (performed 1579), the anonymous Queen's men play, *The True Tragedy of Richard the Third* (1594), and at least one lost ballad

significant implications for the perspective that the playwright adopted in the text: as some commentators suggest that the text was written as Tudor propaganda against the Last of the Plantagenets. Here is how Harold Brooks summed up these issues: "In so far as the play is a tragedy, it is tragedy of the medieval *casus* type. Primarily it is a drama of history, moralised according to the Tudor political idea of the providentially-ordered process that brought Richmond and his successors to the throne."[3]

But what is even more significant is that Shakespeare generalized the available historical accounts and combined them with the tradition of the medieval Vice or Machiavelli. Even though the structure of the play was quite modern for the Renaissance, reviving classical examples by Seneca, it still contained significant influences from medieval morality drama which adds a twist to the history: the audience were not only presented with the despotic king, but with someone who is an embodiment of the Devil. Richard III, the main protagonist of the tragedy, knows for certain who he is from the very beginning. He is determined to act as a villain, and therefore he proudly identifies himself with the medieval Vice[4] or the Scourge of God.[5] However, similarity with the stereotypical "bad guys" ends quickly, because Shakespeare intends to develop a more complicated personality: his protagonist commits a "sin" of wishing to be someone else, of escaping, negating, and rejecting his true self (and escaping true responsibility) by simply becoming an icon of evil. His aim is well defined, and his means are plain to see. In order to become a king, he assumes the position of an anti-Christ,[6] and begins to play tricks with people's

---

(1586). Each retelling adds and subtracts, framing Richard's story within different designs." James R. Siemon, "Introduction" to *King Richard III*, ed. by James R. Siemon, London: Methuen Drama 2009 (*Third Series, Arden Shakespeare*, vol. 16), p. 53.

[3]   Siemon, "Introduction" to *King Richard III*, p. 76.

[4]   Ibid., p. 100: "Happe identifies Avarice in *Respublica* as the first Vice to fulfill all functions characteristic of the type. He is a 'homiletic showman, intriguer extraordinary, and master of dramatic ceremonies'; his method is always deceit and guile; his purpose the 'translating into vivid dramatic image the habitual self-deception or blindness of mankind to the real nature of the temptations to which it succumbs.' He displays the trick of tears and laughter. His weeping feigns his affection and concern for his victim; his laughter, for the benefit of the audience, declares the triumph of his subtle fraud and scorn for the puny virtue of humanity. Yet he attracts the audience's attention and even sympathy, both by embodying its own destructive and anti-authoritarian impulses, and by engaging the audience in a conspiratorial relationship with him, a relationship strengthened as the plays explored increasingly secular themes and were presented in aesthetic rather than in homiletic form." It is quite clear from the passage that the character expresses ultimate and pure evil, which has no rational or moral explanation. This is, indeed, a figure of the devil incarnated.

[5]   Ibid., p. 103: "The fact of bad, tyrannical kings had to be reconciled with the rule of a benevolent Deity; some scriptural references and some classical combine to create the concept of the 'flagellum Dei.' This is the ruler whose personal wickedness (freely chosen) makes his actions a means of expressing the divine will, by chastising and mortifying a sinful people; the chastisement done, the scourge is in turn destroyed. Famous scourges remarked on in literature included Herod and Nero, …Tamburlaine."

[6]   Ibid., p. 109: "Theologically, it is not God who condemns Richard to suffer for the nation's ills. It is Richard who elects to become an anti-Christ, whose free choice of evil is also (by the familiar Christian paradox) the means by which God brings about good."

destinies. Here lies his second great mistake. At first, Richard plays God, but later on God will play with Richard.

I.

King Richard, "that poisonous bunchback'd toad,"[7] or a "lump of foul deformity,"[8] a "bottled spider,"[9] where bottled meant swollen, pointing to Richard's hunchback. In this collocation the spider signifies the poisonous nature of the Duke of Gloucester. In the opening soliloquy Richard adds to his self-presentation: "I that am not shaped for sportive tricks / Nor made to court an amorous looking-glass."[10] These lines, also indicating the future king's lack of physical fitness, draw attention to Richard's attitude to courtly affairs: he is not a leisurely man of the court, his body does not allow him to engage himself in "sportive tricks," which in Elizabethan times meant "sexual games"[11] and recreation, and he is not successful in conquering female hearts. From the very first lines, he draws attention to his physical deformity: "I am a curtailed of this fair proportion / Cheated of feature by dissembling Nature[12] / deformed, unfinished, sent before my time."[13]

But the assumption that Richard is merely a medieval Vice leads to over-simplification. Vice does not need any rational explanation of his deeds, but it shares some features with an *eiron*—a cunning and skillful pretender and rhetorician. A mixture of those two models allows Richard to pretend as well as to have a simple and straightforward excuse for his villainy: "And therefore, since I cannot prove a lover, / To entertain these fair well-spoken days, / I am determined to prove a villain / And hate the idle pleasures of these days."[14]

Two remarks must be made at this point. Richard's self-presentation is meaningfully ambiguous. When he says that he is "determined" to prove a villain on the one hand he can mean "historical causation (the modern sense of 'determined,' here of course derived from the early modern legal sense of 'limited,' 'set by cause') and, on the other hand, it stands for a voluntarily 'self-fashioning,' personal resolution, the freedom to determine one's own destiny."[15] Thus, he either sees himself as being subordinate to Fate or simultaneously decides to show everyone

[7] Shakespeare, *Richard III*, Act I, Scene iii, lines 50–1.
[8] Shakespeare, *Richard III*, Act I, Scene ii, line 58.
[9] Shakespeare, *Richard III*, Act I, Scene iii, line 47.
[10] Shakespeare, *Richard III*, Act I, Scene i, lines 14–15.
[11] See comment to line 14, Siemon, "Introduction" to *King Richard III*, p. 126.
[12] This particular passage brings up a whole series of images, which relied on Elizabethan beliefs that harmony in nature reflected the divine plan. Richard's appearance is disproportional, irregular, ugly—these were the visible signs of the viciousness of his character. As a part of his deceptive plan, Richard presents his deformity as a cause of his villainy, but in fact he is evil by definition.
[13] Shakespeare, *Richard III*, Act I, Scene i, lines 20–1.
[14] Ibid., lines 28–31.
[15] Graham Holderness, *Shakespeare: The Histories*, New York: St. Martin's Press 2000, p. 82.

how eager he is to prove his villainy. Graham Holderness interprets this opening soliloquy as "an elegy for the loss of heroic past, a warrior nostalgia that laments the passing of war, and expresses a witty and scathing contempt for the boredom and triviality of peace."[16] But we need to question this analysis by asking who Richard is after all: a soldier or a courtier; a prospective king or a member of the royal family fighting for power; maybe a lover or just a murderer? Does he himself know who he is? He is sure that his motives are evil, but maybe what he cannot deal with is a mere boredom of a soldier who cannot find his place in peacetime.

Soon after, Richard will prove to be an extremely skillful manipulator. His first task is to spread suspicion and pour mistrust into the audience's mind, and he does so by becoming a mediator between them and the action on stage. Theatrical asides become his main weapon in this struggle for the audience's approval. Right after his introduction, the audience receives a new confession, which this time concerns Richard's plot against his brother Clarence:

> Plots have I laid, inductions dangerous,
> By drunken prophecies, libels and dreams,
> To set my brother Clarence and the king
> In deadly hate the one against the other:
> And if King Edward be as true and just
> As I am subtle, false and treacherous,
> This day should Clarence closely be mewed up...[17]

The following dialogue between brothers serves a perfect example of dramatic irony, since the audience already know about Gloucester's treason; it also provides an excellent instance of verbal irony. Clarence is sincerely surprised by the king's decision, since apparently the cause of his imprisonment in the Tower is a dream interpreted by the king's wizard. What could be more ungrounded and unreasonable for a man of court than to be charged on the grounds of a dream, interpreted by a wizard and pushed forward by a woman? The whole conversation reminds one more of a conversation between two gossips than a farewell between two brothers. Richard repeatedly stresses that he is in the same situation as his brother and can easily be imprisoned. This is the argument on which Richard builds his intimate relations with Clarence:

> I'll tell you what; I think it is our way,
> If we will keep in favour with the king,
> To be her men and wear her livery:
> The jealous o'erworn widow and herself,
> Since that our brother dubb'd them gentlewomen.
> Are mighty gossips in this monarchy.[18]

A repeated usage of the pronouns "we, our, them" juxtapose the two men against "her"—the queen—and her followers. At this point the audience is more than just a

16   Ibid., p. 81.
17   Shakespeare, *Richard III*, Act I, Scene i, lines 32–8.
18   Ibid., lines 77–83.

little confused. Gloucester keeps using cunning word play. His "jokes" cut deeply; they mock both the victim of his plot and God's power to save the sinner: "Well, your imprisonment shall not be long; / I will deliver you, or else lie for you."[19]

For the Christians who long to be united with their heavenly maker life may indeed seem an "imprisonment" and death "a delivery." Also, one finds in these words a troubling echo of the Lord's Prayer: "and deliver us from evil." The equivocation in Richard's pun contains a confession of the murderous plan which will make Clarence's imprisonment short and disclose the means employed by the villain. Richard's next step is to make the audience his accomplices: "Go, tread the path that thou shalt ne'er return. / Simple, plain Clarence! I do love thee so, / That I will shortly send thy soul to heaven, / If heaven will take the present at *our* hands."[20]

It has been noticed that although in this passage vital political claims have been made, none of his statements is devoid of humor. Graham Holderness believes that "Richard's humor derives from his self-confident mastery of the situation, his sense of superiority to his foolish and trusting brothers; and from a kind of creative zest at his own capacity to initiate and manage change, using…that shadow-world of dream and prophecy of which he himself has no apprehension."[21]

Scene I ends with a monologue which was probably delivered on the empty stage. It is not clear who should be the addressee of that speech. Since there are no special stage directions in the text, the actor is free to follow his intuition. Yet, towards the end of the scene, and especially with the final entry, Richard as a character establishes a pattern which will remain a guideline of the whole play. He assigns and sets the roles for himself, the audience, and other characters. Gloucester chooses to be a director of the play; he assumes that he has the power to play with people's lives. This kind of assumption situates him above the events which take place on stage. In fact, there are two "Richards" present—one is the king's brother, an ugly and evil person who walks around the court as a shadow of the legitimate ruler, and no one knows what he is plotting; the other one is the Richard of the soliloquies and asides. The latter is a plotter and an ironist, staging the play for his own delight and for the audience. It is a dangerous part, since Richard also becomes a manipulator and an observer of human fates and, as we have argued earlier, he assumes the role reserved only for God. Nevertheless, he needs the audience, he cannot be satisfied with bare successes of his villainy. He shares everything with those who are watching the performance, forces them to become his accomplices, and at the same time allows them no more freedom than to watch him act. Gloucester seems to abolish the invisible line between himself and the audience, inviting them into his conspiracy; however the audience will have to discover that this line cannot be erased.[22]

19 Ibid., lines 113–14.
20 Ibid., lines 117–20.
21 Holderness, *Shakespeare: The Histories*, p. 86.
22 I am referring of course, to the modern theater and stage, where there are three parts which are reserved for the performance: the auditorium for the audience, the stage for the actors and the intermediate space—if the curtain is closed there is still a strip of stage on which an actor can stand. There, he is alone and from there he can mediate with the audience. The Shakespearean apron stage, without doubt, increased communication between actor and audience.

Scene II starts with a verbal skirmish between Anne and Richard. She openly curses him and at first glance seems to be perfectly aware of his nature. She portrays Richard as an embodiment of Satan, although it is not quite clear whether it is an expression of her grief or a penetrating, indeed, prophetic insight into Gloucester's soul. Addressing the guards who carry a coffin with her husband's body, she exclaims: "Alas, I blame you not; for you are mortal / And mortal eyes cannot endure the devil."[23] Later her accusations are more straightforward, she does not seem to have any restraint in the choice of her wording: "Avaunt, thou dreadful minister of hell! / Thou hadst but power over his mortal body, / His soul thou canst not have; therefore be gone."[24]

This is one of the numerous instances emphasizing Richard's diabolical associations. Anne refers to him as an agent of Hell. For her, there exists no other explanation of the infinite cruelty which dwells in him. Anne addresses Gloucester as "Foul Devil" who "has made the happy earth thy hell."[25] It is astonishing that Richard never denies her statements. Nevertheless, he alters her perception, commenting on her lamentations in such a way that she would appear as a woman who is on the point of madness. Their furious exchange based on vivid imagery and the contrast between a vicious devil and innocent angel appears to be completely reversed by Richard. According to him, if Anne is an angel, why can she curse so violently? Richard-Devil sharpens the opposition by using the name of Saint Paul instead of a curse.[26] Towards the end of this verbal exchange, Anne loses, even though she gets the villain's confession and confirmation of the murder of her husband. The wooing of Anne, against all odds proves to be successful, to the general surprise not only of the viewers but also of Richard himself: "Was ever woman in this humour woo'd? / Was ever woman in this humour won?"[27] "Humour" does not necessarily mean Anne's raging mood, but skillful rhetorical irony, an argument due to which Richard wins the heart of a woman. As Muecke points out, the word "humour"—can simply denote situational irony. He recalls, for instance, that "Johnson...while discussing *Henry IV* part 2, act V, i, lines 90–93, uses the word 'humorous,' instead of 'ironic' which a contemporary critic would have used there. There is something humorous in the fact that the author tells the spendthrift to count the days on the basis of time taken by the debt trail."[28] Yet, it has also been noticed by other critics that "Anne

---

[23]   Shakespeare, *Richard III*, Act I, Scene ii, lines 43–4.
[24]   Ibid., lines 45–7.
[25]   Ibid., lines 51–2.
[26]   It has been noted that Richard curses repeatedly and mainly uses the name of St. Paul. Here is how Holderness comments on this: "If Richard had studied St Paul as frequently as he swears by his name, he would naturally be familiar with the theological paradox explicated in the Epistle to the Romans, that 'so many of us as were baptized into Jesus Christ were baptized into his death' (VI.3). Grotesquely, Clarence is baptized, but into death, not life; in wine, not water." Graham Holderness, *Shakespeare: the Histories*, p. 87.
[27]   Shakespeare, *Richard III*, Act I, Scene ii, lines 227–9.
[28]   Douglas Colin Muecke, "Ironia: podstawowe klasyfikacje [Irony: Basic Classifications]," in *Ironia*, ed. by Michał Głowińskiego, Gdańsk: Słowo/obraz terytoria 2002, p. 55. (My translation.)

succumbs to Richard's wooing partly because he is attractive, but she would not have fallen so readily into such a terrible mistake if she too had not been corrupted."[29]

Richard's soliloquy at the end of Act I, Scene ii begins to show the pattern of asides with the help of which an *eiron* character will be building the tension within dramatic irony. Olivier in his screen adaptation of the play makes Richard speak directly to the camera and in this way creates a sense of intimacy between the audience and the villain. Such intimacy can also signify one more role that Richard plays—he is the ironist who needs the audience (that is what Kierkegaard would call the desire of immediacy). Tillyard has also observed a similar pattern in the play and made a significant remark summarizing the relationships between the ironist and the audience:

> Like most ironists, Richard secures the audience "on his side" and yet involves us even further when (again like most ironists) he betrays our trust, and turns out to be way beyond us, leaving us embarrassed as Baudelaire did: *"Vous! Hypocrite lecteur; mon semblable! Mon frere!"* Our condemnation of evil is involved in our recognition of our brotherhood with it.[30]

Scene iii of the first act serves as an introduction to court life. Even if a contemporary audience is lost in who belongs to which "party," who hates whom and for what reasons, it is absolutely clear that the atmosphere is tense and that Richard has already became famous for his conspiracies. The purpose of the scene may seem unclear at the beginning—it would have been unnecessary if its only justification were to show that the majority of the court is against Richard. However, two things become clear as the scene develops: even though everybody is aware of Richard's evil intentions, none can actually guess what he is plotting or if he is plotting anything at all. Richard's double face becomes even more apparent when he reveals his ideas to the audience and states that the quarrel between him, the queen, and her brothers that took place a minute previous was not just a mere incident. He planned it, and he needed it to fulfill his plan: to murder Clarence and later blame the queen and her party for that deed and get out of the whole affair clean. He can even find some allies for his future plans in Hastings, Derby, and Buckingham.

Until Act III Gloucester is in the shadow of the action which develops with tremendous speed: the slaying of Clarence, death of the current king, a growing uncertainty amongst citizens concerned about the future and a growing terror in the royal house. Unexpectedly, the Vice finds a helper, Lord Buckingham, who turns out to be politically flexible and reacts quickly to the changes at court. But, the hand of a puppet master is present everywhere; so, even when Richard is not on stage he remains present in other character's consciousness. He reappears in Act III, Scene i in full blossom and right away plunges into asides. The young prince Edward has just arrived and awaits the coronation. In case the audience had forgotten that Richard had worked out a long-term plot, he reminds us about it in his conversation with Edward. He offers the prince a stay in the Tower while awaiting the upcoming

---

29   Siemon, "Introduction" to *King Richard III*, p. 110.
30   Ibid., p. 109.

ceremony: "So wise so young, they say, do never live long."[31] Here, the whole
fragment is worth quoting, since in the asides he confirms our suspicions that the
Tower is not a refuge but a place of execution:

> Prince Edward: But say, my lord, it were not register'd,
> Methinks the truth should live from age to age,
> As 'twere retail'd to all posterity,
> Even to the general all-ending day.
> Gloucester: [Aside] So wise so young, they say, do never live long.
> Prince Edward: What say you, uncle?
> Gloucester: I say, without characters, fame lives long.
> [Aside] Thus, like the formal Vice, Iniquity,
> I moralize two meanings in one word.[32]

The first aside definitely introduces rhetorical irony, which can be understood only
by the audience. The second merely reinforces the first. Here, Richard does not
continue the conversation with the child but rather wishes to communicate with
those who are watching him. He reminds us that we are a part of his conspiracy
and that it is time for us to learn his tricks. Besides, comparing himself to a "formal
Vice," Richard emphasizes that even though "he appears something different from
the conventional and obvious Vice of the popular stage, he is imitating the method of
that role; he is inviting the appreciation of the audience for his dexterity in deceit."[33]

The plot against Hastings and later the fall of Buckingham provide us with
splendid examples of a wider, cosmic irony embedded in the structure of the play.
The circumstances devised by Richard make other characters question God and see
the universe as a hostile place, an arena of a constant struggle for survival. Such is
the situation of Hastings who devises the punishment for himself:

> Gloucester: I pray you all, tell me what they deserve
> That do conspire my death with devilish plots
> Of damned witchcraft, and that have prevail'd
> Upon my body with their hellish charms?
> Hastings: The tender love I bear your grace, my lord,
> Makes me most forward in this noble presence
> To doom the offenders, whatsoever they be
> I say, my lord, they have deserved death.
> Gloucester: Then be your eyes the witness of this ill:
> See how I am bewitch'd; behold mine arm
> Is, like a blasted sapling, wither'd up:
> And this is Edward's wife, that monstrous witch,
> Consorted with that harlot strumpet Shore,
> That by their witchcraft thus have marked me.[34]

---

[31]   Shakespeare, *Richard III*, Act III, Scene i, line 80.
[32]   Ibid., lines 75–83.
[33]   Footnotes to line 82, *Richard III: Third Series (Arden Shakespeare)*, p. 215.
[34]   Shakespeare, *Richard III*, Act III, Scene iv, lines 59–72.

The situation reminds one of the typical scenes from fairytales, where a noble king asks the villain to name the punishment for a certain crime after which the crimes of the villain are disclosed. Here, however, the roles are reversed: it is a villain who is a king and who sets up a faithful servant. And although at first glance one can think that Hastings falls victim to blind fate, one should not forget that in fact it is Richard himself who once again turns the wheel of fortune. He is the plotter and the ironist; he punishes and never forgives. Gloucester does not leave any place for Fortune to cast the lot in the case of Buckingham, either. And again, his accomplice becomes a toy in the hands of a capricious master plotter.

The final question one is bound to ask is: why does Richard fall in the end if he appears to be so efficient in managing evil tricks? By saying that he is "evil," Richard denies himself the possibility of finding his true and complex self. The king thinks that he can govern Fortune with the laws of logic, a plot, a plan. And for a while Fortune seems to obey him. But fate is not just a blind necessity; it is a "nothing of anxiety"—as Kierkegaard once called it.[35] When the ghosts of the people whom he had murdered come to haunt Richard on the eve of the final battle, he is not only anxious about his new situation, but he suddenly sees the nothingness and emptiness that awaits him. The moment when he allows fear to overwhelm his imagination, he surrenders to Fate. Then the roles are reversed, and Richard begins to be controlled by Fate. Now, Fortune is on the side of Richmond, as one of his supporters proclaims: "Fortune and victory sit on thy helm!"[36]

The final scenes of the play take place on the field of Bosworth. The gentry rises against Richard and even though he keeps up the appearance of a strong and powerful king, reminding everyone that "the king's name is a tower of strength,"[37] a seed of mortal doubt has already began to sprout in his heart: "Up in my tent! Here will I lie to-night / But where tomorrow?"[38] The space of the stage is divided; almost simultaneously we see the tents of the opposing armies. In one of them Richmond falls peacefully asleep; the other becomes a prison-house for the restless Richard haunted by the ghosts of his victims. The spirits condemn the usurper to "despair and die" while at the same time they assure his dreaming opponent that his cause is just.[39] Yet, it is not the triumph of the good and the banishment of tyranny which is emphasized in this act. The core concept for understanding the downfall of the villain is the despair to which he is condemned. Kierkegaard would have said that at this moment Richard wakes from immediacy into the sufferings of despair:

> What do I fear? myself? there's none else by.
> Richard loves Richard; this is, I am I.
> Is there a murderer here? No—yes, I am:
> Then fly. What, from myself? Great reason why—
> Lest I revenge. Myself upon myself?
> Alack, I love myself. For any good

---

[35]   *SKS* 4, 399 / *CA*, 96.
[36]   Shakespeare, *Richard III*, Act V, Scene iii, line 79.
[37]   Ibid., line 14.
[38]   Ibid., lines 7–8.
[39]   Ibid., lines 115–53.

That I myself have done unto myself?
O, no! Alas, I rather hate myself
For hateful deeds committed by myself!
I am a villain: yet I lie, I am not.
Fool, of thyself speak well: fool, do not flatter.
My conscience hath a thousand several tongues,
And every tongue brings in a several tale,
And every tale condemns me for a villain.
Perjury, perjury, in the high'st degree
Murder, stem murder, in the direst degree;
All several sins, all used in each degree,
Throng to the bar, crying all, Guilty! guilty!
I shall despair. There is no creature loves me;
And if I die, no soul shall pity me:
Nay, wherefore should they, since that I myself
Find in myself no pity to myself?
Methought the souls of all that I had murder'd
Came to my tent; and every one did threat
To-morrow's vengeance on the head of Richard.[40]

The first striking feature of this monologue is that it is not addressed to the audience. Richard is now talking to himself, since his self-centeredness does not allow him to perceive events otherwise. Even the sky is empty because Richard had left no space for God to listen to the sinner or "deliver him from evil"; as we have argued, the proud king had reserved this place for himself. But he forgot that "God needs no human being."[41] (Notably, Kierkegaard glosses this witty remark with a statement which redeems the hierarchy overturned by the proud individual: "how highly embarrassing to be Creator if it turned out that God came to need the creature.")[42] Furthermore, a great deal is happening in this short soliloquy. His question "myself upon myself?" in line 186 gains new meaning if one recalls what Queen Elizabeth back in Act II draws upon herself: "I'll join with black despair against my soul / And to myself become an enemy."[43] This is a verdict which Richard wished to have avoided, but he is not able to. In search for self-justification he remembers about his promise of proving a villain. However, if in the opening monologue Richard proclaims himself evil, here he evokes two contrary feelings by crying in the first line "perjury," as if rejecting all charges against his villainy, claiming that it is brought on him by "tales." He does not want to be guilty as charged, but rather he is a falsely accused—this is how he reassures himself. But there comes the second line with a different voice, which says "murder"—Richard cannot undo what had been done. Such internal debates were typical of morality plays and were meant to educate the audience. But Richard continues announcing that in this case he "shall despair"—this time it sounds like a commitment leading him to self-destruction.

---

[40]   Ibid., lines 183–206.
[41]   *SKS* 7, 127 / *CUP1*, 136.
[42]   Ibid.
[43]   Shakespeare, *Richard III*, Act II, Scene ii, lines 35–6.

II.

Kierkegaard did not comment extensively on the *Tragedy of Richard III*, but the few passages available offer incredibly insightful critical analysis of the play and its protagonist. As early as in *Fear and Trembling*, Kierkegaard's pseudonym Johannes de silentio turns to the character of Richard III in order to exemplify the discussion of the "demonic" type of human nature. The demonic is an extreme aesthetic form of inwardness, which is contrasted with the religious faith of Abraham:[44]

> In that kind of thing, Shakespeare is and remains a hero. That demoniac, the most demonic figure Shakespeare depicted but also depicted in a matchless way—Gloucester (later Richard III)—what made him demonic? Apparently his inability to bear the sympathy heaped upon him from childhood. His monologue in the first act of Richard III has more value than all the systems of morality, which have no intimation of the nightmares of existence or of their explanation.
>
> > ...I, that am rudely stamp'd, and want love's majesty
> > To strut before a wanton ambling nymph;
> > I, that am curtail'd of this fair proportion,
> > Cheated of feature by dissembling nature,
> > Deformed, unfinish'd, sent before my time
> > Into this breathing world, scarce half made up,
> > And that so lamely and unfashionable
> > That dogs bark at me as I halt by them;
>
> Natures such as Gloucester's cannot be saved by mediating them into an idea of society. Ethics actually only makes sport of them...[45]

This comment shows how deeply Kierkegaard was impressed by the dramatic *personae* of the king and how precisely he caught the way in which Richard's character was constructed. As Joel Rasmussen rightly points out, since "a demoniac discloses himself without understanding himself"[46] "the category itself is borne by its exemplification."[47] The reference is more to a category than to a specific person, to the idea of the demonic, a type. On the other hand, accepting negativity, calling oneself "evil" the individual proves his lack of self-knowledge. After all, no certainty is available with regards to what constitutes the inner self, where doubting is not a negative experience, for freedom lies in it. Richard is not concerned with such matters. He is too limited to see beyond what is right and wrong in the narrowest sense of these words. At the same time, Gloucester is too weak to be called an ironist in the way in which Kierkegaard understands this term. Let us not forget that for the

---

[44] For more see Joel D.S. Rasmussen, "William Shakespeare: Kierkegaard's Post-Romantic Reception of 'the Poet's Poet,' " in *Kierkegaard and the Renaissance and Modern Tradition*, Tome III, *Literature, Drama and Music*, ed. by Jon Stewart, Aldershot: Ashgate 2009 (*Kierkegaard: Sources, Reception and Resources*, vol. 5), pp. 185–215.

[45] *SKS* 4, 194 / *FT*, 105–6.

[46] *SKS* 4, 190–1 / *FT*, 101.

[47] Rasmussen, "William Shakespeare: Kierkegaard's Post-Romantic Reception of 'the Poet's Poet,' " p. 193.

Danish philosopher being a subject means being a Christian, and he believes that "Christianity teaches the way to become subjective."[48]

Richard keeps the title of "ironist" in the dramatic sense of the term. But his irony is immediate and requires approval. Even in the final scene, Richard concentrates only on himself; his attachment to the accidental and the immediate is too strong, and this prevents him from having a reflective view of the situation. But there is also a place for a Kierkegaardian ironist in this play. As has already been said, Richard has mute accomplices who are encouraged by him to reflect upon the situation—the audience of the performance. It is they whom we should consider the true ironists. They are capable of surveying the whole situation; therefore, they are capable of accepting and rejecting corruption, hatred, love, suffering, guilt, and despair.

What de silentio omits is the puzzling relation between Anne and Gloucester, yet Kierkegaard does not forget this scene, which is one of the most beautiful wooing scenes in the history of literature, and returns to it in "Guilty/Not Guilty," published under the pseudonym of Father Taciturnus:

> How did it happen that Richard III could overpower the woman who was his sworn enemy and change her into his lover? And why, I wonder did he do it? Was it politics? Was the derision with which he ponders the ease of his conquest politics also? When he dwells on his own deformity with the passion of despair, was it self-examination, whereby he would perceive himself fit to be king? No, it was a hatred of life; it was by the power of the spirit that he wanted to scoff at nature, which had scoffed at him; he wanted to hold nature up to ridicule together with its invention of erotic love and love of the beautiful, for he, the injured one, he, the cripple, he, the desperate one, he, the devil, wanted to demonstrate, despite language and all the laws of life, that he could be loved. Then he learned, then he discovered that there is a power that works upon women with certainty, *the power of falsehood and lies*, when they are declared with the flame of wild enthusiasm, with the unhealthy excitement of lust, and yet with the chilling coldness of the understanding, just as the strongest wines are served cooled with ice. He himself hated, and yet he aroused erotic love even though women do not like someone like that but are disgusted with him and succumb to him only when dizzy and stunned.[49]

There are more questions than answers in this passage, yet with one phrase the philosopher's pseudonym captures exactly the nature of the relationship between Anne and Richard. She is seduced by "the power of falsehood and lies." In the journal entry which refers to the draft of the *Stages on Life's Way*, there are some further deliberations:

> I know you, you horrifying thoughts, which still are alien to my being, I know that one can infatuate her with words, I understand how Richard III could overpower a woman who was his sworn enemy and change her into his mistress, I know that there is nothing that works so effectively on her as untruth, a lie, when it is rendered with the flaming of wild enthusiasm, with the noxious excitement of lust, I know it; she actually does not love such a person, she almost loathes him, but she becomes dizzy, drugged, she surrenders. It was as if an evil spirit wanted to bring me into his power (for these

---

48   Ibid., p. 131.
49   *SKS* 6, 327 / *SLW*, 352–3. (My emphasis.)

spiritual trails run down and one becomes weary of shrieking, weary of crying, weary of raging, if nothing come of it.) It already offered me as deposit a presentiment of superhuman powers by which I would accomplish great things—in that way rescue my pride and save my honor. Oh, it is a hard road, the transition from being larger than life in the power of evil to being nothing, nothing whatsoever, less than nothing and even less than nothing through the antecedent aberrations of thought.[50]

Jozef Tischner (1931–2000), a Polish priest and philosopher greatly influenced by Kierkegaard, pays much attention in his *Philosophy of Drama* to the psychology of the relations between Richard and Anne. His understanding of the wooing scene can shed some light on Kierkegaard's comments of the play. Tischner focuses on several aspects of the scene, the first one appears in the context of the discussion— the presence of evil within a dialogue. Any seduction is a dialogue; it is also a living being, a process in itself. Seduction has both constant elements, such as the roles (the seducer and the seduced), and changing elements, such as persuasion and the perception of the image of the seducer and the seduced. When Anne is faced with the very essence of evil (Richard appears as a liar, murderer, and villain), she does not hide her hatred, and her only wish is to push Gloucester away. Tischner sees in this reaction two possibilities: the first one is that one runs away from the very sight of evil, and the second one is the breaking of the dialogue (by eliminating the possibility of establishing a dialogue with the other).[51] Both reactions are natural: the latter is guided by hatred and the formed by fear. From Anne's perspective the situation is quite clear: she does not wish to have anything in common with the man who killed her husband and his father. Gloucester's intention, on the other hand, is to show Anne that her beauty was a motivation for his deeds. She is his accomplice, and her beauty is supposed to justify his murders and remove his guilt and responsibility. As Tischner summarizes: "Everything Richard said points out that his murders are not a representation of evil but a misfortune."[52] Richard stresses that the existence of Anne's husband was an accidental obstacle to get her love. "By mere suggestion of misfortune Gloucester hides the essence of evil."[53]

Tischner pays attention to the linguistic techniques used during the seduction, which is the flattery, the accusation of the guilt, and a challenge which intends to check whether evil is in fact true. Seduction seen as a dialogue implies a constant growth of reciprocity of all the doubtful facts presented in the language. Both sides go deeper into flattery, increase the accusations, and constantly check whether evil is present. In flattery the central part plays the "underestimated value of the other."[54] Tischner's conclusion matches quite well with Kierkegaard's opinion: Richard was in fact rescuing his honor by shifting the blame on to Anne. When offered a sword to slay Richard, she fails to do so, because she is still trying to prove to herself that she does not have the evil he assigned to her. Yet she is wicked: "any virtue only

---

[50]   *Pap.* V B 116:7 / *SLW*, Supplement, p. 607.
[51]   Jozef Tischner, *Filozofia Dramatu*, Krakow: Wydawnictwo Znak 2006, p. 137.
[52]   Ibid., p. 144 (my translation).
[53]   Ibid. (my translation).
[54]   Ibid., p. 201 (my translation).

seems to be a virtue,"[55] concludes Tischner, "agreeing to be seduced, the human being shows who he or she really is. When one allows seduction, one has denied one's self."[56]

All in all, Richard III did not play any prominent role in the shaping of Kierkegaard's thoughts, but the philosopher's ideas about the play and its main dramatic *personae* provide valuable insights into the nature of the work.

---

[55]   Ibid., p. 204 (my translation).
[56]   Ibid.,

Bibliography

Alapack, Richard, *Sorrow's Profiles: Death, Grief, and Crisis in the Family*, London: Karnak Books 2010, p. 302.

Dewey, R. Bradley, "Seven Seducers: A Typology of Interpretations of Aesthetic Stage in Kierkegaard's "The Seducer's Diary," in *Either/Or, Part One*, ed. by Robert L. Perkins, Macon, Georgia: Mercer University Press 1995 (*International Kierkegaard Commentary*, vol. 3), pp. 159–201.

Garff, Joakim, "The Esthetic is above all my Element," in *The New Kierkegaard*, ed. by Elsebet Jegstrup, Bloomington: Indiana University Press 2004, p. 56.

Kaufmann, Walter A., *From Shakespeare to Existentialism*, Princeton: Princeton University Press 1980, pp. 175–207.

Leon, Céline, "The No Woman's Land of Kierkegaardian Exceptions," in *Feminist Interpretations of Søren Kierkegard*, ed. by Céline Leon and Sylvia Walsh, University Park, Pennsylvania: Pennsylvania State University Press 1997, pp. 154–9.

Malantschuk, Gregor, *Controversial Kierkegaard*, trans. by Howard V. Hong and Edna H. Hong, Ontario: Wilfrid Laurie University Press 1980, pp. 31–2.

Ruoff, James E., "Kierkegaard and Shakespeare," *Comparative Literature*, vol. 20, 1968, pp. 343–54.

Tischner, Josef, *Filozofia Dramatu* [The Philosophy of Drama], Krakow: Wydawnictwo Znak 2006, pp. 137–49.

Robert le Diable:

A Modern Tragic Figure

Telmo Rodrigues

Robert le Diable is the common name of a medieval folk tale with written records dating back to the thirteenth century, although it might have been first produced around the twelfth century. The main character, Robert, is usually associated with the historical figure of Robert (1000–1035), the Duke of Normandy, son of Richard II (963–1027) and father to William the Conqueror (1028–1087). Due to this association, the character is sometimes referred to as Robert of Normandy, although there are very few known links between the tale and the historical character's life.

According to the legend, Robert was the son of the Devil. His mother, seeing her prayers to God to have a child unanswered, promises the soul of her future child to the Devil. From this promise, a child is born: Robert. Since early youth, Robert shows a tendency towards evil that appalls everyone who comes in contact with him. As a grown man his reputation as a murderer, rapist, and thief precedes him, and the mere sight of his figure causes people to flee. Understanding that his mere presence makes people run, Robert turns to his mother for an explanation as to why he behaves in such a way. Upon hearing his mother's account of his conception, Robert decides to travel to Rome in order to have the Pope hear his confession, making his life goal to expiate the sins of his past life. From this point onwards there are two common variations to the story. The first, and the oldest, has Robert becoming a pilgrim and making his way to Rome in order to confess to the Pope. According to this version, Robert plays a major role in three battles to free Rome from the attacks of the Saracens (or Turks, in some versions) and ends his life as a devout hermit after refusing all rewards offered to him, including the hand of the Emperor's daughter.

When one takes into account Kierkegaard's first mention of Robert le Diable, in a journal entry from January 17, 1837,[1] it is clear that it is the second version of the tale that he has in mind. In this second variation of the story, Robert, after seeking the Pope, is advised by the holy father to seek an old hermit who will show him the way to contrition. After seeking out this hermit, Robert is told that his penance requires him to renounce speaking, to take his food from the mouth of dogs, to behave as a madman, never to retaliate when provoked, and to become the Emperor's court fool. In these versions of the story, Robert also saves Rome from three invasions by the Saracens but in disguise; no one recognizes him except the Emperor's daughter

---

[1]   *SKS* 18, 31–2, FF:35 / *KJN* 2, 75–6.

who falls in love with him. The Emperor's daughter, dumb from birth, is the only
one who knows that the mysterious knight who proved so brave in battle is Robert,
and so she is the only one able to understand that his strange behavior is part of his
penance. Eager to know the identity of the mysterious knight, the Emperor promises
the hand of his daughter to the one who proves to be that knight (several versions
introduce schemes as to how that recognition could be attained, the most common
is a wound suffered in battle that was faked by a pretender to the throne). When the
Emperor's daughter is to be married to a man claiming to be the brave knight, she
miraculously regains her voice and reveals Robert's identity as the unknown knight,
allowing their union at the end of the tale and Robert's succession to the throne.

The differences between the versions of the tale seem to be in Kierkegaard's
mind when he makes the reference to Robert le Diable in his journals. While already
concerned with the central idea to be used in his allusion in *Either/Or*, this particular
reference is centered on the Emperor's daughter when Kierkegaard notes: "it is a
very poetic Governance that causes the girl—the one and only person who is in a
position to know what is concealed under Robert le diable's feigned madness (his
penance)—to be mute."[2] This implies that there is a poetical effort in the recreation
of the original version and that the final version to which Kierkegaard seems to allude
has, within it, some kind of poetical individuality. Maybe there is no philological
concern in Kierkegaard's mention, but there is the clear notion that there was an
evolution in making the girl dumb, prolonging, in a sense, the tragedy in Robert's
tale and that that evolution is intended to reinforce the tale as a literary piece. The
modifications made to the story by Kierkegaard may hold, in part, the clue to why
his attention was attracted by the tale since the development of the story incorporates
more and more of the Romantic topics that are so often treated by the author.

The tale is traceable to the thirteenth century, when it circulated as a metrical
poem. Since it is included in *Anecdotes historiques, légendes et apologues tirés
du Recueil inédit d'Étienne de Bourbon*,[3] it could be credited to the friar Étienne
de Bourbon (ca. 1180–1261) in its most uncorrupted form, originally written in
Latin.[4] The popularity of the story seems to have caused a variation in its ending
since it was moved into the form of a *dit*, a custom that turned famous stories into
poems composed in metrical stanzas that could more easily be remembered and
sung. Guillaume Stanislas Trébutien[5] traces the variation in the ending of the tale

2   *SKS* 18, 32, FF:35 / *KJN* 2, 76.
3   Étienne de Bourbon, *Anecdotes historiques, légendes et apologues tirés du Recueil inédit d'Étienne de Bourbon*, ed. by A. Lecoy de La Marche, Paris: H. Loones 1877, pp. 145–8.
4   In a footnote, the editor of the volume calls attention to the fact that this version of Robert le Diable is not the most well known, explaining that in the end Robert ends up as an hermit; this emphasizes the idea that the version in which Robert marries the Emperor's daughter is a later version.
5   Guillaume Stanislas Trébutien, *Le roman de Robert le Diable: en vers du XIIIe siècle*, Paris: Silvestre Libraire 1837. In a later edition of the poem, Eilert Löseth points out some faults in Trébutien's rendition of the poem and proposes a new edition based on two manuscripts. In the introduction to his edition he identifies the two manuscripts containing the tale as: "A, Fr. 253 16 (anc. La Vallière 80); seconde moitié du XIIIme siécle—*Robert le*

to this moment, implying that the second version emerges only in the fourteenth century when the original *roman* began to proliferate orally as a *dit*. Also according to Trébutien, there was a miracle play[6] being performed in the fourteenth century that might have helped the spreading of the new variation (the text of this play was reprinted in Rouen in 1836).

In 1496 a chapbook was printed in Lyon with the title *La Vie du Terrible Robert le Dyable*,[7] a prose version that might have picked up on the most popular versions of the tale. Two more editions followed the next year, both printed in Paris. Chapbook editions circulated widely and became central to the way tales were disseminated and integrated in the folk repertoire. This 1496 edition seems central to the evolution of the tale and the source of many other editions, particularly the translations to Spanish and English.

While there were some known variations of the French tale circulating in England during the fifteenth century, as was the case with the romance *Sir Gowther*, it is only in the sixteenth century that the tale arrives in its best-known versions. Wynkyn de Worde, one of Caxton's assistants, produced two editions of the tale in the early years of the sixteenth century (none dated). One of these editions was a poem reprinted in 1798 by Isaac Herbert.[8] In the introduction to the poem, Herbert refers to his edition as a transcript from what he believes to be the de Worde edition, although he raises doubts about the true author, naming Pynson as a possible author as well. The second de Worde edition seems to be a direct translation from the French prose versions, a very uncommon practice at the time, which might be an indication as to the popularity of the story. During the sixteenth century this popularity grew and by 1529 a miracle play based on *Robert le Diable* was being performed. In 1591, Thomas Lodge published *The famous, true, and historicall life of Robert second duke of Normandy*,[9] a revised version of the folk tale.

As the dates of many of the reprinted works show, in the late eighteenth century and early nineteenth century there was a great revival of medieval traditions, recovering much oral literature as part of a nationalist identity. But the connection to Kierkegaard's use of the tale seems to suggest a different kind of movement and Giacomo Meyerbeer's opera looks like a crucial element in the history of this tale—in that sense, the entry in the journals works like a veiled critique of Meyerbeer's

---

Diable occupe la fin du volume, à partir du fol. 174"; and "B, Fr. 24405 (anc. La Vallière 38); fin du XIVme siécle ou commencement du XVme.—*Robert le Diable* occupe les 25 premiers feuillets." Eilert Löseth (ed.), *Robert le Diable, Roman D'Aventures*, Paris: Firmin Didot et cie 1903, p. i.

6   *Cy commence un miracle de Nostre-Dame, de Robert le Dyable, filz du duc de Normandie, à qui il fut enjoint pour ses meffaiz qu'il feist le fol sans parler; et depuis ot noitre sire mercy de li et espousa la fille de l'empereur*, Rouen: Ed. Frère 1836 (reprinted from fourteenth-century manuscripts of the Bibliothèque du Roi catalogue).

7   P. Mareschall, *La vie du terrible Robert le Diable lequel apres fut nommé Lomme Dieu*, Lyon 1496.

8   Isaac Herbert, *Roberte the Deuyll. A Metrical Romance, from an Ancient Illuminated Manuscript*, London: Eagerton 1798.

9   Thomas Lodge, *The famous, true, and historicall life of Robert second duke of Normandy*, London: Thomas Orwin 1591.

work where the dumb girl is missing. The opera premiered in Paris in November 21, 1831, with libretto by Eugène Scribe and Casimir Delavigne. It became a huge success and was soon being performed in many important European cities (it was performed in Copenhagen as early as 1833, in a Danish translation).[10] The success of the opera seems to have created a philological stir among many scholars, mainly due to its free interpretation of the story's tradition. Scribe's main plot for the opera introduces the Devil himself as Robert's travel companion, a character named Bertram who is identified in the opera as Robert's father. The success of the opera and its departure from the tale's tradition was probably the cause of many French attempts to trace the tale back to its origins, an attempt that Trébutien's edition of the poem and its introduction seem to confirm. On the other hand, it might be the same kind of success that led Gustav Schwab to include the tale in his compilation of German folk tales.[11]

Kierkegaard's connection with Hamlet, Høgne, and Robert le Diable[12] seems peculiar in the sense that, while Hamlet has obvious connections with Denmark, and Høgne is a character in the Nordic folk stories, one might say that Robert le Diable only comes into the German tradition very late, as late as the nineteenth century. True as it may be that since the late seventeenth century there were accounts of the tale in Germany, or of variations on the same, its inclusion in the German tradition seems to date to 1807, in Joseph Görres' *Die teutschen Volksbücher*.[13] David Blamires, along with other scholars, seems suspicious about the importance of the story in the German tradition,[14] mentioning only the existence of a fifteenth-century German version by a Bavarian cleric, a version that was only rediscovered in the late nineteenth century and so could not have been in Görres' mind at the time of his edition. In 1837, when Schwab published his compilation, *Robert le Diable* was once more introduced as part of the German folk tradition, here known as *Robert der Teufel*, which could be a direct cause of the success of Meyerbeer's opera. Again, the reference by Kierkegaard presents a strange problem in the sense that it is not referred to in German, or even in Danish, as the translation of the opera *Robert af Normandiet*; hence it seems safe to assume that Kierkegaard has at least one of the French versions in mind. More important still, it appears to be the popularity of the opera that induced a revival of the tale in the nineteenth century, spreading its influence to countries where it was not a part of the literary tradition and so allowing Kierkegaard to blend it with the two other characters he mentions.

Aside from these philological problems, what connects Hamlet, Robert, and Høgne is the fact that their course of action, and thus their own nature as individuals, is the result of an anxiety that has its roots in their family past. The reference is made

---

[10]   The libretto was translated by Thomas Overskou (1798–1873), as *Robert af Normandiet* (it premiered on October 28, 1833).

[11]   Gustav Schwab, *Buch der schönsten Geschichten und Sagen für Alt und Jung wieder erzählt*, Stuttgart: S.G. Liesching 1837.

[12]   *SKS* 2, 154 / *EO1*, 155.

[13]   Joseph Görres, *Die teutschen Volksbücher*, Heidelberg: Mohr & Zimmer 1807.

[14]   David Blamires, "The Later Texts in Gustav Schwab's 'Volksbücher': Origins and Character," *Modern Language Review*, vol. 94, no. 1, 1999, pp. 110–21.

in the essay "The Tragic in Ancient Drama," and Kierkegaard identifies these three characters as examples of modern tragic figures:

> Greek sorrow, however, like all Greek life, is in the present, and therefore the sorrow is deeper, but the pain less. Anxiety, therefore, belongs essentially to the tragic. Hamlet is such a tragic figure because he suspects his mother's crime. Robert le diable asks how it could happen that he does so much evil. Høgne, whom his mother had conceived with a troll, accidentally comes to see his image in the water and asks his mother whence his body acquired such a form.[15]

These characters are modern tragic figures not because of the consequences of their actions, though they are important, but because they suspect that their course of action depends on someone else's guilt—in the case of these three characters, that of their mothers. The characters' suspicion induces a kind of anxiety that Kierkegaard remarks as an essential part of tragedy, in the sense that, according to his description of anxiety, it exists in the abstract. None of the characters is certain of why they are as they are, but the doubt is the origin of the anxiety that is present in every action they take in the present and that shapes their individuality (Robert le Diable, not by accident, has in his name the epithet that characterizes his behavior). In these characters, anxiety works as an element that moves around sorrow, constantly trying to recognize the reasons for that sorrow; it is, in a sense, a movement of discovery. When the answer is provided, the anxiety dissolves into sorrow, marking the evolution between ancient and modern tragedy. The difference between ancient and modern tragedy lies in the individual character of modern tragic figures, exemplified in Robert le Diable by the way in which the family guilt falls upon his shoulders and by the way in which it is through his actions that that guilt must be expiated. While in the ancient tragedy it is a "little world"[16] that is disrupted by tragic events, in modern tragedy it is the individual and his tragic path that stand at the center, reflecting the way in which mankind evolved, particularly since the advent of Christianity, a crucial element for Kierkegaard's theory since part of the modern tragedy, particularly in Robert's case, lies in the expiation of someone else's sin (Christ was crucified for humanity's sins).

In his attempt to recreate Antigone as a modern tragic character, Kierkegaard explains that the tragic in modern times is provided by the movement between innocence and guilt, a movement that is central in the progress towards pity. In the original *Antigone*, the tragic element is provided by the "echoes"[17] of Oedipus' tragedy and not by the consequences of Oedipus' guilt on the main character. The element of tragedy in Antigone's downfall comes from the parallels between her story and that of Oedipus, reflecting the family's tragic path; Oedipus' guilt does not have a direct influence on his daughter but casts a shadow over the entire family. In a modern tragic character, like Robert le Diable, the sins of the parents pervade the life of their children. Robert is innocent of his mother's guilt, and yet he still acts and makes decisions that turn him into a guilty character—the tragic element lies in the

---

[15]   *SKS* 2, 154 / *EO1*, 155.
[16]   *SKS* 2, 155 / *EO1*, 156.
[17]   Ibid.

movement between his innocence in the way he was conceived and the guilt in his behavior. In a way, the spectator (or reader) identifies with the character's innocence vis-à-vis the parents' guilt and that provides the tragic aspect within stories that are marked by such strong attempts to expiate their characters' obvious guilt.

By choosing Robert le Diable to stand near Hamlet and Høgne as an example of a modern tragic figure, Kierkegaard is pointing out the different ways in which family guilt works in ancient and modern tragedy. But what sets Robert le Diable apart from the other two characters is his relationship with Christianity, something that mirrors mankind's evolution and Kierkegaard's notion that changes in society must be reflected in a new kind of tragedy. In Robert's story guilt is analogous with Christian sin and the expiation of that sin depends on the relationship between the individual and God. So it is not a coincidence that the Emperor's daughter's dumbness is underlined by Kierkegaard as an intensifier of Robert's tragedy, since it reinforces the strength of the individual in modern tragedy: Robert stands alone in his relationship with God, and it is through it that guilt must be expiated. In this sense, by placing the relationship with God in the foreground and thus emphasizing the importance of Christianity in modern society, Robert's story holds within it not only the features that Kierkegaard identifies with modern tragedy but also the reasons why Kierkegaard believes a modern tragedy is needed.

Bibliography

Alexander, Ian W., "An Existential Appreciation of French Literature," *Forum for Modern Language Studies*, vol. 3, no. 2, 1967, pp. 179–83; see p. 179.

Grimsley, Ronald, *Søren Kierkegaard and French Literature*, Cardiff: University of Wales Press 1966, p. 4.

Typhon:

The Monster in Kierkegaard's Mirror

David D. Possen

I. The Monster

Typhon, the root of the English words "typhoon" and "typhus," was the ancient Greek monster-deity responsible for volcanoes, hurricanes, and tempest winds.[1] More benign weather was credited to other gods. In particular, the thunder and lightning attributed to Zeus was welcomed as morally and cosmologically opposed to Typhon's gales and eruptions.[2] The idea, roughly speaking, was that whereas Zeus sends his life-giving storms down from above, Typhon shoots his murderous storms up from below.[3]

It is significant that Hesiod identifies Typhon as the spawn begotten upon Earth (Gaea) by the Pit (Tartarus).[4] That genealogy befits a subterranean beast who wreaks periodic havoc on the world above ground.[5] It also makes Typhon the cosmological-genealogical opposite number to the numerous children of Earth by Sky (Uranus) who populate Greek myth, chief among them the Titan Cronus, Zeus' father.[6]

Typhonic weather phenomena are both deadly and rare. This is explained by the tale of Typhon's rivalry with Zeus. According to Hesiod, Typhon rebelled against Zeus' kingship and nearly managed to wrest control of the world from him and the other Olympians; but Zeus counterattacked with a massive thunderbolt, imprisoning

---

[1]   Hesiod, *Theogony*, vv. 869ff.

[2]   Zeus' stewardship of benign rain-weather is widely attested; for a celebrated example, see Aristotle, *Physics*, 198b18f (II.8). Complicating the above picture, however, is the fact that on one account Typhon's volcanic fire—here the fire of Mount Etna—is itself said to be derived from the thunder and lightning that Zeus had used to imprison him beneath the mountain. See Pseudo-Apollodorus, *Library*, 1.6.3.

[3]   The most exhaustive depiction of the contrast and conflict between Zeus and Typhon is that of Nonnus of Panopolis in Book II of his *Dionysiaca*, especially vv. 436–508. See also Hesiod, *Theogony*, vv. 869–80.

[4]   Hesiod, *Theogony*, vv. 820–1.

[5]   At *Library*, 2.1.2, Pseudo-Apollodorus attributes the same parentage to Typhon's mate, the monster snake-nymph Echidna, kidnapper of unwary travelers (ἥ τοὺς παριόντας συνήρπαζεν). Apollodorus, *Bibliothèque d'Apollodore l'Athénien*, vols. 1–2, ed. by Étienne Clavier, Paris: Delance & Le Sueur 1805, vol. 1, p. 116.

[6]   Hesiod, *Theogony*, v. 138.

Typhon in his father's home, the underworld Pit.[7] The meteorological moral of this story seems to be that even if Typhon, whose name derives from the Greek word for "steaming" (τύφειν), does periodically make his presence on Earth known with volcanic eruptions, and the like, he cannot actually overthrow Zeus' benign rule. At the end of the day, the Sky-god of thunder and lightning will always defeat the Pit-beast of tempest and lava.[8]

In his *Histories*, Herodotus reveals a different side of Typhon: he is the Greek counterpart to the Egyptian storm-god Seth. In the great mythic epic of Pharaonic Egypt, Seth—"Typhon" to Herodotus—murders the god-king Osiris and nearly succeeds in killing Horus, Osiris' son by Isis, as well.[9] Much later Plutarch, musing on the same story in his *Moralia*, reflects on the Greeks' identification of Seth with Typhon. He justifies it as follows: "Typhon is that part of the soul which is impressionable, impulsive, irrational and truculent, and of the bodily part the destructible, diseased and disorderly....The name 'Seth,' by which [the Egyptians] call Typhon, denotes this."[10]

In the history of philosophy, finally, Typhon matters mainly because of the role he plays for Plato as Socrates' emblem for the monstrosity of human ignorance. Early in Plato's dialogue *Phaedrus*, the title character tries to lure Socrates into a playful discussion of Greek myth.[11] Socrates responds that he has no time to busy himself with questions about such beings as Pegasuses or the Gorgons, as he is preoccupied with a matter far more serious than the status of mythological beasts. That is the prospect that he himself is a more horrid beast than the worst monster of Greek myth, namely, Typhon:

> I myself have certainly no time for the business, and I'll tell you why, my friend. I can't as yet "know myself," as the inscription at Delphi enjoins, and so long as that ignorance remains it seems to me ridiculous to inquire into extraneous matters. Consequently I don't bother about such things, but accept the current beliefs about them, and direct my inquiries, as I have just said, rather to myself, to discover whether I really am a more complex creature and more puffed up with pride than Typhon, or a simpler, gentler being whom heaven has blessed with a quiet, un-Typhonic nature.[12]

Socrates' core argument is that it makes little sense for him to devote time to investigating the existence of monsters in the heavens, or in the past, when he still cannot rule out the possibility that a monster even worse than Typhon is lurking in his own soul right now.

[7]   Hesiod, *Theogony*, vv. 820–68.
[8]   Compare Psalm 104:7 and 9 (King James version): "At Thy rebuke [the waters] fled; at the voice of Thy thunder they hasted away....Thou hast set a bound that they may not pass over; that they turn not again to cover the earth."
[9]   Herodotus, *Histories*, 2.156.4.
[10]   Plutarch, *Moralia*, vol. 5, trans. by Frank Cole Babbitt, Cambridge, Massachusetts: Harvard University Press 1936 (*Loeb Classical Library*, no. 306), p. 121 (§ 49, 371b).
[11]   Plato, *Phaedrus*, 229b.
[12]   Plato, *Phaedrus*, 229d–230a. Plato, *Collected Dialogues*, ed. by Edith Hamilton and Huntington Cairns, Princeton: Princeton University Press 1963 (*Bollingen Series*, vol. 71), p. 478.

While Kierkegaard was aware of Typhon's significance in all three of the spheres just discussed—Greek myth, Egyptian myth (as interpreted by Greeks), and the inner world of Socratic reflection—his main interest lay with the Socratic Typhon. The Egyptian Typhon does, as we will see, make one prominent appearance in the *Concluding Unscientific Postscript* (1846). But the bulk of Kierkegaard's Typhon references are to Plato's *Phaedrus* 229e–230a, that is, the remark by Socrates cited above. Accordingly, this article will begin (in Section II) by briefly taking note of Kierkegaard's interest in the Egyptian Typhon-myth, and will then proceed (in Section III) to more detailed consideration of the significance of *Phaedrus* 229e–230a for Kierkegaard's thought. Section IV will round our discussion off with a short conclusion.

II. Kierkegaard and the Egyptian Typhon

In Kierkegaard's day, the philosopher F.W.J. Schelling (1775–1854) described the Typhon [Seth]–Isis–Osiris–Horus cycle as not only the fundamental event of Egyptian mythology, but also an anticipation of Christianity's drama of divine incarnation. Schelling made this claim in his 1842 Berlin lectures on "The Philosophy of Revelation," which Kierkegaard attended in person. Building on remarks by Plutarch, Schelling identified Typhonic evil as the main object of tension in Egyptian myth, with Isis, Osiris, and Horus respectively representing the living God, the dying God, and God reborn.[13] Kierkegaard's detailed lecture notes include the following summary of Schelling's interpretation of the myth:

> The *Egyptian* [mythology] has the most heated battle with the blind principle, which is indeed mastered, but its last strength is consumed in the process. It is Typhon's struggle to the death, [the death of] the material principle. Osiris is the good divinity. Victory is uncertain; at one point, T[yphon] is torn to bits, at another, O[siris]. Only when Horos, the third potency, arrives is T[yphon] overcome. Isis is the principle, linked to God, which hovers between T[yphon] and O[siris] until it gives birth to Horos. T[yphon] himself becomes Osiris. He exists, in fact, only in his opposition to Osiris; when transformed into Osiris, he is invisible, the god of the underworld. The second is Osiris himself. The third is Horos, who is *Geist*.[14]

Though he faithfully recorded this Christian interpretation of the Egyptian Typhon-myth in his notebook, Kierkegaard does not refer to it explicitly anywhere in his published writings.[15] In his *Concluding Unscientific Postscript*, however,

13   F.W.J. Schelling, *Urfassung der Philosophie der Offenbarung*, ed. by Walter E. Ehrhardt, Hamburg: Felix Meiner 1992, pp. 254–56, p. 254: "*Die Ägyptische [Mythologie ist] diejenige, in welcher der heftigste Kampf gegen das blinde Prinzip entzündet ist....Dieses, in der Ägyptischen Mythologie in die höchste Spannung gesetzte, Prinzip ist der ägyptische* Typhon."
14   *SKS* 19, 362, Not11:37–8 / *KJN* 3, 360–1.
15   Unless the line "The parallel with Isis, Osiris, and Typhon does not concern me" (*SKS* 7, 91 / *CUP1*, 92), cited below, is meant to distance Climacus from not only Plutarch's but also Schelling's evaluation of the myth.

Kierkegaard does direct attention to Schelling's main source-text, namely Plutarch. In his *Moralia*, Plutarch draws a rough parallel between the Typhon–Isis–Osiris–Horus cycle and Socrates' account of the origins of Love in Plato's *Symposium*.[16] I say "rough" parallel because Plutarch does not spell out all of the literary equivalences at stake. He merely remarks that Horus, the World-god, resembles Socrates' Eros in possessing an intermediate nature, that is, in ever dying and being reborn, a true child of Want and Plenty.[17]

In the *Postscript*, Kierkegaard's pseudonym Johannes Climacus adopts Plutarch's remark as equally applicable to his own characterization of existence as a synthesis of earthly want and divine plenty:

> The nature of existence calls to mind the Greek conception of Eros as found in the *Symposium*, and which Plutarch correctly explains in his work on Isis and Osiris (§57). The parallel with Isis, Osiris, and Typhon does not concern me, but when Plutarch calls to mind that Hesiod assumed Chaos, Earth, Tartarus, and Eros to be primordial entities, it is very correct in this connection to recall Plato. Here erotic love manifestly means existence or that by which life is in everything, the life that is a synthesis of the infinite and the finite. According to Plato, Poverty and Plenty begot Eros, whose nature is made up of both. But what is existence? It is that child who is begotten by the infinite and the finite, the eternal and the temporal, and is therefore continually striving. This was Socrates' view—therefore love is continually striving, that is, the thinking subject is existing.[18]

Climacus here correlates Plutarch's account of the birth and nature of Horus, and Plato's account of the birth and nature of Eros, with the genealogy and definitions that he himself is offering for existence and subjective thinking.

This passage is valuable for decoding the *Postscript*. For our present purpose, however, it merely marks the end of the line. Climacus grants Typhon only tangential significance as the dark foil to Isis, Osiris, and Horus. By extension, perhaps, Typhon might also be said to represent a kind of abyss against which genuine existence and subjective thinking are organized. But the latter thought remains undeveloped, as it "does not concern" Climacus. If we wish to find loci where Typhon is a manifestly central figure for Kierkegaard, then we will have to seek elsewhere. We will need to turn from the Typhon of Egypt to the monster feared by Plato's Socrates.

III. The Monster in Socrates' Mirror—and in Our Own

In a separate article published earlier in this series,[19] I wrote at length about the extraordinary importance of *Phaedrus* 229e–230a—henceforth the "Typhon

---

[16]   Plutarch, *Moralia*, 374d-e (§ 57).

[17]   Ibid.

[18]   *SKS* 7, 91 / *CUP1*, 92.

[19]   David D. Possen, "*Phaedrus*: Kierkegaard on Socrates' Self-Knowledge—and Sin," in *Kierkegaard and the Greek World*, Tome I, *Socrates and Plato*, ed. by Jon Stewart and Katalin Nun, Aldershot: Ashgate 2010 (*Kierkegaard Research: Sources, Reception and Resources*, vol. 2), pp. 73–86.

passage"—to Kierkegaard's Socrates interpretation and philosophy of religion. I there explained that Kierkegaard, following Ferdinand Christian Baur (1792–1860), interprets Socrates' remark about Typhon as evidence that something analogous to the Christian consciousness of sin can already be discerned in Socrates' self-understanding.[20] On that basis, Kierkegaard argued that Socrates, albeit a pagan and millennia out of date, still has much to teach Denmark's Lutherans about what it means to become and be a Christian.[21]

The pages that follow will cover some of the same ground as my earlier article, though with different aims and a correspondingly different methodology. Here my concern is primarily literary, rather than philosophical; my focus is not so much to analyze the relevant passages for their philosophical implications as it is to provide an overview of the fate and significance of Socrates' Typhon over the course of Kierkegaard's authorship. I will thus proceed chronologically, and at a fair clip.

The first two references to Typhon in Kierkegaard's published authorship appeared in 1843, one in each of *Fear and Trembling* and *Repetition*, the twin pseudonymous works published on October 16 of that year. The reference in *Repetition* is brief and occurs in the context of an extended discussion of theatrical "farce" (*Possen*); what is at stake are the human conditions that actors must fulfill for farce to succeed. Here Constantin Constantius, the pseudonymous author, interjects that even to fulfill or evaluate the conditions for being a human being at all is no easy matter. "People will certainly agree," he writes, "if they stop to consider that Socrates, who was particularly strong in the knowledge of human nature and in self-knowledge, 'did not know for sure whether he was a human being or an even more changeable [*endnu mere foranderligt*] animal than Typhon.'"[22] After touching on this point, Constantius veers away again: "In farce, however...."

There is a noteworthy lightness to this aside. This is signaled not only by the brevity of Constantine's interjection, but also by his use of "even more changeable" (*endnu mere foranderligt*)[23] to paraphrase πολυπλοκώτερον καὶ μᾶλλον ἐπιτεθυμμένον ... ζῷον,[24] the Greek phrase in *Phaedrus* 230a that has been classically translated as "a more complex creature and puffed up with pride."

---

[20]   On Baur's reading, the Typhon passage illustrates how "the more deeply consciousness burrows into itself, the more surely self-knowledge encounters the sin that inheres in a human being's deepest essence." Ferdinand Christian Baur, *Das Christliche des Platonismus, oder Sokrates und Christus*, Tübingen, L.F. Fues 1837 (*ASKB* 422), pp. 23–4. On Kierkegaard's relation to Baur, see David D. Possen, "F.C. Baur: On the Similarity and Dissimilarity between Jesus and Socrates," in *Kierkegaard and His German Contemporaries*, Tome II, *Theology*, ed. by Jon Stewart, Aldershot: Ashgate 2007 (*Kierkegaard Research: Sources, Reception and Resources*, vol. 6), pp. 23–38.

[21]   Cf. *SKS* 16, 36 / *PV*, 54.

[22]   *SKS* 4, 37 / *R*, 162–3.

[23]   Kierkegaard appears to have derived this paraphrase from his 1842–43 reading of Wilhelm Gottlieb Tennemann, *Geschichte der Philosophie*, vols. 1–11, Leipzig: J.A. Barth 1798–1819 (*ASKB* 815–826). At vol. 5, p. 302, Tennemann writes merely *ein anderes wandelbareres Thier*. See Kierkegaard's reading notes at *SKS* 19, 395, Not13:28 / *KJN* 3, 393.

[24]   Plato, *Phaedrus*, ed. by Harvey Yunis, Cambridge: Cambridge University Press 2011, p. 37.

The Greek text is in fact more forceful than Constantin's word *foranderligt*, "changeable" or "variable"—which one might use of a chameleon—would suggest. The adjective ἐπιτεθυμμένον is derived from the verb ἐπιτύφεσθαι (literally "to be consumed"), which is itself a derivative of the basic Typhonic verb τύφειν ("to smoke"). It connotes inflammation and violent energy. Elsewhere, we will soon see, Kierkegaard chooses Danish words with darker connotations—*sammensat* ("complex"), which is commonly paired with *Uhyre* ("monster"), and *besynderlig* ("curious"), with its echo of the word *Synd* ("sin")—to describe Typhon and the Typhonic horror that is the object of Socrates' concern.

But there is a slow descent from the chameleon of *Repetition* to the baleful monster of later works. In *Fear and Trembling*, for example, Typhon is already invoked indirectly as a symbol of "evil." In a broadside against contemporary Lutheran writers who are unconcerned about sin, and who in fact preach that human beings have "already attained the highest,"[25] Kierkegaard's pseudonym Johannes de silentio notes that "even in the inherently more irresponsible and less reflective paganism the two authentic representatives of the Greek view of life, γνῶθι σαυτόν ["Know thyself!"], each in his own way hinted that, by penetratingly concentrating on oneself, one first and foremost discovers the disposition to evil. I scarcely need to say that I am thinking of Pythagoras and Socrates."[26] Here the pagan Socrates, together with Pythagoras, is lauded as having come closer to awareness of "evil" than have the nominally Christian targets of Johannes' polemic—in Socrates' case by worrying that he might be a monster worse than Typhon.

At this point I will skip three years ahead in Kierkegaard's authorship, in order to contrast the indirect reference to Socrates' Typhon just cited in *Fear and Trembling* (1843) with a similar reference in the *Concluding Unscientific Postscript* (1846). In the latter text, the pseudonym Johannes Climacus notes dryly that Socrates is said "to have discovered within himself…a disposition to all evil; it may even have been this discovery that prompted him to give up the study of astronomy, which the times now demand."[27] It is noteworthy that "the disposition to evil" (*Dispositionen til det Onde*) referred to in *Fear and Trembling* now appears as "a disposition to *all* evil" (*Dispositionen til* alt *Ondt*).[28] This suggests that we are no longer talking about a mere malicious streak in human nature, but are contemplating the capacity to become malicious without limit: to be as evil as can be, and perhaps even to be evil through and through. As Climacus then admits about himself: "I am a corrupt and corruptible man…."[29]

What explains this change in Kierkegaard's use of Socrates' Typhon from 1843 to 1846? The answer is best sought in *Philosophical Fragments* (1844), a chronologically intervening text also attributed to Johannes Climacus, and which

---

25   *SKS* 4, 190 / *FT*, 100.
26   *SKS* 4, 190, note 1 / *FT*, 100, note.
27   *SKS* 7, 150 / *CUP1*, 161.
28   *SKS* 4, 190, note 1 / *FT*, 100, note; *SKS* 7, 150 / *CUP1*, 161.
29   *SKS* 7, 150 / *CUP1*, 161. For an extended discussion of the philosophical implications of these passages, see Possen, "*Phaedrus*: Kierkegaard on Socrates' Self-Knowledge—and Sin," pp. 78–9.

contains all of Kierkegaard's three remaining references to *Phaedrus* 229e–230a. In these three passages, Socrates is described as, respectively, being uncertain whether he is "a more curious monster [*et besynderligere Uhyre*] than Typhon or a friendlier and simpler being, by nature sharing something divine";[30] not knowing whether he is "a more curiously complex animal [*et mere besynderligt sammensat Dyr*] than Typhon or whether he has in his being a gentler and diviner part";[31] and, finally, being "almost bewildered about himself [*næsten raadvild over sig selv*]," not knowing whether he was "a more curious monster [*et besynderligere Uhyre*] than Typhon, or whether there was something divine in him."[32]

In the context of the argument of *Philosophical Fragments*, these three varying but closely proximate citations and paraphrases connect Socrates' Typhonic worry with the consciousness of sin that Christianity demands. Climacus makes this connection explicit following the final passage. He there analyzes Socrates' Typhonic confusion as a symptom of Socrates' *failure* to attain the consciousness of sin, which can be acquired only by the direct provision of divine grace: "What did [Socrates] lack, then? The consciousness of sin, which he could no more teach to any other person than any other person could teach it to him. Only the god could teach it—if he wanted to be teacher."[33]

The line just cited might be thought to suggest that Climacus' rhetorical aim in citing *Phaedrus* 229e–230a is to *contrast* Typhonic anxiety—the fear that one is evil beyond measure—with the Christian consciousness of sin. But that cannot be the whole story. As I have pointed out elsewhere,[34] Climacus in fact uses strikingly *similar* language to describe Socrates' Typhonic anxiety and the Christian convert's dawning awareness of sin, even where he appears to be pinpointing the difference between them. Whereas Climacus portrays Socrates, we saw above, as "almost bewildered about himself" (*næsten raadvild over sig selv*) in his Typhonic doubt, he recounts the Christian convert's progress as follows: "Through the moment, the learner becomes untruth; the person who knew himself becomes confused about himself [*raadvild over sig selv*] and instead of self-knowledge he acquires the consciousness of sin."[35] While the final words here do indeed contrast Socrates' goal of self-knowledge[36] with the consciousness of sin that the Christian convert gains, the passage's earlier words highlight the similarity between the two, namely, the similarity between being "nearly confused" and being "confused" about the self. Both Christian and Socratic experience, it would seem, are varieties of self-confusion.

We may still presume, of course, that there is an enormous difference between these two forms of bewilderment, a difference which must amount to nothing less than the difference between Christian knowledge and Socratic ignorance. This would be the difference signaled by the modifier "nearly" (*næsten*), the difference

---

30   *SKS* 4, 242 / *PF*, 37.
31   *SKS* 4, 244 / *PF*, 39.
32   *SKS* 4, 251 / *PF*, 47.
33   *SKS* 4, 252 / *PF*, 47.
34   Possen, "*Phaedrus*: Kierkegaard on Socrates' Self-Knowledge—and Sin," pp. 79–83.
35   *SKS* 4, 255 / *PF*, 52.
36   *SKS* 4, 190, note 1 / *FT*, 100, note. See Section I above.

between being confused and being nearly confused about the self. But if we interrogate *Philosophical Fragments* more concretely about the content of this difference—as Climacus himself does when he asks, "What did [Socrates] lack, then? The consciousness of sin"[37]—we learn little more than that it is sin itself that is at stake, and that "only the god can teach it," since sin cannot be made manifest to a human being except by means of revelation.[38] But that implies, in turn, that Climacus himself cannot himself tell us what sin is, and so cannot explain how the state of self-confusion in which a Christian moves "beyond Socrates" differs from Socrates' own state of Typhonic doubt. The same, moreover, is true for the rest of us: we would need to be "confused" in the ordinary sense of the word to imagine that we know the relevant difference between being "almost confused" (*næsten raadvild*) and being fully "confused" (*raadvild*) about ourselves.[39]

If we now step back and survey these invocations of Socrates' Typhon diachronically—moving from *Repetition* and *Fear and Trembling* to *Philosophical Fragments* and its *Postscript*—what we find is a change in how Kierkegaard's pseudonyms make use of the *Phaedrus* passage. While Constantin Constantius depicts Socrates' self-concern with light humor, Johannes de silentio does so more darkly, highlighting the humility of Socrates and Pythagoras as a foil to Golden Age Denmark's brazenly unreflective Christians. Johannes Climacus, finally, draws a firm link between Socrates' Typhonic doubt and the confrontation with one's own sin that true Christianity demands. This is not to say that Climacus conflates the two, but that he highlights the one as a vital human guide to the other. And this, ultimately, is why the monster of Plato's *Phaedrus* mattered so much to Kierkegaard. Typhon is not just any monster; he is the monster in Socrates' mirror—and as such is a reminder of the savage beast that peers back at us out of our own.[40]

IV. The Monster in Kierkegaard's Mirror

Let us conclude by taking one further step back. Let us consider Kierkegaard's use of Typhon as a literary figure in the broadest possible sense, without regard for distinctions among the Typhon of Greek myth, the Typhon of Egypt, or Socrates' Typhon-figure.

Who is the Typhon common to all of these contexts? He is a beast who is both monstrously inhuman and monstrously all-too-human. Typhon is an enemy to be feared and fought, to be fended off and fenced away; but he cannot be eliminated entirely, as his place of confinement is always beneath us, or (as for Socrates) within us. In the Kierkegaardian drama of existence, the "Typhonic element"[41] cannot be

---

[37]   *SKS* 4, 251 / *PF*, 47.

[38]   *SKS* 4, 224 / *PF*, 14–15. See also *SKS* 11, 209 / *SUD*, 96.

[39]   For discussion of the philosophical implications of this result, see Possen, "*Phaedrus*: Kierkegaard on Socrates' Self-Knowledge—and Sin," pp. 79–83.

[40]   See the motto from Lichtenberg at *SKS* 6, 16 / *SLW*, 8: "Such works are mirrors: when an ape looks in, no apostle can look out."

[41]   *SKS* 19, 365, Not11:38 / *KJN* 3, 364.

purged. Its presence must be acknowledged, for it follows us like a shadow, or a reflection.

In *The Sickness unto Death*, Anti-Climacus distinguishes between despair "over" the self and despair "of" the self.[42] In due course, the first of these two kinds of despair—a wish to repudiate or disclaim the self in frustration, in Anti-Climacus' terms, "not willing to be oneself"—turns out to be folly, a failure to face up to the extent to which we are contributing to our own despair. The second kind of despair, on the other hand—despair *of* the self, in which we acknowledge our alienation from our true selves, acknowledge that we lack the capacity to become ourselves on our own—turns out to be useful. Despairing of the self is, we learn, "the condition for healing" despair.[43] "This repenting *of*" is, quite literally, the *of* of repentance [*denne* Om*vendelse*]."[44]

One of the rhetorical goals of *The Sickness unto Death* is to convince its readers to abandon the first kind of despair and embrace the second, healing kind. In the voice of a spiritual advisor counseling a man prone to despairing *over* the self, Anti-Climacus writes: "You are quite right about the weakness [in your self], but that is not what you are to despair *over*; the self must be broken in order to become itself, but quit despairing *over* that…you must go through the despair *of* the self to the self."[45] The man in despair, in other words, should not despair over his manifest weakness—his inner Typhon—and imagine that he can purge himself of it on his own. He should instead despair *of* his true, strong self, and should appeal to God to restore his self to him.

This spiritual counsel is one of Kierkegaard's most potent messages to his readers, and it pervades the Climacus writings as well as *The Sickness unto Death*. Here the figure of Typhon is vital to its articulation. The core message is that we are always already self-alienated beings, wracked by Typhonic civil war, and we cannot ultimately overcome this predicament by brute force. The most we can do—indeed, the only thing we ourselves can do in the hope of changing our situation—is to despair *of* our true selves: to acknowledge our predicament and flee to God's restoring grace.[46]

Unfortunately, laments Climacus, we are short of role models of such flight to grace. The clerics of our age are self-satisfied so-called Christians, ignorant of their ignorance and incapacity and need of grace. As Kierkegaard would later put it, they are modern Sophists.[47] Hence we do best to return to the Sophists' stalwart enemy, Socrates, and his Typhonic anxiety, to find a model of the anxiety about sin that Christianity demands. And so it should be no surprise that this consummately pagan monster makes appearances at some of the most strident junctures in Kierkegaard's

---

[42]   *SKS* 11, 175n / *SUD*, 60–1n.

[43]   *SKS* 11, 175n / *SUD*, 61n.

[44]   Ibid. *Om*, the Danish word for "of," is the first morpheme in the word *Omvendelse*, "repentance."

[45]   *SKS* 11, 179 / *SUD*, 65, emphasis added.

[46]   For more on this message and its sources, see Possen, "*Phaedrus*: Kierkegaard on Socrates' Self-Knowledge—and Sin," pp. 83–6.

[47]   Cf. *SKS* 13, 405 / *M*, 341.

rhetoric on behalf of Christianity. For it is precisely by way of reintroducing his readers to Typhon—the monster who peers out not only of Socrates' mirror, but also out of the literary mirror that Kierkegaard seeks to hold up to his readers' gaze— that Kierkegaard pursues his core polemical aim: to reintroduce Christianity into Christendom.

Bibliography

Howland, Jacob, *Kierkegaard and Socrates: A Study in Philosophy and Faith*, Cambridge: Cambridge University Press 2006, pp. 104–14.

Possen, David D., "F.C. Baur: On the Similarity and Dissimilarity between Jesus and Socrates," in *Kierkegaard and His German Contemporaries*, Tome II, *Theology*, ed. by Jon Stewart, Aldershot: Ashgate 2007 (*Kierkegaard Research: Sources, Reception and Resources*, vol. 6), pp. 23–38; see pp. 31–3.

— "*Meno*: Kierkegaard and the Doctrine of Recollection," in *Kierkegaard and the Greek World*, Tome I, *Socrates and Plato*, ed. by Jon Stewart and Katalin Nun, Aldershot: Ashgate 2010 (*Kierkegaard Research: Sources, Reception and Resources*, vol. 2), pp. 27–44; see pp. 39–42.

— "*Phaedrus*: Kierkegaard on Socrates' Self-Knowledge—and Sin," in *Kierkegaard and the Greek World*, Tome I, *Socrates and Plato*, ed. by Jon Stewart and Katalin Nun, Aldershot: Ashgate 2010 (*Kierkegaard Research: Sources, Reception and Resources*, vol. 2), pp. 73–86; see pp. 73–83.

The Wandering Jew:

Kierkegaard and the Figuration of Death in Life

Joseph Ballan

I. The Wandering Jew: A Christian Legend

Over the centuries, there have been countless variations on the figure of the Wandering Jew (or, in German and Danish, the Eternal Jew (*Der Ewige Jude, Den Evige Jøde*), sometimes also called Ahasverus or Ahasuerus), but the basic structure of the story accounting for his origin is relatively simple. When Jesus is carrying his cross on the way to the hill where he is to be crucified, he stops to rest in front of a Jewish man's house, but this man informs him that he cannot rest there, and so must continue on his dolorous way. As retold in the economical prose of Swedish novelist Pär Lagerkvist's *The Sibyl*, Jesus then says to this man, "Because I may not lean my head against your house your soul shall be unblessed forever....Because you denied me this, you shall suffer greater punishment than mine: you shall never die. You shall wander through this world to all eternity, and find no rest."[1] Although the legend has roots in the Middle Ages, this particular narrative frame, which would provide the basis for modern literary permutations of the older story, originates in a German pamphlet of 1602, the *Kurtze Beschreibung und Erzählung von einem Juden mit Namen Ahasverus*, which notes that Ahasverus had recently appeared in Danzig. In his literary history of the Wandering Jew, George Anderson enumerates seventeen characteristics of this Christian legend that define the modern retellings of it, and that are all brought together for this first time in this document, including the shabby appearance of the character, his taciturn nature, his occupation (shoemaker), the broad knowledge he had accumulated over centuries of wandering, and the observation that, because he knows his fate, "he is seldom seen to laugh or even to smile."[2] This tale epitomizes much older Christian attitudes toward Jewish populations, symbolized, before Ahasverus, by the figure of Cain, condemned to wander the earth because of his sin. Already in the Middle Ages, Robert Chazan notes, Christians interpreted the diaspora of the Jewish people as divine punishment for the rejection of Christ in terms of the Cain story: "the triple themes of fratricide, banishment from the land, and a lifetime of wandering much enriched Christian

---

[1]   Pär Lagerkvist, *Sibyllan*, Stockholm: Bonniers Forlag 1956, pp. 17–18. (English translation: *The Sibyl*, trans. by Naomi Walford, New York: Vintage 1958, p. 12.)

[2]   George K. Anderson, *The Legend of the Wandering Jew*, Providence: Brown University Press 1965, pp. 47–8.

imagery of post-Crucifixion fate,"[3] and perhaps nowhere in such a lasting way than with the character of Ahasverus.[4]

The *Kurtze Beschreibung*, along with three other pamphlets that modify that version's story in some small way or another, make up what Anderson calls, by analogy with the "Faust-book," the kind of book of folk legend often derided and ignored by the "assistant professor," according to Kierkegaard,[5] an "Ahasverus book" formed in the early years of the seventeenth century.[6] Gradually, with the "heightening of anti-Jewish tension," the tale spread to other regions of Europe, including Denmark, where one of these four pamphlets was translated as the *Sandru beskriffuelse*, printed in 1621 and subsequently in 1631 and 1695.[7]

II. Kierkegaard's Sources of Knowledge about the Wandering Jew

Some notes from 1835 enumerate sources on the figure of the Wandering Jew that Kierkegaard hoped to consult for a project, which never came to fruition, that would connect the stories of Don Juan, Faust, and the Wandering Jew.[8] This project itself, as Peter Tudvad notes, may have had a precedent in a work by the right Hegelian Carl Friedrich Göschel,[9] although it cannot be certain that Kierkegaard ever even had access to this book. The aforementioned entry, which contains some of the same bibliographical information as an 1835 entry, includes a list of dissertations submitted to German universities and briefly summarized in Rasmus Nyerup's *Almindelig Morskabslæsning i Danmark og Norge igjennem Aarhundreder*.[10] In his overview of the literature, Nyerup includes variants of the story of "The Jerusalem Shoemaker," as the Wandering Jew was sometimes called in the Nordic countries,[11] in which he was a doorkeeper rather than a shoemaker and named Cartophilus rather than Ahaseurus.[12] Kierkegaard makes brief note of these variants along with the

---

[3]   Robert Chazan, *Reassessing Jewish Life in Medieval Europe*, New York: Cambridge University Press 2010, p. 87.

[4]   The trope of the Wandering Jew has a long history, extending well into the modern period. For example, one of the most notorious films produced by the Nazi regime in Germany was entitled *Der ewige Jude* (1940, directed by Fritz Hippler). It is practically a catalog of ugly anti-Semitic stereotypes. Here, as elsewhere, the "eternity" of the Eternal Jew has become the immutability of Jewish racial characteristics.

[5]   *SKS* 2, 95–6 / *EO1*, 91.

[6]   Anderson, *The Legend of the Wandering Jew*, pp. 52–3.

[7]   Ibid., p. 66.

[8]   *SKS* 19, 95, NB2:12 / *KJN* 4, 91. See Knud Jensenius, *Nogle Kierkegaardstudier. "De tre store Ideer,"* Copenhagen: Nyt Nordisk Forlag Arnold Busck 1932.

[9]   Peter Tudvad, *Stadier på antisemitismens vej. Søren Kierkegaard og jøderne*, Copenhagen: Rosinante 2010, pp. 83–7.

[10]   Rasmus Nyerup, *Almindelig Morskabslæsning i Danmark og Norge igjennem Aarhundreder*, Copenhagen: Brøderne Thiele 1816, pp. 180–3.

[11]   See also the series of poems by Bernhard Severin Ingemann, *Blade af Jerusalems Skomagers Lommebog*, Copenhagen: Andreas Seidelin 1833. *SKS* 17, 107, BB:16 / *KJN* 1, 100.

[12]   Ingemann, *Blade af Jerusalems Skomagers Lommebog*, p. 182.

list of dissertations.[13] There is no evidence that Kierkegaard actually read any of these scholarly works, much less all of them, but it is clear that he was familiar with some of the important Romantic depictions of the Wandering Jew, including a book of folk literature,[14] whose narrative of the Wandering Jew's eventual conversion to Christianity was, according to Anderson, an especially influential document for many of the nineteenth-century writers interested in the Wandering Jew.[15] This volume would have corrected Kierkegaard's earlier assumption,[16] namely, that this fictional character was a product of the Jewish imagination (as Faust is a product of the German imagination, according to the same entry), when it is in fact a Christian legend.[17]

Other German literary depictions of the Wandering Jew known to Kierkegaard and grouped among his sources for the project including Faust and Don Juan are poems by August Wilhelm Schlegel ("Die Warnung")[18] and Wilhelm Müller ("Der Ewige Jude")[19] and Goethe's autobiography, *Aus Meinem Leben*. In the latter, Goethe notes that he had been influenced by books of folk literature, presumably of the sort mentioned above.[20] In the traditional story, Ahasverus meets Jesus for the first time when Christ is on the *via dolorosa*. Goethe planned to write an epic in which the Wandering Jew had known Jesus before this episode. In his re-imagining of the episode, Ahasverus, a man of the world who nonetheless had a "special affection" for Jesus, tries to persuade the Jewish preacher to avoid public proclamation and to live the life of a contemplative. Meanwhile, Christ attempts to reach Ahasverus with his own message through parables. Neither interlocutor convinces the other. These modifications of the story, such that the traditional scene on the road to Golgotha would not be the first time and place that these two characters meet, have the effect of "motivat[ing]" the eventual "despair" of the Wandering Jew, in Kierkegaard's

---

[13]   *SKS* 19, 95, NB2:12 / *KJN* 4, 91.

[14]   Ludwig Aurbacher, *Ein Volksbüchlein. Enthaltend die Geschichte des ewigen Juden, die Abenteuer der sieben Schwaben, nebst vielen andern erbaulichen und ergötzlichen Historien*, vol. 1, Munich: Michael Lindauer 1835. See *SKS* 19, 94–5, Not2:10–11 / *KJN* 4, pp. 90–1.

[15]   Anderson, *The Legend of the Wandering Jew*, pp. 198–9.

[16]   See *SKS* 27, 185, Papir 253 / *JP* 5, 5110.

[17]   *SKS* 19, 94, Not2:10 / *KJN* 4, 90. Bartholomew Ryan suggests that to these works of German Romanticism may be added some poetic fragments of Percy Bysshe Shelley, which Kierkegaard knew in German translation, and that deal with the Wandering Jew. Kierkegaard does not, however, cite the poems in question. See "Percy Bysshe Shelley: Anxious Journeys, the Demonic, and 'Breaking the Silence,' " in *Kierkegaard and the Renaissance and Modern Traditions*, Tome III, *Literature, Drama and Music*, ed. by Jon Stewart, Aldershot: Ashgate 2009 (*Kierkegaard Research: Sources, Reception and Resources*, vol. 5), pp. 221–2.

[18]   August Wilhelm Schlegel, *Poetische Werke*, Heidelberg: Mohr & Zimmer 1811, pp. 196–203.

[19]   Wilhelm Müller, *Vermischte Schriften*, Leipzig: Brodhaus 1830, vol. 1, pp. 162–4.

[20]   Johann Wolfgang von Goethe, *Dichtung und Wahrheit* in *Sämtliche Werke*, vols. 1–40, ed. by Dieter Borchmeyer et al., Frankfurt am Main: Deutscher Klassiker Verlag 1985-, part 1, vol. 14, p. 692. (English translation: *The Autobiography of Johann Wolfgang von Goethe*, trans. by John Oxenford, New York: Horizon 1969, vol. 2, p. 273.)

reading.[21] Then, as Jesus makes his way to the place of the crucifixion, Ahasverus reminds him of his earlier warnings, but in a flash he perceives a momentary glimpse of the glorified Christ, who issues him the condemnation: "over the earth shalt thou wander till thou shalt once more see me in this form."[22] Goethe never brought this idea for an epic of the Wandering Jew[23] to completion, but, as Karin Schutjer has shown, some of the characteristics Goethe ascribes to Ahasverus in this autobiographical context—especially his lack of compassion and inability to see beyond the material world—prefigure the anti-Semitism of *Wilhelm Meisters Wanderjahre*.[24] In the latter, as in Goethe's abandoned epic, Jewish wandering is cast in a negative light, to be contrasted with a "Goethean ideal of existential wandering," which would be compatible with an adherence to Christianity.[25]

The account of the Wandering Jew interpreted most closely by Kierkegaard is a translation of a German book published in 1797, which tells of the adventures of the Jerusalem shoemaker during the many centuries for which he has been alive.[26] In this narrative, the Wandering Jew recounts the story of one journey for each of the seventeen centuries of his life. We shall have more to say about Kierkegaard's evaluation of this text in a moment. Ahasverus is a main character in the play *Halle und Jerusalem* by Achim von Arnim, and the portrayal of the Wandering Jew in this work as a sinner on the way to forgiveness and even redemption may have influenced Kierkegaard's understanding of the legendary character.[27] Following Aurbacher's *Volksbüchlein*, von Arnim's Ahasverus, who is a particularly nasty sinner who not only spits in the face of Christ but rapes a woman, eventually becomes a Christian and is tasked with the conversion of the Jews to Christianity. Finally, although Kierkegaard does not discuss the work, it should be mentioned that his mentor Poul Martin Møller worked on a project entitled *Ahasverus* during the years 1836–37, of which only two short series of fragments resulted,[28] and in which the Wandering Jew becomes a stand-in for contemporary nihilism,[29] and a figure that may have

---

[21]   *SKS* 17, 107, BB:16 / *KJN* 4, 100.
[22]   Goethe, *Dichtung und Wahrheit*, p. 693 (*Autobiography*, pp. 274–5).
[23]   Without engaging Goethe's text directly, Kierkegaard agrees with Goethe's judgment regarding the suitability of the epic form for this character: *SKS* 19, 94, Not2:7 / *KJN* 4, 90.
[24]   Karin Schutjer, "Beyond the Wandering Jew: Anti-Semitism and Narrative Supersession in Goethe's *Wilhelm Meisters Wanderjahre*," *German Quarterly*, vol. 77, no. 4, 2004, p. 392.
[25]   Ibid., p. 390.
[26]   Anonymous, *Den evige Jøde*, trans. by Andreas Christian Alstrup, Copenhagen: Stadthagens 1797.
[27]   See "Achim von Arnim: Kierkegaard's Encounter with a Heidelberg Hermit," in *Kierkegaard and his German Contemporaries*, Tome III, *Literature and Aesthetics*, ed. by Jon Stewart, Aldershot: Ashgate 2008 (*Kierkegaard Research: Sources, Reception and Resources*, vol. 6), pp. 16–7. Achim von Arnim's play is also notable for the fact that it is one of the first versions of the legend to conclude with the death of Ahasverus.
[28]   Poul Martin Møller, *Efterladte Skrifter*, vols. 1–3, Copenhagen: C.A. Reitzel, 1839–43, vol. 3, pp. 328–30.
[29]   George Pattison, *Kierkegaard, Religion, and the Nineteenth Century Crisis of Culture*, New York: Cambridge University Press 2002, pp. 79–81.

been modeled on the young Kierkegaard.[30] As Finn Gredal Jensen notes, however, the notion that Møller viewed Kierkegaard as an incarnation of Ahasverus remains "highly speculative," as would any hypotheses regarding exchanges that the two writers might have had regarding the Wandering Jew.[31]

III. Kierkegaard's References to the Figure of the Wandering Jew

Kierkegaard's notebooks attest to an early fascination with this legendary character. For example, in 1835, prompted by a passing reference to the "Eternal Wanderer from Jerusalem" in Jakob Peter Mynster's preface to Frederik Christian Sibbern's *Efterladte Breve af Gabrielis*,[32] which suggests that that novel's main character differs from Goethe's Werther in that he is not suicidal, preferring the fate of the Wandering Jew to dying as the miserable man he currently finds himself to be, Kierkegaard wonders why it had become common to refer to a particular contemporary as being a Don Juan type, while no one would think of describing someone as being like an Ahasverus, even though there seem to be contemporary "individuals...who have taken upon themselves too much of the Eternal Jew's nature."[33] The absence of the literary figure of Ahasverus from the popular imagination is regrettable, Kierkegaard seems to think, because the modern age is an "age of despair," which is to say, the "age of the Eternal Jew."[34] This question about the ongoing significance of a legendary character gives an indication of Kierkegaard's apparent project to revive the figure of the Wandering Jew in a modern context, connecting it to two other fictional characters existing outside of Christianity: Faust and Don Juan. Each represents, as "ideas," one of "three tendencies for life outside of religion.[35] The entries in *Journal BB* to which we have referred several times, grouped under the heading "Literature on the Wandering Jew," are found in between two longer sections entitled "Literature on Faust" and "Literature on Don Juan." This project would seem to have met the same eventual fate as Goethe's planned epic based on the figure. As Jon Stewart suggests, Faust, Don Juan, and the Wandering Jew are all "symbols of disharmony—they are all alienated from traditional belief and custom and thus are not at home in the world."[36] In an early formulation of the project of reading these three figures together, Kierkegaard suggests that the "single individual" cannot reach

---

[30]   Frithiof Brandt, *Den unge Søren Kierkegaard*, Copenhagen: Levin and Munksgaard 1929, pp. 454–9.

[31]   Finn Gredal Jensen, "Poul Martin Møller: Kierkegaard and the Confidant of Socrates," in *Kierkegaard and his Danish Contemporaries*, Tome I, *Philosophy, Politics and Social Theory*, ed. by Jon Stewart, Aldershot: Ashgate 2009 (*Kierkegaard Research: Sources, Reception and Resources*, vol. 7), pp. 134–5.

[32]   Frederik Christian Sibbern, *Efterladte Breve af Gabrielis*, Copenhagen: C. Graebe 1826.

[33]   *SKS* 19, 95, Not2:14 / *KJN* 4, p. 91.

[34]   *SKS* 27, 208, Papir 257:3.

[35]   *SKS* 27, 134, Papir 140 / *JP* 1, 795.

[36]   Jon Stewart, *Kierkegaard's Relations to Hegel Reconsidered*, New York: Cambridge University Press 2003, p. 103.

the "moral" or "religious" stages without each of these figures becoming "mediated" in his or her life in the aesthetic stage.[37]

Among the sources having to do with this literary figure, listed in the entry in question, the excerpts from poems by Schlegel and Müller are especially indicative of the Wandering Jew's importance to Kierkegaard. Yet in contrast to their contemporary, Goethe, these poets consider Ahasverus separately from the Christian theological context of the traditional narrative. From Schlegel, Kierkegaard copies these lines, spoken from the perspective of Ahasverus: "I am not young, I am not old, / My life is no life...."[38] And from Müller: "I have already seen everything / but cannot find peace."[39] This entry simply quotes these "profound words" from the two poets, but in their brevity they indicate what seems to define the figure of Ahasverus for Kierkegaard: the endlessness of despair, which for Kierkegaard, if not for Schlegel and Müller, is a life lived in defiance of God. Another entry which contains quoted material referring to the Wandering Jew without commentary[40] likewise suggests that such was Kierkegaard's primary understanding of the figure: from E.T.A. Hoffmann's short story "Master Flea," when Peregrinus Tyss, the main character, is presented with an invention that would permit him to perceive the thoughts of other people simply by looking at them, he wonders, "will not this fateful gift [of mind-reading] impose on him [who possesses it] the terrible fate of the Wandering Jew, who roamed through the world's colorful tumult without joy, without hope, without sorrow, in dull indifference, the very death's head of despair, as though he were traversing a dreary and inhospitable wilderness?"[41] As is the case with the poems of Schlegel and Müller, in this excerpt, the scene of punishment so crucial to earlier renditions of the legend is absent. These Romantic sources suggest that to Kierkegaard, the Wandering Jew was, in Simon Podmore's words, "a motif of abject immortality,"[42] but that the *condition* of abjection is more significant than its etiology.

That the Wandering Jew is an embodiment of despair for Kierkegaard can be seen from several other entries. Meditating on the poetics of the *Faust* legend, and in particular on those adaptations of it which end with the suicide of the titular character, whom the early Kierkegaard understood as the mediation of the figures of Don Juan and the Wandering Jew,[43] Kierkegaard takes the side of Goethe in opting against this conclusion. The logic of the Faust character is such that "it is the counterweight of the whole world that should crush him, as with D. Juan—or end with despair (the Wandering Jew). Despair is Romantic—not punishment as in the case of

---

[37]   *SKS* 27, 134, Papir 140 / *JP* 1, 795.

[38]   Schlegel, *Poetische Werke*, p. 201. See *SKS* 17, 108, BB:20 / *KJN* 1, 101–2.

[39]   Müller, *Vermischte Schriften*, vol. 1, p. 162. See *SKS* 17, 109, BB:20 / *KJN* 1, 102.

[40]   *SKS* 19, 94, Not2:9 / *KJN* 4, 90.

[41]   Ernst Theodor Wilhelm Hoffmann, *Ausgewählte Schriften*, Berlin: G. Reimer 1828, vol. 10, p. 287. (English translation: "Master Flea," *The Golden Pot and Other Tales*, trans. by Ritchie Robertson, New York: Oxford University Press 1992, p. 367.)

[42]   Simon Podmore, *Kierkegaard and the Self before God*, Bloomington: Indiana University Press 2011, p. 92.

[43]   *SKS* 19, 94, Not2:7 / *KJN* 4, 90.

Prometheus."[44] It is crucial to note that Kierkegaard here opposes punishment and despair as (apparently disjunctive) possibilities for the characters under discussion. Punishment is the key note of the Wandering Jew legend in many of its adaptations, and it is significant that Kierkegaard does not read the story didactically, like many of his sources do (for example, Aurbacher, Goethe, Nyerup, and even Schlegel), making punishment of Ahasverus by Christ the main event.

Yet the fact that the Wandering Jew shares with Faust and Don Juan the characteristic of being outside religion altogether[45] (not merely outside Christianity, as the basic narrative frame of the legend has it) indicates that Kierkegaard does not entirely ignore the fact that his fate results from a punishment. Two biblical references to which Kierkegaard links the Wandering Jew support this observation: "the fig tree that Chr[ist] bids wither away"[46] (Matthew 21:18–20; Mark 11:12–14, 20–21) and the "petrified wife of Lot."[47] Unlike most of what Kierkegaard makes about the Wandering Jew, these biblical figures, cited without commentary, echo more traditional theological depictions of Ahasverus as a man whose fate is recompense for rejecting God in the person of Christ. A third biblical cross-reference, however, is more ambiguous: in 1839, that is, at least two years after Kierkegaard was most actively pursuing a philosophical or literary use for this fictional personage, he muses that, if the character of Barabbas, about whom the biblical texts tell us rather little, was developed at greater length, "in many ways, he could have become a counterpart to the wandering Jew…God knows whether or not he became a Christian."[48] Like Barrabas, Ahasverus is a Jew, but unlike Ahasverus, we do not know anything about his eventual relation to Jesus of Nazareth and his disciples. Taken together, these biblical citations make the question on which the interpretation of Kierkegaard's use of the Wandering Jew turns a bit more complicated. That question is, how closely did Kierkegaard adhere to the hermeneutic principle common to his readings of Faust and Ahasverus alike and articulated in 1835: "this legend [of Ahasverus as told in *Ein Volksbüchlein*], which has an altogether Christian tinge to it, can be separated out from this religious-ascetic aspect [that is, presumably, simply the fact of its Christian provenance, of which he had been ignorant mere days before],[49] just as has happened with Faust?"[50] It is this principle that governs Kierkegaard's use of this legendary character as an embodiment of despair, but what are the limits of this poetic transformation of Ahasverus? How can the latter (along with Faust) be at once a symbol of life outside Christianity *and* the central character in a story that can be stripped of its "religious aspects?" We shall return to this question in the concluding section of the article.

The longest and perhaps most telling of Kierkegaard's written engagements with the source material at his disposal is the discussion of the anonymous variation

---

44   *SKS* 17, 49, AA:38 / *KJN* 1, 43.
45   *SKS* 27, 134, Papir 140.
46   *SKS* 19, 95, Not2:13 / *KJN* 4, 91.
47   *SKS* 17, 107, BB:19 / *KJN* 1, 101.
48   *SKS* 18, 8, EE:6 / *KJN* 2, 4.
49   *SKS* 27, 185, Papir 253 / *JP* 5, 5110.
50   *SKS* 19, 94, NB2:10 / *KJN* 4, 90.

on the Ahasverus legend mentioned above. That book's conceit is that four young
people from four different nations meet the Wandering Jew at a recent fair in Leipzig.
The children become excited when they discover they are speaking with the famed
individual, and at their request, he tells them of his many travels over the world and
through the centuries, but with the limitation that he is "not allowed to stay in any
one city longer than three days."[51] This conversion of the legend into an entertaining
yarn about the adventures of a man who lives forever draws sharp criticism from
Kierkegaard, and it highlights what he thinks is a common problem with modern
adaptations of the character: the transformation of the "*eternal* Jew" into a "*temporal*
Jew."[52] As with Faust, Kierkegaard both presupposes and sets to work what we
might call a poetics of the Wandering Jew. That is to say, he operates according to
the principle that there is a correct way to use this character in a modern context
and that there are also incorrect ways to do so. In the case of this particular modern
retelling, the incorrect narrative tendency is to make the main character subject to
what could be called a *sempiternal* temporality, according to which the eternity for
which Ahasverus must wander the earth is a span of time whose only endpoint is
the return of Christ. Because no one knows that date, the time of Ahasverus' life
is seemingly endless. In contrast to this idea of quantitatively relative eternity,
Kierkegaard posits a notion of the Eternal Jew's eternity that would account for the
affective state proper to an endless existence. "What is lacking" in the anonymous
account of the Wandering Jew cum storyteller is "that which signifies the deepest,
most silent despair, the eye that is far more inwardly turned than the one that grasps
external objects as such."[53] The earthly eternity proper to Ahasverus is a qualitative
eternity, and it corresponds to the subjective state of a despair that is closed in upon
itself. Given the narrative framework of the story as he finds it in the anonymous
translation of a German retelling of the legend, the only way of redeeming this "very
badly exploited" conceit would, according to Kierkegaard, be to show, in contrast
to the young people's enthusiasm for interesting stories, the ultimate insignificance
of everything about which the storyteller had seen in the course of his long life
"compared to the sorrow he bore, which he could never, at any moment, alleviate by
expressing it."[54] The problem with this adaptation of the legend, as with others, is the
absence of the element of despair from the characterization of Ahasverus.

By the time Kierkegaard published *Either/Or* in 1843, he still found it useful
to think about Faust and Don Juan in relation to one another.[55] Together, the two
are "the titans and giants of the Middle Ages," and as such they nicely form a neat
conceptual opposition one to the other: "Don Juan is the expression for the demonic
understood as the sensuous; Faust is the expression for the demonic understood as the
spiritual that the Christian spirit excludes."[56] Earlier, in 1835, Kierkegaard posited
Faust, not simply in contraposition to Don Juan, but as the embodiment of *both* Don

51   Anonymous, *Den evige Jøde*, p. 4. See *SKS* K17, 23 / *KJN* 1, 403.
52   *SKS* 17, 108, BB:19 / *KJN* 1, 101.
53   Ibid.
54   Ibid.
55   *SKS* 2, 94 / *EO1*, 89.
56   *SKS* 2, 95 / *EO1*, 90.

Juan and the Wandering Jew, being the "most mediate" of the three. Compared with the figure of Don Juan, and especially in light of Kierkegaard's portrayal of him, it appears less self-evident that the Wandering Jew is similarly immediate. Perhaps the Wandering Jew's immediacy here is simply the immediacy characteristic of Judaism, in Hegelian terms; that is to say, perhaps Kierkegaard is thinking here of an interpretation of the Jewish theological conception of an unmediated absolute. In the absence of longer elaboration on the immediacy of the Wandering Jew, however, it is difficult to say with certainty. In any event, in the essay "Silhouettes," Kierkegaard finds the difference between (Goethe's) Faust and Don Juan refracted in the women with whom they are romantically involved. The difference between Elvira and Margarete is not so much a difference between two individual female characters, but between the "impression" made upon each of them by her corresponding lover, "due not so much to the difference in the two feminine natures as to the essential difference between a Don Juan and a Faust."[57] Perhaps because, unlike Don Juan and Faust, he corresponds to no feminine nature (i.e., he makes no "impression" on any woman), the Wandering Jew appears to have dropped out of this project of comparison entirely, and all that remains of Kierkegaard's interest in him by this point is to be found in the staging of the short essay, "The Unhappiest One."

Before that piece eventually determines that unhappiness consists in a way of dwelling within time in such a way that one is absent from oneself, that is, absent from oneself in the present, the speaker, addressing the "Συμπαρανεκρωμένοι," entertains the possibility that the unhappiest person would be the one who could not die. Such a possibility is exactly what "the legend says about the Eternal Jew."[58] Soon after this reference to the well-known legend, however, the speaker immediately dismisses this hypothesis, because "death is the common fate of all humanity,"[59] and therefore the fictional case of Ahasverus is not useful for thinking about questions of happiness and unhappiness. After everything that the young Kierkegaard had read and thought about the Wandering Jew, the latter makes one single, brief appearance in his published work, only to be quickly whisked off the stage of the text to make room for a different line of argumentation about the nature of unhappiness.

Yet it is possible to assert that Ahasverus reappears incognito in a much later text. The problem of the relationship between subjective suffering and the possibility of dying resurfaces in *The Sickness unto Death*, and, while nowhere does that book mention the Wandering Jew, it is difficult not to think of him in the context of the description of the despair of the one who hopes for death, who despairs over himself to the point that he wishes to rid himself of himself, but cannot die.[60] Tudvad suggests that, in addition, the description of the form of despair associated with "infinitude [*uendelighed*]"[61] is an "obvious allusion to Ahasverus' eternal wandering and to the dispersion of the Jews throughout the world."[62] Yet the analysis of the despair

57   *SKS* 2, 201 / *EO1*, 205.
58   *SKS* 2, 214 / *EO1*, 220. Translation slightly modified.
59   *SKS* 2, 214 / *EO1*, 221.
60   *SKS* 11, 134 / *SUD*, 18.
61   *SKS* 11, 146–9 / *SUD*, 30–3.
62   Tudvad, *Stadier på Antisemitismens Vej*, p. 161.

of infinitude proceeds, in this text, in terms of the "fantastical," and it is unclear in what ways the Wandering Jew's will, knowledge, or feeling could be shown to be "fantastical," so any thesis about a discreet reappearance of Ahasverus in *this* chapter of *The Sickness unto Death* will be speculative. Nonetheless, whether or not he was explicitly alluding here to this legendary character, it is likely that the account of living death, evoked earlier in the text as the form of despair as such, marks the fullest fruition of his long-standing meditation on the Wandering Jew.

If the predominant trait of the Wandering Jew in Kierkegaard's early writings is, following the Romantics' depiction of him, a certain form of despair, two final allusions to the legendary personage in the *Nachlass* signal at once a more theological appropriation of the character and an identification with him on the part of Kierkegaard.[63] They show that Kierkegaard's final understanding of the Wandering Jew's identity depends upon his existing outside of Christianity but nonetheless having the capability to lead people to become Christians. In 1845, he elides Moses, Ahasverus, and himself in describing their common role of "leading pilgrims to the promised land" without entering it themselves.[64] To give the Wandering Jew this role of leading a pilgrimage clearly shows the influence of von Arnim's play *Halle und Jerusalem*, it being the only adaptation of the legend known to Kierkegaard in which Ahasverus brings people to Jerusalem. The final reference to this figure in Kierkegaard's writings comes in 1849 which, together with the possible allusions to Ahasverus in *The Sickness unto Death*, suggests that possibly sometime during the years 1848 or 1849 he had revived his earlier meditations on the Wandering Jew. Reflecting on the position of his pseudonym Johannes Climacus with respect to Christianity and Christendom, and noting that the use of this pseudonym puts Kierkegaard himself in the somewhat paradoxical position of laboring for the sake of the Christian message without "letting [him]self be taken over by Christianity," Kierkegaard considers that maintaining this difficult stance in his writing might necessitate his becoming like "the legendary Wandering Jew—myself not a Christian in the final and decisive sense of the word, yet leading others to Christianity."[65] As with the 1845 reference, here the despair of the Wandering Jew fades into the background as he becomes a figure for a position of externality in relation to Christianity that paradoxically allows him to serve the Christian message in a unique way. Once again, we see the influence on Kierkegaard of von Arnim's depiction of Ahasverus as one whose wandering is not aimless, but leads pilgrims to salvation.

---

[63]   There is one other later reference to the Wandering Jew, which neither resembles the other references nor constitutes an extensive engagement with the figure: Kierkegaard explains Adolph Peter Adler's "doctrine of the moment" as a kind of *carpe diem* mentality, whose "dizziness" Kierkegaard attempts to capture in the following words: "seize the moment, it depends on the moment, in the next moment it will be too late, and then you will go your entire life like the Wandering Jew" (*SKS* 15, 236 / *BA*, 29). Translation slightly modified.

[64]   *Pap.* VI B 40:33 / *JP* 5, 5797.

[65]   *SKS* 22, 337, NB13:92 / *JP* 6, 6523.

IV. Interpreting Kierkegaard's Reading of the Wandering Jew

These last two references to Ahasverus, having little to do with despair as such, demonstrate that the legend of the Wandering Jew meant different things to Kierkegaard at different points in his life. Nonetheless, as we have seen, the majority of Kierkegaard's references to this figure suggest that the Wandering Jew stands, for Kierkegaard, above all, as an embodiment of the despair of a life lived outside of relation to God. As George Pattison points out, in showing how the Wandering Jew represents a form of despair that is particular to modernity, the modernity of this figure is more salient, for Kierkegaard, than his Jewishness. Pattison writes, "Kierkegaard's concern with the Wandering Jew...aims at articulating a condition that belongs to the inner destiny of all who inhabit the condition of modernity."[66] He is not, in the main, attempting to articulate a racial or confessional condition. This is not to say that the charge of anti-Semitism cannot be leveled against Kierkegaard, but only that his use of this particular literary trope seems pitched elsewhere, and that the issue of Kierkegaard's anti-Semitism must be adjudicated on other grounds. As characteristic of modernity, in Pattison's interpretation, the ultimate, endless purposelessness of Ahasverus' wanderings is the keynote of Kierkegaard's reading of this character as revelatory of the modern condition.

In particular, the story of Ahasverus illustrates a clear connection between a self's eternal dimension and its despair; in many versions of the story, the main character's despair takes shape as an eternal form of earthly existence, an eternal inability to die. Kierkegaard likewise posits a link between the eternality of the soul and despair over the inability to die: "if there were nothing eternal in a man, he could not despair at all."[67] Yet in its traditional theologico-didactic form, the story would have limited usefulness for Kierkegaard's analysis of despair, for the Wandering Jew's fate is traditionally said to result from *punishment* for a previous rejection of Christ. That is, his endless wandering is a condition that has been imposed upon him, not an outcome arising organically, as it were, from a life lived in defiance of God. In characterizing the estrangement of living death, Anti-Climacus, by contrast, does not describe it as divine punishment. In addition to offering a possible explanation for the relative neglect of this character in later texts, and even in earlier ones, if we compare the references to the Wandering Jew to references to Don Juan and Faust, perhaps this limitation of the traditional narrative frame, in view of Kierkegaard's own authorial purposes, led him to favor variations like von Arnim's, in which the seemingly endless wandering of the legendary personage is not an unalterable destiny. Von Arnim's Ahasverus redeems himself and his wandering. Perhaps this limitation of traditional versions also accounts for Kierkegaard's crucial claim that it is possible, in the nineteenth century, to extract a message from the legend, peeling away its historically "theological-ascetic" wrapping.[68] Kierkegaard appears to think that this legend can be used within a theological project—specifically, it can be used

---

[66] Pattison, *Kierkegaard, Religion, and the Nineteenth Century Crisis of Culture*, p. 94.

[67] *SKS* 11, 136 / *SUD*, 20.

[68] *SKS* 27, 185, Papir 253 / *JP* 5, 5110.

to symbolize a life outside religion—without adapting wholesale all the theological purposes or implications of earlier uses of the narrative.

Bibliography

Brandt, Frithiof, *Den unge Søren Kierkegaard. En Række nye Bidrag*, Copenhagen: Levin & Munksgaards Forlag 1929, pp. 347-80; pp. 414-4; pp. 433-7; pp. 455-9.

Harket, Håkon, "Kierkegaards evige jøde," *Innøvelse i Kierkegaard. Fire Essays*, Oslo: Capellen Akademisk Forlag 1996, pp. 119–49.

Jensenius, Knud, *Nogle Kierkegaardstudier. "De Tre Store Ideer,"* Copenhagen: Nyt Nordisk Forlag Arnold Busck 1932, pp. 64–124.

Pattison, George, *Kierkegaard, Religion, and the Nineteenth Century Crisis of Culture*, New York: Cambridge University Press 2002, pp. 72–95.

Podmore, Simon, "To Die and yet Not to Die: Kierkegaard's Theophany of Death," in *Kierkegaard and Death*, ed. by Patrick Stokes and Adam Buben, Bloomington: Indiana University Press 2011, pp. 47–51.

Tudvad, Peter, *Stadier på antisemitismens vej. Kierkegaard og jøderne*, Copenhagen: Rosinante 2010, pp. 55–165.

Xerxes:

Kierkegaard's King of Jest

Ana Pinto Leite

I. Introduction

Xerxes I, in old Persian Khshayarsha (519–465 BC) was a Persian king (486–465 BC). He was the son of Darius I and Atossa, daughter of Cyrus, the founder of the Archaemenid Empire. Xerxes, who was the first son born to Darius after his accession to the throne, was preferred by his father to his elder brother Artobazanes, probably because he was Cyrus' grandson.[1]

Xerxes' first task as a king was to crush a revolt in Egypt, and there are also accounts of a Babylonian revolt.[2] Yet Xerxes is best known for his unsuccessful invasion of Greece. This was the continuation of his father's expedition, which was defeated by the Greeks at Marathon (490 BC). Darius' aim was to punish the mainland Greek sympathizers of the Ionian Revolt and to secure Persia's rule in that region.[3]

After thorough preparations, Xerxes gathered an enormous army and fleet.[4] The Persians won a battle at Thermopylae in mid-August 480 BC and pillaged Athens on September 21,[5] but they had to retreat because a lost naval battle at Salamis, on September 29, left the men without supplies.[6] Mardonius, Xerxes' cousin and brother-in-law, was defeated at Plataea on August 27. He was killed, and his army had to retreat.[7] Xerxes retired to Susa and Persepolis, in Persia. He was murdered in 465 BC, together with his oldest son, Darius; one of his other sons, Artaxerxes, succeeded him.[8]

Xerxes has a reputation as a weakling and a womanizer, which is due mainly to the way he is portrayed in Greek sources. Modern research suggests, though, that

---

[1]   See Amélie Kurt, *The Persian Empire: A Corpus of Sources from the Archaemenid Period*, London and New York: Routledge 2010, p. 239; pp. 244–7.

[2]   Ibid., p. 239; pp. 248–50.

[3]   Ibid., pp. 239–40; pp. 250–1.

[4]   Ibid., p. 240; pp. 250–1.

[5]   Ibid., pp. 261–70.

[6]   Ibid., p. 240; pp. 270–2.

[7]   Ibid., p. 241; pp. 281–2.

[8]   Ibid., pp. 242–3; pp. 306–8.

he was a respectable king.[9] He completed and extended Darius' palatial structures at Susa and Persepolis, and carved a rock inscription near Lake Van, in a place prepared by Darius.[10] Furthermore, the texts written by Xerxes show the importance of royal ideals, putting emphasis on the debt of loyalty subjects owed to the empire, which shows that imperial ideology grew stronger under his rule.[11]

II. Kierkegaard's Textual Sources

Kierkegaard's references to Xerxes I are based on two texts: the *Histories* of Herodotus and the biblical Book of Esther.[12] Herodotus, known as the "Father of History," was the first significant Greek historian. He was born around 485 BC in Halicarnassus (modern Bodrum), lived in several places and died around 424 BC in Thurii, southern Italy (Magna Graecia). He also traveled a lot, as far as Babylon, in order to gather information for his life's work, the *Histories*, where he narrates the war between the Greeks and the Persians.

The *Auction Catalogue* shows that Kierkegaard owned several copies of an edition with the Latin name *Herodoti Halicanassei Historiarum libri IX Musarum nominibus inscripti*,[13] which contains the Greek text and a Latin translation. Kierkegaard also owned Friedrich Lange's (1779–1854) German translation, *Die Geschichten des Herodotus*.[14] There are secondary sources that must be mentioned, especially volume 1 of Karl Friedrich Becker's (1777–1809) *History of the World* in

---

[9]   In Amélie Kurt's words, Xerxes was "an heir worthy to continue the work started by his father and entrusted to him." Ibid., p. 241; pp. 300–6.

[10]   Ibid., pp. 300–4.

[11]   Ibid., pp. 241–2; pp. 304–6.

[12]   This book is in the Ketuvim, the third section of the Tanakh, the Jewish Bible, and is also a part of the Christian Old Testament. It is the story of Esther, a Jewish girl who becomes Queen of Persia and prevents genocide against her people. The Book of Esther is read aloud during the celebration of Purim.

[13]   The first volume, which contains the Greek text, was edited by Friedrich Wolfgang Reiz (1733–90). It is divided into two parts, the first of which was published in 1778. The edition was completed by Gottfried Heinrich Schäfer (1764–1840): volume 1, part 2 was published in 1800 and volume 2 (the Latin translation) in 1820. The individual parts of volume 1 were also edited independently. In fact, we find several copies of the Reiz-Schäfer edition in *The Auction Catalogue*. There is a copy in two volumes, *ASKB* 1116. In the appendices we find again a copy of the first volume of the Reiz-Schäfer edition of *Historiarum* (*ASKB* A I 158–159) and an unspecified stereotype edition of Herodotus (*ASKB* A II 37–39). Finn Gredal Jensen disagrees with the dates indicated by the editor H.P. Rohde and also points out that it is a matter of dispute whether the books indicated in the appendices actually belonged to Kierkegaard. See Finn Gredal Jensen, "Herodotus: Traces of *The Histories* in Kierkegaard's Writings," in *Kierkegaard and the Greek World*, Tome II, *Aristotle and Other Greek Authors*, ed. by Jon Stewart and Katalin Nun, Aldershot: Ashgate 2010 (*Kierkegaard Research: Sources, Reception and Resources*, vol. 2), pp. 247–62, see pp. 249–50.

[14]   *Die Geschichten des Herodotus*, vols. 1–2, trans. by Friedrich Lange, Berlin: Realschulbuchhandlung 1811–12 (*ASKB* 1117). See Gredal Jensen, "Herodotus: Traces of *The Histories* in Kierkegaard's Writings," p. 250.

J. Riise's Danish translation,[15] since it is sometimes impossible to determine whether Kierkegaard took the images he uses in connection with Xerxes directly from the *Histories* or from Becker's rewritings.[16]

There is also one biblical reference made in connection with Xerxes, namely, when Kierkegaard mentions King Ahasuerus from the Book of Esther, who has traditionally been identified with Xerxes I.[17]

III. References to Xerxes in Kierkegaard's Writing

The first mention of Xerxes in Kierkegaard's work is in the preface of *Either/Or*, where the fictional editor Victor Eremita describes how he accidentally found the papers containing the texts he is now presenting. Eremita bought an old desk and, while trying to open a drawer that was stuck, he thought it would be a good idea to use a hatchet. Although the drawer remained closed, another compartment sprung open—and he found the papers. Eremita describes his rage while trying to open the drawer: "The blood rushed to my head; I was furious. Just as Xerxes had the sea whipped, so I decided to take dreadful revenge. A hatchet was fetched. I gave the desk a terrible blow with it."[18]

In "In Vino Veritas," the first part of *Stages on Life's Way*, Constantin Constantius uses the same expression while defining "jest": "to challenge a woman, what is that, who does not know that it is a jest, just as when Xerxes had the sea whipped."[19] In a late journal, *Journal NB28*, we find an allusion to this very same image, in the last reference to Xerxes in Kierkegaard's writings (1854):

> The abundance of talk about how blessed it is to have a personal God is like all the other hypocrisy one hears. In one sense, yes, but in another it is far easier to have a blind fate to deal with, for in blind "fate" there is nothing inciting; one has to be as insane as Xerxes to be incited by the sea and natural forces.[20]

These passages refer to an episode in *Histories*, 7.34–5. In this part of the book, Xerxes prepares a new invasion of Greece after his father's defeat at Marathon.

---

[15]   *Karl Friedrich Beckers Verdenshistorie, omarbeidet af Gottfried Woltmann*, vols. 1–12, trans. by J. Riise, Copenhagen: Fr. Brummer 1822–29 (*ASKB* 1972–1983), vol. 1. See Gredal Jensen, "Herodotus: Traces of *The Histories* in Kierkegaard's Writings," p. 250.

[16]   The *Histories* were in later times divided into nine books, named after the muses. One can be sure that Kierkegaard read Book 8, "Urania," and Book 9, "Calliope," because he listed them in his university entrance exam. However, as Gredal Jensen points out, there are no references to these two books in his writings. As far as Xerxes is concerned, all the passages Kierkegaard refers to are contained in Book 7, as we shall see in the next section. See Gredal Jensen, "Herodotus: Traces of *The Histories* in Kierkegaard's Writings," p. 249.

[17]   See Robert J. Littman, "The Religious Policy of Xerxes and the 'Book of Esther,' " *Jewish Quarterly Review*, New Series, vol. 65, no. 3, 1975, pp. 145–55, see pp. 145–8.

[18]   *SKS* 2, 13 / *EO1*, 6.

[19]   *SKS* 6, 52 / *SLW*, 49.

[20]   *SKS* 25, 281, NB28:89 / *JP* 2, 1437.

In order to cross the Hellespont, he has two bridges built using flaxen cables and papyrus. Herodotus narrates:

> No sooner had the strait been bridged than a great storm swept down and broke and scattered all the work. When Xerxes heard of that, he was very angry, and gave command that the Hellespont be scourged with three hundred lashes, and a pair of fetters be thrown into the sea.[21]

A different image of Xerxes can be found among the material of *Either/Or*, Part Two. It appears in a comment on Johan Ludvig Heiberg (1791–1860), a Danish poet and critic who wrote a review of *Either/Or*: "Prof. Heiberg is also in the habit of 'holding judgment day in literature.' Have you forgotten what happened to Xerxes? He had even taken scribes along to describe his victory over little Greece."[22] A draft version of the preface to *Works of Love* contains a similar reference to Xerxes:

> That mighty Eastern emperor intended to perform so many and so great exploits that he had to take along a large number of writers in order to make complete and accurate reports. This would all have been fine and would have worked if the emperor's numerous and great exploits had amounted to something and if in any case he had taken along an adequate number of writers. But Christian love! It is so unlike that mighty Eastern emperor.[23]

The use of scribes refers to Herodotus (Book 7, Chapter 100), where Xerxes examines his army and fleet personally, before the battle against the Greeks. He questions his men, and his scribes write it all down.[24]

Xerxes is also mentioned in the last part of *Stages on Life's Way*, "Guilty/Not Guilty?" The pseudonym Frater Taciturnus writes: "Darius or Xerxes, no matter which one, had a slave who reminded him about waging war against the Greeks."[25] This is, however, a reference to Darius, Xerxes' father. In the sketch to "Patience in Expectancy," the second of the *Two Upbuilding Discourses* from 1844, Kierkegaard also writes "Xerxes" while referring himself to Darius: "Great men like Xerxes and others have a slave to remind them to do this and that."[26] This is a reference to Book 5 in *Histories*, where Herodotus narrates the revolt of the Ionians against Persian

---

[21]   The most probable source was Friedrich Lange's translation, *Die Geschichten des Herodotus*, vol. 2, pp. 159–60. See also Herodotus, *The Persian Wars*, vols. 1–4, trans. by A.D. Godley, New York: Putnam 1921–24, vol. 3, pp. 347–9. As Gredal Jensen points out, Kierkegaard could also have read Becker's *Verdenshistorie*, p. 106: "*Herodotus* tells (VII B 35 Cap.) that *Xerxes* not only had the construction foreman [of the bridges] executed but also had the sea given three hundred lashes and had a pair of foot-irons thrown into it; an account or rumor, which certainly was believed and retold by the freedom-loving Greeks because the despotism which they so despised thereby showed itself in all its vileness." Cited in Gredal Jensen, "Herodotus: Traces of *The Histories* in Kierkegaard's Writings," p. 257n.

[22]   *Pap.* IV B 41 / *EO2*, Supplement, p. 402.

[23]   *SKS* 20, 167, NB2:65 / *JP* 3, 2409.

[24]   See *Die Geschichten des Herodotus*, vol. 2, pp. 183–4. See also Herodotus, *The Persian Wars*, vol. 3, p. 403.

[25]   *SKS* 6, 274 / *SLW*, 295.

[26]   *Pap.* V B 197 / *EUD*, Supplement, p. 447.

rule, and how the Athenians helped them. Darius swore vengeance against the latter, and, according to *Histories* (Book 5, Chapter 105) had a slave who reminded him of that every day.[27]

A reference to a different source is made in a journal entry from 1850. Kierkegaard mentions Ahasuerus, the King of Persia from the Book of Esther, who, as explained before, has been traditionally identified with Xerxes I.[28] We read, "The story of Ahasuerus, who repudiated Queen Vashti because of her pride."[29] In the first chapters of the Book of Esther, Ahasuerus gathers princes and servants from all Persia and Media in a big feast,[30] and orders his wife Vashti to display her beauty before them, which she refuses to do.[31] Vashti is banned,[32] and Esther becomes the king's second wife.[33]

Kierkegaard mentions this story in connection with a commentary on Matthew 22:14:[34] "Hugo d. St. Victore's[35] commentary on the words: Many are called but few are chosen, is excellent (see Helfferich, Mystik, pt. II, p. 319)."[36] This commentary establishes a connection between the verse from Matthew and the verses in the Book of Esther where Ahasuerus chooses his new queen.[37]

IV. Overall Interpretation of Kierkegaard's Use of Xerxes

As one can easily see, Kierkegaard is not concerned with developing a coherent character. Some of the references are not even accurate, as they refer to Darius, not Xerxes. The reason for this is that Kierkegaard uses Xerxes to illustrate or to explain his ideas in different contexts. This heterogeneity is most evident in the contrast between Ahasuerus, from the Bible, and a Xerxes from the *Histories*. It is true that both are, in fact, despots: Ahasuerus demands from the queen that she shows herself to the guests and punishes her for disobedience, while Xerxes orders that the sea be whipped because a storm destroyed his bridges. However, Kierkegaard does not emphasize Ahasuerus' arrogance: he puts the weight on the queen's disobedience,

---

[27]   See *Die Geschichten des Herodotus*, vol. 2, p. 59. See also Herodotus, *The Persian Wars*, vol. 3, p. 127.

[28]   See note 15. The name "Ahasuerus" also designates the "wandering Jew," a figure from medieval legends sometimes described as Pontius Pilate's doorman, sometimes as a shoemaker in Jerusalem who mocked Jesus while carrying the cross, and was then cursed to walk the earth until the Second Coming. See *SKS* 19, 95, Not2:12 / *JP* 5, 5112.

[29]   *SKS* 23, 21, NB15:21 / *JP* 4, 3941.

[30]   Esther 1:3–7. See *The Bible. Authorized King James Version with Apocrypha*, Oxford: Oxford University Press 1997, pp. 597–8.

[31]   Esther 1:11–12.

[32]   Esther 1:19.

[33]   Esther 2:17.

[34]   *The Bible. Authorized King James Version with Apocrypha*, p. 32: "For many are called, but few are chosen."

[35]   Hugh of Saint Victor (ca. 1096–1141) was a German Augustinian mystic.

[36]   *SKS* 23, 21, NB15:21 / *JP* 4, 3941.

[37]   Esther 2:1–18. See *Holy Bible. New Revised Standard Version with Apocrypha*, New York and Oxford: Oxford University Press 1989. pp. 598–600.

calling it pride. Kierkegaard is interested in the fact that this concrete situation can be used to help explain the verse in question from the Gospel of Matthew ("For many are called, but few are chosen"[38]), without being concerned with Xerxes as a historical figure or even as a literary character.

In other cases Kierkegaard borrows from Herodotus the description of Xerxes as an arrogant tyrant, who is punished for his *hubris*—the arrogance of thinking he would win for sure—with defeat. We find this image when Kierkegaard is depicting Heiberg.[39] The similarities between what Kierkegaard criticizes in Heiberg and Xerxes are obvious, once one understands the reason for Kierkegaard's dislike of Heiberg. Despite the fact that Kierkegaard did not like Heiberg's review of *Either/Or*, his break with Heiberg cannot, as George Pattison points out, be seen merely in personal terms.[40] Kierkegaard's literary, philosophical, and religious concerns are completely incompatible with Heiberg's aesthetic thought. The source of Kierkegaard's exasperation regarding Heiberg is, however, his position as an authority figure.[41] Heiberg judges *Either/Or* in the following manner: "It is an unpleasant, tasteless walk, on which one constantly has the feeling that one wants to get away from the person who is holding one by the arm."[42] It is in this context that Kierkegaard compares Heiberg to Xerxes, because both are examples of people who imagine they are in complete possession of the truth: Heiberg thinks he can write in the name of everyone by using the pronoun "one," and Xerxes is completely convinced he is going to win the war.

Kierkegaard's treatment of Xerxes clearly goes beyond what we find in the *Histories*. Kierkegaard develops an image of Xerxes as an insane person, a true example of jest. In "In vino veritas," Constantin Constantius argues it is a jest for a man to challenge a woman, because there cannot be a true correspondence between men, whose function is "to be absolute, to express the absolute" and women, who "consist in the relational."[43] This form of contrast is used in a journal entry to criticize those who affirm they are blessed to have a personal God, and yet do not understand the implications of this.[44] Kierkegaard explains that there is a relation between having a personal power and being constantly in temptation. If there is, on the contrary, only blind "fate," nothing can be inciting, except if one lets oneself be incited by natural

---

[38] Matthew 22:14.

[39] This theme is explored in George Pattison, "Johan Ludvig Heiberg: Kierkegaard's Use of Heiberg as a Literary Critic," in *Kierkegaard and His Danish Contemporaries*, Tome III, *Literature, Drama and Aesthetics*, ed. by Jon Stewart, Aldershot: Ashgate 2009 (*Kierkegaard Research: Sources, Reception and Resources*, vol. 7), pp. 169–87; see p. 169; pp. 180–1. It is also mentioned in George Pattison, *Kierkegaard, Religion and the Nineteenth-Century Crisis of Culture*, Cambridge: Cambridge University Press 2004, p. 45; p. 143; p. 230; p. 242.

[40] Pattison, "Johan Ludvig Heiberg: Kierkegaard's Use of Heiberg as a Literary Critic," p. 179.

[41] Ibid., p. 180.

[42] Johan Ludvig Heiberg, "Litterær Vintersæd," *Intelligensblade*, no. 24, March 1843, p. 289, cited in Pattison, "Johan Ludvig Heiberg: Kierkegaard's Use of Heiberg as a Literary Critic," p. 180.

[43] *SKS* 6, 50–2 / *SLW*, 48–9.

[44] *SKS* 25, 281, NB28:89 / *JP* 2, 1437.

forces, like Xerxes did. The common thread between both situations (to challenge a woman or to let oneself be incited by natural forces) is that there is a disproportion in behavior. We find the elements that constitute this image in the *Histories*, when Xerxes punishes the sea; but Kierkegaard transforms an overconfident ruler into an example of jest.

Kierkegaard's references to Xerxes are scarce and do not form a coherent whole. Apart from the mention to Ahasuerus from the Book of Esther, and the reference to Book 5 of Herodotus' *Histories*, which is in reality a reference to Darius, Kierkegaard's references to Xerxes are centered on just two images from Book 7. He employs them to illustrate or exemplify his ideas, taking them out of their original context. Kierkegaard's Xerxes is therefore sometimes an exaggerated version of Herodotus', since Kierkegaard's concern was not to remain faithful to the sources or even to create his own character, but mainly to use stereotyped aspects of Xerxes as a means to illustrate categories, like jest, or represent specific features of human beings, like Heiberg's arrogance.

Bibliography

Gredal Jensen, Finn, "Herodotus: Traces of *The Histories* in Kierkegaard's Writings," in *Kierkegaard and the Greek World*, Tome II, *Aristotle and Other Greek Authors*, ed. by Jon Stewart and Katalin Nun, Aldershot: Ashgate 2010 (*Kierkegaard Reasearch: Sources, Reception and Resources*, vol. 2), pp. 249–51; pp. 256–8.

Holm, Søren, *Græciteten*, Copenhagen: Munksgaard 1964 (*Søren Kierkegaard Selskabets Populære Skrifter*, vol. 11), p. 85.

Pattison, George, "If Kierkegaard is Right About Reading, Why Read Kierkegaard?," in *Kierkegaard Revisited: Proceedings from the Conference "Kierkegaard and the Meaning of Meaning It*," ed. by Niels Jørgen Cappelørn and Jon Stewart, Berlin: Walter de Gruyter 1997 (*Kierkegaard Studies Monograph Series*, vol. 1), p. 297; p. 307.

— *Kierkegaard, Religion and the Nineteenth-Century Crisis of Culture*, Cambridge: Cambridge University Press 2004, p. 45; p. 143; p. 230; p. 242.

— "Johan Ludvig Heiberg: Kierkegaard's Use of Heiberg as a Literary Critic," in *Kierkegaard and His Danish Contemporaries*, Tome III, *Literature, Drama and Aesthetics*, ed. by Jon Stewart, Aldershot: Ashgate 2009 (*Kierkegaard Research: Sources, Reception and Resources*, vol. 7), p. 169; pp. 180–1.

Zerlina:

A Study on How to Overcome Anxiety

Sara Ellen Eckerson

I. Introduction

Zerlina is a character from Mozart's opera *Don Giovanni* (*Il dissoluto punito ossia il Don Giovanni*), K 527, which premiered in Prague in 1787, with libretto by Lorenzo Da Ponte. The libretto and adaptation exclusively used by Kierkegaard is the one by Laurids Kruse from 1807.[1] Zerlina is described as a beautiful and charming peasant girl, who is about to be married when she and her bridegroom Masetto run into Don Giovanni. Her innocence and naïveté do not protect her against Don Giovanni's advances, and she is seduced in the famous duet, "Là ci darem la mano" (There we will entwine our hands), *duettino* No. 7.[2] This duet is very important for the opera because it is where Don Giovanni demonstrates his art of seduction. The aria also works as a touchstone because it is where the two actors playing Don Giovanni and Zerlina are able to show their acting talents. Zerlina is not portrayed as anything spectacular, but an ordinary peasant girl; Don Giovanni choosing her and seducing her in the duet is not seen as making her into someone special. After being seduced, Zerlina is left bewildered and perplexed as to what happened, how it happened, and by the end does not find herself to blame.

Kierkegaard's appropriation of the character of Zerlina appears in relation to a discussion of the opera as a whole and her role among the other characters, specifically her duet "Là ci darem la mano." Other aspects he focuses on are related to the staging of the opera, the actresses, and the mistakes they made while playing Zerlina that led to inaccurate representations of her character.

II. Influential Texts

The translation/adaptation Kierkegaard used of *Don Giovanni* is by Laurids Kruse, *Don Juan, Opera i tvende Akter bearbeidet til Mozarts Musik* (Copenhagen 1807). The other text relevant for his description of Zerlina is Heinrich Gustav Hotho's

---

[1]   Laurids Kruse, *Don Juan, Opera i tvende Akter bearbeidet til Mozarts Musik*, Copenhagen: Boas Brünnich 1807.

[2]   Wolfgang Amadeus Mozart, *Il dissoluto punito ossia il Don Giovanni: Dramma giocoso in zwei Akten. Libretto: Lorenzo Da Ponte, KV 527, Klavierauszug*, German translation by Walther Dürr, Kassel: Bärenreiter 2005 (BA 4500a), pp. 100–5.

Vorstudien für Leben und Kunst.[3] In addition, the numerous performances of the opera *Don Giovanni* that Kierkegaard saw before the completion of "The Immediate Erotic Stages or the Musical Erotic" (1843) and "A Cursory Observation Concerning a Detail in Don Giovanni" (1845)[4] were extremely influential for his writings on Zerlina; thus specifically the performances he attended at the Royal Theatre in Copenhagen roughly between the years of 1831 and 1832 must be taken into account.[5]

III. Zerlina in Kierkegaard's Writings

In *Either/Or* "The Immediate Erotic Stages or the Musical-Erotic," Zerlina is described first by A as an *ordinary peasant girl*, which is important in the perspective of the entire opera, and the role of her seduction in it. For A, it is to misunderstand Mozart if Zerlina is seen as special; it is incorrect for Zerlina to be seen as anything but ordinary from an aesthetic or any other point of view. In A's perspective, Zerlina is kept as insignificant as possible in the scope of the opera.[6] Specifically, Zerlina cannot be seen as a peasant girl heroine emerging from the sensuous seduction that is crucial to the opera; Zerlina is just an ordinary girl who can satisfy Don Giovanni's needs in that moment. She is qualified as a woman who is young and beautiful, a characteristic she shares with many other women; however, what interests Don Giovanni about her is actually something even more ordinary, a quality that she shares with every woman.[7]

Zerlina's ordinariness is also shown in another common trait Zerlina has with other women, which is that she is dangerous to Don Giovanni after she has been seduced by him in the same sense that Elvira is.[8] Another example of her ordinariness and bewilderment is how she is unable to describe the power that attracts her to

---

[3]   Heinrich Gustav Hotho, *Vorstudien für Leben und Kunst*, Stuttgart and Tübingen: Cotta 1835 (*ASKB* 580), pp. 92–147, specifically pp. 109–10.

[4]   *SKS* 2, 53–136 / *EO1*, 45–135. "En flygtig Bemærkning betræffende en Enkelthed i Don Juan I–II," *Fædrelandet*, nos. 1890–1, May 19–20, 1845, columns 15147–52, 15155–9. *SKS* 14, 67–75 / *COR* 28–37.

[5]   For additional information regarding these performances, see Elisabete M. de Sousa, "Wolfgang Amadeus Mozart: The Love for Music and the Music of Love," in *Kierkegaard and the Renaissance and Modern Traditions*, Tome III, *Literature, Drama and Music*, ed. by Jon Stewart, Aldershot: Ashgate 2009 (*Kierkegaard Research: Sources, Reception and Resources*, vol. 5), pp. 137–63; p. 141. According to Sousa (p. 144), there were a total of 70 performances of *Don Juan* using Laurids Kruse's libretto between the years of 1827 and 1845. Although there is no exact number, Kierkegaard is presumed to have started attending performances as a teenager and continued to attend performances of *Don Juan* until the early 1850s, see p. 141.

[6]   *SKS* 2, 100–1 / *EO1*, 96–7. A makes a reference to Hotho, who has understood the necessity of Zerlina being an ordinary girl; however, A believes he has missed the fundamental reason for why this is the case.

[7]   *SKS* 2, 101 / *EO1*, 97.

[8]   *SKS* 2, 100–1 / *EO1*, 97–98.

Don Giovanni.[9] A writes about Don Giovanni's power in relation to Zerlina, and the situation created by Zerlina's wedding. Among the other descriptions of how Don Giovanni involves himself in all the fun and games of the wedding, is that he acts as the groom for Zerlina.[10] Later, A details the kind of erotic relation Don Giovanni has with Zerlina: she is in his power because she is afraid of him.[11]

When describing how Don Giovanni resonates everywhere in the opera, A makes the frequently cited comment that Don Giovanni resonates in Zerlina's anxiety (*Angst*).[12] This is further described with A's theory regarding the characters of the opera as celestial bodies that revolve around Don Giovanni (the sun), half-illuminating their bodies; this is explained such that the side of the character turned toward Don Giovanni is illuminated, leaving the other side dark. A anticipates an incorrect interpretation of his theory, an interpretation that would understand him to be saying the characters of the opera are like abstract passions. For an example of what this would look like, A writes that according to this incorrect interpretation, Zerlina would be (the abstract passion of) "irresponsibility."[13]

Zerlina appears only in passing in "The Seducer's Diary" when Johannes is describing the moment that is most seductive. He claims the moment is the wedding day of a bride. Zerlina is mentioned because in the time before the bride meets her groom in the church to be married, there is a moment that makes "even an insignificant girl significant," even an ordinary girl like Zerlina "becomes something."[14] Zerlina is used to show her appeal as a bride and thus an aspect of why she is attractive to Don Giovanni; it also pertains to her power and strength in *Don Giovanni* even as a peasant.

In "A Cursory Observation Concerning a Detail in Don Giovanni," published in *Fædrelandet*, nos. 1890–91, on May 19–20, 1845,[15] A speaks about a specific performance he saw of Don Giovanni.[16] We find A making this ordinary peasant girl into something more significant, similarly to Johannes' comment, though it is more

---

[9]   *SKS* 2, 105 / *EO1*, 101. Here A writes that with her response "No one knows" to his question, "By what power does he enthrall you?," he ironically, though truthfully, answers her "Well spoken my child! You speak more wisely than the wise men of India…and the trouble is that I cannot explain it, either."

[10]   *SKS* 2, 105 / *EO1*, 101–2.

[11]   *SKS* 2, 127 / *EO1*, 125.

[12]   *SKS* 2, 122 / *EO1*, 119. Although Zerlina's anxiety is spoken of in this passing form, it is of importance in *The Concept of Anxiety*, when Kierkegaard is speaking about anxiety as a sympathetic antipathy (*SKS* 4, 348 / *CA*, 42); The Hongs makes a connection (*CA*, Explanatory Notes, p. 235, note 47) to a journal entry that is reminiscent of Zerlina's anxiety (*Angst*) in this passage of *Either/Or*, Part 1: "Anxiety is a desire for what one fears…anxiety is an alien power which grips the individual, and yet he cannot tear himself free from it and does not want to…anxiety makes the individual powerless" (*SKS* 18, 311, JJ:511 / *KJN* 2, 286).

[13]   *SKS* 2, 126 / *EO1*, 123–4.

[14]   *SKS* 2, 424 / *EO1*, 436–7.

[15]   *SKS* 14, 67–75 / *COR* 28–37.

[16]   See *SKS* 14, 74 / *COR*, 277. It is a performance of the version by Laurids Kruse (Copenhagen 1807) at the Royal Theater seen at some point between February 1845 and May 8, 1845.

explicit: he forces the reader to pay special attention to her.[17] The article, which serves as a review, is primarily about Zerlina and Don Giovanni, their relationship, and specific actors/singers who have played their parts. The article additionally shows A/Kierkegaard's ability to make musical criticism and demonstrates his sharpness in regard to particular points. Furthermore, the article is surprising because of how precise it is, considering it is by someone who claims not to be a musical expert.[18] In the review, A makes it clear that the duet between Zerlina and Don Giovanni from the first act ("Là ci darem la mano") is very important for the opera as a whole, and the spectator has great expectations for it.[19] A also explains that Mozart composed this aria particularly well, because Zerlina is shown not to have the qualities of individuality that define a different kind of character (a quality like this would be a violent passion in a desire shared by two persons).[20] Instead, Zerlina's seduction is described like a quiet marriage that does not create any kind of commotion.[21] A then goes on to describe the situation that was created: Zerlina has been seduced, but she cannot figure out how it happened, and this creates a mental strain for her, precisely because she cannot explain it. For A, Zerlina's inability to explain is extremely important,[22] and he gives an example of this. To do so he recalls an old performance he had seen of *Don Giovanni*, and criticizes the actress Madame Kragh[23] when she sang "No, I will not" with great resolve. Singing in this way is entirely against A's conception of Zerlina because, for him, Zerlina is actually bewildered, puzzled, and baffled right from the start.[24] It is important that Zerlina not be seen as making a reflection at this point, which A describes in his own footnote to the passage. Here he reflects on the structure of the opera; Zerlina's appearance in the opera gives Don Giovanni a moment to catch his breath because unlike the other characters, Zerlina

---

[17]   A actually concludes his review by sympathizing with the reader because he has made an aesthetic interpretation of Zerlina, which many find unimportant (*SKS* 14, 75 / *COR*, 36).

[18]   See *SKS* 2, 72 / *EO1*, 65.

[19]   *SKS* 14, 69 / *COR*, 28–9.

[20]   *SKS* 14, 70 / *COR*, 30.

[21]   *SKS* 14, 70 / *COR*, 30. This statement is reminiscent of *SKS* 13, 211–12 / *M*, 163–4: Zerlina is referred to very briefly to when Kierkegaard quotes something Don Giovanni says to Zerlina. The quotation is, "true happiness resides only in the tender arms of a blameless wife." This situation is used specifically as a comparison to Juliane who seduces Fredrik and the church, see Mark Lloyd Taylor, "The Hermit Emerges Victorious: Contempt for Women in Kierkegaard's Attack Upon the (Male) Ecclesiastical Establishment," in *The Moment and Late Writings*, ed. by Robert L. Perkins, Macon, Georgia: Mercer University Press 2009 (*International Kierkegaard Commentary*, vol. 23), pp. 199–238; specifically pp. 210–11.

[22]   *SKS* 14, 70 / *COR*, 30.

[23]   Ibid. See the Hongs' note (*COR*, Explanatory Notes, p. 277), "Boline Abrahamsen Kragh (1810–1839) played the role of Zerlina, 1833–1839."

[24]   *SKS* 14, 70 / *COR*, 30. The line sung is a quotation from Kruse, *Don Juan*, Act I, Scene 13. Kierkegaard describes Zerlina's perplexity before, during, and after the seduction when writing about what it is to be sacrificed, and when referring to the "thousands of spontaneous enthusiasts who have been sacrificed," where the lowest and highest resemble each other. However, he states the lowest is like Zerlina: "I want and do not want." See *SKS* 26, 79, NB31:104. The Zerlina citation, as indicated by the editor, is to Laurids Kruse, *Don Juan*, p. 33.

is not against him.[25] Zerlina's subsequent seduction is then one of two types: difficult and dangerous, or just a seduction of a lovely peasant girl, done in an artful and child-like way. Mozart thus ties the characters of Zerlina and Don Giovanni together in a spontaneous and purely musical relation, without lessening the effect of the other characters in the opera.[26]

A continues the theme of Zerlina's bewilderment and innocence when he quotes the line following, "Masetto's soul will bleed."[27] He writes that there is no deep sympathy expressed in this line, but rather it must be accompanied by spontaneous movements, that is, holding her apron, or Zerlina pushing away Don Giovanni's advances. This in turn helps to understand the way Zerlina and Masetto's relationship works.[28] Developing the topic of Zerlina and Masetto's relationship, A says Zerlina's aria "Batti, Batti, o bel Masetto"[29] should not be seen as a circumstance of reconciliation after a quarrel, because Zerlina does not yet have the "presence of mind" to be reconciled. In fact, she is quite afraid when she is left alone on stage shortly after the "Batti, batti" aria with Don Giovanni's impending arrival thereto.[30] Thus Zerlina uses the "Batti, batti" aria to help Masetto feel better about her and about himself, although she remains unsure about everything, which puts her innocence into question. Zerlina's naiveté must be kept vivid; even after the pseudo-reconciliation with Masetto, Don Giovanni returns with his tricks such that Zerlina must go back to Masetto much in the same state as she was before the "Batti, batti" aria.[31] The result of consoling Masetto leads her to believe the problem is not with her, but that Masetto and Don Giovanni are enemies.[32] To complete the picture of the relationship between Zerlina and Masetto, A writes about what it would be like visiting Madame Masetto after a few years time.[33]

---

[25]   These characters are specifically Donna Anna, Elvira, and the Commendatore.

[26]   *SKS* 14, 70–1 / *COR*, 30–1.

[27]   *SKS* 14, 71 / *COR*, 31. From, "Là ci darem la mano," in Kruse, *Don Juan*, p. 11. The line constitutes Zerlina's first reply in the duet.

[28]   *SKS* 14, 71 / *COR*, 31.

[29]   Kruse, Act I, Scene 21; *Don Giovanni*, Bärenreiter (BA 4550a), Act I, Scenes XVI–XX, No. 12, pp. 155–61. English translations of this aria vary greatly, see "Canst thou see me, unforgiven," in Wolfgang Amadeus Mozart, *Don Giovanni: Opera in 2 Acts, English-Italian Text*, New York: Alfred Publishing 1985 (Kalmus edition K 06314), pp. 106–10 and No. 12 Aria, "You are jealous, you are cruel," in Wolfgang Amadeus Mozart and Lorenzo da Ponte, *Don Giovanni: A Comic Opera in Two Acts*, trans. by Edward J. Dent, Oxford: Doblinger Vienna with Oxford University Press 1938, p. 26. Due to the wide variance in translations, commentators generally refer to this aria by its Italian title.

[30]   See *SKS* 6, 26 / *SLW*, 19 (mentioned above).

[31]   This reference is to the "second reconciliation" between Zerlina and Masetto as shown through Zerlina's aria "Vedrai, carino," in *Don Giovanni*, Bärenreiter (BA 4550a), Act II, Scene VI, pp. 288–91, see also "If you will promise me not to mistrust me" Act II, No. 18 Aria, in Mozart, *Don Giovanni: A Comic Opera in Two Acts*, trans. by Dent, p. 47.

[32]   *SKS* 14, 71 / *COR*, 31.

[33]   He describes her as adorable and delightful; however, she remembers the day of her wedding as a great confusion, with a lot of movement, with Don Giovanni wishing to have a word with her, and at the end of it Masetto and Don Giovanni would have killed each other, had she not been there to stop it (*SKS* 14, 71 / *COR*, 31–2).

A develops Zerlina's bewilderment, describing the fact that her confusion regarding what is both the physical and the moral, leaves her at a distance from Donna Anna and Donna Elvira. Zerlina is not sufficiently disturbed about what happened. She takes part in everything and finds companionship with the aristocratic ladies, not seeing herself as beneath them, although she is a simple peasant. She also takes part in hunting down Don Giovanni. However, she does not do so because he seduced her, but because he was mean to Masetto, in the same way Leporello hit Masetto: it is because of the people who have done wrong to Masetto that she wishes to seek revenge.[34] Zerlina also has an inability to understand Elvira. Even after Elvira presents all of her *pathos* to her, Zerlina understands Don Giovanni better than she does Donna Elvira. Thus Kierkegaard describes it as crucial that the actress not overreact or show anxiety because of what Elvira has said to her. Instead, the actress should show surprise.[35]

To conclude the review, A comments on the character of Don Giovanni related to how, and to whom, he must sing, which is important for developing the dynamic between Don Giovanni and Zerlina. The comment is given from a chorographical and aesthetic perspective. A uses the duet between Don Giovanni and Zerlina as an example. In this instance, Don Giovanni is supposed to sing to Zerlina.[36] In terms of acting, Don Giovanni must not be too quick in the seduction, nor be too obvious because Zerlina would pick up on it; rather, he can play on her naiveté. In the duet, he must grab Zerlina's attention naturally and with the music. He is able to see that she actually is falling for him although she feigns not to be.[37] In the duet, the seduction is immediate, musical, and a thoroughly enjoyable game for Don Giovanni. A emphasizes the importance of Zerlina's portrayal such that when she is seen and heard on stage with Don Giovanni, she creates a kind of euphoria for the spectator. This euphoria is a result of the spectator trying to see her as a sincere character.[38] Nevertheless, when she is seen with Masetto, there is a humorous aspect to her situation because she seems always to be getting into trouble like a child.[39]

Elsewhere in his works, Kierkegaard describes moments related to Zerlina's character in more detail. For example, Zerlina is mentioned in *Stages on Life's*

---

[34]   *SKS* 14, 71 / *COR*, 32. Reference to Leporello striking Masetto is found in the editor's footnote: Kruse Act II, Scene 7. However, it is not actually Leporello who strikes Masetto but Don Giovanni dressed as Leporello, see "Zitto! Lascia ch'io senta," Act II, Scene V, Recitative, in Mozart, *Don Giovanni,* Bärenreiter (BA 4550a), pp. 282–4, and "Quiet! Just let me listen," Act II in *Don Giovanni: A Comic Opera in Two Acts*, trans. by Dent, Act II, pp. 45–6.

[35]   *SKS* 14, 73 / *COR*, 33. A does not elaborate on what Elvira says, or where precisely he means in the opera, but it strongly suggests the moments following, "Là ci darem la mano," Act I, Scene X, and how Zerlina should act during Elvira's "Ah fuggi il traditor" in *Don Giovanni*, Bärenreiter (BA 4550a), pp. 106–7; pp. 108–10, respectively.

[36]   *SKS* 14, 73 / *COR*, 34.

[37]   Don Giovanni is able to see Zerlina's "unwillingness is a camouflaged surrender" (*SKS* 14, 74 / *COR*, 35–6).

[38]   The spectator is "trying in vain to apply the earnest category to her" (*SKS* 14, 75 / *COR*, 36).

[39]   *SKS* 14, 75 / *COR*, 36.

Way, specifically in "In vino veritas": Victor Eremita says it is when we hear other people going away that we become most solitary. He uses Zerlina's situation in *Don Giovanni*, in Act 1, Scene 18, as a comparison, when she is left alone on stage, and the chorus is slowly disappearing. One can hear the solitude as the sound fades away, and solitude comes about.[40]

IV. Commentary

The way an actress performs the part of Zerlina is an important thread in Kierkegaard's commentary on Zerlina, especially in "A Cursory Observation," which serves as a useful text from a musicological and philosophical perspective. In respect to Zerlina, he is more focused on the performances of the actresses and peculiarities of their performances.[41] One critic has explored this point, focusing on Kierkegaard's attention to the method and voice of the actress who plays Zerlina. In short, an actress must conceal the fact that she is reflective when playing the character of Zerlina and has to hide herself.[42] It is pointed out that the actress playing Zerlina must not reveal herself to be a reflecting individual, that is, that she, in Zerlina's shoes, would otherwise be horrified by the cruelties Don Giovanni did to Donna Elvira and show sympathy for her. In addition to these aspects, it is worth emphasizing the importance Kierkegaard ascribes to the gestures the actors make while on stage, specifically the characters of Don Giovanni and Zerlina in the duet "Là ci darem la mano." The details of these gestures are recognizable to Kierkegaard's modern reader when imagining performances made in our modern times. However, it must be remembered that in the texts that emphasize Zerlina, Kierkegaard is describing very

---

[40]   *SKS* 6, 26 / *SLW*, 19. This moment is more developed when Kierkegaard is describing the scene, what he calls "the most solitary scene," because Zerlina "*becomes* alone," since Masetto has stepped away and the chorus has slowly disappeared. This is what begins what Kierkegaard terms, "Zerlina's little part." This is when she sings, "Tra quest'arbori celata si può dar che non mi veda" (If I hide among these trees...), cited by the editor as Kruse, *Don Juan*, I, 18, p. 57; see *Don Giovanni*, Bärenreiter (BA 4550a), Act I, Scene XVIII, pp. 170–1. Kierkegaard compares the disappearing of the chorus, which heightens the effect of Zerlina's solitariness, to the "distant clattering of a carriage," which gives the impression that others are leaving. It is a situation that Kierkegaard describes as "a purely musical situation...like the nature–solitude that tempts erotic love" (*Pap.* V B 168, p. 282 / *SLW*, Supplement, p. 531). This idea is developed again in a draft in which Kierkegaard describes the fading away of the chorus, where Zerlina and "the sound and solitude come into existence as a musical situation"; see *Pap.* V B 171:1 / *SLW*, Supplement, p. 533.

[41]   See Janne Risum, "Towards Transparency: Søren Kierkegaard on Danish Actresses," in *Kierkegaard and his Danish Contemporaries*, ed. by Jon Stewart, Berlin and New York: Walter de Gruyter 2003 (*Kierkegaard Studies Monograph Series*, vol. 10), pp. 330–42; see p. 334; p. 339.

[42]   Joseph Westfall, *The Kierkegaardian Author: Authorship and Performance in Kierkegaard*, Berlin and New York: Walter de Gruyter 2007 (*Kierkegaard Studies Monograph Series*, vol. 15), p. 27; p. 29.

specific performances of *Don Giovanni* in Copenhagen between 1829 and 1845.[43] To place his critique in its appropriate nineteenth-century setting and the corresponding operatic choreography, it is of significant insight into Kierkegaard's commentary to note the way in which Mary Ann Smart explains how this choreography was made in direct relation to the music that was played. First, music would provide pace in controlling the movements of an actor, but secondly, music had an ability to work on a more intimate level in the meaning of gestures, "pinning itself to a particular character or sequence of movements in order to guide the spectator's attention, sending us signals about where to look or what to feel while looking at a body on stage."[44] It is this kind of physical–musical relation that Kierkegaard is getting at in his description of the way the actors should move their body in "Là ci darem la mano."

However, Kierkegaard is also criticized for his statements related to women desiring to be seduced by Don Giovanni and the utilization of the "Là ci darem la mano" aria to support this as the ultimate example of Don Giovanni's abilities. Don Giovanni's false earnestness in his promises, explicitly on display in the aria "Deh Vieni alla Finestra" (Come, come to the window)[45] is claimed better to portray the reason why a woman would want to be seduced by Don Giovanni.[46] The snag in the proposal of "Deh Vieni alla Finestra" compared to "Là ci darem la mano" is that it lacks the vocal and bodily interaction Kierkegaard describes in such detail, thus making it a less powerful manifestation of Don Giovanni's talent for seducing women in Kierkegaard's account. In addition it also lacks the display of charm involved in the active participation and dialogue between the characters involved in the seduction as demonstrated by Zerlina and Don Giovanni in "Là ci darem la mano."

Another theme Kierkegaard discusses in relation to Zerlina, which is often taken up by critics, is her difference in class standing in comparison to the other *donnas* of *Don Giovanni* and her relative indifference to this fact.[47] Theodor W. Adorno

---

[43]   On a performance in May 1845, see Westfall, *The Kierkegaardian Author: Authorship and Performance in Kierkegaard*, p. 147. See also ibid., p. 151. For a discussion regarding Madame Kragh (the "old" Zerlina, 1829–39), Ulricha Augusta Stage (as Zerlina, February 23, 1845), and the confusion regarding who played the part of Zerlina between the date of Kragh's death (1839) and the date when Stage replaced her (as Zerlina in 1845), see ibid., footnote 40, p. 151, and Risum, "Towards Transparency," p. 334.

[44]   Mary Ann Smart, *Mimomania: Music and Gesture in Nineteenth-Century Opera*, Berkeley: University of California Press 2004, pp. 5–6. For additional detail on Kierkegaard's description of Zerlina in his review, see Sousa, "Wolfgang Amadeus Mozart: The Love for Music and the Music of Love," p. 150.

[45]   See *Don Giovanni*, Bärenreiter (BA 4550a) Act II, Scene III, No. 16, Canzonetta, pp. 268–71. Don Giovanni sings this *canzonetta*, or short vocal piece, accompanied by a mandolin outside the window of Donna Elvira's maidservant.

[46]   See Irving Singer, *Mozart & Beethoven: The Concept of Love in their Operas*, Baltimore: Johns Hopkins University Press 1977, pp. 50–1. This is used as part of Singer's criticism of Kierkegaard's treatment of *Don Giovanni*.

[47]   See Daniel Herwitz, "Kierkegaard Writes his Opera," in *The Don Giovanni Moment: Essays on the Legacy of an Opera*, ed. by Lydia Goehr and Daniel Herwitz, New York: Columbia University Press 2006, pp. 120–1.

famously transforms Zerlina into a representative of class differences and a country simpleton versus city refinement, in his "Huldigung an Zerlina."[48] When commenting on Adorno's text, Berthold Hoeckner, also reflects on the musical structure of Zerlina's arias, which is simple and an illustration of her social status compared to the ladies of a higher social standing.[49] As A describes, for Don Giovanni, Zerlina is a woman like any other and is not preoccupied with her being a peasant or not.

Karl Hammer, highly influenced by Kierkegaard in the writing of his chapter on *Don Giovanni*, describes the entrance of Zerlina and Masetto, their wedding party, and their *joyful recklessness* and *innocent gaiety*.[50] Her being charming, young, and inexperienced draws the spectator's attention to her right away. In this way she has also been characterized as an "easy victim"[51] for Don Giovanni's tricks. Nevertheless, these elements add to her general likeability and explain why the spectator might want to apply an earnest category to her, as Kierkegaard describes. In addition to this first impression, her sensuousness is brought out and put on display during the duet "Là ci darem la mano," where she becomes not only likeable, but also sensuous, and dramatically as well as musically interesting. Furthermore, what can be noted from a musical-erotic standpoint is how Zerlina does not reflect on her seduction, Don Giovanni, or her anxiety such that she remains happy-go-lucky without succumbing to a burden like that which Donna Elvira carries. When A speculates what it would be like to make a visit to "Madame Masetto" in the future, we see Zerlina came out unscathed after the ordeal of Don Giovanni entering and leaving her life. The same argument cannot be so easily made for the other characters of the opera, thus we indeed see something extraordinary in this ordinary peasant girl.

---

[48]   Theodor W. Adorno, "Huldigung an Zerlina," in *Musikalische Schriften IV*, vol. 17 of *Gesammelte Schriften*, vols. 1–20, ed. by Rolf Tiedemann, Frankfurt am Main: Suhrkamp 1971–86), pp. 34–5.

[49]   Berthold Hoeckner, "Homage to Adorno's 'Homage to Zerlina,' " in *The Don Giovanni Moment: Essays on the Legacy of an Opera*, ed. by Lydia Goehr and Daniel Herwitz, pp. 211–23, specifically pp. 214–15.

[50]   Karl Hammer, "Don Giovanni," in his *W.A. Mozart—eine theologische Deutung: Ein Beitrag zur theologischen Anthropologie*, Zürich: EVZ–Verlag 1964, p. 211.

[51]   T.H. Croxall, "Kierkegaard on Music, A Paper based on Kierkegaard's Essay 'De umiddlebare erotiske Stadier, eller Det Musikalsk–Erotiske' from 'Enten Eller,' Vol. I," in *Proceedings of the Royal Musical Association*, 73rd session (1946–47), Leeds: Whitehead & Miller 1947, pp. 1–11; p. 9.

Bibliography

Cartford, Gerhard M., "Kierkegaard and Mozart: a Study," in *Cantors at the Crossroads: Essays on Church Music in Honor of Walter E. Buszin*, ed. by Johannes Riedel, St. Louis: Concordia Publishing House 1967, pp. 121–40; see p. 126.

Croxall, T.H., "Kierkegaard on Music, a Paper based on Kierkegaard's Essay 'De umiddlebare erotiske Stadier, eller Det Musikalsk–Erotiske' from 'Enten Eller,' Vol. I," in *Proceedings of the Royal Musical Association*, 73rd session (1946–47), Leeds: Whitehead & Miller 1947, pp. 1–11; see p. 9.

—— "Kierkegaard og operaen 'Don Giovanni,' " in *Dansk Musiktidsskrift*, vol. 31, no. 1, 1956, pp. 3–9; see p. 8.

Davini, Simonella, "Arte e critica nell'estetica di Kierkegaard," in *Aesthetica Preprint: Periodico quadrimestrale del Centro Internazionale Studi di Estetica*, Palermo: Presso la Facoltà di Lettere e Filosofia dell'Università di Palermo, no. 69, 2003, pp. 1–78; see pp. 52–5; p. 68.

Hammer, Karl, "Don Giovanni," in his *W.A. Mozart—eine theologische Deutung: Ein Beitrag zur theologischen Anthropologie*, Zürich: EVZ–Verlag 1964, pp. 211–13; pp. 216–22; p. 224; p. 227.

Herwitz, Daniel, "Kierkegaard Writes His Opera," in *The Don Giovanni Moment: Essays on the Legacy of an Opera*, ed. by Lydia Goehr and Daniel Herwitz, New York: Columbia University Press 2006, pp. 120–1; p. 125.

Leon, Céline, "The No Woman's Land of Kierkegaardian Seduction" in *Either/Or, Part One*, ed. by Robert L. Perkins, Macon, Georgia: Mercer University Press 1995 (*International Kierkegaard Commentary*, vol. 3), pp. 229–50; see p. 231; p. 243; p. 247.

—— *The Neither/Nor of the Second Sex: Kierkegaard on Women, Sexual Difference, and Sexual Relations*, Macon: Mercer University Press 2008, p. 36; p. 46; p. 56; p. 66; p. 234.

Liessmann, Konrad Paul, *Ästhetik der Verführung. Kierkegaards Konstruktion der Erotik aus dem Geiste der Kunst*, Vienna: Sonderzahl 2005, pp. 36–7; p. 150.

Pattison, George, *Kierkegaard, the Aesthetic and the Religious: From the Magic Theatre to the Crucifixion of the Image*, Basingstoke: Palgrave Macmillan 1992, pp. 98–9.

—— "Søren Kierkegaard: a Theater Critic of the Heiberg School," in *Kierkegaard and his Contemporaries: The Culture of Golden Age Denmark*, ed. by Jon Stewart, Berlin and New York: Walter de Gruyter 2003 (*Kierkegaard Studies Monograph Series*, vol. 10), pp. 319–29; see p. 325.

Petersen, Nils Holger, "Søren Kierkegaard's Aestheticist and Mozart's *Don Giovanni*," in *Interart Poetics: Essays on the Interrelations of the Arts and*

Media, ed. by Ulla–Britta Lagerroth, Hans Lund, and Erik Hedling, Amsterdam: Rodopi 1997, pp. 167–76; see p. 173.

Risum, Janne, "Towards Transparency: Søren Kierkegaard on Danish Actresses," in *Kierkegaard and his Contemporaries: The Culture of Golden Age Denmark*, ed. by Jon Stewart, Berlin and New York: Walter de Gruyter 2003 (*Kierkegaard Studies Monograph Series*, vol. 10), pp. 330–42; see p. 334; p. 339.

Singer, Irving, *Mozart & Beethoven: The Concept of Love in their Operas*, Baltimore: Johns Hopkins University Press 1977, p. 28; pp. 50–1.

Sousa, Elisabete M. de, "Wolfgang Amadeus Mozart: The Love for Music and the Music of Love," in *Kierkegaard and the Renaissance and Modern Traditions*, Tome III, *Literature, Drama and Music*, ed. by Jon Stewart, Aldershot: Ashgate 2009 (*Kierkegaard Research: Sources, Reception and Resources*, vol. 5), pp. 137–67; see p. 150.

Taruskin, Richard, *Music in the Seventeenth and Eighteenth Centuries*, Oxford: Oxford University Press 2010, p. 495.

Taylor, Mark Lloyd, "The Hermit Emerges Victorious: Contempt for Women in Kierkegaard's Attack Upon the (Male) Ecclesiastical Establishment," in *The Moment and Late Writings*, ed. by Robert L. Perkins, Macon, Georgia: Mercer University Press 2009 (*International Kierkegaard Commentary*, vol. 23), pp. 199–238; see pp. 210–11.

Tschuggnall, Peter, *Sören Kierkegaards Mozart-Rezeption: Analyse einer philosophisch-literarischen Deutung von Musik im Kontext des Zusammenspiels der Künste*, Frankfurt am Main: Peter Lang 1992; pp. 131–3; p. 136.

Westfall, Joseph, *The Kierkegaardian Author: Authorship and Performance in Kierkegaard*, Berlin and New York: Walter de Gruyter 2007 (*Kierkegaard Studies Monograph Series*, vol. 15), p. 27; p. 29; pp. 147–64.

Williams, Bernard, "Don Giovanni as an Idea," in his *On Opera*, New Haven: Yale University Press 2006, pp. 31–42; specifically pp. 33–4; pp. 40–1.

Index of Persons

Mozart, Wolfgang Amadeus (1756–91),
Austrian composer, 18, 125, 169–79,
257–67.
Don Giovanni, 18, 174–5.
The Magic Flute, 169–79.
The Marriage of Figaro, 174–5.
Müller, Wilhelm (1794–1828), German
poet, 237, 240.
Münchhausen, Karl Friedrich Hieronymus,
Baron von (1720–97), German
nobleman, 139–54.
Mynster, Jakob Peter (1775–1854), Danish
theologian and bishop, 184, 239.

Nemesis, 60, 62, 155–62.
Nero, i.e., Nero Claudius Caesar Augustus
Germanicus, born Lucius Domitius
Ahenobarbus (37–68), Roman
emperor, 163–7.
Niels Klim, 49–55.
Nietzsche, Friedrich (1844–1900), German
philologist and philosopher, 28–9.
Nitsch, Paul Friedrich Achat (1754–94),
German historian, 134, 191.
Nyerup, Rasmus (1759–1829), Danish
literary historian and linguist, 236,
241.

Oedipus, 219.
Oehlenschläger, Adam (1779–1850), Danish
poet, 65–9, 71.
Olsen, Regine (1822–1904), 36–7.
Ophelia, 37.
Osiris, 224–6.
Ovid, i.e., Publius Ovidius Naso
(43 BC–AD 17), Roman poet, 189.

Palfery, Simon, 88–90.
Papageno, 169–79.
Pattison, George, 245, 254.
Per Degn, 181–6.
Pezza, Michael (1771–1806), Italian
brigand, 115–16.
Pfitzer, Nicolas, 97.
Philemon, 189.

Philostratus of Lemnos (known also as
Philostratus the Elder)
(ca. 190–230), Greek writer, 164.
Pilate, 92–3.
Pindar, 156.
Plato, 189–91, 194–6, 224–6, 230.
Plutarch, 224–6.
Podmore, Simon, 240.
Polański, Roman, 86.
Ponte, Lorenzo de (1749–1838), Italian
opera librettist and poet, 257.
Prometheus, 187–98, 241.
Pythagoras, 228, 230.

Rasmussen, Joel D.S., 89, 209.
Raspe, Rudolf Erich (1736–94), German
writer and scientist, 140–1, 145.
Richard II (963–1027), Duke of Normandy,
215.
Richard III (1452–1485), King of England
from 1483–85, 199–213.
Richardson, Samuel (1689–1761), English
writer, 96.
Riise, Johan Christian (1794–1875), Danish
translator and editor, 251.
Robert le Diable, that is, Robert, the Duke
of Normandy (1000–1035), 215–21.
Rohde, Peter P. (1902–78), Danish author,
5.
Rossel, Sven, 44.
Rötscher, Heinrich Theodor (1802–71),
German theater critic and theorist,
16, 19–20, 23, 31–2, 100.
Rousseau, Jean-Jacques (1712–78), Swiss-
born French philosopher, 96.
Rudelbach, Andreas Gottlob (1792–1862),
Danish theologian, 184.

Saint Margaret of Antioch, 96.
Saint Margaret of Cortona, 96.
Schelling, Friedrich Wilhelm Joseph von
(1775–1854), German philosopher,
225–6.
Schikaneder, Emanuel (1751–1812),
German-Austrian actor, 173.

Wagner, Heinrich Leopold (1747–79),
    German dramatist, 96.
Waldorff, Jessica, 169, 173.
Wandering Jew, 116, 235–47.
Waser, Heinrich (1714–77), German
    translator, 3–5.
Weidmann, Paul (1744–1801), Austrian
    author, 97.
Wiebel, Bernhard, 141.
Wieland, Christoph Martin (1733–1813),
    German poet, 4, 14.

Wilde, Oscar (1854–1900), 143, 148, 150.
William the Conqueror (1028–87), 215.
Worde, Wynkyn de (died 1534), English
    printer and publisher, 217.

Xenophon, 190.
Xerxes, 251–7.

Zerlina, 257–67.
Ziegler, Friedrich Wilhelm (1761–1827),
    German actor and dramatist, 17.

Index of Subjects